# FIELD E... IN SOCIAL WORK

WITHDRAWN

## CONTEMPORARY ISSUES AND TRENDS

Edited by

DEAN SCHNECK, University of Wisconsin-Madison

BART GROSSMAN, University of California at Berkeley

URANIA GLASSMAN, Adelphi University

WITH AN INTRODUCTION BY

ALFRED E. KADUSHIN, University of Wisconsin-Madison

**KENDALL/HUNT PUBLISHING COMPANY**
4050 Westmark Drive    Dubuque, Iowa 52002

# DEDICATION

This book is dedicated to the memory of

## DR. HELENE FISHBEIN
### 1927-1986

Dr. Fishbein was the Director of Field Instruction at the Adelphi University School of Social Work for ten years, Associate Professor, and Chair of the New York Area Directors of Field Instruction. She inspired many field instructors, students, and colleagues with her commitment to quality field education.

She was one of the founders of the Field Instruction Symposia presented at the Council of Social Work Education since 1985. This volume stands as her legacy.

She was a gracious presence among us.

# TABLE OF CONTENTS

# PREFACE

Whenever field directors, field instructors, and faculty assemble to consider our educational enterprise, there emerges a camaraderie born of a shared experience and a common struggle. Whether at national symposia, regional field director groups, or field instructor recognition and training events, meeting, networking and consulting always seem to affirm our efforts and enhance our morale.

This has certainly been true during the past five years as the informal national network of field educators and directors have come together in national symposia and regional forums to present and discuss research on field education, innovative curriculum models, and critical instructional issues. The resultant scholarly productivity and organizational development of the national network have coalesced to produce this volume. In a very real sense, it represents the collective effort of forty-two authors, all of whom are experienced field instructors and educators, or field directors from diverse schools and social agencies across the United States and Canada.

This book features a selection of thirty papers focusing on field educational models, issues, research, administration, and teaching methods. The topics reflect the broad spectrum of field education and will be of interest to field directors and faculty, agency field instructors and training directors, fieldwork students, agency directors, and social work deans and directors. The content will be helpful for:

* developing new field work programs
* implementing new curriculum models in the practicum
* meeting the needs of a changing student body
* resolving instructional issues
* serving as a general reference on field education

A special feature of this text is an introduction by Emeritus Professor Alfred Kadushin of the University of Wisconsin-Madison. He calls attention to the perennial importance placed upon field instruction by social work students, and discusses the more complex and demanding nature of field instruction in comparison to agency supervision. The book is organized into four major parts:

CONCEPTUAL FOUNDATIONS FOR FIELD EDUCATION
FIELD INSTRUCTION MODELS
FIELD INSTRUCTION ROLES AND PROCESSES
EDUCATIONAL ISSUES

Earlier versions of these papers were selected through a juried review process or as keynotes for presentation at the 1987 and 1988 National Field Work Symposia of the Annual Program Meetings of CSWE. They have been updated and revised for publication. The express purpose and intention of the authors and the editors is that this volume advance the mission and enhance the quality of field education.

Dean Schneck
Madison, Wisconsin
April 29, 1990

# ACKNOWLEDGEMENTS

First, we wish to acknowledge the contributions of our authors and their reference group, the national network of field educators, directors, and field instructors. Their friendship and encouragement, well as their valuable ideas and scholarship have literally allowed this project to become a reality. They are our esteemed colleagues, and we are proud to be associated with them.

We wish to recognize the support of members from the National Clearinghouse on Field Education, an earlier "incarnation" of the national network whose purpose, the pursuit of excellence in field education, survives and is reaffirmed by this book.

The theater of activity and medium for the presentation of the original papers contained in this book were the National Field Work Symposia at the Annual Program Meetings of CSWE. We wish to commend and thank the Council for its recognition and support of national affinity groups to convene in an annual forum for the exchange of educational research and scholarship. Beginning in 1985 with the post-conference institute and continuing from 1987 to present as the National Field Work Symposia, these occasions have provided a concentrated and integrated format for the exploration and advancement of field education for social work practice.

Whenever a project of this sort is attempted involving dozens of authors from across the United States and Canada, a necessary prerequisite is the moral and infrastructure support provided by one's school. It is thus fitting that we thank our respective schools at the University of Wisconsin-Madison, Adelphi University, and the University of California at Berkeley. We are proud to be affiliated with institutions that value and support both field education and scholarship.

We feel a special kinship with Brad Sheafor and Lowell Jenkins for their intellectual leadership, friendship and support of this endeavor. The publication of their book, QUALITY FIELD INSTRUCTION IN SOCIAL WORK in 1982, provided both an example and a foundation for this current effort.

We were especially honored that Alfred Kadushin would value our efforts and participate in this project. It is not surprising, however; for he has been a consistent supporter, participant, and thoughtful critic of field education for four decades. At both the national and local level, we have never known Al to decline an invitation to address field instructors and educators and to share his wealth of knowledge and insights on social work supervision and field instruction. He has our thanks, our respect and our affection.

We wish to acknowledge with fondness and regard and to thank Betty S. Zeps, field program assistant at the School of Social Work of the University of Wisconsin-Madison for her dedication, hard work, and competence, not only in the preparation and copy editing of the final manuscript, but also for her many years of staffing assistance to the national field network and the field work symposia. Because she is so literate and professional, Betty far surpasses the pale of the ordinary.

Dean, Bart, and Ronnie, April 29, 1990

# INTRODUCTION

## FIELD EDUCATION IN SOCIAL WORK: CONTEMPORARY ISSUES AND TRENDS

**Alfred E. Kadushin, Professor Emeritus**
**University of Wisconsin-Madison**

There is a general consensus that field instruction is the most significant, most productive, most memorable component of social work education. Within the general consensus this conclusion is most vehemently and most enthusiastically supported by social work students - present and former.

From the very beginning of professional training for social work the "practical and theoretical were yoked together."[1] And Mary Richmond in calling for the establishment of a program of education for social work said that "it never should be forgotten that emphasis is to be put on practical work rather than on academic requirements."[2]

Everyone recognizes that "knowing about", however sophisticated the knowledge, gets you only so far and falls short of the responsibilities of a profession. A profession has the community's mandate to do something about, to take some action in response to some situation of concern to the community. "Doing" implies "know how" which, while it requires "knowing about", goes considerably beyond knowledge and is of a different order of things. And "knowing how", which gives meaning and significance to "knowing about", can only be competently learned through doing. Skills imagined and enacted vicariously in the mind in the class can be only practiced in the flesh in the living interchange with a client.

Only in the translation of knowledge into practice, acquired in the field, does social work education achieve professional justification. A book devoted to a study of field instruction is thus a fitting tribute to the importance of this component of education.

But a collection of studies such as this on field instruction models, roles, process, and issues providing a conceptualization of field instruction calls attention to the fact that field instruction is a complex phenomenon requiring serious study. Field instruction, while similar to agency supervision, is even more complex and more demanding than agency supervision. While both field instructors and agency supervisors engage the three principal cluster functions of supervision--administra-

---

[1] Albert W. Wright, "The New Philanthropy," PROCEEDINGS OF THE NATIONAL CONFERENCE ON CHARITIES AND CONNECTIONS, 1896, p. 5.

[2] Mary Richmond, "The Need for a Training School in Applied Philanthropy" in PROCEEDINGS OF THE NATIONAL CONFERENCE OF CHARITIES AND CORRECTIONS, 1897.

tive, educational and supportive functions--their effective implementation is even more difficult for field instructors than it is for agency supervisors.

Administratively, the agency supervisor deals primarily with the agency organization as a closed system with a limited role set--administrator, supervisor, direct service worker. The field instructor has to deal with a number of organizational systems in complex interrelationship and a more heterogenous roles set with a larger number of actively involved participants. In addition to the agency in which the student is placed and in which the field instructor is based, there is the Department or School of Social Work and beyond that the university (college) with which the school or department is affiliated. The role set includes not only student, field instructor and agency administrator, but also faculty liaison, field director and school faculty. The organizational complexities and interpersonal relationships that need to be dealt with is clearly more convoluted for the field instructor.

In the balance between administrative, educational and supportive tasks, the field instructor gives clear priority to education. But not only is the demand for educating the student-supervisee more consequential for the field instructor, the nature of the demand itself is more arduous. The necessity for conceptualizing practice so that it can be clearly communicated in terms of applicable generalization is more frequently required of the field instructor than the agency supervisor. The field instructor more frequently needs to be a skillful teacher in addition to being a skillful social work practitioner.

The requirement for providing effective supportive supervision demands more from the field instructor than it does from the agency supervisor. The social work student, as contrasted with the agency supervisee, has not as yet developed any sense of confidence in his/her ability to be of help, has not as yet achieved a sense of identity as a social worker, is as yet in the process of making a commitment to social work and may still be uncertain about professional choice. The student, as contrasted with the agency supervisee, is more dependent, more anxious, making the painful transition from lay attitudes and values to social work professional attitudes and values, struggling with unnerving attacks of self-awareness more frequently than the agency supervisee. The field instructor is likely to require a greater sensitivity to student's unsettling, upsetting feelings and needs to devote time and energy in dealing with them, than does the agency supervisor interacting with the agency supervisee.

And, yet despite the fact that field instruction is more demanding, more complex, requiring more varied skills than agency supervision, it has received less study, less attention by social workers, a contention validated by a review of the social work literature. Between 1981 and 1989, **Social Work Abstracts** listed only 45 articles under the index heading of "field instruction", "field education" or "field work." The total number of entries on field instruction during the decade constituted three tenths of one percent of the 13,000 articles cited in **Social Work Abstracts**. This book is a valiant and successful effort to redress this imbalance.

# PART I: CONCEPTUAL FOUNDATIONS FOR FIELD EDUCATION

## INTRODUCTION

Field education for social work practice has had a time-honored and quintessential presence in social work over the past century. It has evolved during a most remarkable century of human history, and has been analyzed and illuminated by many of social work's most thoughtful and visionary pioneers. Interestingly, it has occupied over time positions of greater and lesser status and prominence in social work education. Portraying the history of field education goals and ideals against the backdrop of social, educational, and practice realities is Schneck's major theme in *Ideal and Reality In Field Education*. The lineage of mission and purpose statements through the past century yields "portraits in time of cherished ideals cast against the backdrop of the realities of the day" and impels us to ponder the imponderable: what lies ahead for social work practice and education, particularly field education? Reflections on this question are discussed by Schneck in the concluding section, "2000 and Beyond". He speculates, "There is little more to be gained on a grand scale by studying the role and structural features of field education . . . nothing less than the development and true integration of knowledge-based practice interventions in field education will suffice."

Conceptual foundations in field education are those sets of ideas, principles, and constructs which underpin and inform practice and the educational process. They fall into four major areas in Part I.

The first area concerns the constituent actors, common elements, and organizations--their interaction and political economy. These would necessarily include faculty, field directors and field staff from the schools; field instructors and educational coordinators within the agencies; the affiliational structures and relationship; field students, including their interests, past experience, and talent; and the complex of larger organizations such as CSWE, NASW, and state and federal social welfare agencies and institutions which influence and shape field education. These constituencies each present their needs, resources, and intentionality for field education. Their interaction or political economy is the theme developed by Grossman in *Themes and Variations: The Political Economy of Model Building*. The dynamic interplay and balancing of these constituencies clearly emphasizes the centrality of field education in meeting the mission and aspirations of the students, the school and the profession. As he states, ". . . the structure of a given field program depends upon a variety of forces and circumstances in the school and community, some of which can be manipulated and few of which can be controlled. We can most usefully discuss fieldwork decision-making in a relative rather than an absolute perspective." Grossman then proceeds to describe and discuss the common elements and environmental influences which shape the character and operation of field instruction programs.

The second area of conceptual foundations considers the educational philosophy and value attributed to experiential learning in social work education.

13

This is the major theme of Mesbur and Glassman's *From Commitment to Curriculum: The Humanistic Foundations of Field Instruction* as they discuss humanistic perspectives and experiential education in social work. They trace the historical roots to the early part of the century when "learning through doing" sought to unify knowledge and values through personal growth and development. As they state, "In social work education, the student must learn to combine knowledge with values toward honing the conscious use of self. The aim of field instruction is the integration of knowledge and practice endeavors so that practice wisdom and an emotional internalization of the professional role result." Following a discussion of the ideas of the early advocates of humanistic and experiential learning (John Dewey, Bertha Reynolds, Mary Richmond) and more recent theorists (Malcolm Knowles, David Kolb, Donald Schon, Marion Bogo and Elaine Vayda) they define a set of guiding principles for content and educational process in a field instruction curriculum. They conclude with a discussion of future directions and dilemmas in the advance of humanistic education and experiential learning in social work education.

The third area analyzes the cognitive process of learning, and the integration of theoretical knowledge and concepts with professional decision-making and intervention. The application of abstract theories, concepts, and ideas has attracted the concerted attention and reflection of social work educators for at least a half a century. Bogo and Vayda in *Developing a Process Model for Field Instruction* briefly discuss this history in the context of describing a national field instruction study undertaken in Canada. Its goals were the development of a comprehensive approach to field instruction and the improvement of service delivery. Given the regional diversity of Canada, the challenge was the inclusion of "generic concepts which would be relevant across the country." They cite the school-agency interface in field instruction as an avenue for "the transfer of new knowledge and service methods to the service providers" in a mutual exchange because "practice experience informs the development of new knowledge . . .". They then discuss the model of field instruction practice which evolved from the Canadian national project. Their model, the integration of theory and practice loop (ITP), was adapted from the work of Kolb, who envisioned a problem-centered learning process and cycle anchored in direct pexperienced. Their approach, while recognizing that "field instruction is a branch of social work practice which possesses a distinctive blend of knowledge, values and skills", places the emphasis more on the learning process than on specific content. They discuss The cognitive looping process in the ITP model and its acceptance and implementation by Canadian field instructors and social work faculty. They provide instructive examples of how a social worker would identify and connect to theoretical knowledge bases given different practice scenarios.

In the *Integration of Learning in Field Education: Elusive Goal and Educational Imperative*, Schneck considers the same phenomenon and imperative from an instructional perspective. He traces the notion of integration of learning vis-a-vis the evolution of social work education over the past century. The integration of theoretical knowledge and concepts was "seen as an instrumental goal in the long struggle to move away from an apprenticeship training model toward a knowledge-based professional education model." Given the explosion of socio-behavioral knowledge over the past 30 years, the goal of knowledge-guided practice or empirically based practice depends largely upon the success of the integration of theoretical and conceptual knowledge in the practice situation and field experience. Following a discussion of the mechanistic and holistic perspectives of integration, Schneck presents a teaching-learning model for the integration of learning in field education. The model, "places emphasis on the understanding of the nature of the learning sources and knowledge needs within the students' experience and the skillful use of teaching-learning methods and processes to facilitate synthesis." The model is illustrated by four paradigms which "identify the major content components in field education, the ideological, conceptual, emotional, and behavioral with individual and group teaching/learning activities suggested for the integration of learning." He argues for a learning environment in which the teacher or supervisor demonstrates and models a cognitive process which blends various knowledge sources into a coherent understanding or construct which can be applied to the specific practice situation.

The final conceptual foundation area reflected in Part I deals with the content or curriculum for field education. What is the intellectual product of the practicum? The nature of the knowledge content in field education is addressed by several authors in this section including Mesbur and Glassman, Bogo and Vayda, and Schneck. They recognize the importance, yet complexity, of applying general theoretical knowledge and concepts to specific practice situations and call variously for extrapolated constructs, custom tailoring, coherent understandings, and personalistic integrations of perceived knowledge, values, and personal experience. All of these foundations seek a cognitive operational process and internalization which links the specific to the general. It seems to be the state of the art. While social work knowledge and research is becoming more specific in focus, by and large, most practice situations confronted by social workers with all of their situational dynamics and variables are not informed by a definitive body of knowledge. To be sure, there is a lot of practice wisdom and experience "in the real world"; but for the most part, this also has not been defined or validated. It should be recognized, in balance, that this state of affairs does not distress many experienced practitioners who understand the limits of science and empiricism in guiding practice. They remind us that social work practice requires the artful application of knowledge and values within a creative and intuitive process.

Schneck ponders this dilemma in *Ideal and Reality In Field Education* when he states, "we may be poised at the next evolutionary stage of our development as a profession, that is the infusion and refinement of knowledge in practice settings. Field instruction and post-graduate training programs could become the center of this endeavor." The notion of instructive protocols for practice as content lessons in field education is postulated as the necessary next step in field education. This could be particularly helpful in the advance of practice in emerging problem areas. He conjectures that, "field education could become the primary medium for the bridge between the university function to generate and disseminate knowledge (the educational ideal) and the professional practice function to apply and refine knowledge in specific applications (the practice reality)."

The potential for practice leadership through field education is the theme of Schneck's *The Leadership Opportunity in Fieldwork for Responding to Change*. Here, the case is made for the fieldwork enterprise contributing practice innovation to the ever-pressing social problems of the day. He states that "field work, that is practice and education in the field provides a continuing opportunity to work at the nexus of change, that lively juncture of the practical and the ideal, the real and the unrealized, the intuitive and the empirical." He discusses the challenge, the compelling imperative given today's problems, and the structural organizational place of field education in highlighting the leadership opportunity.

In examining conceptual foundations in these major areas, all of the authors affirm the centrality of field instruction in practice education and innovation. Clearly it needs to be more than personal growth, skill rehearsal, or a laboratory for classroom theory, though these are important components. Our primary purpose is to teach the next generation of social work practitioners to comprehend and assist a more complex and problematic world than we would have ever imagined a generation ago when most of us were field students. When well done, field education transcends the art-science, theory-practice, and school-community dichotomies; and not only obtains an open, stimulating, and supportive learning environment for students, but also comprises the matrix from which true progress can emerge.

# IDEAL AND REALITY IN FIELD EDUCATION

Dean Schneck, *University of Wisconsin-Madison*

The evolving and colorful mission of field education can be imagined as a mediating construct among the interacting forces and dynamics of social, educational and practice ideals and realities. The expressed goals of the apprenticeship, field work, field instruction or field education as it has been variously called over the past century reveal a core statement of the overall purpose of social work education as they seem portraits in time of cherished ideals cast against the backdrop of the realities of the day. As we struggle with our current realities in teaching and administering field programs, we necessarily act within our own particularistic spheres of influence, demands and resources, perhaps recalling our own experiences as a field student.

It seems fitting to pause for a moment to reflect upon this classic interaction of ideal and reality and to examine some of the historic, as well as the more recent expressions of the mission for field education. This seems wise, not only to pay homage to those who went before, but also to consider what may be ahead.

The lineage and continuity of field education ideals through a century of arguably most dramatic and compelling social, cultural, and technological change, represent a remarkable tradition, often timeless in the relevance of its vision. Although clearly accommodating to contextual realities, the mission and strivings of our elders strike resonant chords indeed. Consider the following:

> With more than 25 years of experience in schools of social work, with 29 schools in a 10-year-old association, with a professional organization of 4,200 members and 43 chapters, with probably 25,000 professional social workers in the United States, and a possible need for 3,000 new workers each year--education for social work is today facing problems of increasing magnitude and complexity. (Conrad, 1930, p. 148-149)

This quote from Irene Farnham Conrad, then director of the Syracuse, New York, Community Chest, is taken from the first edition of the **Social Work Year Book 1929.** Her article chronicles more than a quarter century of organized social work training activities and closes with the following questions:

> How are the universities which are proposing to organize schools of social work to be helped in their plans? What should be the relationship between specialized schools and the general schools of social work? Professional education will ever be a joint undertaking involving the agency, the profession, and the school. . ." (p. 154)

17

The following figure attempts to depict the complex matrix in which field education has always been embedded. It is possible to visualize to some extent how the mission statements for field education have developed, and why, given the nature of social, educational, and practice variables, it is so difficult to predict what lies ahead.

## FIGURE 1: Ideal and Reality Matrix in Field Education

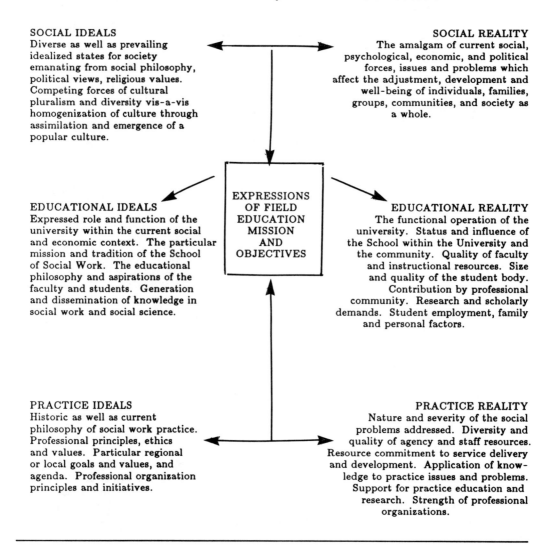

SOCIAL IDEALS
Diverse as well as prevailing idealized states for society emanating from social philosophy, political views, religious values. Competing forces of cultural pluralism and diversity vis-a-vis homogenization of culture through assimilation and emergence of a popular culture.

SOCIAL REALITY
The amalgam of current social, psychological, economic, and political forces, issues and problems which affect the adjustment, development and well-being of individuals, families, groups, communities, and society as a whole.

EXPRESSIONS OF FIELD EDUCATION MISSION AND OBJECTIVES

EDUCATIONAL IDEALS
Expressed role and function of the university within the current social and economic context. The particular mission and tradition of the School of Social Work. The educational philosophy and aspirations of the faculty and students. Generation and dissemination of knowledge in social work and social science.

EDUCATIONAL REALITY
The functional operation of the university. Status and influence of the School within the University and the community. Quality of faculty and instructional resources. Size and quality of the student body. Contribution by professional community. Research and scholarly demands. Student employment, family and personal factors.

PRACTICE IDEALS
Historic as well as current philosophy of social work practice. Professional principles, ethics and values. Particular regional or local goals and values, and agenda. Professional organization principles and initiatives.

PRACTICE REALITY
Nature and severity of the social problems addressed. Diversity and quality of agency and staff resources. Resource commitment to service delivery and development. Application of knowledge to practice issues and problems. Support for practice education and research. Strength of professional organizations.

The early advocates for field training instinctively called for apprentice experiences and programs in the provision of material benefits and friendly visitation to the poor and needy. However, many sensed the need for the utilization and the development of knowledge and theory. In noting what may be the earliest reference to training, Conrad states:

> As early as 1893, in her paper on "The Need of Training Schools for a New Profession" at the International Congress of Charities in Chicago, Anna Dawes emphasized the relation between successful social work by any agency and the preparation of its workers. Four years later Mary E. Richmond, in her paper "The Need of a Training School on Applied Philanthropy" [**Proceedings, National Conference of Charities and Corrections, 1897**], advocated a professional school for social workers, affiliated with a university but having freedom to emphasize practical features of the subjects taught. (p. 149)

Clearly, many of our continuing issues and debates concerning the integration of theory and practice, the dynamic between specific skill and generalizable concept, the role of intellectual ability, personality, and suitability for the profession have a seminal presence in the early discussions of the nature of field education. Mildred Sikkema, a noted historian and consultant in field instruction, writing for the Council in 1966, discusses the purpose and structure of professional education a century ago:

> The early advocates of training for "applied philanthropy" in the United States envisioned a "life vocation" for educated young men and women. In the 1890's training for this new profession was perceived as including academic instruction and "practice under expert guidance." The leaders who were interested in the development of training programs that would combine general principles with practice were clear that the new training must include opportunities for the student to:
>
> * have prolonged, intimate contact with the people served by philan-thropic agencies;
> * take part as a representative of an agency in giving the service it offered;
> * learn this practice under the regular supervision of people rich in experience. (Sikkema, 1966)

The regard for formal academic instruction and field practice in the development of a "life" vocation is readily apparent. Training program were designed to provide first-hand knowledge and exposure to the poor and their living conditions so as to foster professional responsibility and the inculcation of altruistic values and commitment. Sikkema describes the historical focus of field work by saying:

The main thesis was that field work provided an opportunity for both paid and volunteer workers to obtain intimate knowledge of the poor and of actual social and economic conditions. It was believed that only through continuing contact, as a representative of an agency under expert guidance over an extended period of time, could a charity worker develop:

* conviction about the needs of the poor;
* the quality of caring about the poor as individuals possessing human dignity and the capacity to use opportunities for creating a more satisfactory life;
* a sense of individual social responsibility through an evolving social consciousness;
* conviction that the use of an orderly method and organized procedures of helping would enhance rather than destroy the personal, sympathetic factor in helping; and
* habits of mind and work considered essential in carrying out the work of the agency effectively and efficiently. (p. 3)

There we have the purpose, structure and content of field education as conceived almost 100 years ago. A more recent historian, Aase George, in the Sheafor and Jenkins volume (1982), reflects upon the early literature in field education:

When one reads the papers written by early leaders in the field of social work on the need for training schools, it is clear that learning through doing was always seen as an important part of education for social work. Mary Richmond, for example, in 1897 called for a permanent group of instructors to direct the work of students, giving them theory and practice together. She pointed out that while many learned from doing, learning by doing alone is not efficient and must be supplemented by theory.[1]

Around the country, in major cities such as New York, Boston, Chicago, St. Louis, Cleveland, and Philadelphia, visionary pioneers in charity organizations and settlement houses sponsored and founded independent training centers and programs primarily in family casework which gave rise to some of the most prominent schools of social work in the country. Though a unifying theory of method and process had yet to be articulated, the mission statements for practice and apprenticeship training clearly called for the amelioration of individual and family needs as well as for social reform and social statesmanship.

Beginning in the 1920's and through the 30's, social ideals as well as educational and practice ideals were shaped by major historic events which in turn refocused field training. These included, of course, the return home of the troops

---

[1]The citation is from Mary Richmond's work, "The Training of Charity Workers," The Charities Review, Vol. 6 (June, 1897).

after World War I, the industrial and economic expansion of the 20's, the pervasive impact of psychoanalytic theory of personality upon social work practice and field supervision, and finally the economic collapse and great depression of 1929 and the 30's. During this period social casework specialties began to emerge in response to the practice needs in various institutional areas. George discusses some of the specializations as follows:

> Medical social work had developed in Massachusetts General Hospital in Boston and Bellevue Hospital in New York as early as 1905; and one of the early schools, Simmons, was especially noted for education appropriate for that area of practice. Psychiatric social work had also developed out of the introduction of the psychoanalytic theory of personality, the efforts to rehabilitate shell-shock victims of World War I, and the mental hygiene movement which led to the establishment of mental guidance clinics in the twenties. Smith College School of Social Work, which has always been known for its education of psychiatric social workers at Boston Psychopathic Hospital, wished to establish training to meet the needs of the hospital program. Child welfare, school social work, and Red Cross work were among early specializations. Public administration was also recognized early as a special field, and later in the depression years of the 1930's, when the Federal Emergency Relief Administration was sending students to schools of social work to be educated for public welfare positions, field work in the area also became important. (p. 40-41)

Practice and training for mainstream social casework, however, became preoccupied with the inner experience and personality development relegating social reform and social justice concerns to a backwater eddy, not to reemerge until the 40's. In clarifying the transitional impact upon field work, Sikkema (1966) states:

> The earlier organizing concept of the goal of field work as that of gaining knowledge, developing attitudes, and understanding values within the context of social and economic conditions was replaced in this second period by an emphasis on understanding those served within the context of psychoanalytic and psychiatric knowledge. (p. 4)

The seeds of the next stage of evolution were already sown in the debate between professional development versus personality development as the goal of field work. The confusion over the aims of field work, whether upon the personal growth or the professional behavior of the student, or perhaps personal growth as the foundation for professional behavior, belied the impact of psychoanalytic theory and training; and had its analogue in the practice conception of the day.

In the dissonant clash between ideal and reality in the 30's and 40's, historic realities of unimagined proportions necessitated a rethinking of the purposes of social work practice. Sikkema noted:

The depression of the 1930's and World War II imposed human experiences that forced social work educators to reflect soberly upon the social responsibility of the profession in the conflict between the interests of the individual and the collective social interest. Sharply and urgently asked in the 1940's was whether the profession had a responsibility to attack problems of the social structure. Equally significant was the question of the social responsibility of individual members of the profession. (p. 5)

During the 40's "middle ground" syntheses began to be seen in the work of Charlotte Towle and Virginia Robinson. In the "Supervision" chapter of her classic, **Common Human Needs** (1945), Charlotte Towle states:

In supervision, which is essentially a teaching-learning situation, that is, an educative process, *we rely heavily on the principle that a new intellectual orientation may influence feeling and hence action.*[2] Conditions are particularly favorable for this outcome when the intellectual orientation is largely gained through or accompanied by experience which affords opportunity for the immediate demonstration and use of the ideas. For this reason, *the teaching aspects of supervision within a social agency afford a challenging opportunity for the realization of educational aims.* (p. 101)

Robinson (1936) saw the process of practice learning as occurring through the effective reorganization of attitude following the integration of new knowledge with feeling. Clearly the mutuality and reciprocity between the cognitive and the affective were being envisioned.

The post-war era of the late 40's and 50's can be viewed as a period of revitalization, expansion, and professionalization of social work education and field instruction. Much attention was given to the development and utilization of practice and educational theory, and the standardization of a two-year Master's program. Early beginnings of baccalaureate education were seen including field instruction, and the advancement of the field instruction component from an apprenticeship model to education for professional practice was initiated. Sikkema characterizes this period as follows:

The die was cast and the goal was clearly stated: education for the profession rather than apprenticeship. ... Attention was focused over a long period of time on the identification of content for field teaching, organized often around social work method. ... Attempts were made to create an educational focus by developing devices for

----

[2]For further discussion see Charlotte Towle, "Underlying skills of case work today," SOCIAL SERVICE REVIEW, Vol. 15, No. 3, 456-41; appears also in PROCEEDINGS OF THE NATIONAL CONFERENCE OF SOCIAL WORK, 1941, 254-266.

"integrating" class and field work. . . . The notion of field work as a course for which objectives could be identified, content selected, and learning opportunities planned continued to be discussed--and strong convictions both for and against it persisted.

As if a harbinger of things to come, the emerging concept of professional identification with the purposes of social work rekindled interest in the student's development of social consciousness and social responsibility. Though not widely incorporated into field education at the time, the notion of professional self, with its implicit prerogative to define problems more broadly and act autonomously, clearly provided a rationale and legitimacy for the thunderous era of activism in the 60's and early 70's. (Sikkema, p. 7)

During the 60's, the dialectic between ideal and reality became strident, and divisive. If field work can be visualized as a bridge between social ideal and reality, then that bridge in the 60's was stressed and strained by overload and contortion. The cultural and generational awakening to the ills and injustices of society stirred inner convictions and ideals to external expression and activism. In the transformation, ideals often seemed less important than idealism. Perceptions of reality became ahistoric and absolute; and liberal relativism and incrementalism became not only irrelevant and inadequate, but were viewed as co-optation.

Much of this bombast, of course, was not heard until the middle part of the decade; the early 60's more approximated the developmental period of the 50's. The expansion of social work practice in traditional areas as well as its extension to new problem areas created new jobs and professional roles for social work. It was a halcyon era for social work education. Federal demonstration and training grants to stimulate the development of practice in emerging areas provided large amounts of financial support to schools of social work, faculty, and students. The 'War on Poverty' stimulated the social welfare "industry," and many states had work/study and stipend programs to "rush to market" Master's level social workers for practice in state and local agencies.

Economically, it was a time of low inflation and unemployment; and the supply/demand equation clearly favored the supply sector. It was not uncommon for large state and private agencies to send recruiters around the country to visit schools of social work and interview prospective graduates.

Against this backdrop of frantic and petulant energy, idealism, and absorption in the present, some very thoughtful and creative work was done in the conceptual development of field education. During most of the decade, CSWE, with support from the National Institute of Mental Health and the Children's Bureau of HEW, sponsored several national conferences and symposia events which brought together distinguished faculty, field directors, and deans to explore field teaching and learning and to promote innovation in structure, educational process, and knowledge development in the field component.

This was the era of the teaching/learning centers in many schools around the country with their concomitant initiatives for the integration of knowledge and research with the field experience, the opportunity for practice research, and for the extension of practice to underserved communities and populations. Great attention was paid to faculty roles and staffing patterns, curriculum objectives and sequencing, adult education principles, and conceptual frames of reference for field instruction. Several schools around the country were experimenting with faculty field instructors teaching units of students based in social agencies, community service centers, or teaching/learning centers. Clearly the apprentice model, steeped in tradition and imbued with sentimental value, came under scrutiny and, in the minds of some, irreverent challenge. (Cassidy, 1969).

Taken in sum, these efforts went far beyond earlier orthodoxy to utilize the developing knowledge base in curriculum development and learning and communication theory to bring field instruction solidly into accord with modern educational ideals and objectives. In a way, Katherine Kendall set the agenda for the 60's in a thoughtful and heuristic paper published in 1959, but presented in 1958 at a fiftieth anniversary dinner honoring social agencies who had participated in the field work program at the University of Chicago. She asserted:

> We need have no fear of discussion and analysis of the costs of social work education, particularly its field instruction component --*if* we have an intelligible rationale and attainable objectives for our pattern of field instruction, *if* we have well-thought-out goals and evaluation procedures for student performance, and *if* we have a clearly delineated method of field teaching which achieves the educational purposes of the university and, at the same time, contributes to professional service in the agency. Let the two faces of Janus look squarely at what goes into the production of a well-qualified social worker and why. We can then add up the costs and go on from there to assess whether they are too high or too low in relation to the benefits which accrue to the university, to the community, and to society as a whole. (1978)

Eleven years later at the close of the 60's, Helen Cassidy (1969) of Tulane University, site of much experimentation in field instruction and host of a major national symposium, stated in the symposium proceedings:

> The last decade has seen a proliferation of effort and an explosion of field instruction experimentation. Liberated from old bonds, schools have advanced along uncharted but interesting areas of knowledge probing in field instruction. As we might have suspected, this time-honored piece of the curriculum has withstood dissection and analysis exceedingly well. The study of its potential, still in an early stage, seems to offer infinite possibilities for richness and usefulness.

Though perhaps overshadowed by the turbulent waves of social protest of the day, major advances were seen in the articulation of educational ideals for field instruction. It was an impressive period.[3]

During the 70's and the 80's, as if recoiling from the 60's, the pendulum of social reality with social ideals trailing closely behind, moved back toward the center and then perhaps to the right of center. Decade markers are, of course, arbitrary historical time frames. Actually the early 70's rode on the momentum of the 60's and resembled it in some ways; yet, change was in the air. Gradually, our ideals were viewed as unrealistic. The collective impact of social and economic retrenchment, double digit inflation and interest rates and Watergate, diminished our dreams and deflated the social welfare enterprise. Demographic changes, particularly the aging of the baby boomers into their post-college young adult roles focused attention on employment, employability, and individual needs. Just as youth in the 60's acted discontinuously from the values of the fifties, the materialism and individualism exhibited by many mid-seventies and eighties youth seemed disconnected, even oblivious to the vaunted idealism of the sixties. The popular manifestations, of course, were seen in changes in dress, music, drug usage, and personal and political values.

Political and economic realities forced social work to retreat from many of its earlier commitments. We learned the language of compromise; terms such as "cost benefit analysis", and "zero-based budgeting" came into our vocabulary. Once placed in a defensive posture, it was not surprising to see protective reactions and accommodations on the part of some social workers and organizations.

Paralleling these retreats, many Schools of Social Work saw a decline in their application rates and (though few spoke of it), perhaps, a deterioration in the overall quality of the applicant pool. Most schools, of course, had precious little stipend support to offer students and often the faculty saw erosions in their salary base due to the inability of compensation packages to keep up with inflation. Despite the encouraging upturn of application rates in some schools recently, are we attracting our share of the "best and the brightest"? Are we seeing a true resurgence of altruism or are we engaging in wishful thinking? Some will point to the increased volunteerism and community awareness of many of today's youth in 90's problems (homelessness, AIDS, ecology, underclass youth) and say "aye." Others, noting demographics, especially the aging of the "baby boomers", shifting political sentiments, and economic realities, will say regrettably, "nay." We see some expansion of job opportunities for our graduates (and faculty), but the salaries are usually far below comparably educated graduates in other fields. The jury is still out.

---

[3]See for example, **Modes of Professional Education** (New Orleans: School of Social Work Tulane University 1969); **Field Learning and Teaching: Explorations** in Graduate Social Work Education (New York, Council on Social Work Education, 1968); **Field Instruction in Graduate Social Work Education: Old Problems and New Proposals** (New York: Council on Social Work Education, 1966); Betty Lacy Jones, ed. **Current Patterns in Field Instruction in Graduate Social Work Education** (New York: Council on Social Work Education, 1969); and Virginia Franks, **The Autonomous Social Worker**, Occasional paper No.1 (Madison: University of Wisconsin-Madison School of Social Work, 1966).

Viewing the impact of all this on field instruction and field educators, the inescapable conclusion is that we have been through a hard time! Though the austerity imposed on our endeavors by the social reality of the past fifteen years has cost us dearly, we are bowed but not broken. George (1982) summarizes the 70's as follows:

> While interest in maintaining and improving the educational quality of field instruction continued in the 1970's, there was not the level of activity in sharing exploratory studies and research at professional meetings and through publications that marked the 1960's. This was probably related to the decrease in availability of funding through government grants and the termination of the CSWE project on field instruction and learning in the 1960s. Faculty responsible for field instruction programs have expressed a need for more consultive help and planned meetings to consider common problems and their solution. (p. 54)

It should be noted that social, practice, and educational realities are not universal; there is often unevenness and regional exceptions to the prevailing reality. During the 70's and 80's, many schools had significant bright spots in their evolution. Regional practice needs and the well-being of local economies encouraged the development of social service programs and innovative educational programs in many schools. Moreover, we would be very remiss if we did not recognize the courageous and creative efforts of social workers and field educators around the country which were mounted to combat the unconscionable cutbacks in social programs and their deleterious effects upon the citizenry.

In field education, there were two notable developments during this period--one organizational and the other scholarly. Beginning in 1977 and continuing approximately through 1980, a valiant effort on the part of several distinguished field educators resulted in the establishment of the National Clearinghouse on Field Education. During this period, the Clearinghouse served as a vehicle for communication and dissemination of unpublished educational materials for field work administrators, coordinators, and instructors in social work education. At the risk of omitting someone, the "principal movers" were Norma Berkowitz of the University of Wisconsin-Madison; Reva Fine Holtzman of Hunter College; Lowell Jenkins of Colorado State University, Fort Collins; Rosalie Mollenhauer, then at the University of Texas-Austin; Helen Cassidy of Tulane University; and Margaret Schutz-Gordon of the University of Kansas. The supporting constituency group, called the National Alliance of Field Coordinators and Administrators, sponsored several roundtable conferences at APM's and regional conferences which focused on the pursuit of excellence in field education.

Norma Berkowitz captured the sense of the initiative well in her "Personally Speaking" column in the National Clearinghouse Newsletter:

> The birth of the Clearinghouse and the National Alliance was the result of a need for people with a common problem (field instruction

and/or administration) to come together and share information and experience. Both came into being as self-help developments at a time when those involved in field instruction felt impotent and isolated in a time of rapid re-examination and change in social work education. (1979, p. 3)

The sad and inevitable outcome was that the National Alliance and *National Clearinghouse Newsletter* ended in approximately 1980 due to a lack of financial and program support from CSWE and the schools. There did not exist at the time sufficient resources to sustain an independent organizational structure or association of field educators. When one considers the noble intentions and dedicated efforts of this group of our colleagues, it is clear that they deserved better.

The continuing efforts of field instructors, educators, and administrators to provide valuable and effective learning experiences to students were aided immeasurably by the publication in 1982 of Brad Sheafor's and Lowell Jenkins' **Quality Field Instruction in Social Work: Program Development and Maintenance**. Their stated intention was:

> . . .to present a comprehensive view of the multiple dimensions of field instruction and to fill a significant gap in social work literature--the lack of a single volume providing an overview of the purpose, structure, and tasks required for student learning." (Preface, ix)

This volume has become a source book, rich in practical as well as theoretical knowledge of field instruction. Their formulation of the mission of field education is best expressed in their words:

> A vital part of social work education is field instruction. Field instruction is an experiential form of teaching and learning in which the social work student is helped to: (1) consciously bring selected knowledge to the practice situation; (2) develop competence in performing practice skills; (3) learn to practice within the framework of social work values and ethics; (4) develop a professional commitment to social work practice; (5) evolve a practice style consistent with personal strengths and capacities; and (6) develop the ability to work effectively within a social agency. (p. 3)

In concluding this historical review of the mission of field education, it is readily apparent that we owe a large debt of gratitude to those notable authors and innovators who shared their observations and wisdom in the published written record. It also prompts a conjecture that there exists within the archival annals and bulletins of our social agencies, universities, and libraries, a body of unpublished statements which contains comparable aspirations for field education as envisioned by many outstanding educators and practitioners. It would be most interesting to read their versions as well. Clearly, we are in very good company--yesterday and today.

## 2000 AND BEYOND

Very soon, we will be experiencing the conjuncture of two milestones, one centennial and one millennial. During the decade of 1990-2000, we will note, if not celebrate, the centennial of field education in social work. The exact date is difficult and perhaps arbitrary to specify; but undoubtedly it will occur within this period. At the end of our centenary decade, we will surely mark the passing of the millennium as we enter the year 2000 A.D. It will be a date of little significance in the geologic age of the planet; nonetheless, we will ceremonially note it as a major marker in human time on New Year's Eve, 1999.

Most of us, with a little luck, will still be teaching and administering field programs (and/or doing other things). As we make this collective journey to the year 2000 and beyond, what will we witness, influence, and experience in field education? Will there be any grand leaps forward or elegant new formulations from the interplay of ideal and reality? I think, yes; of necessity, there must be. However, they will not occur, in my opinion, in the re-statement and codification of the basic elements of field education. There is little more to be gained, on a grand scale, by studying the role and structural features of field instruction. There are, to be sure, many variable applications of these common elements and creative syntheses within program missions throughout the country; but this is essentially good educational program development. It represents the necessary, but not the sufficient, condition for a quantum leap forward.

Practice, as we all know, is becoming ever more complex. Many problems are interrelated; and there is much new knowledge being developed in recombinant disciplines which did not even exist 20 years ago. The world is changing very quickly with the acceleration of technology, migration, ecological and demographic imperatives, macroeconomic and geopolitical restructuring and shifts in balances of power and population. These factors and others will yield very complicated problems in living and survival which will demand all the available talent and perseverance of the next generation of social workers.

Within our universities, we have seen a generation of growth in specialty-trained Ph.D.s. Many have more publications upon receipt of their doctorates or shortly thereafter than some faculty had when granted tenure twenty years ago. Often, their research and scholarly work is sharply focused and empirical. Much has promise for practice, but only if it can be utilized in specific practice applications underpinned with a solid conceptual rationale and taught to students and prac-titioners.

Where better for knowledge diffusion and integration to occur than in field education and staff development of practitioners. We know, regrettably, that many practitioners read very little of the professional literature and participate even less in research. Practice and research imperatives in the future may well advance a crucial ethic of professional practice--that is, for practitioners as well as educators and researchers to share responsibility for the development and improvement of practice knowledge and methods. I have commented:

> Knowledge can inform practice, but practice can also reform
> knowledge. The knowledge-building process can and should go both
> ways. We may, at times, have a better configuration of practice,
> construed artfully and intuitively in field work . . . We are often
> forced to confront new problems and persistent human needs in the
> absence of definitive guidance from academic or empirical sources.
> . . . Ultimately, innovations from practice as well as those derived
> from research must stand on their respective merits. (see *Leadership*,
> p.78, this volume)

In the future, field education could become the primary medium for the bridge
between the university function to generate and disseminate knowledge and innovation (the educational ideal) and the professional function to apply and refine
knowledge in specific practice applications (the practice reality).

We may be poised at the next evolutionary stage in our development as a
profession, that is, the infusion and refinement of knowledge in practice settings.
Field instruction and post-graduate training programs could become the center of
this endeavor. Professions evolve and proceed through stages of development from
informal to formal, from intuitive and practical to empirical and theoretical, replete
with ritual, tradition and ideals. Rothman and Jones (1971) have noted:

> . . . Professions generally in their development and maturation move
> from a period when (a) education is controlled by practitioners and
> heavily emphasized skill and apprenticeship, (b) to a period of
> independent professional schools, when skill and theory are given
> somewhat equal treatment, and finally (c) to a period when education
> is centered in the university under university control and intellectual
> concepts, and principles are given greatest emphasis. (p. 46)

They hypothesized in 1971 that social work was in a middle phase and ought to shift
to a "new balance" which "would also include class and field but with a heavier
weighting on the academic-knowledge side" (p. 47). They cite William McGlothlin
(1960):

> In general, then, the trend of the curriculum in the various profes-
> sional fields is to move toward greater emphasis on knowledge,
> concepts, and principles, with proportionately less emphasis on
> detailed instruction in the skills of practice or on special techniques.

In considering these developmental paradigms for the professions, one senses an
incomplete cycle, a missing linkage from the conceptual back to the actual, as if
refined abstractions need not be re-affirmed in their matrix phenomena.

The ability and success of researchers to disseminate knowledge and of
practitioners to adapt new knowledge to their needs has fascinated and frustrated
both constituencies during the "knowledge explosion" of the post-war period.
Research on the attitudinal, purposive, and perceptual differences of researchers and

practitioners, the disjuncture and estrangement that often occurs between these constituencies, the articulation of roles and processes for the transmission of knowledge (consultants, collaborators, specialists, etc.) has preoccupied many educators, theorists, and researchers.[4]

The positing of a change agent for the utilization of research in practice has been characterized as follows:

> Of all the suggestions for obtaining research utilization, the establishment of a linkage mechanism in the form of a change agent or agency is the most strongly advocated by many writers. Linkage is basically a series of two-way interactions that connect user systems with resource systems (Havelock, 1969). The articulating force can either overlap the two sides, or bridge the gap between the research and the practitioner. (Bhola, 1965)

That "change agent", that "articulating force" could be the field instructor or educator recycling knowledge back to practice. Clearly, knowledge generation without a cycle back to practice would become irrelevant and practice without the infusion of new knowledge from the university would become anaemic and outmoded. The paradigm is already well represented in our professional language by "knowledge-guided practice" or "empirically-based practice". In this context, the role of change agent has been thus expressed:

> His [sic] influence is variously transmitted through cognitive knowledge transfer, attitudinal reeducation, and behavioral performance modification. He may be part of the knowledge-producing system, the knowledge-user system, or both systems, not to mention the contextual social system. In short, he is a catalyst of change, and a potentially powerful linking force in the continuous effort to put knowledge to practical and innovative use. (*Putting Knowledge to Use*, p. 61-62)

We have progressed historically from an early recognition of the value of new knowledge through an ascendant phase of the development of knowledge of and for practice. It seems now that the next major advance must be to find ways to incorporate that knowledge into practice. Similar initiatives have been advocated earlier; Mildred Sikkema in 1964 defined "two pivotal objectives" in her proposal for "innovation". Stated in educational terms, they are:

* affirming in performance the integration of thinking with feeling and values as a basis for professional activity; and

---

[4]See **Putting Knowledge to Use: A Distillation of the Literature Regarding Knowledge Transfer and Change** (Los Angeles, Human Interaction Research Institute in collaboration with the National Institute of Mental Health, 1976).

\* affirming in performance a grasp of the underlying structure and significance of complex knowledge, of the connections among the parts of a whole. (p. 10)

A few years later, at the Symposium on *Modes of Professional Education* in 1969, Herbert Aptekar, in discussing knowledge to be introduced into teaching centers, stated:

What I am saying here is that there is a form of learning, which when seen in its mature development is thought of as practice wisdom. This form of learning is the domain of the practicum. In it, there are many specific items of knowledge: some strictly factual and informational; some involving understanding of people, of one's own self and of clients; some pertaining to community and society; some concerned with the profession as such and the way organizations and institutions within the profession function; some strictly technical in character and concerned with the possible ways of doing the same thing; but all put together in a recognizable package which should be labeled "professional behavior." (p. 88-89)

Teaching-learning centers were often able to structure student experiences in ways which synthesized this vision of professional behavior. At the same symposium, Samuel Finestone (1969) in defining the knowledge development potential for field teaching and learning noted:

. . . the major point is that knowledge transmission and knowledge building should go on in the field as well as the class. . . . Effective learning requires that the student be given opportunities to practice that which he is expected to learn in the context which is salient for him. He must learn and practice in the model which combines service and knowledge building. (p. 124)

In reflecting upon the preparation for thoughtful practice, he went on to say:

Social Workers have to live and practice and learn in the context of uncertainty and the hypothetical. . . . If we wish practitioners to be prepared to participate in knowledge-building efforts, perhaps we should directly provide such experiences as part of field teaching and learning. (p. 125, 127)

Though ardently advocated and readily accepted by many in field education, the realization of this goal has been elusive. Taken as a whole, our knowledge infusion efforts in field instruction are largely under-developed. The content for practice may be inconsistent or often unspecified. I suggest this is not because of a lack of skilled and dedicated practitioners and educators or field practice opportunities, but a lack of widely held and validated practice content.

Scott Briar (1969) evidenced this concern over twenty years ago as he discussed the teaching center concept:

> The experienced practitioner and the new student alike correctly recognize that what they need most of all is knowledge that will increase their effectiveness in bringing about the changes they and their clients seek, and they also see clearly that all too little such knowledge is available either in the classrooms or the journals of their profession. (p. 72)

He further stated that in the teaching center design:

> . . . the practice activities conducted under the aegis of the center should be innovative and experimental, at the leading rather than the trailing edges of practice. (p. 74)

## PRACTICE PROTOCOLS IN FIELD EDUCATION

It is the belief of this author that nothing less than the development and true integration of knowledge-based practice interventions in field education will suffice. By this, I mean the specific application of social work and social science knowledge to human problems (individual, family, group, community, societal) in the form of instructive protocols as content for field learning. Generic methods and process, human behavior and social environment, treatment methods and skills, and social problem and policy content are the knowledge sources; but, they will need to be fashioned into specific applications for practice and taught as content in field instruction.

It will not be sufficient only to pose interesting questions and infer knowledge sources. Field instructors and faculty will be challenged to configure actual interventions for the various practice dilemmas we face and to teach these guides to students. Our students yearn for this kind of knowledge, and we owe them and their clients rigorous and creative syntheses.

The depiction below illustrates the place of practice protocol:

| EDUCATIONAL IDEAL | PRACTICE PROTOCOLS IN FIELD EDUCATION | PRACTICE REALITY |
|---|---|---|
| Research, theory and knowledge generation, and diffusion to social work practice | Knowledge, value, and skill based interventions for specific practice applications | Old and new practice problems and need for innovation to improve service quality and effectiveness |

The notion of protocols as guides for practice suggests units of learning assembled in prescriptive and procedural terms incorporating relevant knowledge and practice interventions. It could be argued that this is too much of a "cook book" approach to practice. The rhetorical response while recognizing the cautionary note would indicate that the validity of this criticism would depend upon the degree of specificity and flexibility allowed. In truth, most of us need recipes, though we assume the chef's prerogative of adding a little more or less of something to achieve a desired result. Else, we start "from scratch" every time.

In the actual practice situation, there would, of course, be room for judgement and intuition. Given the current state of our application of knowledge, we are nowhere near the point of having to fear overspecification. A particular teacher or instructor might be overly specific or rigid; but that is a teaching problem. In a recent national Field Work Symposium, I summarized:

> But all of our heartfelt strivings, our well-designed structures, and our refined processes will come to naught if we do not disseminate a strong and visionary message for practice. For in field practice, the medium is only part of the message. The rest of the message must of necessity illuminate the problems which are so pressing and the practice which we hold so dear. Else, we may not endure as a profession in the new millennium. (see p. 78)

The foregoing represents an ideal for the "illuminating message" and how it can be blended into the quintessential mission of field education to prepare knowledgeable and effective social workers. If we advance along this path, quickly and with conviction, we will not only endure, but prosper as a profession in our next century and the world's new millennium.

## BIBLIOGRAPHY

Aptekar, Herbert H. (1969) "Differentiating types of knowledge introduced in the classroom and teaching centers," in MODES OF PROFESSIONAL EDUCATION: FUNCTIONS OF FIELD LEARNING IN THE CURRICULUM. TULANE STUDIES IN SOCIAL WELFARE, Vol. XI New Orleans: School of Social Work, Tulane University.

Berkowitz, Norma, ed. (September, 1979) THE NATIONAL CLEARINGHOUSE ON FIELD EDUCATION NEWSLETTER. Vol. 1, No. 2.

Bhola, H.S. (1965) A CONFIGURATIONAL THEORY OF INNOVATION DIFFUSION. Columbus: Ohio State University.

Briar, Scott (1969) "Teaching Center design as a function of curriculum objectives", MODES OF PROFESSIONAL EDUCATION: FUNCTIONS OF FIELD LEARNING IN THE CURRICULUM. Tulane Studies in Social Welfare, Vol. XI New Orleans: School of Social Work, Tulane University.

Cassidy, Helen (1969) "Foreword" to MODES OF PROFESSIONAL EDUCATION: FUNCTIONS OF FIELD LEARNING IN THE CURRICULUM. Tulane Studies in Social Welfare, Vol. XI New Orleans: School of Social Work, Tulane University.

Conrad, Irene F. (1930) "Education for Social Work" in SOCIAL WORK YEAR BOOK 1929, Fred S. Hall and Mabel B. Ellis, eds. New York: Russell Sage Foundation.

FIELD LEARNING AND TEACHING: EXPLORATIONS IN GRADUATE SOCIAL WORK EDUCATION. (1968) New York, Council on Social Work Education.

FIELD INSTRUCTION IN GRADUATE SOCIAL WORK EDUCATION: OLD PROBLEMS AND NEW PROPOSALS. (1966) New York: Council on Social Work Education.

Finestone, Samuel (1969) "Field teaching and knowledge development" in MODES OF PROFESSIONAL EDUCATION: FUNCTIONS OF FIELD LEARNING IN THE CURRICULUM. Tulane Studies in Social Welfare, Vol. XI New Orleans: School of Social Work, Tulane University.

Franks, Virginia (1966) THE AUTONOMOUS SOCIAL WORKER. Occasional paper No. 1, Madison: University of Wisconsin-Madison School of Social Work.

George, Aase (1982) "A History of Social Work Field Instruction: Apprenticeship to Instruction." in Sheafor and Jenkins, QUALITY FIELD INSTRUCTION IN SOCIAL WORK: PROGRAM DEVELOPMENT AND MAINTENANCE. New York: Longman.

Havelock, R.(1969) PLANNING FOR INNOVATION THROUGH DISSEMINATION AND UTILIZATION OF KNOWLEDGE. Ann Arbor: University of Michigan Institute for Social Research.

Jones, Betty Lacy, ed. (1969) CURRENT PATTERNS IN FIELD INSTRUCTION IN GRADUATE SOCIAL WORK EDUCATION. New York: Council on Social Work Education.

Kendall, Katherine A. (1978) REFLECTIONS ON SOCIAL WORK EDUCATION, 1950-1978. New York, International Association of Schools of Social Work.

McGlothlin, William (1960) PATTERNS OF PROFESSIONAL EDUCATION. New York: G.P. Putnam's Sons.

MODES OF PROFESSIONAL EDUCATION: FUNCTIONS OF FIELD LEARNING IN THE CURRICULUM. (1969) Tulane Studies in Social Welfare, Vol. XI New Orleans: School of Social Work, Tulane University.

PUTTING KNOWLEDGE TO USE: A DISTILLATION OF THE LITERATURE REGARDING KNOWLEDGE TRANSFER AND CHANGE. (1976) Los Angeles, Human Interaction Research Institute in collaboration with the National Institute of Mental Health .

Richmond, Mary. "The Training of Charity Workers," THE CHARITIES REVIEW, Vol. 6 June, 1897.

Robinson, Virginia P. (1936) SUPERVISION IN SOCIAL CASEWORK: A PROBLEM IN PROFESSIONAL EDUCATION. Chapel Hill, NC: The University of North Carolina Press.

Rothman, Jack and Jones, Wyatt (1971) A NEW LOOK AT FIELD INSTRUCTION: EDUCATION FOR APPLICATION OF PRACTICE SKILLS IN COMMUNITY ORGANIZATION AND SOCIAL PLANNING. New York: Association Press.

Schneck, Dean (March, 1987) "The Leadership Opportunity in Fieldwork", presented at FIELD WORK: NEXUS OF CHANGE IN SOCIAL WORK EDUCATION, Annual Program Meeting of the Council on Social Work Education.

Sheafor, Brad and Jenkins, Lowell (1982) QUALITY FIELD INSTRUCTION IN SOCIAL WORK: PROGRAM DEVELOPMENT AND MAINTENANCE. New York: Longman.

Sikkema, Mildred (1966) "A Proposal for an Innovation in Field Learning and Teaching," FIELD INSTRUCTION IN GRADUATE SCHOOL WORK EDUCATION: OLD PROBLEMS AND NEW PROPOSALS. Council on Social Work Education. This section is adapted from her unpublished dissertation: "The Objectives of Field Work in Social Casework, 1989-1955" University of Chicago, 1964.

Towle, Charlotte (1945)  COMMON HUMAN NEEDS.  New York: National Association of Social Workers.

# THEMES AND VARIATIONS: THE POLITICAL ECONOMY OF FIELD INSTRUCTION

Bart Grossman, *University of California at Berkeley*

## INTRODUCTION

"Fieldwork is one of the most discussed, most deprecated, least understood, most praised and least easily described courses in graduate Schools of Social Work," Margaret Schubert comments in her introduction to FIELD INSTRUCTION IN SOCIAL CASEWORK (1963). Her statement is as true over a quarter of a century later, and, I would predict, it will continue to be true so long as we have fieldwork in Social Work education.

Fieldwork is at the nexus of change in social work education. The choices that a school makes about its mission, goals, and resources, the needs and commitments of community agencies, and the hopes and dreams of students meet in the field practicum. The decisions we make concerning the structure of field education will be affected by all these forces.

Our task as field educators is to effectively use community resources in training our students to apply knowledge gained at school to practice in the field. How do we develop and maintain the structures that link the school and the field? Usually under pressure, reactively, or sticking with the tried and true. Sometimes we are able to find a creative way to lash oddly shaped bits and pieces together into a coherent whole.

In the 60's and early 70's, the days of Title XX and other forms of soft money, field work experiments abounded. It seemed then that we were on the verge of significant modifications in the basic structure of Social Work education and of the place of field work within that structure. With faculty-led field units and field teaching centers, it seemed that the schools would continue to expand their role in the teaching of practice in the field.

By the late seventies, this situation had changed drastically. Today there are fewer resources available to maintain the status quo. Opportunities to perform curricular experiments are rare. As Social Work educators we are less focused on improving curricular models, than we are on preparing students to cope with the overwhelming problems that surround us.

Even when resources are available, proactive change in field work is hard to achieve. The traditions of field instruction are strong. After working to install a structured approach to field instruction in one school, Laura Epstein commented that no matter what she did, the apprenticeship model seemed to come back. It is extremely difficult to convince faculty and agency field instructors that their prejudices about fieldwork are prejudices. Why the CSWE standard of 900 hours; why not 800, 2000? Why two placements in two years - why not one, four, or a rotation like medical training in some facilities? We might ask - what does the research suggest? In fact, there are very few comparative studies. Program comparisons are hard to do and there is little incentive to do such research when it so often seems that changing field structures would be impractical, unworkable, expensive, unpopular with students and unacceptable to agencies.

We may agree with Sheafor and Jenkins (1982) that all field instruction programs in social work education have a common purpose: "linking classroom learning with practice activities so that the new social workers can effectively engage in knowledge and value guided practice." However, the structure of a given field program depends on a variety of forces and circumstances in the school and the community, some of which can be manipulated and few of which can be controlled.

We can most usefully discuss fieldwork decision-making in a relative rather than an absolute perspective. "A political economy perspective," says Hasenfeld, "views organizational decision-making as a response to economic and political pressures within and outside of the organization." If we apply such a perspective to field instruction, we should have a clearer view of the factors influencing our decisions. We may be better able to separate our purposes from our means and be able to think more clearly about the long run as well as current realities.

My primary purpose in this paper is to clarify the discussion of field work decision-making by providing a common set of elements of field instructional programs and the environmental factors that influence these elements. I will also apply this perspective in analyzing some field program processes.

## COMMON ELEMENTS IN FIELD INSTRUCTION PROGRAMS

Before we discuss the factors that influence our decisions we ought to have a common understanding of the structural elements involved in field instruction about which we make decisions. We can then look at different program models as variations on common themes.

A set of these elements was developed for an Institute on Field Instruction taught by Helene Fishbein of Adelphi University, Dean Schneck of the University of Wisconsin at Madison and I in 1985. The list was generated as an extension of our three distinct models. These elements go beyond addressing the fundamental questions of how much field work is included and how the time is arranged (i.e. block vs. concurrent, full time vs. part time, etc.).

### 1.   Agency Selection

What are the selection criteria and mechanisms for finding, choosing, and preparing agencies to work with students and the school? How, and to what degree, is agency choice related to the mission of the school, the needs and interests of students, and the knowledge and connections of faculty? What do we expect of the agency in terms of its support of student learning and field instructor training? How do we work with non-traditional (and non-Social Work) settings?

2.    **Field Instructor Selection**

What are the selection criteria and mechanisms used for finding, training, and preparing instructors? What qualifications and commitments do we demand? What sorts of training, support, and recognition do we offer?

3.    **Agency-School Relations**

How do we maintain communication, accommodate change, evaluate, and cope with tensions due to divergent interests and missions? What is the role (and status) of faculty in regard to field liaison activities? What vehicles exist for agency input and school-agency collaboration? What is the nature and duration of the commitment between the school and the agency?

4.    **Student Placement Process**

How much control is exercised by the school, the student, and the agency? How is information about agencies shared with students and information about students shared with agencies? Who within the school (faculty, field director, field liaisons) plays what role in placement? What procedures characterize the exchange between the student, agency, and school in making a placement (eg: pre-placement interviews, field fairs, the existence of student stipends, etc.)?

5.    **Student Preparation**

How much responsibility does the school (vs. the agency) take in orienting the student to practice roles and the field context? How (and how much) is the beginning of field articulated with course content?

6.    **Planning and Monitoring the Student Field Experience**

What devices exist (such as learning agreements, contracts, etc.) to define the placement? How are these devices developed and approved? How is the school oversight role managed (eg: field director, faculty liaisons, field consultants, written reports, etc.) and structured (agency visits, phone contacts, group meetings, etc.)? What happens if there are problems between the student and the agency?

7.    **Evaluation**

How, when, by whom, and according to what standards is the student's performance evaluated? Who plays what role in grading?

8. **Integration of Learning**

How active is the school in helping the student to learn from field work? What vehicles exist to promote integration of learning (integrative seminars, field meetings, faculty field instructors, learning centers, etc.)?

## ENVIRONMENTAL ELEMENTS THAT INFLUENCE FIELD DECISIONS

Given this organized way of looking at the elements of a field instruction program, it would be useful to also have a common framework for viewing the local factors that influence field program decisions. We can conceive of the task environment of the field program in a School as having the following elements that influence its decisions:

1. **The School Curriculum** - The formal learning expectations and the educational mission of the school.

The curricular mission can be quite specific or very general, and the mission may be treated perfunctorily or seriously in decision-making. For example, many schools have a mission statement which focuses on preparation for public social services practice. How many of these schools place most of their students in public agencies?

Another issue is the fit between the school mission and agency availability. In Skolnik's 1985 report of the CSWE Field Education Project, a comprehensive study of field instruction, a frequently reported difficulty was finding settings that could offer a generalist experience. A generalized curriculum can be specific in its demands on the field. There are particular strains when the curriculum moves into areas for which appropriate settings do not exist, adequate supervision cannot be secured, or the curriculum fails to keep pace with changes in a field of practice.

2. **The University or College** - The frame of reference and reward system that influences school priorities towards practice, teaching, research, and, therefore, field work.

For example, if the University, or the division of the University in which the School or Department of Social Work is located is heavily committed to research, it is unlikely that faculty will be rewarded for emphasizing practice. In such a situation the liaison role may be a relatively low priority, as suggested in the study by Smith, Faria and Brownstein (1986). The role may be particularly burdensome to junior faculty members struggling to achieve tenure, to whom it is frequently delegated. In Skolnik's study, lack of support for field education among academic colleagues was rated one of the top five problems affecting field instruction.

3. **The Students** - The interests of students and the frequent clash between student plans and the objectives of the curriculum.

Traditionally, students have cited the field as the most important aspect of social work education. Students find the pragmatic, hands-on world of practice more relevant than the theoretical world of the classroom. The relationships they have with field instructors are often the most intimate and powerful relationships they will have with an educator. For example, Fortune, et. al. (1985) found that students' positive perception of their supervisors was the single most important influence on their satisfaction in field work.

However, the interests of students can be problematic. In a study of eight Masters programs, Rubin and Johnson (1984) found that a great majority of entering students wanted the MSW as a route to becoming private practice psychotherapists. This clash of purposes between students and many schools' missions creates difficult choices for the field. We may insist on placing students in public settings and encounter overt resistance or sabotage that undermines field learning. We may find some agencies training students for roles that the school does not define as central to its mission. We may be faced with losing agencies prized by students that feel the curriculum does not prepare students to deliver psychotherapeutic services.

Added to these problems is the reality that today's students have less financial support (especially in the form of agency stipends) and more family responsibilities than past generations. Their academic and practice background may be more limited, and part-time and other extended programs may further restrict the placement opportunities for particular students.

4. **Field Resources** - The amount and type of financial and personnel resources available for agency finding, linkage and program development.

Since the days of Title XX, field resources have been shrinking. It is difficult to tell how many actual FTE's are devoted to field work in a given school. Smith, et. al, (1986) report three Master's programs in which all the liaison work is done by the Practicum Director. Most other programs use faculty liaisons, but the liaison workload varies widely. Reported numbers of field students counted as a course equivalent ranged from 6 to 30. A few schools still have field units or teaching centers, but the large majority rely on agency staff as field instructors. So, many Field Directors rely on resources that may be fragmented and over which they have little control.

5. **The Agencies** - The number, type, and stability of agencies, and the nature and extent of their commitment to student training.

Locating and securing appropriate field settings was the second largest problem mentioned in Skolnik's sample. There are many strains in the school-agency relationship. Schools and agencies may be in substantial conflict about the proper domain of the Social Work profession and, therefore, disagree about what preparation students should receive for placement and what they should learn in the field.

In addition to questions of "program fit," funding cutbacks have restricted training in agencies. Client populations with higher levels of acuteness must be served in shorter periods with fewer resources. Training departments have been reduced or eliminated and many field instructors receive no credit from the agency for the time they spend supervising students. Agencies are constantly retooling, adding staff and programs to adapt to new funding priorities, and frequently in too much turmoil to absorb field students.

6. **Competing Sources of Professional Training** - competition among Schools of Social Work and between social work and other professions resulting in less availability of MSW or even degreed professionals to serve as field instructors.

Increasingly, inroads are being made by Psychologists, Marriage, Child, and Family Counselors, and Nurses in fields formerly dominated by social workers. Some of this change is the effect of deprofessionalization and some of it is the increasing reluctance of social workers to work in public sector agencies, to serve the poor, or to perform such activities as discharge planning and case management.

Also affecting competition in recent years are social work licensing laws which create a pool of post-graduate interns who will serve for little or no wages in exchange for supervisory hours required for licensure or certification for third party payment.

In summary then, we can characterize the key aspects of the environment as: 1) The Curriculum, 2) The University or College Environment, 3) The Students, 4) Field Resources, 5) The Agencies, and 6) Competing Sources of Professional Training.

## COMMON ELEMENTS AND ENVIRONMENTAL INFLUENCES

Although I would like to be able to offer a grand scheme linking field elements and environmental factors and suggesting the right program decision for every circumstance, in light of the fragmentary and largely anecdotal information that is available, such a step would be premature and presumptuous. I hope that the community of field educators will flesh out this matrix by sharing the things that have been learned and observed. Therefore, I wish to share some of my observations about how some environmental influences are reflected in particular field elements and how these factors may be influenced to achieve field work purposes.

### School Mission and Field Resources

In theory, the curricular mission of the school should be the key organizing principal for its field practicum. Perhaps the purest such approaches are the few remaining examples of school-staffed learning centers in which students deliver services under faculty supervision and with faculty models. The mission of a given school of social work, however, does not necessarily represent a consensus among faculty. If there are divisions, the sharpest ones are often between those faculty with a practice focus and those who are more concerned with policy. A mission statement may represent a paper victory for one group or may include both by saying nothing definite about either.

In practice, the principal field liaison resources of most schools are practice-oriented faculty, and in some schools the field program operates a sort of shadow curriculum in which students, clinically-oriented faculty, and treatment agencies focus together on clinical issues that may not be featured in the classroom curriculum. This sort of disparity has much to do with frequent student perceptions that there is little integration between field and classroom. It also plays a role in the reported lack of support for the field by academics.

It can be dangerous for the field program to ally itself with the perspective of any particular segment of the faculty or the agency community. The Field Director would be better advised to seek an array of agencies that match the school's mission so that the field program is not perceived as detrimental to the educational objectives of any significant group of faculty. Faculty members may be recruited to help in finding new types of agencies and interesting students in settings that have not been popular.

Where there are inconsistencies between the mission and agency realities, we would do well to bring these issues back to the faculty in a timely way, asserting our expertise as field educators who understand what must be done to create appropriate field learning opportunities. If it is clear to all faculty that the field program supports the school's educational goals as they see them, it is more likely that the school will make an adequate commitment to the field. When the faculty disagree, the field may raise but not resolve the issue.

## Working with Field Instructors

While agencies and individual field instructors both play crucial roles in field instruction, schools have choices about which of these elements will be seen as more central to the organization of the program. There are two extremes: a mentorship approach in which one develops individual field instructors over time through extensive training and follows them if they change jobs, and an agency-based approach in which one stays with agency systems using qualified persons as field instructors, providing support, consultation or more limited formal training and supplementing the work of field instructors with school-based seminars or field units.

Field educators should consider the design and intensity of training for field instructors in terms of the expected longevity of field instructors in the program and the possible impact that training has on continuing service. In environments where workers are constantly changing jobs, few agencies are stable for very long, and new service programs seem to emerge by the hour, we cannot rely upon an orderly sequence of training and development for the field instruction role. Instead we need the resources to individualize our approach, e.g., a field faculty model. In more stable practice communities, structured training may be a better incentive to keeping field instructors involved, and may be successful in teaching them a perspective that the school wishes to foster. If only limited and fractionalized liaison resources are available, field directors may need to rely strongly on formal training.

The expectations that the school has for field instructors need to be adjusted to the time and preparation that these professionals have for this specialized role. In these days of limited agency resources, the schools may have the obligation and opportunity to take more responsibility for student learning in the field through more careful student preparation and on-going processing of field experiences with the faculty. At the same time, it is important that the work of field instructors be recognized and supported through formal gatherings, written communications, and involvement in the life of the school. Sometimes we forget that contact with the school can, in itself, be very rewarding to practitioners, if only as a respite from the pressure of agency life.

## Preparation and Integration of Learning

Preparation for placement is an area in which the schools can play a direct and often unchallenged role. It is difficult to argue than an orientation to practice is outside of the school's responsibility. If time is taken to prepare students with a perspective about the profession, the field of practice, and the learner role in field work, they should be able to make better educational use of field experiences. At Berkeley, we have developed a delayed entry model with eight weeks of introductory seminars. We have enriched our resources for this function by using selected field instructors as presenters and panelists in introductory sessions. The pattern works reasonably well and seems to have helped us introduce students to a broader conception of the role and mission of social work than is acquired by immediate introduction to one practice setting. There was and continues to be some agency discomfort with the shortened first year program and we have continued to make efforts to adjust the model without surrendering our purpose. At other schools, I have seen shorter but more intensive preparation approaches.

Another important contribution to student perspective is the addition of an on-going field seminar in which students can share, compare, and critically analyze field experiences. With faculty guidance, students can more consciously integrate field practice with social work theory. These groups also become important emotional supports to students at a time when the stresses in field agencies are great and agency staffs and field instructors are less able to notice and respond to student distress. If resources are lacking in the field program to mount such seminars, other faculty or even senior field instructors may be recruited.

## Monitoring and Evaluation

The development of clear learning agreements including specific learning goals and tasks is another important vehicle through which the school can assert its educational mission without great resource expenditure. This approach, structured by the school's teaching objectives and augmented by special student interest and legitimate agency requirements, makes explicit a three-way negotiation.

Any time the field program makes a process explicit, it gains additional influence over that process. Students and agencies may disagree with the school about the wording of a particular competency, for example, but if it is possible to modify the wording in the development of a learning agreement, they are unlikely to ignore the goal entirely. In fact, this modified learning goal will probably get more attention than it would have gotten in its original form.

One important source of bonding between school and agency is a clear message from field staff that it is sharing with the agency the task of gate-keeping for the profession. The use of a learning agreement with explicit learning goals and tasks clarifies the basis of student performance evaluation. In these litigous times, all of the parties ought to have the protection of a clear, written agreement. Without a "paper trail" of this sort it may be impossible for the school and agency to support one another in dealing with unsatisfactory student performance.

## Agency-School Relations

The primary goal of field administration is generally to secure and maintain an adequate number and array of appropriate field opportunities. If competition is an issue, the school must concern itself with marketing its wares in the field. What can it offer to agencies that will be attractive? If we contribute resources to the agencies that are congruent with the school's mission and faculty we can strengthen the school's link to the field and reinforce acceptance of the mission. For example, if there is an emphasis on research in the curriculum, the school might offer assistance with agency-based research.

Because field instruction is, in the words of Sheafor and Jenkins "too often relegated to a second class citizenship in higher education," field educators may build alliances with agencies in isolation from the school. This approach can be self-defeating because it can encourage disjointed educational experiences and resentment of the field by other faculty members. Instead, the field director and/or field faculty can create new resources, secure relationships with settings, and overcome competition by working to link the school and agencies.

## Placement Process

The process of placing students provides a good example of a practice strongly influenced by regional differences. The New York area directors have turned local competition into a strength by collaborating in setting placement policies. They forbid the practice of pre-placement interviews. If I tried to do that in second year placements I would probably be lynched by the students, the agencies, or my own staff. Our second year competition is largely with other professions making cooperation less possible. The tradition of interviews is compatible with a market in which there are both many choices and many choosers; lots of supply and lots of demand. As in the area of agency selection, one may be limited if the market is limited, but one can still be active in preparing students for interviews, directing the form of agency feedback and playing an advocacy instead of a broker role in the process of placement.

## Field Dependency and University Support

The influence of the university is generally experienced through faculty attitudes and resources. Small fractions of the time of faculty members who are principally concerned with survival and advancement by publication are not useful resources for aggressive agency recruitment. If the university environment is not supportive of attention to the field, field educators will be more dependent on the resources of agency staff and may also have less incentive to be selective in choosing agencies and field instructors.

In an environment in which the field is a low priority for faculty, the field program is likely to be more strongly influenced by the agencies ad by student interests. The model of the field is likely to be what Hale (1969) called the "work model" in which field work is oriented to a particular role in the agency, rather than a practicum model in which the agency is an applications laboratory for classroom learning.

This condition of dependency on the field is reinforced when there is significant competition for agency spaces among schools and professions. There are feedback effects of such dependency as well, for over time students will demand that the classroom pursue directions that are congruent with the field experience.

The conclusion is rather obvious. If a school is interested in having a clear curriculum direction, it had better look to its staffing of the field. A field program may be able to obtain greater support and resources from the school if it charts a direction clearly related to the mission of the school, for example, developing new placements in areas related to a new specialty. It makes little sense for a school to mount a program initiative, however, without working closely with the practice community to assure the existence of appropriate field resources.

In order to obtain ongoing support and recognition, field educators will also need to demonstrate a commitment to the modus operandi of the University. In a research institution, it is important that we do research about our work, and that we write. Where classroom teaching is highly valued we should teach and teach well. In this way we identify with the educational enterprise without losing our connection to the world of practice. This is the dual focus of the field educator, to be part of the academic world and part of the world of practice, and to find creative ways of blending the needs and interests of both.

Field instruction, like politics, is an art of the possible. We need to stay grounded in sound educational principles and remain clear about our mission. We also need to recognize that what we do must fit into a complicated network of persons and institutions, none of which share exactly our perspective or our priorities.

When you put it that way it sounds an awful lot like Social Work, doesn't it?

## BIBLIOGRAPHY

Brian, S. (1969) The Learning Center in Social Work Education. In MODELS OF PROFESSIONAL EDUCATION: FUNCTIONS OF FIELD LEARNING IN THE CURRICULUM. Tulane Studies in Social Welfare Vol. 11, New Orleans: School of Social Work, Tulane University, 231-235.

Fortune, A.E., Feathus, C.., Rook, S.R., Scrimenti, R.M., Smollen, P., Stemerman, B., and Tucker, E.L., (1985) Student Satisfaction with Field Placement. JOURNAL OF SOCIAL WORK EDUCATION. 21(3), 92-102.

Hale, M.P. (1969) Curriculum Models for Social Work Education. In MODES OF PROFESSIONAL EDUCATION: FUNCTIONS OF FIELD LEARNING IN THE CURRICULUM. Tulane Studies in Social Welfare Vol. 11, New Orleans: School of Social Work, Tulane University, 211-227.

Schubert, M. (1963). FIELD INSTRUCTION IN SOCIAL CASEWORK: A REPORT OF AN EXPERI-MENT. Social Service Monographs, 2nd Series, School of Social Services Administration, University of Chicago.

Sheafor, B.W., and Jenkins, L.E. (Eds.) (1982). QUALITY FIELD INSTRUCTION IN SOCIAL WORK. New York: Longman.

Skolnik, L., (1985) FINAL REPORT: FIELD EDUCATION PROJECT. Council on Social Work Education.

Smith, H.Y., Faria, G. and Brownstein, C., (1986) Social Work Faculty in the Role of Liaison: A Field Study, JOURNAL OF SOCIAL WORK EDUCATION. 22(3) 68-79.

# FROM COMMITMENT TO CURRICULUM: THE HUMANISTIC FOUNDATIONS OF FIELD INSTRUCTION

Ellen Sue Mesbur, *Ryerson Polytechnic Institute*
Urania Glassman, *Adelphi University*

## INTRODUCTION

Field instruction in social work provides students with the opportunity to apply and experience the accumulated practice knowledge and wisdom of the profession for their clients' well being. Through learning by doing students can make initial efforts to creatively enact social work values and vision. It is within the field instruction process that the "ideal" becomes an achievable reality through the meeting of the affective and the observable. By viewing the field instruction experience systematically, educators have been provided with rich possibilities for building knowledge through a synthesis of practice theories, models, and experience. Despite differences in school curricula, regional service needs, and service deliveries, certain common and unifying themes have continued to permeate the field education literature. Educational principles are extracted from these themes which will enable our increasing proactivity as we operationalize the diverse field curricula in our schools. However, any educational model we endeavor to conceptualize must be viewed and evaluated through the lens of its utility for creative practice. We must remain mindful, as Dean Schneck recently stated, that "... all of our heartfelt strivings, our well-designed structures, and our refined processes will come to naught if we do not disseminate a strong and visionary message for practice." (1987, p.4).

## HUMANISTIC EDUCATION AND EXPERIENTIAL LEARNING IN SOCIAL WORK

Social work education has traditionally embodied a two-pronged approach to professional learning: encouraging the assimilation of knowledge and values through the classroom setting and the assimilation of skills through a field work practicum. This direct exposure by the student to social work practice is in essence a form of experiential learning, that is, the gaining of knowledge pertaining to or deriving from personal experience. Since the days of Mary Richmond, "learning through doing" has held an important place in social work education. Influenced by the work of John Dewey and his associates, social work educators developed guiding principles for social work supervision, pursuing a learning model linking education, work, and personal development. Charlotte Towle and Bertha Reynolds, early exponents of the humanistic and experiential learning tradition, viewed this kind of learning in supervision as "an individualized growth and change process based on personal experience" (Eisikovitz and Guttman, 1983, p.52).

In social work education the student must learn to combine knowledge with values towards honing the conscious use of self. The aim of field instruction is the integration of knowledge and practice endeavors so that practice wisdom and an emotional internalization of the professional role result. Field instruction focuses on, 1) learning through experience, 2) reflecting upon one's practice, 3) developing a cognitive framework to inform practice, and 4) enhancing self awareness of one's impact upon client systems by an application of new knowledge and behaviours. Ultimately, social work education seeks to develop a professional with a degree of personal autonomy. This is a goal well suited to humanistic educational methods, for in social work education learners and their experiences are central to the achievement of professional goals. Knowledge in social work cannot be transmitted without a corresponding process of integration by a thoughtful, independent practitioner, eager to learn how to translate knowledge and values into action.

In viewing each person as unique, humanistic education places its emphasis upon the validity and worth of each person's experience and contribution. Humanistic principles have permeated the field of adult education and are inherent in the values of the social work profession. These include notions of democracy, of individual freedom, of responsibility, and of shared humanity. "...The whole focus of humanistic education is upon the individual learner rather than a body of information (Elias & Merriam, 1980, p. 122)."

In their commitment to developing the whole person, not just the cognitive segment, humanists and social work educators stress the importance of the affective component of learning, while not denying the importance of acquiring knowledge. By ignoring the affective element of learning, educators may be creating what Jacques Barzun (1969) called "the intellectual half-man." Therefore the goal is to stimulate the affective aspects of the student so as to develop "persons who understand themselves, who understand others and who can relate to others." (Patterson 1973).

In this kind of education, the instructor is viewed as a facilitator of learning rather than solely a provider of information. As facilitator, the educator must to plan ahead to create the conditions within which learning takes place. The educator must also trust students to assume responsibility for their learning (Rothman, 1973). There is considerable evidence that the teacher must engage each learner first and foremost by connecting with his motivation and investment, and second with his own particular learning bent or favored mode of learning" (Somers, 1971, p.52).

Humanistic educators share a similar philosophy about the individual as a learner. The focus on learners' personal needs has, perhaps, been most strongly articulated by Carl Rogers (1961, 1969, 1983). Rogers' strong belief in the need for a facilitator to be totally non-directive guides his understanding of the learning process. Learners require a highly supportive and respectful environment to be able to recognize their needs, to begin to explore them and to understand the constraints of early negative learning experiences. Other practitioners in the human growth movement also share Rogers' commitment to being non-directive about what learners choose to examine, along with the view that the facilitator should behave authentically. Their major difference lies in their more interventionist approach to facilitating learning (Boud, 1987, p. 226). This orientation commits the field instructor to devolving authority, to transferring it so that it is shared equally by all participants in the learning process. It sends as well the message for practice to strongly support the right of the participant in the helping process to determine his or her own goals within it.

Originating in the works of Dewey, Lewin, and Piaget, experiential learning theory emphasizes the use of a social science base to further translate humanism into educational methods. This view of learning gives primary emphasis to the centrality of experience in the learning process. To quote Dewey, (1938) "...the fundamental unity of the newer philosophy is found in the idea that there is an intimate and necessary relation between the processes of actual experience and education" (p.20). Attempting to understand the enactment of democratic values through action research and the laboratory training method, Lewin notes that it is the dialectical tension between immediate concrete experience and analytic detachment that enables learning to occur (Kolb, 1984, p.11). Lewin left a legacy of ideas affirming the validity of subjective experience and emphasizing "that feelings as well as thoughts are facts" (Kolb, p.11). Piaget, in his work on cognitive development in childhood, describes how intelligence is shaped by experience. Bruner (1964, 1966), Kohlberg (1969), Perry (1970), and Loevinger (1976) have extended Piaget's work into the realm of adult learning processes. Experiential learning theories, then, attempt to specify those processes and conditions involved in the acquisition of knowledge through experience. According to Kolb:

> ...learning shapes the course of development...by the level of integrative complexity in the following four learning modes: 1) Affective complexity in concrete experience results in higher-order sentiments. 2) Perceptual complexity in reflective observation results in higher-order observations 3) Symbolic complexity in abstract conceptualization results in higher-order concepts. Finally, 4) Behavioral complexity in active experimentation results in higher order actions (Kolb, p.140).

The structural bases of the learning process involve two dimensions. The first is a prehension dimension which includes two dialectically opposed modes of grasping experience. One mode is through the direct apprehension of immediate concrete experience. The other mode is through indirect comprehension of symbolic representations of experience. The second dimension of the learning process is that of transformation, which includes two dialectically opposed modes of transforming experience, one via intentional reflection, the other via extensional action. The learning process at any given moment in time may be governed by one or all of these process interacting simultaneously (Kolb, 1984).

It is easy to see the breadth of integration that occurs and the time that is consumed in an experiential learning process in the field. This integration is similar to what occurs in the social work helping relationship, offering the student a unique opportunity to experience an appreciation and respect for the process per se. Coleman (1976), suggests that experiential learning, though more time consuming, appears to be less easily forgotten than cognitive approaches.

Brown (1980) distinguishes three types of experiential learning; all three have applicability in field education. In the first, *"How To" Learning*, the learner goes through a constructed experience in order to learn a previously defined concept or skill. *Role Socialization*, refers to the assimilation of a professional role. Through their practitioner, students are guided towards an appreciation of the elements necessary to this role, includes the acquisition of professional values. In *Learner Managed Experiential Learning*, the learner develops objectives and resources, participates in the experience, and then incorporates this learning into a "personal body of theory and practice that can be drawn upon in future action" (Brown, 1980, p.53).

In considering Kolb's and Brown's typologies, it becomes obvious that not all experiential learning is alike. Curricula must be designed differentially if professional schools wish to make the most effective and efficient use of experiential learning. Kolb, in a synthesis of the work of Dewey, Lewin and Piaget, identifies the common characteristics which define the nature of experiential learning. He suggests that learning is best conceived, not in terms of outcomes, but rather, in terms of a continuous process, grounded in experience. Experiential learning is a holistic process of adaptation to the world in that it requires the resolution of conflicts between dialectically opposed modes of adaptation. Involving transactions between the person and the environment, experiential learning is ultimately about the process of creating knowledge. As Kolb states, "Learning is the process whereby knowledge is created through transformation of experience" (Kolb, p.38).

With emphasis on the process of adaptation and learning, rather than on outcomes or specific content, a field practicum can provide opportunities for students to go beyond facts, theories, and procedures to make sense of uncertain, unique or conflict-ridden practice situations through a process Schon (1987) calls "reflection-in-action". If knowledge is a transformation of experience, continuously created and recreated rather than acquired or transmitted, then through reflection-in-action, students in a field practicum can devise new methods of reasoning, can construct and test new categories of understanding, strategies of action or ways of framing problems (Kolb, p.39). Because this process we are discussing transforms experience in both its objective and subjective forms, it is more accurate for educators to consider it "relearning" rather than learning. Our role as educators is not only to impart new ideas for consideration, but to dispose of or modify old ones.

If professional knowing is viewed as "thinking like a social worker", then along with requisite facts and procedures, students must also learn "the forms of inquiring by which competent practitioners reason their way, in problematic instances, to clear connections between general knowledge and particular cases" (Schon, 1987, p.39).

## ANDRAGOGY: A SYNTHESIS OF HUMANISM AND EXPERIENTIAL LEARNING

Andragogy is derived from the Greek word "andras" or man, and has emerged as a coherent body of theory and technology based on assumptions about adults as learners. Andragogues define education "not as a process of transmitting knowledge, but as a process of inquiry -- mutual, self-directed inquiry" (Knowles, 1972, p.36). Knowles' concepts are rooted in the early humanistic views of Dewey and Lewin, as well as the more recent conceptions of the humanistic psychologists such as Rogers and Maslow.

Pedagogy involves the use of child development theories and learning theories to devise methodologies for teaching children. Knowles (1972) notes that the term "pedagogy of adult education" is a contradiction in terms, but suggests that most adults, including people in professional programs, have been taught as if they were children. So often our students come to us carrying a personal educational history of dehumanization. These students are especially sensitive to infantilizing approaches in field education. Yet their troubles are blamed on them rather than upon the educational approach.

Knowles proposes a number of assumptions to help professionals best utilize andragogical concepts in social work education. His first suggestion arises from his recognition that in growth towards maturity, a person's self concept moves from dependency to increasing self-directedness. "...Those students who have entered a professional school have made a big step toward seeing themselves as essentially self directing...[and] identified with an adult role" (p.34). Educators must examine curricular structures to ensure student input has been included. If it has not, the adult status of the learner has been denied.

Knowles affirms personal experience as an important resource in learning. Experiential teaching techniques require learners to analyze their own experiences. Timing in developing learning experiences that coincide with the learner's tasks is essential. Neglect of this element may interfere with the student's continuing readiness to learn. Adults tend to have a problem-centred perspective to learning which often requires an immediacy of application. This orientation suggests that curricula for the adult be organized around problem areas. Each year might begin with field experiences which then move towards an exploration of underlying principles and theory. Foundation knowledge can then be further broadened, followed by a deeper application of skill in the field.

The andragogical approach places the individual goals of learners central to the teaching/learning process. This structure may take many forms, but fundamental to it is the necessity for a supportive interpersonal learning climate and the need for learners to clarify their goals, plan learning programs, identify available resources, clarify evidence of achievement, and develop evaluative procedures. The teacher's (or facilitator's) role is to help the learner define learning needs and respond to them. The facilitator is not necessarily the "expert" who provides knowledge about the learner-defined task, but rather someone who can provide support and assistance to learners as they find their way through the learning process. This approach emphasizes "freedom as learners" and derives from a reaction against traditional teaching "which places the learner in the position of responding to what a teacher provides" (Boud, 1987, p.225).

It must be noted that while violation of these principles is more easily ignored by the student in the classroom through various withdrawal techniques, the view of the learner as a child in the field experience creates an insufferable situation for the student, and is often one of the primary reasons a placement may be terminated. It is equally insufferable for clients when these principles are violated by practitioners. Yet, when a student participates in andragogical learning approaches he or she is more readily available to respond to client agendas rather than his or her own.

## Field Education and Andragogy: A Promising Partnership

The principles of andragogy have particular relevance for social work field education. The practicum is rich with opportunities for promoting an environment favorable for adult learning. It is problem-oriented, requires action, reflection and evaluation and generally expects and rewards initiative and self-direction.

Early on, Bertha Reynolds applied the work of Dewey to the development of a humanistic framework for social work education. She notes, "Learning is an art, which is knowledge applied to doing something in which the whole person participates...there is invariably a gap between knowing a thing and being able to do something with it. (Reynolds, 1942, p.69). Her major contribution to social work education was the identification of five stages in the field education learning process: 1) acute self-consciousness; 2) developing a sink or swim attitude; 3) comprehending what is needed in the situation (though not always being able to perform the task); 4) acquiring professional expertise; 5) gaining the ability and confidence to teach others.

Frey and DuBois (1972) outline similarities between social work and adult education. These include such common objectives as enabling individuals and groups to develop relationships and move towards self-actualization. They suggest that adult education could democratize or loosen traditional forms of social work supervision by encouraging personal growth and self-actualization.

Gelfand, Rohrich, and Nevidan (1975) report results of a training course based on andragogical principles for workers at the Children's Aid Society of Metropolitan Toronto. Workers planned their own learning experiences through diagnosing their learning needs, developing interest groups, and negotiating appropriate learning trials with training resource persons. "Research results strongly suggested that this course was effective in promoting personal growth (self-actualization) and in developing worker strengths in self-and-other awareness, and problem-solving" (Gelfand, Rohrich, and Nevidan, 1975, p.61).

Price (1976) suggests that adult learning principles can help schools of social work move towards an expanded frame of reference (p.111). While self determination and adult learning principles are in many ways parallel, Price finds that self-determination as a principle is "more prevalent in the social work literature concerned with practice than with education" (p.105). She vpoints out this omission may be related to the issue of accountability. "Arriving at a balance between encouraging the student's natural bent and requiring a standard of performance from the profession's value system must somehow be achieved (p.108).

Lowy (1983) developed a phase model of supervision, defining supervision as "...a learning and teaching process designed to incorporate and integrate the various dimensions of the professional role of social work (p.56)." Included are the ethics, methods for working with the gamut of client systems (p. 56). He notes that, "A major task remaining for social work is to design and test empirically a phase theory of supervision (p.59)."

Eisikovitz and Guttman (1983) adapt Dewey's experiential learning continuum. They conceptualize a model of learning through experience containing five components: 1) placing the supervisee in a demanding reality context; 2) supporting the supervisee's need to learn and master the acquisition of specific practice skills; 3) allowing the utilization of skills in responsible challenging action; 4) developing critical analysis and reflection of experience; and 5) developing abstractions, principles and generalizations. They suggest that their model, in ordering stages of learning and offering rules that govern action, can be seen as a practice theory (p.61).

Bogo and Vayda (1986) adapt Kolb's work to learning in social work education. They suggest that the integration of theory and practice is a cyclical process involving four elements: retrieval, reflection, linkage to professional knowledge, and professional response.

These writings all acknowledge the relevance of adult education principles to the education of social workers, both in the classroom and in the field. However, it has not been until quite recently that we have seen social work field education literature move beyond a description of principles and a consensus on their usefulness to the actual development of teaching-learning models.

## COMPONENTS AND PROCESSES OF A FIELD INSTRUCTION CURRICULUM

The field instruction experience includes two distinct yet interrelated components. The first focuses upon content, within the field curriculum and within its learning objectives. The second component focuses upon process within educational methodology. Several principles of field instruction have been identified that delineate these two components.

### EDUCATIONAL CONTENT: PRINCIPLES GUIDING SELECTION AND USE

PRINCIPLE 1: *The field curriculum must be seen as the operationalization of the school's curriculum* by both faculty and agency personnel. There must exist a strong commitment by both faculty and agency to curriculum content, to viewing the student as an adult learner, and to implementing the field curriculum through mutually agreed upon educational methods.

PRINCIPLE 2: *The field curriculum cannot be an appendage to the school's curriculum*, existing simply to meet agency demands. Rather, it must stand as a fully developed and integrated component of a cohesive curriculum plan, built on a comprehensive vision for practice. The school's field education structure should not foster an abdication of responsibility, permitting the agency to teach one mode of practice while the school teaches another.

PRINCIPLE 3: *The field instruction curriculum requires a strong faculty commitment* to its content and implementation. These criteria should be developed and agreed upon by faculty curriculum development processes.

PRINCIPLE 4: *Agency practice should be consonant with the school's curriculum and professional standards*. These standards include serving a broad spectrum of the community and its underserved populations, and staying alert to discriminatory agency practices in the treatment of clients and students.

PRINCIPLE 5: *The field curriculum must include clear objectives* translatable into criteria for student performance.

## EDUCATIONAL PROCESS:  PRINCIPLES FOR A FIELD CURRICULUM

PRINCIPLE 6: *The delivery of the field curriculum depends on the mutuality and commitment* of the field instructors, agencies, and faculty to teach the next professional generation.  Faculty and field instructors should be familiar with andragogical designs and learning approaches.  In the midst of all that appears diverse, a unifying perspective of practice approaches and educational principles must be translated into educational structures and administrative procedures that clarify curriculum and educational method.

Principles Pertaining to School, Agency and Students:

PRINCIPLE 7: *The treatment of students in the practice setting needs to be based on non-authoritarian methods.*  It is important for the agency and the field instructor to place a high value on student input by including students in staff meetings and in its informal get-togethers.  Schools should also educate agencies towards using andragogical designs. (This can be achieved through seminars in field instruction.)

PRINCIPLE 8: *The curriculum should translate performance criteria into descriptive behaviours and clear expectations,* not merely attitudes and stances.  When supported and interpreted by the faculty consultants, clear expectations of the student can facilitate the evaluation process, enabling educator and student to gain collective clarity about student performance. Making curriculum objectives available to students in a timely manner helps them to be proactive in considering their learning endeavors.  Sharing with students educational assumptions guiding learning designs can also catalyze the learning process.

PRINCIPLE 9: *Mutually developed and clearly defined field assignments can help illustrate concepts learned in class.*  The more clearly the assignment is conceived, the more easily developed is a conscious use of self that is not over-whelmed by trial and error or negative learning experiences.

PRINCIPLE 10: *Evaluating student performance in the field involves the student, field instructor and faculty field consultant* in a reciprocal process. Learning contracts developed with the student can focus the evaluation process.

Principles Pertaining to Student and Field Instructor Transaction:

PRINCIPLE 11: *The educational assessment occurring between student and field instructor has two components, skills and learning style.*  The first involves recognizing student needs in relation to learning knowledge, skill, role, and practice patterns.  In arriving at a mutual assessment it is important to view gaps in practice as undeveloped areas rather than as deficiencies.  The second component involves the faculty member and student together determining the best methods for student learning, the elements that facilitate or impede this learning.

PRINCIPLE 12: *The learning contract is an educational tool well-suited to the field work practicum.*  The student has an opportunity to formalize learning goals, to indicate how achievement of the goals will be identified, and to develop criteria for evaluation.

PRINCIPLE 13:  *The field instruction conference helps the student scrutinize his or her own practice, and allows an exploration of alternative modes of helping.* It centers upon the student as practitioner rather than upon management of a case. Exploring varied approaches engages the student's creative energy, and reflects the view that practice is learned by struggling to create a style of one's own, not by imitating the field instructor.

PRINCIPLE 14:  *Direct feedback can be an important catalyst in developing the conscious use of self.* Feedback, to be most useful, should be specific. It should be linked to behaviour with clients, agency and field instructor. It should also be offered in a supportive atmosphere.

PRINCIPLE 15:  *The evaluation process is a collaborative effort by the student and field instructor.* It begins with an evaluation conference in which the criteria for performance clarify growth and identify learning goals. The student and field instructor each prepare for the conference, sharing perceptions and issues. The field instructor's written evaluation provides the next step. Evaluations should not be written without the sharing provided for in the conference. Opportunity for the student to react to and joint signing should be built into field instruction designs.

PRINCIPLE 16:  *Process recording continues to help student and field instructor scrutinize practice and enhance self-awareness.* It can make clear student learning patterns and permit an evaluation of the use of self in the conference which can help the learner explore alternative approaches. Using process recording as a means for assigning value judgments to student actions is not consonant with andragogical education designs. Process recording differs from audio-taping and video-taping because, by its very nature, it forces the active re-examination of prior interactional phenomena.

PRINCIPLE 17:  *Video tapes, and newer, experientially-oriented methods depend on the spontaneity of the field instructor.* These methods need to be developed and more systematically used. However, their utilization requires active participation by the learner, hard to achieve without commitment to andragogical educational methods.

PRINCIPLE 18:  *Role Play is useful in an open environment that values risk-taking.* Role rehearsal is a helpful way of trying out a feared or newer approach. In assuming the client role, the student's empathetic awareness is sharpened. Watching the field instructor try his or her hand at the role offers the student another perspective.

**CONCLUSION:  FUTURE DIRECTIONS OR--DO WE PRACTICE WHAT WE PREACH?**

There seems to be common acknowledgement of the relevance of adult education principles for the education of social workers, both in the classroom and in the field.  However, only recently has the literature begun to move beyond descriptions of principles and consensus upon their usefulness to a development of teaching-learning models for social work field education based upon these principles and concepts.  Four dilemmas in social work field education have come to light:

The first dilemma is the ambivalence toward humanistic education and experiential learning.  In this ambivalence, our concern with quality control takes centrality.  When all else fails, we abandon humanistic principles and rush to be judgmental and evaluative.  It is as if humanistic educational principles negate standards for excellence!

The second dilemma revolves around the old habits of the supervisory process, rooted in the diagnostic school and incorrectly translated by inexperienced personnel into control of the student.  The integrity of the learner may be denied structurally, for example, by preventing consultations with other agency personnel, or by expecting the student to imitate the field instructor's approach to practice.  Both circumstances stifle the student's potential creativity.

The third dilemma is the inherent lack of a systematic epistemology of knowledge for the profession.  A phenomenological perspective would foster an understanding of how we arrive at our knowledge of both practice and educational phenomena, resulting in greater congruence between our espoused theories and the assumptions that govern our daily interactions. Once our profession can more readily identify that perspective, our experientially-based educational methods will be grounded in a philosophical theory that values intersubjective experience.

The fourth dilemma is rooted in lack of proper action-research tools for the understanding of how practice is performed in the practice world.  This lack is due to our improper conceptions about knowledge and research.  Schon (1983), taking a phenomenological approach to the theory of knowledge, challenges professionals to search for "...an epistemology of practice implicit in the artistic, intuitive processes which some practitioners bring to situations of uncertainty, instability, uniqueness, and value conflict (p.49)."  This search is guided by a specific process of "reflective conversation with the situation (p.268)," and draws its impetus from Giddens (1976).  Schon's methodology is an attempt at a hermeneutic analysis which "brackets" the inter-subjective phenomena to be studied so they can be experienced through a new lens.  This approach enables the practitioner to reflect-in-action, thereby becoming a researcher in the practice context.

The act of learning is a highly personal endeavor, with perception assuming a key role in this act. Individuals perceive selectively, accounting for what is learned in an educational setting.  Personal goals and attitudes affect this perception, and self concept promotes or inhibits learning.  Assuming then that the motivation for learning in the adult social work student is intrinsic, field instructors are challenged to provide options for students in all aspects of the field experience, thereby framing learning choices within the context of agency structure, client needs, and student desires.

# BIBLIOGRAPHY

Barzun, Jacques (1971) "The Problem of the Intellectual Half-Man". Harold C. Lyon, Jr. (Ed.) LEARNING TO FEEL--FEELING TO LEARN. Columbus, Ohio: Merrill.

Bogo, Marion and Vayda, Elaine (1986) THE PRACTICE OF FIELD INSTRUCTION IN SOCIAL WORK. Theory and Process. Toronto: University of Toronto Press.

Boud, David (1987) "The Facilitator's View of Adult Learning". David Boud and Virginia Griffin (Eds.) APPRECIATING ADULT LEARNING:FROM THE LEARNER'S PERSPECTIVE. London: Kogan Page.

Brown, Gerald (1980) "Three Types of Experiential Learning: A Non Trivial Distinction". NEW DIRECTIONS FOR EXPERIENTIAL LEARNING. Vol. 8, pp.47-58.

Brown, G.I. (1976) THE LIVE CLASSROOM: INNOVATION THROUGH CONFLUENT EDUCATION AND GESTALT. New York: Penguin.

Bruner, Jerome S. (1966) ON KNOWING: ESSAYS FOR THE LEFT HAND. New York: Atheneum.

Coleman, James S. "Differences Between Experiential and Classroom Learning". In Morris T. Keeton, et al (Eds.) EXPERIENTIAL LEARNING: RATIONALE, CHARACTERISTICS, AND ASSESSMENT.

Dewey, John (1938) EXPERIENCE AND EDUCATION. Kappa Delta Phi.

Eisikovitz, Zvi and Guttman, Eva (Spring, 1983) "Toward a Practice Theory of Learning Through Experience in Social Work Supervision." THE CLINICAL SUPERVISOR, Vol. 1, no. 1, pp.51-63.

Elias, John and Merriam, Sharon (1980) PHILOSOPHICAL FOUNDATIONS OF ADULT EDUCATION. New York: Robert Krieger Co.

Frey, Louise and Dubois, Eugene (August, 1972) "Adult Education and Social Work: What They Can Learn From One Another". JOURNAL OF CONTINUING EDUCATION AND TRAINING, Vol. 2, no. 1.

Garland, James; Jones, Hubert and Kolodny, Ralph (1973) "A Model for the Stages of Development in Social Work Groups" in Saul Bernstein, (Ed.) EXPLORATION IN GROUP WORK. Boston: Milford House.

Gelfand, Bernard; Rohrich, Sandy; Nevidan, Pat and Starak, Igor (Fall, 1975) "An Andragogical Application to the Training of Social Workers". JOURNAL OF EDUCATION FOR SOCIAL WORK, Vol. 11, no. 3, pp.55-61.

Giddens, Anthony (1976) NEW RULES FOR SOCIOLOGICAL METHOD. New York: Basic Books.

Goldstein, Eda (1984) EGO PSYCHOLOGY AND SOCIAL WORK PRACTICE. New York: Free Press.

Heron, J. (1973) "Re-evaluation and Counselling: Personal Growth Through Mutual Aid". BRITISH JOURNAL OF GUIDANCE AND COUNSELLING, 1, 2.

Knowles, Malcolm (1970) THE MODERN PRACTICE OF ADULT EDUCATION. New York: Association Press.

Knowles, Malcolm (Spring, 1972) "Innovations in Teaching Styles and Approaches Based Upon Adult Learning". JOURNAL OF EDUCATION FOR SOCIAL WORK, PP.32-39.

Kohlberg, L. (1969) "Stage and Sequence: The Cognitive Developmental Approach to Socialization", D.A. Goslin, ed. HANDBOOK OF SOCIALIZATION THEORY AND RESEARCH. Chicago: Rand McNally.

Kolb, David A. (1984) EXPERIENTIAL LEARNING. EXPERIENCE AS THE SOURCE OF LEARNING AND DEVELOPMENT. Englewood Cliffs, N.J.: Prentice Hall.

Loevinger, Jane (1976) EGO DEVELOPMENT. San Francisco: Jossey-Bass.

Lowy, Louis (Spring, 1983) "Social Work Supervision: From Models Toward Theory". JOURNAL OF EDUCATION FOR SOCIAL WORK, Volno. 2. pp.55-62.

Maslow, Abraham (Summer, 1979) "Humanistic Education", Two Articles by Abraham Maslow. JOURNAL OF HUMANISTIC PSYCHOLOGY, Vol. 19, no. 3, pp.13-24.

Patterson, C.H. (1973) HUMANISTIC EDUCATION. Englewood Cliffs, N.J.: Prentice Hall.

Perls, F.S. (1969) GESTALT THERAPY VERBATIM. Moab, Utah: Real People Press.

Perry, William (1970) FORMS OF INTELLECTUAL AND ETHICAL DEVELOPMENT IN THE COLLEGE YEARS. New York: Hold, Rinehart and Winston.

Price, Hazel G. (Winter, 1976) "Achieving a Balance Between Self-Directed and Required Learning". JOURNAL OF EDUCATION FOR SOCIAL WORK, Vol. 12, no. 1, pp.105-112.

Richmond, Mary (1917) SOCIAL DIAGNOSIS. New York: Russel Sage Foundation.

Reynolds, Bertha (1942) LEARNING AND TEACHING IN THE PRACTICE OF SOCIAL WORK. New York: Farrar and Rinehart.

Rogers, Carl (1969) FREEDOM TO LEARN. Columbus, OH: C.E. Merrill.

Rogers, Carl (1961) ON BECOMING A PERSON. Boston: Houghton-Mifflin.

Rogers, Carl (1980) A WAY OF BEING. Boston: Houghton-Mifflin.

Rothman, Beulah (Spring, 1973) "Perspectives on Learning and Teaching". JOURNAL OF EDUCATION FOR SOCIAL WORK, Vol. 9, no. 2.

Schneck, Dean (March, 1987) "The Leadership Opportunity in Fieldwork for Responding to Change'. A paper presented at Field Work: Nexus of Change in Social Work Education. Field Work Symposium, Council on Social Work Education, St. Louis.

Schon, Donald A. (1987) EDUCATING THE REFLECTIVE PRACTITIONER. San Francisco: Jossey-Bass Publishers.

Schon, Donald A. (1983) THE REFLECTIVE PRACTITIONER. HOW PROFESSIONALS THINK IN ACTION. New York: Basic Books.

Schutz, W.C. (1975) ELEMENTS OF ENCOUNTER. New York: Bantam.

Shulman, Lawrence (1982) THE SKILLS OF SUPERVISION AND STAFF MANAGEMENT. Itasca, Illinois: Peacock.

Siporin, Max (1984) "A Future for Social Work Education", in Miriam Dinnermam and Ludwig L. Geismar (Eds.), QUARTER-CENTURY OF SOCIAL WORK EDUCATION. NASW, ABC-CLIO, CSWE.

Siporin, Max (1982) "The Process of Field Instruction" in Bradford Sheaffer and Lowell Jenkins (Eds.), QUALITY FIELD INSTRUCTION IN SOCIAL WORK. New York: Longman.

Somers, Mary Louise (1971) "Dimensions and Dynamics of Engaging the Learner". JOURNAL OF EDUCATION FOR SOCIAL WORK. Vol. 7, no. 3.

Towle, Charlotte (1954) THE LEARNER IN EDUCATION FOR THE PROFESSIONS. Chicago, Ill,: University of Chicago Press.

# DEVELOPING A PROCESS MODEL FOR FIELD INSTRUCTION[1]

Marion Bogo, *University of Toronto*
Elaine Vayda, *York University*

Concern with the quality of field instruction has occupied social work educators both in the United States and Canada for some time (Sheafor & Jenkins, 1982). In 1979 at the Annual Conference of the Canadian Association of Schools of Social Work (C.A.S.S.W.), a group of educators expressed concerns about the lack of knowledge regarding the state of field instruction in schools across the country. Accordingly, a two-year study, sponsored by Health and Welfare Canada, was undertaken to collect and collate data about field practice gathered from faculties, field co-ordinators, field instructors, agency administrators, and students.

One major gap identified by the survey was the absence of a consistent and comprehensive training program for field instructors at the field preparation level (Thomlison, Watt & Kimberley, 1980). Field instructors claimed that "they need more skills to perform their roles more adequately" (Thomlison, Watt & Kimberley, p. 45). The survey revealed that 25% of field instructors in the sample did not have a professional social work degree and 47% of the responding field instructors were in the first or second year of instructing students.

It seemed evident that the development of a comprehensive approach to field instruction and training was needed. Such a program could yield immediate benefits to field instructors who were asking for guidance in how to achieve their task as field educators. In addition an objective would be the long-range improvement of service delivery. It could be argued that one factor leading to the improvement of social service delivery is the transfer of new knowledge and service methods to the service providers and that the interface of field teachers with the professional schools of social work is one avenue for such a transfer. Practice experience informs the development of new knowledge so the exchange must be mutual. Field practice instructors along with academic faculty, must assume responsibility for guiding students to integrate practice theory and to develop professional judgment.

Health and Welfare, Canada funded a project to produce a national curriculum base for use by Canadian schools of social work in providing educational activities for social work practitioners to enhance their competence as field practice educators. Canada is characterized by regional diversity which effects the mandate, focus, and resources of particular educational programs. Therefore it was essential to establish a network structure which would facilitate ongoing and frequent consultation and feedback. The final product had to include generic concepts which would be relevant across the country.

---

[1]A version of this paper has been published in the CANADIAN SOCIAL WORK REVIEW, Vol. 6, No. 2, Summer, 1969, pp. 224-232; and is printed here with their permission.

Eighteen schools of social work agreed to participate in the project, which required them, through their field co-ordinators, to gather information from relevant field practice constituencies and to communicate these data to the project. Data analysis revealed that all schools have materials which identify practicum objectives or generic content, outline the structure of the practicum, and define the role responsibilities of the principal actors, student, field instructor and faculty representative. Though the words and emphases differed, similar trends were apparent in the materials.

While most schools held occasional orientation meetings or workshops for field instructors, only a few schools offered ongoing seminars, courses, or support groups for field instructors. Almost no documentation existed on the content, structure, or process of these activities. Some schools did not report any training. Schools generally provided reading lists on field instruction. Only one school stressed a commitment to a specific theoretical approach to social work practice and expected field instructors to understand that approach. Schools in under-serviced remote areas identified severe resource problems that necessitated the use of persons holding non-social work degrees as field instructors.

Some field co-ordinators reported the problems of developing and offering a quality field education program in academic environments that did not value field education in social work professional education. In some schools, therefore, the practicum appeared to be an under-resourced area. It is not surprising to note that the field co-ordinator role is marked by considerable turnover. During three years of the project, one third of the co-ordinators changed roles. These conditions ultimately effect the quality of social work education and the practice competence of the graduates of these programs.

This paper will now examine the model of field instruction practice developed through the project. Social work education provides opportunities for students to learn about the components of social welfare and social work practice; to think critically and analytically about social issues and concerns; and to apply knowledge through competent practice. Social work education in the field shares these objectives with academic courses. However, the point of departure is the practice event. The experience of observing and participating in social work activities provides the context and data for cognitive, affective, and behavioural learning. Field instructors, like all social work educators, help the student to make connections between knowledge and practice.

Early social work educators were concerned with the nature of field education and the relationship between field instructor and student (Berengarten, 1961; Reynolds, 1942; Towle, 1954). Analyses of approaches to field instruction have appeared in recent social work literature (Bogo & Vayda, 1987; George, 1982; Jenkins & Sheafor, 1982; Wijnberg & Schwartz, 1977). Education for social work, as with other professions, began with apprenticeship training. The *apprenticeship approach* appears to focus on behaviours and strategies but omits reflective and conceptual activities. This model does not direct attention to the importance of the awareness of one's own values and assumptions nor does it encourage identification of theoretical concepts as guides to action. The *growth-therapeutic approach* was prominent as a result of the influence of psychoanalytic theory on social work education and practice (Robinson, 1962; Hamilton, 1954). Field instructors encourage students to be reflective and to disclose personal issues elicited by the social work process. Research on this style of supervision found that a focus on personal issues was considered stressful and objectionable (Kadushin, 1974; Rosenblatt & Mayer, 1975). The *role systems approach* (Wijnberg & Schwartz, 1977) shares many similarities with the principles of andragogy (Knowles, 1972). The transactional nature of the relationship between student and field instructor assumes primary importance. This approach is egalitarian, collaborative and stresses the necessity of positive and negative feedback. This model does not explicitly address a conceptual base for practice. The *academic and articulated approach* emphasizes knowing and understanding the professional knowledge base (Jenkins & Sheafor, 1982). In the academic approach the field instructor must be informed of course content, the faculty liaison must carry the major educational responsibility. This approach may dilute the reflective aspect of practice. In the articulated approach faculty and field instructor must agree on the content and sequence of learning and field experience. This necessitates considerable investment in time and personnel which may be unattainable given the current reality of financial restraint. A *competency-based approach* focuses on concretizing a particular professional knowledge base in the form of measurable behaviours (Arkava & Brennan, 1976). In a comparative study Larsen and Hepworth (1980) found that students taught in this method performed at a higher overall level of competency and had confidence in their skills.

None of the models developed in the literature seemed totally adequate to the achievement of the task of helping the student to integrate theory with practice. Implicit in the preparation of students for service in the field is a process whereby the information, knowledge and critical, analytic base acquired by students in the academic part of professional education must be translated into an ability to arrive at a professional decision in a service context. Each school has developed a unique philosophy of education, specific curriculum objectives and specific practicum regulations and procedures. However, field instruction is more than a structural arrangement between academy and agency where actors follow a set of procedures. Field instruction requires more than providing an example for a student to observe and emulate as in apprenticeship training between a master teacher and an apprentice, and more than establishing a facilitative relationship between student and field instructor.

What is required is a model that illuminates the process of field instruction and provides a systematic and structured approach. It should assist field instructors in examining their own practice and that of their student's, as well as student and field instructor interaction. The organizing principle was the belief that field instruction is a branch of social work practice which possesses a distinctive blend of knowledge, values, and skills which can be articulated and learned. It was obvious that a universally relevant generic approach to field instruction must focus more on the process than on the specific content of the practicum sequence. What was required was a structured approach that would be applicable to all levels of practice, both direct and indirect, to traditional and non-traditional settings, whether urban or rural, and to BSW and MSW education.

Practitioners, as they become educators, must be able to examine their own practice and communicate the thoughts, attitudes, values, and feelings that effect the actions they take. As practitioners many of these actions have become "second nature," so that plans and behaviours appear, to the observer, to evolve naturally. In fact, professional behaviour is based on implicit ideas and beliefs that the practitioner has developed through their own educational and practice experience. This "integrated knowledge" must now be identified and clarified so that the field educator can communicate it to the student. The instructor then transfers this process into field instruction, as, together with the student, they examine the student's practice and search to articulate the knowledge useful to understand and guide the student's intervention. In field education the student and instructor participate in an interactive process where the experiential data provided by the practice and policies of the agency, the field instructor's practice, and especially the student's practice provides the context for extracting the components of values, attitudes, concepts, mandate, feelings, behaviours, and examining and analyzing these elements.

It seemed obvious that this is where the field teacher begins and where students and field instructors return again and again. This suggested a looping process which is cumulative, multidimensional, and tentative. The work of Kolb (1984) argued that adult learning theory builds on the premise that learning is stimulated by a problem which needs to be solved and is therefore rooted in the practice experience. He suggested a cycle which moves from the concrete experience to observation and reflection, to abstraction and generalization and then to the formation of hypotheses to be tested. This cycle is both active and passive, concrete and abstract. We adapted the Kolb cycle to be specifically applicable to social work. The result is the Integration of Theory and Practice Loop (ITP) which begins with retrieval, loops to reflection, then to linkage, and then to professional response. Since social work practice is generally ongoing, the loop returns to retrieval and the process begins again but informed by the preceding experience with the loop. The model is to be conceptualized as having a temporal and spatial dimension.

## I.T.P. LOOP (INTEGRATION OF THEORY AND PRACTICE)

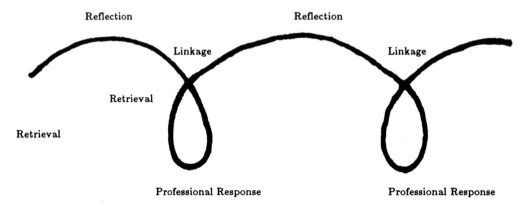

Reflection          Reflection

Linkage          Linkage

Retrieval

Retrieval

Professional Response          Professional Response

**Retrieval** summons the recall of the information, the facts describing any given practice situation. The social worker or student recalls a professional situation both as participant as well as observer. Retrieval may involve the facts of an initial encounter or may involve observations of reactions to a professional response that had evolved from the preceding encounter. The methods of retrieval include observations made through recall and verbal reports, process and summary recording, audio or video tapes, live supervision, or co-working experiences. The content can include details about the specific setting and circumstances, interpersonal communications, and cultural, economic, or political factors.

**Reflection** starts with personal associations to the encounter deriving from life experiences, the student's feelings, thoughts, and assumptions regarding the retrieved data. For example, cultural, class, and sex biases must be identified so their influence and power can be understood and controlled. The field instructor must help the student identify practice behaviour in relation to its effect on the client system and give feedback to the student that is empathetic, clear, and related to the learning objectives. Feedback should be reciprocal, in that it invites dialogue.

**Linkage** is that part of the ITP loop which calls forth the cognitive associations of both the student and the field instructor to the retrieved data and the associations considered through reflection. Both field instructor and student attempt to identify and label knowledge that they believe will help explain and understand the data and the feelings that have been evoked. This process is analytical. It is a search for concepts learned by the student or practiced by the field instructor which derive from theoretical bases such as ecological systems, structural analysis, empowerment theory, psychodynamic theory, communication theory, or developmental theory. The purpose is to encourage the student to partialize and select from competing concepts what is needed to construct a cognitive system of understanding that fits what has been retrieved and subjected to reflection. It is the goodness of fit of a working hypothesis that both student and field instructor must agree upon.

**Professional Response** is the selection of a plan that will inform the next encounter the student has with this specific situation. This plan must derive from the preceding process; it is an exercise in "if this...then that." Since the process is applied to complex human events, it remains tentative and is subject to revision, modification, or abandonment based on subsequent work.

The ITP loop should provide a structure for the integration of cognitive and affective processes which we believe form the core of social work practice. It permits these two processes to be unhooked and hooked again through a conscious analytic process. In addition, it will succeed whether one chooses to focus widely on a global problem or concern or narrowly on a specific episode of student-client communication. For example, it can be used to focus on a single interchange in a family therapy interview, or the focus can be widened to examine a case management problem, or to consider a neighbourhood analyses of significant actors in order to develop an effective strategy for community development. Data can be analyzed using more than one approach, helping the student make comparisons between the effect of two or more different models on problem definition and intervention targets or plans. For example, examining a request for housing using an individual task-centered approach which would direct intervention to the particular client can be contrasted with a structural analysis which would in addition direct worker and client to take action aimed at eradicating the causes of the housing shortage.

The loop can be used to teach social work practice at any level of intervention with a variety of populations, purposes, and settings. It can be microscopic or macroscopic depending on what facts are retrieved. The choice of a lens and the degree of magnification depends on the practice activity and the specific intent of the field instructor.

In presenting the ITP loop to field instructors and social work faculty across Canada, we have found that linkage seems the most difficult to comprehend and the most controversial. There seems to be a belief that practice is either radical or traditional, an old social work battle cry that refuses to be silenced. We believe that linkage encourages students to bring to the practicum knowledge from the classroom or a specific perspective for assessment of a situation which may be somewhat different from the practice knowledge base of the field instructor. By suggesting that both field instructor and student need to review all knowledge that may be relevant to a situation, the opportunity exists for learning that no single approach or formulation is applicable to any situation without considerable custom tailoring. Assessment and therefore intervention must consider not only the client's inter-actions, but the helping system itself, and societal biases and blockages. Strategies flow from a full consideration of explanatory theories and remain tentative and uncertain.

Both faculty and field educators may wish for a simpler time when greater uniformity of thought existed among faculty and agency. The issue of 'fit' between class and field has a long and tortured history in North American social work education. Each school of social work has the responsibility to communicate to the field instructors its philosophical and theoretical approaches, the content of courses, and to decide the degree to which it hopes to achieve congruence between what is taught in the school and what philosophical and theoretical approaches inform the practice of social work in the field.

A British social worker has written that "the integration of theory and practice is a unique and intuitive process but the social worker must be articulate about the problems and her thinking, citing the specific and selecting from the general. ...The worker uses theoretical knowledge not to apply formulae, but to construct coherence from immediate complexity" (England, 1986). For example, in identifying isolation as a concern where an individual seems to have no supportive network, we are connecting to a knowledge and value base affirming that human isolation is an unhealthy state. In identifying a sense of powerlessness to alter noxious conditions of living, we link to a theoretical base which teaches that change can occur through understanding the institutionalization of oppression and empowering collective action to exert pressure on those institutions. In identifying a struggle between adolescent and parent we link to a theoretical base that examines appropriate developmental stages and behaviours for individuals and family members and the effect of recurring dysfunctional transactions on maintaining a power struggle. In identifying a hospital team headed by a physician who wants beds immediately even if it means sending a patient to an inappropriate facility, we link to the knowledge that a client problem can be created by the system charged with the resolution of problems. In working with family caregivers of the chronically ill, we link to the knowledge that counselling without some attention to the provision of concrete relief will be of little benefit. These are examples of practice wisdom, but they are at the same time examples of applied theory.

The ITP loop can provide field instructors with a tool to examine and articulate the links between their thoughts, values, feelings, and behaviours as field instructors. It can also be utilized to review the student-field instructor encounter itself in order to uncover blockages to the attainment of learning objectives. We are aware that relationship is an integral ingredient of field instruction and when trust is not established at the outset learning is impeded. Learning and teaching styles do vary and field instructors and students need to spend some time looking for differences in expectations and in approaches to problem-solving. It is not necessary that there be total consistency for learning to take place, but it is essential that differences be identified so that clear communication is possible. Gizynski (1978) looks at three areas where field instructors need to develop self-awareness; dependency needs, differences in style, and awareness of values. The field instructor can use the ITP loop to sharpen self-awareness in these areas by responding to the internal cues that something in the supervisory sessions is not going well or seems unclear. By retrieving this cue and the related feelings and looking for what may be contributing factors, such as value conflicts, learning style disparities, or incompatible expectations around dependent/independent behaviour, the field instructor can engage with the student in a process of resolution.

In summary, we set out to develop a model for field instruction which can be used to analyze the union of practice wisdom or intuition with social work knowledge and values through a cognitive process. Use of the loop should culminate in a reuniting of the two processes when the professional response is applied to the situation in the next encounter. We believe that social work is both an art and a science. It is necessary to insist that field instructors and students understand, through an active process both the affective and cognitive components that influence the choice of a professional response. It is also necessary that they understand the tentativeness of that response as it is applied through a dynamic and complex human encounter.

In order for field instruction to build on and augment the classroom experience, it is important that schools provide for ongoing field instructor training and monitoring as well as the more traditional orientation sessions and manual which most already provide. This may set the stage for the establishment of field instruction as a generic social work practice role.

## BIBLIOGRAPHY

Arkava, M. L. and Brennan, E. C. eds. (1976) COMPETENCY-BASED EDUCATION FOR SOCIAL WORK: EVALUATION AND CURRICULUM ISSUES. New York: Council on Social work Education.

Berengarten, S. (1961) "Educational Issues in Field Instruction in Social Work," SOCIAL SERVICE REVIEW, 35(3), 246-257.

Bogo, M. and Vayda, E. (1987) THE PRACTICE OF FIELD INSTRUCTION IN SOCIAL WORK: THEORY AND PROCESS - WITH AN ANNOTATED BIBLIOGRAPHY. Toronto: University of Toronto Press.

England, H. (1986) SOCIAL WORK AS ART. London: Allen and Unwin Publishers Ltd.

Gizynski, M. (1978) "Self Awareness of the Supervisor in Supervision," CLINICAL SOCIAL WORK JOURNAL, 6(3), 202-210.

George, A. (1982) "A History of Social Work Field Instruction: Apprenticeship to Instruction," in QUALITY FIELD INSTRUCTION IN SOCIAL WORK, (eds.) Bradford W. Sheafor and Lowell E. Jenkins. New York: Longman, 37-59.

Hamilton, G. (November 1954) "Self-Awareness in Professional Education," SOCIAL CASEWORK, 35, 371-379.

Jenkins, L. E. and B. W. Sheafor (1982) "An Overview of Social Work Field Instruction," in QUALITY FIELD INSTRUCTION IN SOCIAL WORK, (eds.) Bradford W. Sheafor and Lowell E. Jenkins. New York: Longman, 3-20.

Kadushin, A. (1974) "Supervisor-Supervisee: A Survey," SOCIAL WORK, 19, 289-297.

Knowles, M. (Spring, 1972) "Innovations in Teaching Styles and Approaches Based on Adult Learning," JOURNAL OF EDUCATION FOR SOCIAL WORK, 8, 32-39.

Kolb, D. (1984) EXPERIENTIAL LEARNING: EXPERIENCE AS A SOURCE OF LEARNING AND DEVELOPMENT. Englewood Cliffs, New Jersey: Prentice Hall.

Larsen. J. A. and Hepworth, D. (Spring 1980) "Enhancing the Effectiveness of Practicum Instruction: An Empirical Study," JOURNAL OF EDUCATION FOR SOCIAL WORK, 18, 50-58.

Reynolds, B. C. (1942) LEARNING AND TEACHING IN THE PRACTICE OF SOCIAL WORK. New York: Farrar and Rinehart, Inc.

Robinson, V.R. (Ed.) (1962) JESSIE TAFT: THERAPIST AND SOCIAL WORK EDUCATOR Philadelphia: University of Pennsylvania Press.

Rosenblatt, A. and Mayer, J. E. (1975) "Objectionable Supervisory Styles: Students' Views," SOCIAL WORK, 20, 67-73.

Sheafor, B. W. and Jenkins, L. E. (1982) QUALITY FIELD INSTRUCTION IN SOCIAL WORK. New York: Longman.

Thomlison, B., Watt, S. and Kimberley, D. (October 1980) TRENDS AND ISSUES IN THE FIELD PREPARATION OF SOCIAL WORK MANPOWER. Ottawa, Canada: The Canadian Association of Schools of Social Work.

Towle, C. (1954) THE LEARNER IN EDUCATION FOR THE PROFESSIONS: AS SEEN IN EDUCATION FOR SOCIAL WORK. Chicago, University of Chicago Press.

Wijnberg, M. and Schwartz, M. C. (Fall 1977) "Models of Student Supervision: The Apprentice, Growth, and Role Systems Models," JOURNAL OF EDUCATION FOR SOCIAL WORK, 13, 107-113.

# INTEGRATION OF LEARNING IN FIELD EDUCATION: ELUSIVE GOAL AND EDUCATIONAL IMPERATIVE

Dean Schneck, *University of Wisconsin-Madison*

The integration of learning in field education has received considerable attention and advocacy by many distinguished authors in social work education. Perhaps because it is so inextricably linked to educational policy and teaching issues, the topic of integration occurs in many historical and developmental discussions of curriculum structure and content. In its earliest discussion and inferences, integration was seen as an instrumental goal in the long struggle to move away from an apprenticeship training model toward a knowledge-based professional education model. Aase George (1982) states:

> Mary Richmond, for example, in 1897, called for a permanent group of instructors to direct the work of students, giving them theory and practice together. She pointed out that while many learned from doing, learning by doing alone is not efficient and must be supplemented by theory.[1]

Mildred Sikkema (1966), an oft-quoted historian of field work, in examining the early training of charity workers (1898-1918) notes:

> Occasional reference was made in field work evaluations to such abilities as "intellectual grasp" of the purpose, nature, and methods of the work and the problems presented, or a "grasp" of the unity between purpose and program. Although probably not widely recognized at the time, these ideas suggested educational goals of field work. Viewed in today's frame of reference, they carry the notions of integration of thinking with feeling and values, and of recognition of the connectedness of things, of a unity between the parts and the whole.

During the twenties and thirties, education for social casework was dominated by psychoanalytic theory (a particular irony given the social chaos of economic depression). Emphasis was placed on the personality growth and development the student, and the primary medium was the relationship between the field supervisor and the student. In the subsequent debate over whether task accomplishment or personal growth was the main objective of field work, a blended perspective developed. Sikkema states:

---

[1]Aase George cites from Mary Richmond, "The Training of Charity Workers," THE CHARITY REVIEW, Vol. 6 (June, 1897), 308-321.

One concept of the relatedness evolved later as Charlotte Towle's formulation of integration task-integrative capacity in the learning process. Virginia Robinson formulated it as the integration of thinking and feeling in practice or, of learning as the behavioral outcome of the student's reorganization of attitude that follows incorporation of knowledge. (p.5)

During the forties and fifties, field work became field instruction with CSWE curriculum statements calling for educational standards for field instructors. In addition to specified content on method, process and professional attributes, mechanisms for the integration of class and field were utilized to achieve the educational focus. George states:

For example, course outlines were shared with field instructors and seminars on new class content were provided for them. Student integration of class and field was also one approach. Class assignments calling for analysis of field experience in terms of class content and periodic written reports on field experience, relating it to reading and class content were among the devices used. (p. 47)

Commenting on integration during the same era, Sikkema states:

Attempts were made to create an educational focus by developing devices for "integrating" class and field work. Inevitably, these attempts led to the questions: what was to be integrated and by whom? Another concept of integration was abroad, too, in field work: the integration that was assumed would take place in the student in the learning process. (p. 6)

In the sixties and the seventies, major advances in the conceptualization of practice (social problem focus, generalist approach, the autonomous social worker) were often paired with experiential models of field instruction. These included teaching-learning centers staffed and sponsored by the schools but located in the community, project models, and faculty-based field units, multi-method in approach, focused on major social problems. Though not without role strains between the schools and community agencies, these innovative models ushered in major advances in field instructional content, educational process, and the integration of learning.

One such project specializing in community organization and social planning was developed by Rothman and Jones (1971), and called for a structured two-year field experience sequentially designed to provide laboratory-observational skill development and simulation experiences as well as a community practicum. They identified as a major learning problem "the discrepancy between what is learned in the classroom and what is learned in field." (p. 42). They state:

The commonly held assumption is that field work provides an opportunity to apply the theory learned in the classroom to actual situations and real problems. Logically there are four possible relationships between class and field:
1. Class and field integrate.
2. Class and field supplement each other.
3. Class and field are unrelated.
4. Class and field are in conflict.
. . .Given the dominant field-instruction pattern currently followed by a majority of the schools, we would hypothesize that, of the various possible relationships detailed above, class and field in general supplement each other rather than integrate. (p. 44)

Field teaching centers were established by many schools during the sixties in an active attempt to bring faculty and classroom content literally closer to the problems as well as to enhance the integration of learning for students. They were often based in low-income communities, neighborhood centers, housing projects, and large health and mental health settings. Traditional classroom content, methods, and research classes were taught in the centers.[2] School- or agency-based field units under the direction of a faculty member afford a consistent opportunity for the integration of learning. A field unit of students (usually 8-15) is located in a large agency or based in the school with placements in several different agencies within a particular field of practice, social problem area, or major methodology. The faculty from the school have responsibility for the selection and design of field placements, share in the supervision, monitoring and evaluation of the student with the agency supervisor, and teach an integrative practice seminar for the field unit. The integration of learning can be fostered in tutorial sessions and field unit seminar activities.[3]

The interaction of faculty with agency supervisors in a field teaching center or a field unit can be very productive, not only for a more congruent field experience for the student, but also for the development of practice knowledge, research and innovative services. An example would be the Queens field instruction center in Long Island, New York. This center coordinates multi-year and multi-agency field placements for students from the New York area schools through a consortium of health, mental health, and community agencies. As described by Lurie and Pinsky (1973), interagency instructional teams of faculty and agency field instructors assist students in integration of field and classroom content through learning center seminars. The collaboration of faculty and agency field instructors

---

[2]See Aase George, in Sheafor and Jenkins; and **Modes of Professional Education: Functions of Field Learning in the Curriculum.**

[3]See, for example, Virginia Franks, **The Autonomous Social Worker**, Occasional Paper #1, School of Social Work, University of Wisconsin-Madison, 1967, originally presented at the APM of CSWE, Jan. 1966, in New York City.

in the Queens center also allows for better coordination and expansion of student-provided services in many problem areas.

Any recent accounting of the integration of learning must credit the impetus provided by new perspectives in adult education, particularly andragogical approaches. These ideas have their roots in education and are articulated for social work by Malcolm S. Knowles (1972). He characterizes the andragogical approach as being student-centered, problem-focused, readiness-oriented, and facilitated by a learning climate oriented toward collaboration, comfort, authenticity, and trust. In this approach, close collaboration between student and teacher in educational planning and delivery could certainly be seen to augment the integration of learning. Social work education with its emphasis upon self-determination, student entitlement and prerogatives is easily drawn to such an instructional perspective.

A lucid discussion on the integration of learning is provided by Michael S. Kolevzon (1975) in his report of a study on the integration of research content with the field experience. He provides a discussion of the organic and mechanistic perspectives of integration. Organic integration is the natural process by which people perceive relationships between events and experiences and internally order them into a meaningful whole, unique to the individual. This subjective and internal process, of course, allows for the distinct possibility that the learner may order his experiences and perceptions in an alternative manner or with different meanings from those intended by the teacher. The mechanistic perspective assumes that the internal organization within the student can be facilitated by structural curriculum methods and techniques which aid purposive integration. Kolevzon comments that though the organic and mechanistic perspectives seem contradictory, mechanistic techniques are often cited in the educational literature as a way to aid the organic integration of learning. (p. 61)

Indeed, though an organic or holistic integration is sought within the student, structural teaching methods have considerable utility, though they can be counter-productive in the extreme. A case can be made (which I will state later) that structural mechanisms in excess actually stifle learning and, particularly, innovation.

Most of the literature on the integration of learning advocates educational methods which can be classified by the following principles:

a.  **Synchrony**--the timing or sequencing of matched content and field experiences.

b.  **Harmony**--the articulation of a shared practice perspective or frame of reference between the field and classroom experiences.

c.  **Congruency**--the conceptual fit of class content with the field learning experience.

d.  **Contiguity**--the attempt to bring together the locus of field and classroom learning by having classroom content taught in agencies or field learning centers.

e.  **Reciprocity**--the mutuality of influence or impact between the classroom content and the field experience.

These principles are carried out in curriculum design and by various methods including:

1. coordinated teaching outlines and syllabi,
2. faculty/agency instructional teams,
3. teaching and content sequencing and coordination mechanisms,
4. dual or triple teaching assignments for individual faculty (field, methods, problems course),
5. special learning opportunities such as conferences, symposia, field trips, and combined class/field seminars.

A fanciful analogy which may be instructive would be to liken our efforts in the integration of learning to the artistry practiced by a skilled painter or musician. A painter manipulates color, style, composition, stroke and technique, while a musician uses tonal quality, chords, harmonies, and tempo. These elements are blended to express a message, an idealized image, a vision, mood or sentiment. Yet, painting lessons or musical training will not produce an artistic expression in the absence of talent and a holistic ideal.

## A TEACHING-LEARNING MODEL FOR THE INTEGRATION OF LEARNING IN THE FIELD

The model which follows places emphasis upon understanding the nature of the learning sources and knowledge needs within students' experience and the skillful use of teaching-learning methods and processes to facilitate synthesis. This perspective relies upon spontaneity and teaching skill; pre-determined structure provides only a place to begin, not a way to learn.

The paradigms represent an attempt to identify the major content components in the field experience, i.e., the ideological, conceptual, emotional, and behavioral, with individual and group teaching-learning activities suggested for the integration of learning. These are portrayed over four major process stages which pair the student learning needs with the social work process tasks in the preparation/engagement phase, the problem solving phase, the intervention/change phase, and the stabilization/disengagement phase.

There is inevitably some overlap and repetition in the various stages as there is naturally in field teaching. In identifying the teaching-learning activities, the objective was to describe activities and techniques which have potential for the integration of the various components. They are choices, not prescriptions. Implicit in these paradigms is a reciprocal cycle of inquiry from the specific to the general or abstract so that a more coherent understanding and internalization occurs within the student.

The integrative teaching-learning activities are not model-specific; they could be employed in different structural models of field education. Teaching methods for the integration of learning should ideally respond to rather than dictate the pace and learning styles of the students. To the extent possible and reasonable, we should take our cues from the needs and readiness of our students as they practice in the selection of teaching-learning activities. This is the most difficult and exciting kind of teaching. It calls for flexibility, an awareness of individual and group process, and an ability to spontaneously adjust content and format to capture the learning moment.

At the CSWE Field Education Institute in 1985, I stated:

> My basic thesis is that the integration/generalization of conceptual content and problem-specific knowledge in the field practice experience requires a faculty guided and modeled inductive/deductive intellectual process. . . . Such a model demands frequent opportunities for faculty and student individually and in group situations to practice this approach to learning using field problems in a peer group, problem-solving and consultation process.

If innovation is based on the reordered formulation of perceived reality, we should consider the alternatives which may occur in our students' synthesis of their practice experiences. They occasionally might "put it together" in a better way.

This approach requires us to know well the elements of the learning experience, to consciously employ a range of integrative teaching and learning methods, and to provide the stimulation, support, and example needed to achieve a productive, even creative, understanding derived from a full and rich field learning experience.

Chart A:   **PREPARATION/ENGAGEMENT PHASE**

**IDEOLOGICAL**

Assess current attitudes and political views
toward clients and social problems.
Identification of relevant personal values
and religious beliefs.
Exposure to professional ethics
Personal expectations.
Identify/explore case related value issues.

**INDIVIDUAL/GROUP TEACHING-LEARNING ACTIVITIES**

Orientation and exposure to agency setting,
staff and programs.
Value discussion/clarification.
Interviewing practice and role-play (video).
Problem assessment/exploration discussion.
Identification of knowledge needs and methods choices.
Problem solving and process simulation exercises.
Case observations with supervisor or mentor.
Case sharing with supervisor or faculty.
Initial client contacts.
Case examples and discussion.
Individual and group supervisory conferences.
Discussion of professional role vis-vis
previous work experience.
Opportunity to discuss initial assumptions and
expectations about client problems and professional roles.

**CONCEPTUAL**

Initial social problem, research &
human development knowledge.
Understanding of social work
process stages.
Information on agency programs
and structures.
Agency policies and procedures.
Understanding of student
expectations.
Initial exposure to methods and
techniques.

**BEHAVIORAL**

Level of social skills
from life experience.
Level of work skills from
previous employment.
System/entry/negotiation skills.
Professional role behaviors.
Initial communication and
interviewing skills.
Assertive and expressive
behaviors.

**EMOTIONAL**

Performance anticipation/anxiety.
Previous emotional experiences in general.
Re-activation of old personal struggles.
Connection to existing personal problems or needs.
Subjective response to client needs and problems.
Security and credibility.

Dean Schneck, 1990

Chart B:  **PROBLEM SOLVING PHASE**

IDEOLOGICAL

Resolution of situational value/ethical issues.
Clarification of professional responsibilities.
Juxtaposition of personal values, religious beliefs, and political views vis-a-vis professional role expectations.

INDIVIDUAL/GROUP TEACHING-LEARNING ACTIVITIES

Case presentation and consultation.
Structured problem solving and value clarification exercises -- case related.
Explore and apply relevant theoretical knowledge.
Evaluate interventive method and technique choices.
Anticipate barriers, outcomes, and consequences of interventive decisions.
Discuss subjective responses and interference with professional role.
Case sharing with supervisor, faculty or mentor.
Review similar case histories or practice examples.
Assess and possibly visit potential resources.
Develop and evaluate several alternative case formulations and plans.
Observe or record student interviews for content and technical feedback.
Evaluate and resolve practical value considerations.
Simulate or role-play (video) case related interventions and techniques.

CONCEPTUAL

Assessment of problem dynamics.
Consideration of motivation and change potential.
Knowledge of interventive roles and methodologies.
Knowledge of community resources and natural helping systems.
Understanding of problem solving process.
Conceptualization and refinement problem definition.
Initial decisions on scope of interventions.
Planning of interventions and identification of barriers.

BEHAVIORAL

Data collection and planning skills.
Contracting/negotiation skills.
Outreach and motivational skills.
Meaning attribution skills.
Supportive skills.
Decision-making/priority skills.
Professional influence.

EMOTIONAL

Tolerance of ambiguity and resistance to premature closure in the problem solving process.
Emotional response to client needs and problems.
Identification and transference issues.
Subjective reactions to case choices and issues.
Reassurance needs.

Dean Schneck, 1990

Chart C:  **INTERVENTION/CHANGE PHASE**

IDEOLOGICAL

Pragmatic/operational value issues.
Ends/means questions.
Idealism *vs.* reality confrontations.
Value conflicts among principled professionals.
Exposure to possible ethical breaches of others.
Reaction to insufficient resources and compromised goals.
Challenges to personal values, political views or religious beliefs.

**INDIVIDUAL/GROUP TEACHING-LEARNING ACTIVITIES**

Frequent supervisory/consultative conferences.
Modification of case plan and objectives.
Discussion of practice norms, judgements, vis-a-vis case assignment and learning needs.
Consideration of client responses, unexpected developments and consequences.
Explore student concerns relating to case responsibilities, decision making or value matters.
Demonstrate application of theoretical knowledge and resource information to practice situation.
Identify important process components from immediate practice experience.
Use simulation exercise to overcome student resistance or to develop sufficient competence.
Provide suggestions for dealing with resources or institutions such as courts, schools, law enforcement agencies, employers.
Provide feedback and support on task performance and skill development.
Provide relative sense of progress and improvement vis-a-vis school and agency expectations, initial skill level, and student's own goals.
Provide perspective on role stressors, such as reasonable levels of effort, limits of responsibility, client demands, bureaucratic frustrations, delivery system problems, etc. to prevent unneeded stress or anxiety.

**C O N C E P T U A L**

Understanding of process and the client's experience.
Awareness of case plan and objectives.
Operational problem solving and decision making.
Application of practice theory, research, and knowledge.
Reformulation of problem definition as interventions proceed.
Understanding of case management and coordinative responsibility.
Being mindful of unintended consequences.
Balance of change and stability.

**B E H A V I O R A L**

Apply intervention methods and various techniques to accomplish case objectives.
Enact professional responsibility with increasing autonomy.
Exert professional influence with client and resource systems.
Expand interviewing, treatment and communication skills.
Assert observations and opinions with professional staff.
Coordination and management skills.

EMOTIONAL

Experience "in vivo" practice responsibilities, successes, failures, and frustrations.
Emotional reactions to practice demands, crises, excitement.
Self-confidence and self-criticism questions.
Emotional response to difficult problems, harsh realities, lack or resources.
Reassurance and support needs.

Dean Schneck, 1990

Chart D: **STABILIZATION/DISENGAGEMENT PHASE**

**IDEOLOGICAL**

Reflection and reevaluation of personal values, political views, and religious beliefs.
Value attributions to client outcomes, agency efforts, and resource systems.
Review of ethical conflicts encountered.
Practice and program policy implications.

**CONCEPTUAL**

Meaning attributions to practice experiences and client outcomes.
Outcome evaluation of service plan.
Review of what actually happened and consequences for clients.
Restate problem formulation in retrospect.
Knowledge of termination/separation dynamics and resistances.
Generalize experiences to practice concepts, principles, process and policy.
Identify knowledge and skills gaps of the student and the profession.

**INDIVIDUAL/GROUP TEACHING-LEARNING ACTIVITIES**

Help students see the importance of a well-done termination and separation process for the client particularly the stabilization, generalization of of learning and separation components.
Use case reviews and discussion to discern process issues, techniques used, and theoretical knowledge which was applied.
Consider retrospectively alternative case formulations and intervention choices not chosen, i.e., "the road not taken".
Extrapolate SW principles, policies, concepts, and values from the case experiences, making inductive and deductive linkages with specific examples.
Identify knowledge and skills areas with each student for improvement and development.
Review student accomplishment in achieving service objectives, client benefits, and changes.
Assist student in gaining perspective of their achievements vis-a-vis a broader practice framework.
Discuss personal/professional value conflicts flowing from their immediate experience.
Assist student with professional or career choices.

**BEHAVIORAL**

Evaluate and reinforce change efforts and growth with clients.
Deal with dependency or resistance of the client or self.
Strengthen client self-reliance and coping skills.
Anticipate and prepare client for new or continuing problems.
Solifidy resources linkages.
Generalize new social skills to potential situations.

**EMOTIONAL**

Reaction to situational ethics.
Termination/separation issues and ambivalences.
Feelings of satisfaction, achievement, disappointment, loss, or regret.
Self-evaluative or self-worth questions.
Suitability and career choice/direction issues.
Assess affective responses to clients' problems and agencies.

Dean Schneck, 1990

**BIBLIOGRAPHY**

Franks, Virginia (1967) THE AUTONOMOUS SOCIAL WORKER, Occasional Paper #1, School of Social Work, University of Wisconsin-Madison, originally presented at the APM of CSWE, Jan. 1966, in New York City.

George, Aase (1982) "A History of Social Work Field Instruction: Apprenticeship to Instruction.: in Bradford W. Sheafor and Lowell E. Jenkins (eds.) QUALITY FIELD INSTRUCTION IN SOCIAL WORK. New York: Longman, Inc.

Knowles, Malcolm S. (Spring, 1972) "Innovations in Teaching Styles and Approaches Based on Adult Learning." JOURNAL OF EDUCATION FOR SOCIAL WORK.

Kolevzon, Michael S. (Spring, 1975) "Integration Teaching Modalities in Social Work Education: Promise or Pretense?" JOURNAL OF EDUCATION FOR SOCIAL WORK.

Lurie, Abraham and Pinsky, Sidney (Fall, 1973) "Queens Field Instruction Center: A Field Instruction Center for Multi-Level Education in Social Work." JOURNAL OF EDUCATION FOR SOCIAL WORK.

Richmond, Mary. "The Training of Charity Workers," THE CHARITY REVIEW, Vol. 6, June, 1897

Rothman, Jack and Jones, Wyatt (1971) A NEW LOOK AT FIELD INSTRUCTION: EDUCATION FOR APPLICATION OF PRACTICE SKILLS IN COMMUNITY ORGANIZATION AND SOCIAL PLANNING. New York: Association Press.

Schneck, Dean (February, 1985) "Improving the Integration of Classroom and Field Education," presented at MODELS OF FIELD EDUCATION: EXAMINING THE COMMON ELEMENTS. Post-conference Institute, CSWE-APM.

Sikkema, Mildred (1966) "A Proposal for an Innovation in Field Learning and Teaching," in FIELD INSTRUCTION IN GRADUATE SCHOOL WORK EDUCATION: OLD PROBLEMS AND NEW PROPOSALS. New York: CSWE.

# THE LEADERSHIP OPPORTUNITY IN FIELDWORK FOR RESPONDING TO CHANGE

Dean Schneck, *University of Wisconsin-Madison*

If the business of social work is social problems and social change, we should be very busy indeed. Everywhere we are confronted by new problems and old dilemmas. We see disturbing violence in families; we wonder how we'll make headway against poverty, particularly among minority and underclass populations. We have deinstitutionalized the mentally ill and now find many floundering helplessly on the streets. Our prisons are so crowded that we must discharge many legal offenders untreated and often dangerous back into the community. We take some comfort in our advances in serving the elderly but now realize many become impoverished with catastrophic illness; and we face potentially the most serious public health problem in recent history--AIDS. Yet, somehow, incredulously, we are not as busy as we should be.

We have seen in many areas a net loss of social work positions, and a waning of our influence. Certainly, the federal government's commitment to practice development and education has withered away. Some states and localities have increased in real terms their support of the human services, but most have not. Notions of social responsibility are changing. Many policy makers and legislators from the right and the left, even "War on Poverty" liberals have rediscovered self-reliance, the work ethic and competitiveness. The challenge of framing these ideological initiatives against our long-standing commitment to social justice will be complicated.

Supposedly, we are in a continuing, albeit "slow growth" economic recovery. We have seen national policy and priorities shift away from social provision and benefits for the needy to individual responsibility, opportunity, and the social contract. Our graduates, will likely earn $22-$30,000, while comparably educated engineers, computer technicians, and MBAs earn $40-$60,000. Somethings's amiss. Yet, the building blocks of progress remain. Critical social problems need attention more than ever; the market place is open; and the resources of our country are easily sufficient.

Fieldwork, that is, practice and education in the field, provides a continuing opportunity to work at the nexus of change, that lively juncture of the practical and the ideal, the real and the unrealized, the intuitive and the empirical. Social work education began in the field, is oriented to problems from the field, and ultimately is measured by its contributions to practice in the field. Are we seeing the kind of practice leadership and innovation which would inspire political support and social commitment?

Fieldwork is often viewed as the requisite laboratory for the integration of other discrete parts of our curriculum. Social policies, human behavior over the lifespan, social work values and ethics, practice methodologies and techniques, and research comprise the elements which the field experience is expected to synthesize into a meaningful whole. These elements are often portrayed as the major determinants of practice with fieldwork being the resultant medium for the integration.

I propose that field practice can and should be an equal co-variable in the determination of the agenda for education. Knowledge can inform practice, but practice can also reform knowledge. The knowledge-building process can and should go both ways. We may, at times, have a better configuration of practice, construed artfully and intuitively in fieldwork than would be had by the integration of existing, perhaps even outmoded, ideas and methods. On that occasion, our obligation would be to "disintegrate" the configuration, articulate the policy, method, and content issues back to the classroom and researchers. After all, our innovations arise from the response to new problems, the redefinition of old problems, the formulation of more effective policies, and the crafting of better methods and techniques.

We are often forced to confront new problems and persistent human needs in the absence of definitive guidance from academic or empirical sources (e.g., AIDS, homelessness, cocaine addiction). We have the prerogative to experiment with alternative policy responses or practice approaches without a priori empirical verification. Thus doing, our ethical responsibility is to specify openly what we are doing so that others can examine, criticize or validate. If practice is to be ever dynamic, then our theories and practice methodologies must also be so, even if we must push upstream to the tributary sources of theory to reform them. Thus, the opportunity for practice leadership in field education is ever present. Ultimately, innovations from practice, as well as those from research, must stand on their respective merits. Time and scrutiny serve us all a lesson in humility.

In field education, we necessarily attend to the training objectives of our schools, construct a responsible and relevant field model, arrange agency placements and supervisory resources, and, of course, look after out students properly. These never-ending duties produce nothing less than the grand medium for our educational endeavors. But all of our heartfelt strivings, our well-designed structures, and our refined processes will come to naught if we do not disseminate a strong and visionary message for practice. For in field education, the medium is only part of the message. The rest of the message must of necessity illuminate the problems which are so pressing and the practice which we hold so dear. Else, we'll not endure as a profession in the new millennium.

# PART II: FIELD INSTRUCTION MODELS

## INTRODUCTION

The previous section examined basic theoretical concepts and perspectives that underlie field education in social work. Field educators may sometimes feel a bit "sheepish" discussing conceptual foundations. If we are honest we must admit that much in our program designs is as rooted in tradition and pragmatism as in theory and empiricism. We should not be embarrassed, for it is the peculiar task of fieldwork to blend the ideal and real in social work education. We balance these two poles in creating and sustaining our programs while we teach our students to balance them in their practice.

However, if we are to survive and grow in field education roles, we must be able to set and achieve significant goals related to improving field program design and implementation. To do this we must surely find, in the words of the old A.A. prayer, "the strength to change what we can change, the serenity to accept what we cannot change, and the wisdom to know the difference."

Rather than try to change everything that can be changed at once, we may select an aspect of the field program for modification or we may try an alternative structure in one area of a multifaceted program. If we plan well, evaluate carefully, and promote successful innovations effectively, such experimentation may, in time, alter an entire program.

The sources of innovation lie in close attention to the weaknesses and strengths of our particular field structures, openness to the work of our colleagues, and sensitivity to the opportunities and limitations in our own environments. The following papers offer illustrations of field educators blending the ideal and the real to achieve innovations in field design. While they vary in scope, each demonstrates how theory may suggest alternatives but need not limit creativity.

Marshack and Glassman challenge traditional assumptions about the mechanism through which field instructors teach. They find in the pressures of shortened agency time frames, reduced training resources, and heightened demands for accountability, an impetus to expand beyond the one-to-one tutorial approach. Employing the educational concept of andragogy and the practice principle of client self-determination, they develop the foundation for models of group field instruction and task supervision.

Norberg and Schneck describe a "dual matrix" model of linkage between a school of social work and a large, multi-unit psychiatric hospital. This system operationalized the often avowed but seldom achieved ideal of a mutual partnership between agency and school in field education. The dual matrix is designed to respect and support the unique contribution of each institution while providing students with a coherent, integrated field experience.

In "Field Units Revisited," Conklin and Borecki demonstrate that an idea from the past can be an innovation when it is rediscovered and retooled by thoughtful field educators. The paper describes field units in a large public school system, a child protective agency, and a YWCA. In any fieldwork discussion among faculty, it is almost inevitable that pained reference will be made to the disappearance of field units due to federal funding cuts. Conklin and Borecki show that this structure need not be lost given the creativity to adapt it to current realities.

There are few empirical comparisons of alternative program models in the fieldwork literature. Grossman and Barth contrast a traditional immediate entry program and a delayed entry approach. The delayed entry first year model was instituted to prepare students for practice with a strong core of professional social work knowledge and values. While the authors encountered difficulties which required design modifications, they found that enhanced school-based preparation can be congruent with a strong, agency-based component.

Perhaps the most sacred of scared cows in field instruction is the one-to-one tutorial style of supervision/field instruction. Yet, this pattern has also been criticized as overly hierarchical and dependency inducing. Kaplan demonstrates the strength of group supervision in creating a richer and more democratic learning environment. Her specific guidelines and process descriptions anchor group supervision in a classic social group work perspective.

Much has been written in recent years about the resistance of social workers to the use of social work research technologies. Gantt, Pinsky, Rosenberg, and Rock describe a well-organized collaborative effort between a social work school and a large medical center, designed to link research and practice education in the field. The authors illustrate how the Practice Research Center drew students, agency staff, faculty to generate significant practice related research on issues of hunger and moral development in children.

The next two papers offer broad perspectives on goals, structure, and relationships between undergraduate and graduate field instruction models. Mesbur provides a broad historical overview of the debate concerning baccalaureate social work training. She considers six basic elements of undergraduate field programs, suggesting basic requirements and offering alternative strategies in each area:

1) selection of agencies;
2) selection of field instructors;
3) characteristics of field experiences;
4) theoretical components of field instruction;
5) training of field instructors; and
6) evaluation of student performance.

Social work organizations and theorists have sought to define differences between graduate and undergraduate social work education in terms of knowledge and skill development. Kilpatrick's investigation of differences and similarities between undergraduate and graduate field instruction models found that with regard to objectives, knowledge base, practice skills, integration and agencies, there seem to be more similarities than differences.

Finally, McClelland reviews the literature on field program innovations since the 60's. He finds design variations driven by three forces: changing educational philosophy and technology, changing student needs and interests, and the need to respond to retrenchment and change in social service institutions. McClelland also remarks on the continued strength of the traditional model and the tendency of innovations to erode in the face of environmental pressures.

The breadth of McClelland's perspective draws us to perhaps the most important questions in field model design. While as field educators, we may be proud of our ability to manage limitations, how can we guard against expediency? How do we assure that all our creative approaches, paradigms, and structures produce quality field experiences? And how do we keep our models directed toward the goal of educating social workers who can effectively serve disadvantaged persons and manage and improve our social service systems.

# INNOVATIVE MODELS FOR FIELD INSTRUCTION: DEPARTING FROM TRADITIONAL METHODS

Elaine Marshack, *Hunter College, City University of New York*
Urania Glassman, *Adelphi University*

## INTRODUCTION

Field education in social work has been characterized by placement of each student with a single field instructor in one field setting for an academic year. Deriving from its apprenticeship origins, the intensive one-to-one teaching relationship came to reflect the long-term clinical practice model which predominated in social work for many years (Berkman and Carlton, 1985). More recently educational models grounded in role systems and adult learning theories and responsive to changing service delivery have led to innovation in field education.

This paper explores some innovative approaches to the field instruction of students. It sets the stage for innovation, looks at field instruction within an andragogical framework, and presents two alternative models--group field instruction, and secondary and task supervision.

### THE CURRENT PRACTICE CONTEXT

Social work practice has undergone dramatic changes in recent decades. Long-term practice models have yielded to flexible use of varied methods within short time frames, placing a premium on rapid assessment and disposition. It is increasingly expected that clients will be active participants in change processes from contracting through evaluation of services. Stringent cost containment, productivity expectations, and accountability measures increase pressures for quick action and independent decision making. Students generally carry heavier and more diverse assignments than they did as recently as the late 70's (Marshack and Rosenfeld, 1986, p.7) and confront such challenging problems as homelessness, AIDS, and child abuse. The average age of students has risen to approximately 30, skewed by the growing numbers of pre-professionals in part-time programs (Rubin, 1985, p.42). While social work administrators remain generally committed to providing field placements, released time and other perks for field instructors have been reduced, making their recruitment more difficult. It is also more difficult for schools to confirm and maintain placement plans; and the turnover of field instructors during, as well as between, academic years has risen drastically.

### FOSTERING INNOVATION: THE AGENCY, SCHOOL, AND EDUCATOR

Faced with shrinking resources and increasing numbers of social service crises in almost every practice arena, social work practice requires flexibility and breadth. Students must be able to maintain their cool, in spite of practice gaps, knowledge gaps, and the simple fact of being students. Student education requires a commitment operationalized through agency and school structures, and implemented by educators who are prepared to take risks. While educational innovation is necessary to keep pace with the changing practice contexts and dwindling resources, the effort necessary to maintain quality field education stretches everyone to their limits.

Developing a field placement for a student entails at least the willingness of agency staff to plan a suitable educational assignment tailored to student learning as well as agency need, and the provision of a qualified field instructor. In a small agency with a single social worker, formal educational structures may be at a minimum. Within larger agencies the development of a complex educational component entails formalizing several structures. An educational coordinator is likely to develop primary and often secondary placements. Group supervision and educational seminars may also be offered. Hospitals and community mental health clinics rely on this format. Further initiatives in very large agencies can lead to the development of consortium structures, and more complex and innovative educational designs. In one instance, a municipal hospital, a state psychiatric facility, and a medical school are linked in this kind of structure and bring groups of students or of field instructors together for seminars.

The school can take a proactive role in designing educational experiences in agency contexts. In working with small programs, the school can bring students or field instructors within geographical proximity together to foster cross fertilization (Fishbein, 1985). The creation of secondary assignments in nearby agencies can offer the breadth not available in the smaller setting. The school may institute a consortium of agencies exposing students to multiple settings, teachers and instructional modalities (Henry, 1975; Gladstein and Wilson, 1980). The singly placed student in a satellite office of an agency can benefit from spending two days a month in the main site attending seminars with other students.

Equally important are the school's efforts to serve as a catalyst for bringing students to under-professionalized or emerging areas of practice, and to stigmatized or underserved populations. University faculty often collaborate with agencies to develop student units and to seek out grants in cutting edge areas. One such grant enabled students to work with Alzheimer patients and their families in multiple settings, including a hospital, a geriatric facility and a community center.[1] A training grant for work/study students in child protective services[2] and student units in shelters for the homeless are further examples.[3] Each of these structures offers a model to students for how to function innovatively in an agency context. More student units for the homeless and those for persons with AIDS are sorely needed as models of field education and service delivery. A seminar for new field instructors may provide stimulus for innovation. Seminars for experienced field instructors

---

[1]grant between Jewish Institute for Geriatric Care and Hunter College School of Social Work.

[2]grant by Suffolk County Department of Social Services to Adelphi University School of Social Work.

[3]grant by NYC Human Resources Administration to Columbia University School of Social Work.

offer opportunities for encouragement of leadership in initiating new models of field education. Whether university or agency based, each educator has a responsibility to encourage innovation. In their roles within agencies, educational coordinators and field instructors can develop newer educational structures, experiment with educational methods, and risk departure from tradition in an atmosphere of partnership with each other and students. The ideologue wedded to a single perspective will close off opportunities for educational experimentation for oneself and for others.

In the school, the field work faculty are challenged to keep themselves and their placement agencies abreast of the latest developments in field education, and to view agency experimentation through the lens of innovation rather than tradition. Fostering the creative use of educational tools such as video playbacks, role plays, and a range of process and summary recordings is vital to student growth. Learning to design and experiment with varied educational structures such as group field instruction, secondary assignments, and task supervision is critical to the enhancement of field teaching.

## EDUCATIONAL PERSPECTIVES FOR FOSTERING INNOVATION

Though it remains the predominant model of field teaching, the tutorial method of field instruction may foster inordinate dependency, infantilize students, "encourage organizational docility and discourage risk taking" (Germain and Gitterman, 1980, p. 299). Hand in hand with reliance on tutorial teaching was the expectation that graduates would continue to be closely supervised during their early years of MSW practice as well.

In contrast, today's graduates are expected to be "professionally reflective, self-evaluating...knowledgeable" (Commission on Accreditation, 1984, Appendix 1, p. 8, item 7.18) and able to "make decisions with self-confidence, minimize their dependency, and stretch their vision to broader professional issues." (Matorin, 1979, p. 156). Are we adequately preparing students to meet the challenge by continuing to rely on a field instructional model which may reward dependency and conservatism? We are clearly challenged to re-examine our teaching methodology.

It is intended in social work field education that a student integrate knowledge and values into conscious use of self in practice. Despite its structural limitations, one-to-one teaching in the field provides a unique opportunity to individualize instruction so as to encourage a student to reflect on practice in a purposeful way that is both intensely personal and yet informed by a defined system of values and knowledge that governs professional self expression. The challenge for the field instructor is to help in the growth of an integrated, creative and self-confident professional self within the context of defined standards and practices.

In its early history the teaching of social work students in the field emphasized learning through the student's adoption of a supervisor's accumulated wisdom and its application to the learner's own practice (Wijnberg and Schwartz, 1977, pp. 107-113; Bogo and Vayda, 1987, pp. 20-24). As psychoanalysis gained influence, there was movement from an apprentice to a growth model in which attention was focused on development of the student's personality as a means to enhance effectiveness in service provision. As a role systems perspective has increasingly influenced social work practice and education, attention has shifted to the mutual responsibilities of field instructor and student for active participation in the teaching-learning situation.

Andragogical principles of education have particular significance for shifting the teaching perspective from an apprentice to a role systems model. Knowles (1972) identified such characteristics of adult learners as self directedness, the reservoir of experience an adult student brings to education, motivation to enhance skills and a focus on problem solving. Bertha Reynolds' (1942) defined several stages in the learning process which helped to normalize such characteristics of early student performance as acute self consciousness and the ability to identify what is needed before being able to do it. She also discussed the importance of mutual decision making in the educational process. Clancy (1985) further asserts the andragogical tenet of student - field instructor mutuality in planning and implementing the learning experience. Shared recognition of the field instructor's expertise rather than psychological coercion will then form a basis for a student's relationships to a field instructor (Wijnberg & Schwartz, 1977, p. 109). These andragogical approaches built upon mutuality and collegiality, motivate the student's initiative and creative energy.

Experiential models of education underpin the learning in field instruction. The learning sequence in experiential education begins with the use of specific situations that are affectively important to the learner. These situations are then focused on to establish the more cognitive general principles. Through the under-taking of the actual assignment the student learns the nuances of practice theory and the connection of theory to the more cognitive general practice principles. Through the field instruction conference, experiential methods such as role play can be used to shed light on prior interactions with clients and to role rehearse for future ones (Glassman and Kates, 1984). Rothman (1973) notes the need for conceptualization and structure in the execution of experiential methods, with a vigilance for linking the experience with concept.

Along these lines, Brown (1980) distinguishes three types of experiential learning which have applicability in field education. The first, "how to" learning, which offers a chance to take part in a series of constructed experiences to learn a concept or skill, may include information and referral, or discharge planning. The second, "role socialization", is more complex, requiring the development of an appreciation for what knowledge, values, and behaviors are necessary for successful practice. Role socialization requires an individualized curriculum for the learner that emanates from a differential educational assessment. The third, "learner-managed experiential learning," entails self-directed agendas that emanate from enhancement of the more complex areas of role socialization.

Kolb, in a vein similar to Brown's, has highlighted four processes in experiential education by levels of integrative complexity. The first level revolves around the experiencing of affect as it becomes understood through a conceptual lens. For example, the student first visiting an in-patient psychiatric facility feels overwhelmed in the environment, and upon reflection with the field instructor develops a way to apply concepts about development and practice to that reality. In the fourth and most complex stage, "active experimentation which results in higher order actions" is emphasized. Here action plans can be re-organized based on prior integrations of affect, action, knowledge and values. By this time the student has gained the ability to guage the kind of support and intervention to offer patients, to utilize personal reactions to clients, work in a team, and affirm the use of a psychosocial assessment in a case review.

## THE NEED FOR NEW MODELS OF FIELD INSTRUCTION

While the incorporation of andragogical principles into field teaching may greatly enhance its effectiveness, it does not change the essential structure of one-to-one field instruction. Models that represent innovations not only in teaching formats but in structures as well have begun to emerge in both schools and placement agencies. These include group field instruction, and task and secondary supervision.

## GROUP FIELD INSTRUCTION

The literature has tended to speak synonymously of group supervision and group field instruction. Group supervision, in contrast to educational seminars, case conferences, and staff meetings, most engages the intense affect of the participants (Shulman, 1984). Its usefulness depends on willingness to expose one's practice through process recording and other modes. Group field instruction is closest to group supervision in interactional processes, affective intensity, and the supervisor's role. However, unlike the supervisor of professionals, the field instructor is required to help students in their struggle to integrate perspective on the professional role and practice technology.

Bertha Reynolds (1942) in developing a framework for educating social workers, utilized group methods that relied upon principles of stage theory in group and educational development. In group learning the educator's principal role centers on creating an atmosphere for work, enabling openness, and engaging conflict towards learning. The educator is required to assess educational needs, stage issues and authority relations. In a major examination of staff development, Blackey (1956) highlights the supervisor's lack of group skill and conceptual framework as the primary obstacle to utilization of group methods for staff development. Application of a group therapy model rather than a group education one undermines the development of group goals, collective problem solving, and learning (Blackey, 1956). Its use reflects the "therapeutic approach" in individual social work supervision discussed earlier (George, 1982). Therefore, Blackey's (1956, p. 35) finding that case materials are used by supervisors to pick apart interventions rather than to establish generalized principles, is not surprising.

Getzel, Goldberg and Salmon (1971) used an approach to staff development similar to Blackey's. They move the educational process of the entire agency away from a supervisory model grounded on a casework framework to an interactional or role systems one, noting that participation in group supervision hastens the develop-ment of practice skill and the flexibility necessary for effective work. Kadushin (1976) affirms the requirement of institutional support by the agency for the supervisory group.

Group field instruction can be used as a primary method of field instruction. Social work groups are known for their effectiveness as learning systems through their processes of mutual aid, consensual validation, and feedback. It has been suggested that individual supervision tends to infantilize the worker (Judd, Kohn, and Schulman, 1962). The group offers opportunity to dissipate the master authority role of the field instructor. In the group the "supervisor seems less the personalized judge, jury and evaluator as he is seen functioning in relation to the cases of others (Judd, Kohn, and Schulman, 1962, p. 102). Members are more readily able to request consultation in a group where resistances to learning are diffused (Kadushin, 1976). The chance for discovering common problems helps the member feel less alone with a difficult situation (Kadushin, 1976). For some students the group offers opportunities to expand limited perspectives (Shafer 1982, p. 222), and develop new insights due to larger numbers (Kadushin, 1976).

This structure provides a greater chance of focusing on relevant case material which is harder to hide in the group. For the group to be maximally effective as a learning structure, its potential power should not be diffused by individual field instruction. When all practice dilemmas are directed into the group then mutual aid can be used optimally for learning.

Group dynamics and group development principles are most effective for sustaining this educational method. Issues of cohesion, inclusion, authority (Glassman and Kates, 1983), power and control (Garland, Jones and Kolodny, 1973), cooperation and competition, will be latent, each or several taking salience at particular times.

In addressing the recurring authority theme that is part of the supervisory process, Shulman (1984) separates the authority of the supervisory role derived from the agency, and the use of the role to develop democratic norms that enhance education in the group, suggesting that the group supervisor need not play an authoritarian role in the group.

The field instructor is required to have knowledge in the areas of social work practice, educational methods, and group methods. Kadushin (1976) identifies the necessity for clear agendas, tasks, and objectives. Educational objectives are identified for and with the group within the context of its stage of development, curricular objectives, and its members increased learning of practice skills. Through joint efforts the field instructor and participants can develop group goals and an evolving group educational assessment that reflect group and member needs.

The field instructor reads process recordings and prepares for meetings by either focusing on excerpts from student records or inviting a single presentation of a process. Consistent with field instruction methods, the focus of learning is the student members, not their clients. Alternative practice approaches are considered, and members are helped to extract general principles. Some meetings can be centered on a common practice theme culled from process records; others can use role play and student video tapes. The field instructor develops educational strategies, and makes educational assessments that include patterns of student practice and learning styles (Fishbein and Glassman, 1986).

The field instructor's use of self will vary according to the stage of group development. In the early stage, when the group works on developing a democratic mutual aid system (Glassman and Kates, 1986) the field instructor will focus more on: a) inviting the collective participation of all including less verbal members; b) responding to group feeling--either to obstacles, avoidance, or positives; c) being sensitive to and encouraging minority opinion to create an open atmosphere that values and encourages difference in practice styles; d) inviting the group to share feelings about the field instructor as authority in the group and as evaluator. Wanting to please the field instructor should be discussed to develop perspective and a broader range of intimacy (Shulman, 1984). e) This newer level of intimacy helps the group set broader learning goals. Once normative, the mutual aid process is used to enhance the purpose related learning activities in the group.                In the later stage, (Glassman and Kates, 1986) to develop a deepening of practice skills and to handle anxiety producing educational agendas, the field instructor will center more on: a) enabling the students to take risks; b) modeling feedback and encouraging its use by members for clarification of practice dilemmas; c) helping members role rehearse and experiment with alternative practice approaches; d) enabling the creative use of conflict among members; e) offering interpretations; f) offering confrontation to either the group or members; g) helping the group use the here and now; h) identifying obstacles to practice that may include projections and self fulfilling prophesies. Self awareness issues which focus on the effects of particular student actions on clients, need air time. Finally, the field instructor will focus on, i) helping the group maintain its educational purpose (Glassman and Kates, 1986).

Skills such as giving support, offering data and facts, and reaching inside silence (Shulman, 1979) will be applied throughout. Shulman (1984, p. 213) has acknowledged the "powerful feelings of inadequacy" the potential group supervisor faces. He suggests that the group supervisor enhances mastery when important social group work principles including surfacing the taboo practice areas that generate worker anxiety, are applied. Group field instruction continues to be underutilized even as a secondary method of education in the field. Given the number of student field placements provided by the collective representation of both our schools--some 800 placements annually--only two settings in 1986 used group field instruction as the primary method. One was a university based agency (Kaplan, 1987); the other was an agency program created in partnership with the school. Two additional settings were added the following year. It is quite certain that a planned effort by the school is necessary to institute the use of group field instruction in the agency.

## TASK AND SECONDARY SUPERVISION

Social agencies gave rise to social work education, and they continue to innovate teaching models. It is largely within agencies that the first major shift in the structure of MSW field teaching, the use of a task or secondary supervisor in addition to a field instructor, has recently occurred. Only now is task supervision being recognized and addressed by schools.

Task supervision may be defined as the teaching in some ongoing area(s) of an MSW student's field practicum by a person additional to the designated field instructor. This task supervisor may be a qualified field instructor who is serving as a secondary teacher, a social worker who does not meet requirements for field instruction or a non-social worker. Excluded from this definition are consultants and leaders of seminar and student groups. The task supervisor may be based in a different unit or agency than the field instructor.

In a survey of field instructors affiliated with one metropolitan area school in 1983, task supervision was reported as being used by 90 individuals, approximately one-third of the total group (Marshack, 1986, p. 46). Task supervision was presented predominately as a means for enhancing the diversity and richness of the educational experience. Sometimes a qualified field instructor was not expert in the primary practice area of a student but a task supervisor was. In other instances, agency needs for service or a field instructor's need to share teaching responsibilities were significant in the decision.

A range of models for use of task supervision was indicated. One design involves a consortium of agencies collaborating to provide a primary assignment for a student in one setting and a secondary in another. Sometimes these consortia involve one field of practice, such as health care, with the intention of broadening student exposure to the range of social work roles in that field (Rehr and Caroff, 1986). Other consortia bring together diverse kinds of social agencies, thus focusing attention on the impact of systems on the delivery of social work services. One, for example, involves a large voluntary hospital and a community center which are geographically adjacent and serve overlapping populations. An unanticipated benefit of this design was respite for students from the emotional demands of hospital services as they deal with more normative client needs in the community center (Gladstein and Wilson, 1980, p.69).

One large consortium of seven agencies, including medical and psychiatric hospitals under both voluntary and public auspices, a geriatric center, a community center, and a child guidance program, has existed since 1971 and provides instruction for up to 100 students from six schools of social work each year (Gladstein and Wilson, 1980; Henry, 1975). Each student has a primary placement in one setting and a secondary in a different one.

Coordination of student planning is a major need in all consortia involving multiple institutions, and in each of the three cited above an individual employed by one of the cooperating agencies carries primary responsibility for planning and administration of the student program.

A more typical model is task supervision within a single agency which exposes a student to different units or service modalities. The task supervisor might have expertise in an area of specific interest or need for student learning such as the intake process, family treatment, group services, community outreach, or administration. As there is an increase in programs which allow work-study students to meet practicum requirements in their employing agencies and as social work continues to move into new arenas, such as industry and political organizations, there may not be staff qualified to serve as field instructors. The primary teaching role is often then carried by school-based faculty or social workers in other agencies, while task supervision is provided by a non-social worker in the placement setting.

In some placement agencies task supervision is a well established practice. More common among the study group were task supervisory plans initiated and administered by field instructors who tended to consult agency rather than school personnel if problems arose. The roles of field instructor and task supervisor were found to overlap heavily in both teaching methodology and content, but field instructors tended to retain overall control of both the student assignment and evaluation processes. The findings suggest that field instructors predominantly inducted task supervisors to perform a broad range of teaching functions similar to their own rather than delimiting their focus within a narrower or more instrumental definition. The roles of the two teachers were, therefore, differentiated primarily by the practice method or area in which teaching occurred and by the field instructor's retention of control for the overall process. This overlap in roles of field instructor and task supervisor placed particular emphasis on the quality of the collaborative relationship between the two.

Most of the participating field instructors had entered into task supervisory plans with enthusiasm, and would choose to do it again. Most, too, evaluated the teaching by a task supervisor as having enhanced student learning, and more than half considered it as greatly enhancing.

Other study findings warrant consideration in implementing use of task supervision. Field instructors with longer prior experience in field teaching were more likely to choose to work with task supervisors again after an initial experience. This preference may be related to the finding that field instructors bore the major responsibility for administering task supervisory plans and inducting task supervisors into their roles. It would be important therefore, to explore whether a worker might prefer to develop knowledge of and comfort with the role of field instructor before attempting to share teaching with a task supervisor.

A further caveat is suggested by the finding that the few field instructors who had been initially unenthusiastic about a task supervisory plan tended to maintain or increase their reluctance during the experience. If a field instructor is reluctant to work with a task supervisor, the basis of the reluctance needs careful exploration before proceeding with such a plan. Among the study group, positive appraisals by field instructors of their collaborative relationships with task supervisors were closely associated with their readiness to work with them again. This suggests that mutual respect and ease in communicating with one another are basic to the comfort of both partners in a shared teaching plan. Conflict or difference may occur, as it often does in triangular relationships, and this possibility makes clarity about respective responsibilities and a plan for ongoing communication essential. Initial discussion about the specific area of a student's practice to be supervised by a task supervisor, the teaching focus and methodology, and plan for the task supervisor's participation in evaluation can be helpful. Unless field instructor and task supervisor can maintain open communication, the student may be caught between conflicting messages from both teachers. Therefore, a field instructor who is anticipating use of task supervision should expect to spend some time conferring about issues in teaching with the secondary supervisor and be prepared to deal directly with any problems which might arise.

If the task supervisor is not a social worker, issues of professional identity and differences between social work and other disciplines in approaching practice are likely to come sharply to the fore and can provide rich content for teaching by a field instructor who remains alert to these potential issues.

In summary, the use of task supervisors not only presents a creative chance to expand the field learning opportunities of social work students, but also dilutes dependency on single field instructors and provides additional role models for students. Secondary instructors "will have insights into the student's practice and will be able to raise questions and make suggestions different from those of the primary instructor." (Hamilton and Else, 1983, p. 40)

In examining the logistics of such plans, it seems appropriate that the primary responsibility for their establishment and maintenance remains with the staffs of practicum agencies, both because the present arrangement seems highly effective and because schools have limited resources for liaison functions with agencies (Rosenblum and Raphael, 1983, p. 72; Gordon, 1982, p. 116). Schools can support the use of task supervision by developing guidelines and providing consultation to practicum agencies. Content about task supervision can be included in seminars for new field instructors, and the support of agency administrators and educational coordinators sought through their participation in advisory committees to the school.

## CONCLUSION

As we examine these innovations, it becomes clear that field teaching methodology needs to be flexibly responsive to changes in the delivery of social services and the realities of both agency and school practice. Collaboration between school and field educators is essential to meet their common goal of preparing social work students to function effectively in an uncertain future.

## BIBLIOGRAPHY

Blackey, E. (1956). GROUP LEADERSHIP IN STAFF TRAINING. Wash., D.C.: HEW.

Bogo, M. & Vayda, E. (1987). THE PRACTICE OF FIELD INSTRUCTION IN SOCIAL WORK: THEORY AND PROCESS WITH AN ANNOTATED BIBLIOGRAPHY. Toronto: Univ. of Toronto.

Brown, G. (1980). Three Types of Experiential Learning: A Non Trivial Distinction. NEW DIRECTIONS FOR EXPERIENTIAL LEARNING, 8, 47-58.

Carlton, T. O. (1985). The Relationship of Practice to Education: Past Constraints and Present Opportunities Shaping Professional Preparation for Health Social Work. In B.Berkman and T. O. Carlton (Eds.), THE DEVELOPMENT OF HEALTH SOCIAL WORK CURRICULA: PATTERNS AND PROCESS IN THREE PROGRAMS OF SOCIAL WORK EDUCATION. Boston: Mass. General Hosp. Institute of Health Professions.

Clancy, C. A. (1985). The Use of the Andragogical Approach in the Educational Function of Supervision in Social Work. THE CLINICAL SUPERVISOR, 3, 75-86.
Commission on Accreditation. (1984). HANDBOOK OF ACCREDITATION STANDARDS AND PROCEDURES. New York: Council on Social Work Education.

Fishbein, H. (1985). THE FIELD INSTRUCTION CENTER. Doctoral dissertation, New York: Yeshiva University.

Fishbein, H. & Glassman, U. (1987) Teaching Field Instructors to Use Group Field Instruction. St. Louis: APM, of the CSWE (unpublished).

Garland, J.; Jones, H.; & Kolodny, R. (1973) A Model for Stages of Development in Social Work Groups. In S. Bernstein (Ed.), EXPLORATIONS IN GROUP WORK. Boston: Milford House.

George, A. (1982). A History of Social Work Field Instruction: Apprenticeship to Instruction. In B. Sheafor, & L. Jenkins (Eds.), QUALITY FIELD INSTRUCTION IN SOCIAL WORK; PROGRAM DEVELOPMENT AND MAINTENANCE (pp. 37-59). N.Y.: Longman.

Germain, C. & Gitterman, A. (1980). THE LIFE MODEL OF SOCIAL WORK PRACTICE. N.Y.: Columbia University.

Getzel, G.; Goldberg, J.; and Salmon, R. (1971). Supervising in Groups as a Model for Today. SOCIAL CASEWORK, 52, 154-163.

Gladstein, M. & Wilson, M. (1980). Three Field Teaching Centers in the Social Health Module. In P. Caroff & M. Mailick (Eds.), SOCIAL WORK IN HEALTH SERVICES; AN ACADEMIC PRACTICE PARTNERSHIP (pp. 65-86). New York: Prodist.

Glassman, U. & Kates, L. (1983). Authority Themes and Worker Group Relations. SOCIAL WORK WITH GROUPS, 6, 33-52.

Glassman, U. & Kates, L. (1984). The Use of Simulation Role Play to Teach Social Work Practice in Groups. Detroit: APM of CSWE (unpublished).

Glassman, U. & Kates, L. (1986) Techniques of Social Group Work. SOCIAL WORK WITH GROUPS. 9, 9-39

Gordon, M. S. (1982). Responsibilities of the School: Maintenance of the Field Program. In B. Sheafor & L. Jenkins (Eds.), QUALITY FIELD INSTRUCTION IN SOCIAL WORK: PROGRAM DEVELOPMENT AND MAINTENANCE (pp. 116-135). New York: Longman.

Hamilton, N. & Else, J. F. (1983). DESIGNING FIELD EDUCATION: PHILOSOPHY, STRUCTURE AND PROCESS. Springfield, Ill.: Thomas.

Henry, C. S. (1975). An Examination of Field Work Models at the Adelphi University School of Social Work. JOURNAL OF EDUCATION FOR SOCIAL WORK, 11, 62-68.

Judd, J.; Kohn, R. E.; & Schulman, G. (1962). Group Supervision: A Vehicle for Professional Development. SOCIAL WORK, 7, 96-103.

Kadushin, A. (1976). SUPERVISION IN SOCIAL WORK. New York: Columbia Univ. Press.

Kaplan, T. (1988). Developing a Model for Group Field Instruction. Atlanta: APM of the CSWE (See this volume)

Knowles, M. (1972). Innovations in Teaching Styles and Approaches Based Upon Adult Learning. JOURNAL OF EDUCATION FOR SOCIAL WORK, 8, 32-39.

Kolb, D. A. (1984). EXPERIENTIAL LEARNING: EXPERIENCE AS THE SOURCE OF LEARNING AND DEVELOPMENT. Englewood Cliffs: Prentice Hall.

Marshack, E. F. (1986). Task Supervision: A Quiet Revolution in Field Teaching of MSW Students. ARETE, 11, 45-50.

Marshack, E. F. & Rosenfeld, D. (1986). Agency Perspectives on Current Practice: Implications for Education. Miami: APM of the CSWE (unpublished).

Matorin, S. (1979). Dimensions of Student Supervision: A Point of View. SOCIAL CASEWORK, 60, 150-156.

Price, H. (1976). Achieving a Balance Between Self-Directed and Required Learning. JOURNAL OF EDUCATION FOR SOCIAL WORK, 12, 105-112.

Rehr, H. & Caroff, P. (1986). A NEW MODEL IN ACADEMIC PRACTICE PARTNERSHIP: MULTI-INSTRUCTOR AND INSTITUTIONAL COLLABORATION IN SOCIAL WORK. Lexington, MS: Ginn.

Reynolds, B. (1942). LEARNING AND TEACHING IN THE PRACTICE OF SOCIAL WORK: Farrar & Rinehart.

Rosenblum, A. F.; & Raphael, F. B. (1983). The Role and Function of the Faculty Field Liaison. JOURNAL OF EDUCATION FOR SOCIAL WORK, 19, 67-73.

Rothman, B. (1973). Perspectives on Learning and Teaching, JOURNAL OF EDUCATION FOR SOCIAL WORK, 9, 39-52.

Rubin, A. (1985). STATISTICS ON SOCIAL WORK EDUCATION IN THE UNITED STATES. Wash., D.C.: Council on Social Work Education.

Shafer, C. M. (1982). The Methods of Field Instruction. In B. W. Sheafor & L. Jenkins, (Eds.). QUALITY FIELD INSTRUCTION IN SOCIAL WORK: PROGRAM DEVELOPMENT AND MAINTENANCE (pp. 215-225). New York: Longman.

Shulman, L. (1984). SKILLS OF SUPERVISION AND STAFF MANAGEMENT. Itasca, Ill.: Peacock.

Wijnberg, M. H. & Schwartz, M. C. (1977). Models of Student Supervision: The Apprentice, Growth, and Role Systems Models. JOURNAL OF EDUCATION FOR SOCIAL WORK, 13, 107-113.

# A DUAL MATRIX STRUCTURE FOR FIELD EDUCATION

Wendy Norberg, *Mendota Mental Health Institute, Madison, Wisconsin*
Dean Schneck, *University of Wisconsin-Madison*

## INTRODUCTION--THE EDUCATIONAL AND POLITICAL PROBLEM

The design and implementation of field models which enable valuable learning experiences for students require not only good intentions but our best planning and negotiating efforts. Field learning opportunities, both clinical and organizational, require the dedication and commitment of agency supervisors, administrators, and school faculty but also depend upon a well designed and functioning structure which accurately accounts for the exchange and balance of knowledge, skills, and professional prerogatives. Such a process forges alliances which can move beyond institutional allegiances to realize the underlying value and potential of collaboration.

It was noted recently: "Seeking not only balance, but harmony and congruence from disparate and potentially competing needs among students, the school and the community, represents a nexus of influence clearly evocative of our finest problem-solving and negotiation skills" (Schneck, "Arbiter", 1990, see p. 234)

In the fall of 1980, two field educators and administrators in Madison, Wisconsin, one in a major mental health institute and the other in a school of social work, were faced with a compelling educational problem and political dilemma. Though not of their making, they resolved to problem-solve and utilize leadership within their respective systems to develop an educationally sound and politically viable field education structure. The principals, a new social service director and a new field director, inherited a placement structure containing many of the classic conflicts which characterize school-agency strife: program and staff transition, resource constraints, role confusion among staff and students, attendant anxiety, and thus, the inevitable estrangement of professional staff from the school. Clearly, excellent learning opportunities in mental health were being jeopardized. The lack of a current and relevant placement structure did not allow the inherent quality of these placements to be realized. Thus the dual matrix structure of field education linking Mendota Mental Health Institute and the School of Social Work, UW-Madison, was initiated.

The purpose of this paper is to illustrate an example of structure and model design in field education. We will discuss the collaborative planning process which was so important in the design of a successful placement model and structure. We will define the objectives and delineate those principles and concepts which we believe can be extrapolated to other settings and similar problems elsewhere. It is our express intention to forthrightly share what we've learned in the hope that it may be of value to others.

## FIELD MODELS AND DUAL MATRIX STRUCTURE DEFINED

It has been noted earlier, "We call many things models in our day-to-day discourse on field education. However, when we examine field education more closely, identifying the various functions, values and educational features, it reveals itself as a complex combination of an educational process, a structural organization, a perspective or conceptualization of practice, and an identified body of knowledge" (Schneck, 1980).

The recognition of these multiple components, not only conceptually but with specific reference and application to our home environments, and the conscious assemblage of an integrated model constitute the elusive ideal in field model development. Whether it resembles a tapestry or frayed loose ends depends upon how well we do our job.

By *dual matrix*, the authors refer to students' membership and participation dually in a school of social work faculty-based field unit and an institute/ community-based student unit group. In this design, students receive supervision, consultation, and mental health practice content both from faculty and professional social workers in mental health. They meet regularly with each seminar group, thereby accruing problem-specific knowledge and practice skills from both constituencies. Faculty teach social problem content in the context of the integrative seminar on campus, and the director of social services and clinical staff of the Institute provide practice and skill content and supervision for the student group at the institute.

This structure has encouraged social problem field units from the school to link with relevant clinical practice units at the Institute to develop excellent field placements in the areas of child, adolescent and adult in-patient mental illness, forensics, sex offender treatment, geropsychiatric care, patient rights, and community-based programs for the chronically mentally ill. The students' learning experience is thus dually imbedded in the university and the community. Both sources provide the knowledge and skills needed to function in a modern, specialized, state mental health facility and later in professional practice.

## HISTORY AND EVOLUTION OF THE STRUCTURE

### A. Evolution of Mendota Mental Health Institute as a Specialized Short Term Treatment Facility

To provide a better perspective of why the dual matrix structure of field education was chosen, it is helpful to share some recent history regarding MMHI as a psychiatric treatment facility. MMHI formally known as Mendota State Hospital had upwards of a thousand patients until the early 1970's. With the introduction of various landmark statutes regarding admission criteria and treatment, changes in existing laws and treatment methods for the mentally ill ("deinstitutionalization"), the census and bed capacity decreased markedly in the 70's and 80's. Today, it is a 273-bed state operated mental health facility providing specialized treatment, training, research and consultation. It is an integral part of the state mental health delivery system and receives referrals from county human services boards and courts throughout the state.

The specialized treatment services are for adult male forensic patients, children, adolescents, adults and elderly. There are eighteen treatment units divided into three program areas: forensics, adult, and child/adolescent. The length of stay varies among units, but the goal is to complete treatment in as short a time as is clinically possible. Overall, there are approximately fifty-one admissions and fifty-five discharges each month.

For each patient there is an assessment, a plan for treatment and discharge planning conducted by a multidisciplinary treatment team. Social workers are responsible for: completing an assessment and identifying the social, psychological, and environmental factors affecting the functioning of each of the patients and their families; formulating a treatment plan based on the assessments of all disciplines; implementing various aspects of the treatment plan which are based on social work expertise, and establishing a discharge plan. The Institute affords an opportunity for exposure to a variety of client types and treatment modalities in a specialized setting with access to social work staff for supervision and professional role models. Recognizing the evolution in the treatment of the mentally ill, we needed to examine the field education model to evaluate its effectiveness and change as necessary in order to better serve students and patients.

## B.  History of the Mendota Mental Health Institute Field Unit

Social work field placements began at Mendota in the 50's. In the early years, several graduate students per year were assigned to Mendota who were primarily supervised by the Director of Social Services. From 1966 until 1976, a staff social worker at Mendota was appointed a faculty member at the UW School of Social Work to teach an agency based and funded field unit which provided on-site supervision to as many as fifteen graduate students. Considerable time was spent with students in tutorial and tandem supervision as well as in weekly group supervision meetings. Students were assigned to various treatment units for practice with patients. Generally, these units were large, diagnostically undifferentiated treatment units for children, adolescents, and adults. Patients were usually grouped by age or gender, with the exception of an alcoholic treatment unit and one specialized unit for severely psychotic and agitated patients.

A clinical unit social worker was identified to supervise the student, though the hallmark learning experiences were often seen in the interaction with the field instructor. This is explained by the unique characteristics and talent of the supervisor, who was (and is) an outspoken and highly accomplished clinical social worker, author, and originator of a creative and controversial model of psychotherapy. His status and reputation within the institution drew the learning dialectic substantially away from the clinical units and to the interaction of the students with himself. Students were required to assert clinical ideas and interview a difficult patient in front of the group each semester. Recall that the dialogue on the purpose of field work in many schools and agencies in the 50's and 60's centered upon the personal growth versus professional development debate.

When this instructor left the Institute in 1976 for full-time private practice and consultation, an inevitable vacuum was created and the field model changed by default to a liaison model. The change took a great deal of adjustment on everyone's part both at the Institute and School. The group supervision conducted by the former instructor was perceived by all parties as fulfilling a very important function. It was the only opportunity for students within the Institute to gather and share experiences and problems of being a student at a large facility.

The new faculty member who assumed responsibility for students placed at Mendota was extremely busy with other duties which included monitoring students placed at other sites and serving as field director. Though an internationally recognized social work educator and expert in mental health, she was unable to devote the extra group supervision time beyond meetings held regularly with students to provide basic theory and methods. It was a difficult transitional problem to solve. Several clinical staff volunteered to continue the group, feeling strongly that it was something that could only be helpful to students if staff facilitated the process. The previous instructor had been a Mendota staff social worker for over 20 years; thus, "ownership" of the unit was at issue. In retrospect it was a very painful time. The focus of the group was never clearly defined. Everyone was so eager to make the process work that little attention was paid to the concrete detail of defining what was to be accomplished. Some of the staff felt they were conducting group therapy with the students; at other times, parenting; and at other times, actually problem solving and teaching.

The liaison model may have been more functional if other resource and transition problems at the School and Institute had not been as difficult for all concerned. Budgetary constraints and personnel changes at the School necessitated three different faculty liaisons during a 4-year period. Also, staff at the Institute began losing interest in student training due to the lack of structure and leadership. Placements were becoming increasingly difficult to arrange; and consistency and stability were major problems. Finally, the lack of a syllabus which defined the content of the learning experience and the student expectations together with considerable ambivalence toward the "outside" faculty role exacerbated the situation.

In 1980, a mutual decision was made to take the time to seriously examine what we were providing students. There was fundamental agreement that problem solving was in order. Thus, a careful analysis of the potential for matching specializations was conducted. The School had field units in place according to various problem areas and fields of practice. For example, field units existed in aging and mental health, child and family welfare, social work with the criminal justice system, interpersonal skills training: socio-behavioral focus, community mental health, and social work with the chronically mentally ill. As indicated, Mendota had specialized treatment units that seemed to correspond substantively with the units of the School.

C.    **History of the Wisconsin Field Unit Educational Model**

Some note of the history of faculty-based field units at Wisconsin is necessary to appreciate the potential pairing connections between the School and the Institute. At the 1980 Annual Program Meeting of CSWE, the model was defined:

> In looking historically at our field education program at the UW-Madison, several major themes and commitments emerge . . . The first is that we have viewed field work as education for professional practice requiring critical analysis, conceptual and problem solving ability as well as training in the traditional skill areas. Secondly, our School has made a major educational and resource commitment to faculty-based field units organized thematically around problem-practice areas, major interventions or methodologies, institutional areas of practice, or around a particular perspective of practice. . . The field unit design provides for students a conceptual basis for practice, and a supportive learning environment for shared learning and consultation (Schneck, 1980).

The unit approach to field teaching with an accompanying small group seminar was originally viewed by our School as a teaching method chosen mainly to augment the progressive and controversial educational objectives of the day, namely that of the "autonomous social worker" and the problem-centered, multi-method, approach to practice (Franks, 1967). This new practice philosophy and perspective is best expressed in the words of Virginia Franks, pioneer field director for the School during the rapid expansion of the 60's, who, acting in concert with Martin B. Loeb, the visionary director at that time stated:

> The philosophic approach of the school supports the idea of "the autonomous social worker", one whose knowledge, skill, and understanding allows for work wherever a social worker is needed whether or not an appropriate agency exists. . . . An essential characteristic of "the autonomous social worker" is the ability to assume leadership in practice development and policy formulation. . . .we are operating on the hypothesis that the field course is not independent, and that the link between the on and off-campus courses must be strengthened for maximum educational results.
>      The concept of providing multi-method learning experiences in the field course has particular significance when viewed in the light of some of our newer problem-centered approaches to field teaching (Franks, pp. 2 and 5).

A reflective view over the past 25 years confirms the wisdom and foresight of Franks and Loeb for their conscious and articulate integration of practice philosophy and teaching methods.

The field unit structure at Madison has certainly undergone evolutionary changes in the ensuing years. The normalization of the field unit delivery structure with its concomitant agency and community linkages, the development of the practitioner-educator career track within the School, the developent of the integrative field seminar as a source of substantive content and practice methods, and the allocation of a "hard money" commitment of .50 teaching FTE for a fifteen-student field unit, have all emerged as important derivative features of the structural model.

The particular irony in retrospect is that the important advances of the autonomous social worker and problem-centered, multi-method practice controversial in the early 60's are now well-accepted and commonplace among schools around the country; whereas the implementing structure of a field unit of students staffed by a faculty member of the School, viewed originally as an instructional method to augment the philosophic choices is now the uncommon feature. This can be explained by its cost in faculty FTE and its attendant educational expectations which draw faculty into the perennial struggle with competing demands from their scholarly work.

### D.  Development of the Dual Matrix Structure

Back to 1980, the negotiations between Mendota and the School proceeded very positively and clearly focussed on building the best educational model that could be developed for students. The shared assumptions of both parties were:

1)  MMHI is a major provider of mental health services in Wisconsin with a high quality social work department firmly committed to the training of social work students;

2)  MMHI placements can afford diverse opportunities for experience in the assessment and treatment of various types of mental illness, development of leadership skills, coordination of community resources, discharge planning and participation in a multi-disciplinary approach;

3)  the School of Social Work has strong expertise and faculty resources in the field of mental health;

4)  the School has a commitment to providing quality field education for students in mental health through its field unit structure.

The foundation of the dual matrix structure is the matching and pairing of clinical treatment units at the Institute with faculty educational field units at the School. This was easily done, at least in concept:

| Clinical Unit–MMHI | | Field Units–SSW |
|---|---|---|
| Training Adolescents for Community Living | | Group Work in Mental Health-- |
| Home and Community Treatment (Social learning theory/behavioral interventions with adolescents and families) | <---------------------> | Social Learning Perspective |
| Geropsychiatric Center | <-------------------------------------> | Aging and Mental Health |
| Adult Psychiatric Service | | Mental Health in Institutional |
| Adolescent Treatment Unit | <----------------------------> | and Community Settings |
| Program for Assertive Community Treatment | | |
| Children's Treatment Unit | <--------------------------------> | Child and Family Welfare |
| Forensics Rehabilitation Service | | Social Work in Corrections |
| Forensics Assessment Unit | <--------------------------------> | and Criminal Justice |
| Community Preparation Service | | |
| Patient's Rights Unit | <-----------------------------> | Social Policy Unit |
| Administration | | |

The obvious missing element was a group learning experience at Mendota for all students placed from the School. It needed to provide immediately relevant practice content, and an opportunity for case discussion and group supervision. Hence the Mendota student unit seminar was revived and reformed. Under the leadership of the social service director at the Institute, a bi-weekly student seminar focused upon orientation, policies and procedures, diagnostic categories and treatment methodologies, psychotropic drugs, ethical and patient rights considerations, and case presentation and consultation. This seminar has evolved to provide the dual anchor, that is, the on-site group learning seminar for field practice content. Greater detail and the role of students in the planning and delivery of the seminar is presented in the next section.

These components, then, formed the basic elements of our plan. We were aided by the consultation from the coordinator of student programs of the Institute, Annette Haney, a psychiatric nurse, who had responsibility for student training programs in all the discipline areas.[1] Once the basic elements of the plan were formulated, the plan was shared with the respective constituencies for discussion, i.e., the School of Social Work field faculty and the MMHI Department of Social Work. This was a necessary step since a common administrative error is the making of a decision that affects others with the expectation that everything will work smoothly even though the affected parties had no opportunity for input.

---

[1]Appreciation and thanks are hereby expressed to Annette Haney, Coordinator of Student Programs, Mendota Mental Health Institute for her time, support, and ideas.

The plan was well-received in both camps though it is fair to say we were "not taking no for an answer." In a sense, we made them "an offer they couldn't refuse," because a strong linkage between the two systems afforded faculty excellent clinical placements (much in demand by students) and gave clinical supervisors at the Institute generally high quality graduate students to supervise (a distinct professional perquisite in our community).

The final step prior to implementation was to gather all relevant parties together for an open forum and an opportunity to meet each other and learn in more detail the respective responsibilities and roles within the newly created structure. In the Fall of 1981, the dual matrix model began. All of the preliminary meetings and planning to develop the infrastructure paid off; the model is now in its tenth year, modified only to accommodate new field unit--clinical unit linkages as necessitated by changes in either system. The next section of the paper addresses in more detail the various aspects of the model.

## DESCRIPTION AND IMPLEMENTATION OF THE STRUCTURE

### A. Structure and Role Features

During the 1980-81 planning phase, the importance of role definitions became readily apparent as the discussion focused on responsibilities within the dual matrix model. The cast of characters included the Director of Social services (DSS), Director of Field Education (DFE), field faculty, clinical unit supervisors, students, field units, MMHI student unit, and the multidisciplinary team as well as other layers of clinical, supervisory and administrative types peering at the process eagerly awaiting the outcome of the negotiations.

Communication and collaboration have been stressed throughout this paper and it certainly was viewed as critical to the success of the newly developed model. Thus, to assure the best possible interactions and relationships of all concerned parties, the important task of defining roles commenced. The following presents role definitions for all primary participants in the dual matrix model of field education:

### Clinical Unit Supervisor and Staff at Mendota Mental Health Institute

The placement of the student occurs within the multidisciplinary treatment team with the exception of an administrative placement which relates to an executive level. This structure provides an opportunity for ongoing practice supervision in a setting rich with expertise not only in social work, but other disciplines as well. The role of the unit supervisor is to: participate in selection and placement of students, orient the student to the unit, assist the student in the development of the learning plan, provide practice supervision, work closely with the field faculty, consult on student growth and development, participate in the evaluation, and provide a good professional role model. The unit supervisor is held accountable per MMHI policy for all aspects of student performance while at the agency which serves as an added incentive to take his/her role quite seriously.

## MMHI Student Group

While a detailed description of the seminar will be provided in the next section, it is important to note that a decision was made to gather the students placed at MMHI together periodically for supplementary group learning opportunities including: institute orientation, discussion of policy and program matters, special learning opportunities, and to provide an opportunity for sharing and consultation among students.

## Field Faculty

The field faculty member is responsible for: student selection and placement, development and approval of learning plans, teaching the integrative unit seminar, providing practice consultation, working closely with unit supervisors, consulting on student growth and development, evaluation and grading, and providing a good professional role model.

## Field Unit

In contrast to the MMHI student unit group, the field unit at the School is comprised of students placed at a continuum of different agencies within a field of practice. This affords a learning environment rich in peer consultation, support, and motivation for student performance and learning. Substantively, it provides an integrative seminar for content presentations by faculty, staff, students and guests.

## Individual Student

The most important person in this process is the student who has dual membership in the field unit at the School and the clinical unit at the Institute. Expectations of the student include clarity in expression of learning needs and interests which lead to the development of the learning contract; meeting pre-and co-requisites especially the pre-placement interviews; cooperating and communicating assertively with staff and faculty; and striving for their best performance in all assignments.

## Department Director at MMHI

The Director of Social Services conducts long range planning with faculty, staff at the Institute, and the Director of Field Education at the School. Her educational responsibilities include the annual contract negotiations, planning with faculty for the Field Fair, placements and orientation; coordinating and teaching the group seminar; consulting, problem solving, and providing administrative support.

### Director of Field Education

The Director of Field Education's role includes responsibility for the placement of all field students at the graduate school; long range planning with faculty, agency supervisors and administrators; contract negotiations, providing consultation and problem-solving to staff, students, and faculty as well as administrative support. Teaching a field unit and an occasional class is also a regular faculty responsibility in addition to administration.

The time spent delineating the roles has paid off many times over. All parties entered the arrangement with a clear understanding of what was to take place. Memos outlining progress were frequently distributed to staff during the process of development of the model. Meetings were held with staff and faculty separately and together to discuss their roles and address their concerns. In the end or actually the beginning, no one was able to claim lack of involvement or participation in the decision-making. Thus, a layer of potential resentment and subsequent sabotage was avoided.

### B. Collaboration of Clinical Unit Supervisor and Field Faculty

Shared functions in this area have already been delineated. What follows will illustrate the basic principles of the process that make it work.

### Preliminary Phase of Placement:

Prior to the arrival of the student, the dual matrix structure necessitates communication on all levels. This is a period of time for faculty and supervisors to become acquainted; to define expectations of the student, the faculty and supervisor; and to learn each others' roles. This phase of the process is important regardless of whether the supervisor/field faculty member is a novice or a veteran of student training. Circumstances change, people change and it is important to discuss these aspects to minimize surprises or conflict.

### Development of Learning Contract:

The faculty member is responsible for theory, methods, and overall integration. The supervisor is responsible for practical application. Both are responsible for developing and maintaining a quality educational package based on the learning goals of the student and the School. Thus, communication avoids duplication or working at cross purposes.

### Implementation of Placement:

It is critical to remain abreast of student performance in the agency as well as in the field unit. Experience has taught us that students can be functioning seemingly well in one area while not performing adequately in the other. To provide an integrated student placement, it is important to share that information, make changes, and provide assistance as necessary. Without ongoing communication, momentum and precious time can be lost that is not retrievable. Students may also take advantage of the situation and manipulate to meet their own sometimes unrealistic demands/needs.

## Evaluation:

For the same reasons, it is essential to include the unit supervisor in the evaluation process. The field faculty member is typically not present at the agency work site where students gain practical application and thus, without feedback, cannot evaluate student progress adequately. Self report of the student is important but decreases significantly in value when not accompanied by a validating report from the clinical supervisor. On rare occasions, the supervisor and field faculty see a student differently. With straightforward communication, these issues do not wait to surface until an evaluation and thus markedly decrease in significance and occurrence.

## C. Educational Process from the Field Fair to Evaluation

It is our belief that preliminary discussion can be as important as what takes place after a student arrives; in fact, it can make or break a placement. The process is simple but it takes time and commitment to every aspect of student training. Equally important to note is that supervision of students by MMHI social workers is **voluntary**. Students are not assigned to staff. A deeply held conviction is that quality training of social work students depends on clinical staff supervising because they want to and they understand the commitment they are making. Therefore, prior to making a decision to supervise, social workers meet with the Director of Social Services to discuss their role.

Primarily, the discussion focuses on the meaning of process supervision. Very simply, they must make a commitment to meet with the student a minimum of one hour per week to deal specifically with issues of practice on the unit (in practice, they meet more frequently due to the close working relationship of the multidisciplinary team on each unit). The structure they choose for the meetings is for each of them to determine; it may include processing audio or video tapes, reviewing paperwork, and problem solving a direction to take with a case. However, it must occur regularly, not catch as catch can, or left to the students to determine when they need consultation. Experience has taught us that leaving it up to the students produces poor quality and inconsistent supervision in many cases since students often find processing their work to be threatening and something that, while helpful, they would just as soon avoid.

Once the DSS has a sense of the number of interested social workers, discussions begin with the Director of Field Education in preparation for the Field Fair which occurs in April of each year. Simultaneously, MMHI and the School of Social Work review and renew their contract. Typically, the contract allows for a maximum of 12-14 placements each year. There have been as few as three students and as many as 12 during the years the dual matrix model has existed. The average has been eight students per year.

In preparation for the Field Fair, a description of available placements is prepared by the DSS. The DFE also prepares a handbook of all available field units, community placements, and policies which is given to all students enrolled at the School each year.

The Field Fair is, for many incoming students, the first opportunity to learn more about available field placements by talking directly with field faculty and agency staff. The DFE begins the afternoon with a brief overview of the field program and placement opportunities. This is followed by students' circulating to tables of agency representatives and field faculty according to interest. They can discuss learning opportunities, expectations, and review written material from the community agencies. The DFE and advisors at the School assist the students in sorting out these issues and narrowing their area of interest.

Students list three preferences for placement in order of priority during the Spring placement process. Prior to listing an MMHI unit, the respective field faculty and unit supervisor must agree. This necessitates contact with the field faculty member and an interview with the MMHI social worker. The interview serves to further expand a definition of the purpose of the placement, to discuss the learning goals of the student, the type of supervision the unit social worker will provide and whether MMHI can provide the learning sought by the student. If all agree, the student registers for the respective field and MMHI unit.

Following the gathering of the field unit for introductions, orientation to the School and expectations, students arrive at MMHI and orientation to the facility is initiated. This phase begins with a general orientation to MMHI. The first session involves introductions, role definitions, review of the MMHI Student Handbook (policies, unit descriptions and other available services at MMHI) and an opportunity to ask questions. The opening session is facilitated by the DSS and DFE. It is important for students to have an overview of the School and the agency before sending them to their respective clinical units. Approximately three additional sessions conducted by the DSS and other relevant Institute staff are scheduled to orient students to major policies and procedures (See Appendix). Simultaneously, students are oriented to each of their MMHI clinical units by the unit supervisor. All of the orientation provides a solid foundation on which to base the specifics of the placement which are developed in the learning contract.

Each student is responsible for writing a learning contract within the framework of the field course objectives. The contract spells out the learning goals of the student and the manner in which each will be accomplished in specific measurable terms. Prior to committing this on paper, the field faculty, unit supervisor, and student meet to discuss the content and make certain the goals are reasonable and achievable. This is followed by implementation of the placement per the prescribed roles. This is the longest phase and the most productive during which students learn and perform clinical social work with patients, families, and groups.

At the end of each semester, the student, supervisor, and field faculty meet for an evaluation based on the learning contract. Some faculty ask unit supervisors for a recommended grade, while others do not. University policy dictates that faculty must assign the grade which is as it should be; the collaboration is what is important. It is MMHI policy that all evaluations be written. The DSS maintains a file for two reasons: future references and assuring that contracting, implementation and evaluation are consistent with established procedures. Occasionally, situations arise in which the DSS and DFE need to become involved due to a personality conflict, poor performance, lack of compliance with policies either on the part of the student or the staff, or the unusual case of emotional disturbance.

At the end of the academic year, just as field faculty and unit supervisors evaluate students, students evaluate the School and the agency both verbally and in writing. The evaluations provide useful feedback for MMHI and the School. The DSS and DFE evaluate comments and make changes as necessary. For example, problems with a particular supervisor, such as lack of supervisory meetings or not allowing sufficient freedom for the student to practice independently, etc., have been handled. Comments pertaining insufficient curriculum in the area of mental health assisted the School in defining a course of action a few years ago.

In summary, this phase of the process can only serve to improve the educational product. One valuable lesson learned was that asking the questions meant all parties had to be prepared to deal with the answers, positive or negative.

### D. Mendota Student Unit Seminar

When the entire structure of field education was studied in 1980--81, there was a commitment on the part of the University as well as MMHI that some type of gathering of the students placed at MMHI served a useful purpose. MMHI was a large facility with much to offer educationally, apart from the specific unit on which the student was placed. Students came from several field units and while each of the units met regularly, there was no other mechanism for all students placed at Mendota to convene to share ideas and problems encountered in direct application of skills.

A mutual decision was made to structure the group meetings in a seminar format. This was logical due to the fact that one consistent complaint of students had been the lack of a focused arena for discussion of mental health issues. Available course work at the University could not include the specific detail the students were asking for and the unit placements at MMHI were not able to provide that detail either due to a need to focus on service provision. However, there were many resources of differing disciplines at hand for teaching at the University and MMHI. Thus, the assumptions about the merit of a seminar were that it would provide:

-structure for provision of detailed coverage of a practice or content topic,
-opportunity for direct application of skills,
-opportunity for sharing information in other practice areas at MMHI,
--opportunity for clinical problem solving,
-opportunity for students to hear and present material,
-opportunity for exposure to other disciplines.

The decision was made that topical content was to be determined jointly by the students and the DSS. Students often have a clear sense of their needs. Also, if they share in the decision regarding content they are more likely to be committed to attending and participating. As indicated in the previous section, students are involved in an extensive orientation phase of placement which takes approximately the first month to complete. Determining seminar topics at the onset of placement is an unreasonable expectation for the students. Therefore, topical content discussion takes place after they have been at the Institute at least a month, have been able to evaluate what their courses will offer including the field unit seminar, and what will take place on their clinical units. See Appendix for seminar outline.

The final orientation meeting determines topics of interest. Often students have difficulty narrowing the field of interest to a manageable focus; it is the role of the DSS to facilitate that process and also obtain enough information regarding their interest to be able to secure presenters. When students have difficulty identifying topics (not often the case), the DSS will resort to seminars previously conducted for suggestions. Most frequently, the seminars have been held every 2-3 weeks for a two-hour period which has been most manageable given other commitments students face. The DSS schedules all the seminars by contacting various presenters, drawing from Institute clinicians, faculty at the U.W. or community agency staff. We attempt to provide coherence and sequencing of the content in order to be useful and timely in their field assignments.

Deviations from the practice outlined thus far are as follows:

1. Today's graduate school sees a variety of students including those who have worked and are returning to school. Students often have a great deal of expertise in certain areas. Therefore, they may volunteer for topics. This has worked well because it gives students an opportunity to present material to others.

2. Students often find case presentation or clinical unit explanation (including a tour) useful. Social workers eventually perform some aspect of this and practicing in field work provides an opportunity to present, have others ask questions and critique the delivery and content of the presentations.

3. The final meeting of the academic year is a group evaluation of MMHI field work which has been previously described. Evaluations since 1981 have been extremely positive about the seminars. Students uniformly have stated the seminars provide content they would not have obtained elsewhere.

## PROGRAM EVALUATION

As indicated, students complete written evaluations for Mendota staff and School faculty at the end of each school year. In analyzing the evaluations, it is necessary to look for related themes which seem to have consistency and repetition during any particular time frame. These, then, can be used consciously for program improvement and clarification. On the positive side, students cited:

1) The availability of a wide range of treatment methods and skills to be learned through the various clinical services;

2) The opportunity to learn specialized knowledge about the various populations being treated and the generalizable value of this content to other settings;

3)      The opportunity to work closely with other treatment disciplines in a coordinated teamwork fashion and learn the specialized nature of the other disciplines;

4)      The opportunity for major professional development and growth in clinical social work;

5)      The opportunity to function as an equal member of a multi-disciplinary treatment team;

6)      The specialized content and application to practice gained in the Mendota Unit seminar provided at the Institute.

On the critical side, several themes emerged, although they were not present during every year. The first had to do with the "goodness of fit" between the clinical unit at the Institute and the faculty field unit. Some students felt that while the faculty field unit seminar contained good general information, it did not provide enough specific information for their practice at the Institute. This reinforces the need for the seminar at the Institute. During the first few years of operation, there were several complaints about the quality and consistency of the clinical unit supervision. In retrospect, this is not surprising since normative practices in this area had not been reinforced for some time. This is not to say that there was not interest and fair treatment of the student; but the regularity and consistency of the supervisory practices varied considerably. This was addressed largely by the assertive expectations coming from the social service director in clarifying the role and function of the clinical unit supervisor. It was set forth as a condition for having a student placed on the unit and monitored closely throughout the year. Fortunately, this has not been a problem for several years.

Another criticism of students was directed at the School; many felt that there was not enough specific clinical coursework available on campus to augment their practice at the Institute. This criticism, together with the clinical unit/field unit matching issue had some credibility and basis in reality. The development of specialized clinical practice in some settings has outpaced the ability of this school (and many other schools) to provide sufficient graduate courses. Schools are often criticized for their inability, or sometimes reluctance, to provide highly specialized clinical content in their courses. It's an old dilemma that goes well beyond the operation of our dual matrix model, but adds continuing impetus for the School to maintain and expand its direct practice courses and clinical content both in field and the classroom. This has been acknowledged in several recent hires during the past few years. Faculty were recruited who had a strong practice background and were interested in teaching coursework in direct practice and mental health. Moreover, pressure from the Institute as well as from other clinical settings in the community, persuaded us to staff certain courses more than once a year, e.g., psychopathology, alcohol/drug abuse, etc.

The final criticism which has been evidenced in student feedback, though not as forcefully as in our reflections, is the regularity and consistency of contact between faculty and clinical unit supervisors during the student's placement. This is a particularly difficult criticism to confront because, as stated earlier, the reliability and implementation of the dual matrix model rests firmly upon a foundation of collaboration and communication. Nevertheless, we feel that our efforts and those of faculty and clinical supervisors need to reinforced in this important area.

As always, there were reasons and rationalizations, some more credible and understandable than others. They would probably be aggregated under three rubrics: time, trouble (lack of), and trust. By time, of course, we mean the actual hours and minutes required to schedule a meeting, travel to the Institute and/or campus, discuss the student's placement performance and how the seminar content and field assignments are complementing each other. By trouble, we mean the absence of student performance problems which would raise the "red flag" and signal the need for an immediate conference. In short, when things are going well, the natural tendency of many is to not pay close attention. The final reason is trust, that is, the mutual accord and respect in the working relationships among faculty and clinical supervisors. Most have worked together for several years and have considerable trust and regard for each other's skill and autonomy. In an ironic twist, it becomes something of a compliment not to trouble each other with a mid-semester meeting with the student.

While many of us can see ourselves falling into one or another of these lapses occasionally, as a pattern or a norm, they would eventually erode the foundation of the dual matrix model, and in subtle as well as obvious ways, deny students the fullness of their learning experience. The integration of learning, as noted earlier, requires an understanding of the mutuality and reciprocity of the knowledge sources available in the classroom and the field setting. This awareness, however, is not sufficient without the conscious and active bridging between conceptual content and the field experience (Schneck, p.67). We believe this responsibility is shared equally by the clinical staff and the faculty. While this can be done conceptually in the classroom or at the Institute, the two principal parties need to have enough contact to know the nature of what they are trying to bridge and integrate. Thus, there is no substitute for consistent contact even if the student is doing very well. If viewed as co-teaching or team teaching, the imperative becomes obvious.

The formalization of one's ideas into a written paper or presentation is supposed to have salutary benefits; and we think we've discovered one. We plan to enlist students in the future to help us (by reading the paper) make the model work more effectively by conveying to them an understanding of the principles upon which the dual matrix structure is founded, i.e., communication and collaboration. Not only will it be facilitative of their placement experience, but it should also provide them with an "object lesson" of these important principles, for many of them will assume practice positions in mental health and hospital settings.

## ANALYSIS AND SUMMARY

The construction of a dual matrix structure for anything elicits a recall of the traditional Zen Buddhist concept of duality--that common detour of consciousness in which the seeker of truth on the path of enlightenment cannot move beyond dualistic perceptions of reality, i.e., black or white, good or bad, male or female. Clearly, any membership or status in dual reference groups (in our case, the University and the Institute) evokes dynamic tensions and, perhaps, identity struggles which need to be balanced in order to achieve the educational benefit and the integration of learning so much desired.

This presents an important and perennial educational question, i.e., how do teachers promote the tolerance of ambiguity, incorporate the necessary diversity of input, and avoid the seduction of one's identity into one camp or the other. How does one accomplish mutuality and integration rather than duality and separatism? The answer seems to lie in the ability of students, agency instructors and faculty to consciously build the conceptual and experiential bridges between the students' field experience and learning needs, and the knowledge and skill resources wherever they lie. This can be accomplished through active, spontaneous, and non-possessive teaching/learning skills and activities. As the teacher in either group seminar setting is able to define the connectedness and model appropriate regard for the other, students will be shown how to prevent barriers in their understanding.

The teaching/learning activities are not magical; they begin with the students' learning needs, background, and preconceptions. All of these seem to come into play when a student assumes a professional role and responsibility within the clinical practice setting.

At the 1987 Field Work Symposium it was noted:

Teaching methods for the integration of learning ideally should respond to rather than dictate the pace and learning styles of the students. To the extent possible and reasonable, we should take our cue s from the needs and readiness of our students in the selection of teaching-learning activities. This is the most difficult and exciting kind of teaching. It calls for flexibility, the perception of individual and group needs, and an ability to spontaneously adjust content and format to respond to student needs (Schneck, p. 67)

In this teaching method, one can validate the dual reference group status, or more simply put, the other side of the students' reality and draw upon same as a valuable learning resource. The appendix includes paradigms which depict teaching/learning activities for the integration of learning in field. These can be employed equally well in a campus-based or an agency-based practice seminar. If an inductive/deductive cycle of inquiry is engendered from the practice reality to concept and theory, then duality and separatism are unable to form as students (and teachers) care less about where they sit than what they understand.

Another lesson in the development of the dual matrix structure was an important reminder of the constant interplay between structure and process. This lesson is, of course, a classic one in social work practice and education; and, here it is again. Our good intentions and willingness to problem solve the intersystem dilemma would have amounted to nothing without a structural outcome which recognized the content, roles, and reciprocal contributions between clinical staff and faculty. Yet our prized structural mechanism would have never been accepted or well-implemented without some of the "eternal" process features of trust, mutual respect, cooperation, tolerance, and commitment. Administrative leadership also visibly affected the desired outcome. While at times, our "third eye" may have mirrored to each of us *pro forma* functioning; nonetheless, the enactment of our respective roles with integrity and diligence was an essential ingredient.

Another major lesson has been to recognize the ever expanding body of theory, research, specialized practice method and skill content available to the modern practitioner in mental health. There is so much for a student (or an agency director or faculty) to know and integrate into one's perspective. Theory and research in mental health, health, alcohol and drug abuse, forensics, paradigms of intervention, delivery system/agency policy, procedures and services, and certainly not the least, clinical practice methodology and techniques all beckon and bewilder the new and old student alike.

## FUTURE DEVELOPMENT

The authors see possibilities in several areas: one ongoing creative endeavor, and the others, important program development changes. Given the assurance that the model is well founded, our primary focus will be the continual exploration of new placement ideas whether these be in different clinical units, administration, or in innovative ways of designing traditional placements through the use of new practice models or experimental methods. In fact, the dynamic nature of the model would allow new pairings of field/clinical units as resources allow and problems dictate.

Another development we are considering specifically pertains to the Institute seminars. Currently, seminars are developed and conducted exclusively for the social work students placed at Mendota. Occasionally, students from other disciplines and students from other field units at the university have expressed an interest in a particular topic of clinical interest. Normally, they have been allowed to attend, so long as there is relevance to their educational needs. Given many requests, we are exploring the possibility of extending the offer to students from other disciplines at the Institute and/or extending the offer to students from other field units in social work if there is sufficient interest on the part of faculty at the School. In either case, the students at MMHI and the Director of Social Services would retain the right and responsibility to determine the topics for the year as they do currently.

Expanding the opportunity in this way may offer another possibility for students to hear highly specific content that they would otherwise not have available to them. The limiting factors would be logistics, scheduling, and availability of student and faculty time. There are usually more open and free colloquia, symposia, guest lectures, and "grand rounds" kinds of opportunities than anyone has time to attend. Students are often employed part time and many have family responsibilities so that the additional time available may be limited; however, expanding the Institute seminar to other students would certainly benefit some, and perhaps increase the availability of resources for the seminar.

Educational quality is ephemeral; it is not achieved once and forever. Students, faculty and staff turn over; educational priorities and resources change and evolve; new practice knowledge becomes available; yet, all of these realities do not alter our basic mission. In fact, they enable it. What the dual matrix structure with its attendant features and principles really does is provide a bridge between two equal and essential parties--the School and the Mental Health Institute--in order that students may secure the best educational product we can deliver.

## BIBLIOGRAPHY

Franks, Virginia (1967) THE AUTONOMOUS SOCIAL WORKER, an Occasional paper of the School of Social Work, University of Wisconsin-Madison, No. 1, presented at the APM of CSWE, January, 1966, New York.

Schneck, Dean (1990) "Arbiter of Change in Field Education: The Critical Role for Faculty," in FIELD EDUCATION IN SOCIAL WORK: CONTEMPORARY ISSUES AND TRENDS. Dubuque, IA: Kendall/Hunt Publishing Company.

Schneck, Dean (March, 1980) "Field Education at Wisconsin-Madison: On Field Education Models and the Wisconsin Experience." A Roundtable presentation at the CSWE-APM, Los Angeles.

Schneck, Dean (1990) "Integration of Learning in Field Education: Elusive Goal and Educational Imperative," in FIELD EDUCATION IN SOCIAL WORK: CONTEMPORARY ISSUES AND TRENDS. Dubuque, IA: Kendall/Hunt Publishing Company.

**APPENDIX A**

Mendota Mental Health Institute Seminar

Wendy Norberg, Director of Social Services
Preceptor, School of Social Work, University of Wisconsin
Madison, Wisconsin

Orientation Phase:

**Part I**

* Introductions
* Slide tape of MMHI clinical programs
* Review of student handbook
* Director of Social Services commentary on roles of clinical unit supervisors, director of social service, and seminars students
* Field Director commentary on role of the student, field director, field faculty and other curriculum connections

Orientation Continues with Sessions in the Following Areas:

**Part 2**

* Medical records policies
* Security policies
* Overview of the Wisconsin Mental Health System
* Admission policies
* Patients Rights
* Health screening
* Safety procedures
* Central work processing

**Clinical Seminar Phase**

Seminars conducted since 1981 have included clinical content presented by various disciplines at the Institute, faculty from the University and community agency staff. The following topics exemplify the seminar:

* Serving as an expert witness in court
* Psychopharmacology
* Personality disorders: Borderline, Antisocial
* Diagnosis and treatment of schizophrenia
* Provocative therapy
* Dealing with the resistive client
* Sexual abuse: Treatment of the perpetrator, Treatment of the Victim(s)
* Child abuse laws" Implications for treatment
* Affective disorders
* Dual diagnosis: MI/DD
* Play therapy
* Working with Families of Schizophrenics
* Suicide prevention
* Discharge planning with community resources
* Deinstitutionalization
* Psychological Testing
* Ethical dilemmas in mental health practice
* Competency to stand trial
* Depression in Adolescents
* Case presentations and/or unit tours by students tying in a case
* Open forum for case consultation as needed by the students

**APPENDIX B**

CONTRACT AGREEMENT BETWEEN
MENDOTA MENTAL HEALTH INSTITUTE AND
UNIVERSITY OF WISCONSIN - MADISON
CONCERNING THE EDUCATION OF STUDENTS IN SOCIAL WORK

Upon signature of this document, Mendota Mental Health Institute and the School of Social Work of the University of Wisconsin-Madison agree to affiliate in the education of students during the period from September 1989 through August 1990 according to the following conditions:

1.     That the Institute will accept no more than 14 graduate field work students from various field units within the School of Social Work for training in its programs each semester. The acceptance of students in based upon the following conditions:
a) unit programming conducive to the learning needs of students and available supervisory time
b) the completion of an interview between the prospective student and MMHI supervisor
c) mutual agreement between MMHI Unit Social Work Supervisors and Field Faculty as to training plans, goals, and time commitments.

2.     That the timetable for student placement be consistent with programming patterns at each facility. Therefore, the following schedule will be adhered to as closely as possible:
a) The Institute will contract with the University in the Spring for the specific number of training slots available for the following Fall.
b) Field Unit Faculty and MMHI unit supervisors will interview prospective students.
c) The University will confirm each placement prior to the onset of the semester. Exceptions to accommodate late arriving students can be made between the MMHI Director of Social Services and the Director of Field Education at the School.

3.     That first year students are required to spend sixteen hours per week in field experience and second year students are required to spend twenty hours in field experience. The bulk of the time will be at MMHI with time allotted for faculty unit meetings away from the Institute.

4.     That the students will receive supervised experience by the Institute Social Work staff with cases/projects in the MMHI unit setting.

5.     That the students progress be evaluated jointly by the Institute staff and faculty of the School of Social Work generally based on the learning contract.

6.     That any problems with individual students or the placement model will be communicated by the representatives of the Institute and the University in an attempt toward early resolution. That any change in personnel representing the University or the Institute in relation to this program will be communicated to the other party.

7.     That the Institute will provide a group and individual orientation for the students.

8.     That students will be made aware of and act to safeguard patients rights, in particular that of privacy by protecting information of a confidential nature.

9.     That the Institute is not liable for sickness or injury benefits to students, but does provide access to its Employee Health Service for students. Liability related to students in field placement will be the responsibility of the University's training program.

10.     That no student will be discriminated against on the basis of race, creed, color, national origin, sex or age.

11.     That this contract is subject to review and renewal by both parties in the Spring of 1990.

12.     The implementation of this agreement will follow the attached basic assumptions and role definitions.

IDEOLOGICAL

CONCEPTUAL

Assess current attitudes and political views
toward clients and social problems.
Identification of relevant personal values
and religious beliefs.
Exposure to professional ethics
Personal expectations.
Identify/explore case related value issues.

Initial social problem, research &
human development knowledge.
Understanding of social work
process stages.
Information on agency programs
and structures.
Agency policies and procedures.
Understanding of student
expectations.
Initial exposure to methods and
techniques.

INDIVIDUAL/GROUP TEACHING-LEARNING ACTIVITIES

Orientation and exposure to agency setting,
staff and programs.
Value discussion/clarification.
Interviewing practice and role-play (video).
Problem assessment/exploration discussion.
Identification of knowledge needs and methods choices.
Problem solving and process simulation exercises.
Case observations with supervisor or mentor.
Case sharing with supervisor or faculty.
Initial client contacts.
Case examples and discussion.
Individual and group supervisory conferences.
Discussion of professional role vis-vis
previous work experience.
Opportunity to discuss initial assumptions and
expectations about client problems and professional roles.

BEHAVIORAL

Level of social skills
from life experience.
Level of work skills from
previous employment.
System/entry/negotiation skills.
Professional role behaviors.
Initial communication and
interviewing skills.
Assertive and expressive
behaviors.

Performance anticipation/anxiety.
Previous emotional experiences in general.
Re-activation of old personal struggles.
Connection to existing personal problems or needs.
Subjective response to client needs and problems.
Security and credibility.

EMOTIONAL

Dean Schneck, 1990

Chart B: **PROBLEM SOLVING PHASE**

IDEOLOGICAL

Resolution of situational value/ethical issues.
Clarification of professional responsibilities.
Juxtaposition of personal values, religious beliefs, and political views vis-a-vis professional role expectations.

INDIVIDUAL/GROUP TEACHING-LEARNING ACTIVITIES

Case presentation and consultation.
Structured problem solving and value clarification exercises -- case related.
Explore and apply relevant theoretical knowledge.
Evaluate interventive method and technique choices.
Anticipate barriers, outcomes, and consequences of interventive decisions.
Discuss subjective responses and interference with professional role.
Case sharing with supervisor, faculty or mentor.
Review similar case histories or practice examples.
Assess and possibly visit potential resources.
Develop and evaluate several alternative case formulations and plans.
Observe or record student interviews for content and technical feedback.
Evaluate and resolve practical value considerations.
Simulate or role-play (video) case related interventions and techniques.

CONCEPTUAL

Assessment of problem dynamics.
Consideration of motivation and change potential.
Knowledge of interventive roles and methodologies.
Knowledge of community resources and natural helping systems.
Understanding of problem solving process.
Conceptualization and refinement problem definition.
Initial decisions on scope of interventions.
Planning of interventions and identification of barriers.

BEHAVIORAL

Data collection and planning skills.
Contracting/negotiation skills.
Outreach and motivational skills.
Meaning attribution skills.
Supportive skills.
Decision-making/priority skills.
Professional influence.

EMOTIONAL

Tolerance of ambiguity and resistance to premature closure in the problem solving process.
Emotional response to client needs and problems.
Identification and transference issues.
Subjective reactions to case choices and issues.
Reassurance needs.

Dean Schneck, 1990

Chart C: **INTERVENTION/CHANGE PHASE**

CONCEPTUAL

IDEOLOGICAL

Pragmatic/operational value issues.
Ends/means questions.
Idealism *vs.* reality confrontations.
Value conflicts among principled professionals.
Exposure to possible ethical breaches of others.
Reaction to insufficient resources and compromised goals.
Challenges to personal values, political views or religious beliefs.

INDIVIDUAL/GROUP TEACHING-LEARNING ACTIVITIES

Frequent supervisory/consultative conferences.
Modification of case plan and objectives.
Discussion of practice norms, judgements, vis-a-vis case assignment and learning needs.
Consideration of client responses, unexpected developments and consequences.
Explore student concerns relating to case responsibilities, decision making or value matters.
Demonstrate application of theoretical knowledge and resource information to practice situation.
Identify important process components from immediate practice experience.
Use simulation exercise to overcome student resistance or to develop sufficient competence.
Provide suggestions for dealing with resources or institutions such as courts, schools, law enforcement agencies, employers.
Provide feedback and support on task performance and skill development.
Provide relative sense of progress and improvement vis-a-vis school and agency expectations, initial skill level, and student's own goals.
Provide perspective on role stressors, such as reasonable levels of effort, limits of responsibility, client demands, bureaucratic frustrations, delivery system problems, etc. to prevent unneeded stress or anxiety.

Understanding of process and the client's experience.
Awareness of case plan and objectives.
Operational problem solving and decision making.
Application of practice theory, research, and knowledge.
Reformulation of problem definition as interventions proceed.
Understanding of case management and coordinative responsibility.
Being mindful of unintended consequences.
Balance of change and stability.

Experience "in vivo" practice responsibilities, successes, failures, and frustrations.
Emotional reactions to practice demands, crises, excitement.
Self-confidence and self-criticism questions.
Emotional response to difficult problems, harsh realities, lack or resources. Reassurance and support needs.

EMOTIONAL

BEHAVIORAL

Apply intervention methods and various techniques to accomplish case objectives.
Enact professional responsibility with increasing autonomy.
Exert professional influence with client and resource systems.
Expand interviewing, treatment and communication skills.
Assert observations and opinions with professional staff.
Coordination and management skills.

Dean Schneck, 1990

Chart D: **STABILIZATION/DISENGAGEMENT PHASE**

IDEOLOGICAL

C
O
N
C
E
P
T
U
A
L

Reflection and reevaluation of personal values,
political views, and religious beliefs.
Value attributions to client outcomes, agency
efforts, and resource systems.
Review of ethical conflicts encountered.
Practice and program policy implications.

INDIVIDUAL/GROUP TEACHING-LEARNING ACTIVITIES

Help students see the importance of a well-done
termination and separation process for the client
particularly the stabilization, generalization of
of learning and separation components.
Use case reviews and discussion to discern process
issues, techniques used, and theoretical knowledge
which was applied.
Consider retrospectively alternative case formulations and intervention choices not chosen,
i.e., "the road not taken".
Extrapolate SW principles, policies, concepts, and
values from the case experiences, making inductive
and deductive linkages with specific examples.
Identify knowledge and skills areas with each
student for improvement and development.
Review student accomplishement in achieving service
objectives, client benefits, and changes.
Assist student in gaining perspective of their
achievements vis-a-vis a broader practice framework.
Discuss personal/professional value conflicts
flowing from their immediate experience.
Assist student with professional or career choices.

Meaning attributions to practice
experiences and client outcomes.
Outcome evaluation of service plan.
Review of what actually happened
and consequences for clients.
Restate problem formulation in
retrospect.
Knowledge of termination/separation
dynamics and resistances.
Generalize experiences to practice
concepts, principles, process
and policy.
Identify knowledge and skills gaps
of the student and the profession.

B
E
H
A
V
I
O
R
A
L

Evaluate and reinforce change
efforts and growth with clients.
Deal with dependency or resistance
of the client or self.
Strengthen client self-reliance
and coping skills.
Anticipate and prepare client for
new or continuing problems.
Solidify resources linkages.
Generalize new social skills to
potential situations.

Reaction to situational ethics.
Termination/separation issues and ambivalences.
Feelings of satisfaction, achievement, disappointment,
loss, or regret.
Self-evaluative or self-worth questions.
Suitability and career choice/direction issues.
Assess affective responses to clients' problems and agencies.

EMOTIONAL

Dean Schneck, 1990

SUMMARY OF EDUCATIONAL ROLES IN WORKING WITH FIELD STUDENTS

**Field Student** <------------> **Field Unit Group**

### Field Student

- Express learning needs and career goals with clarity.
- Meet pre-and co-requisites, especially preplacement interview.
- Cooperate fully with staff and faculty, including incorporation of criticism and feedback.
- Perform ethically and competently in all field assignments.

### Field Unit Group

- Provides environment for group learning activities including problem-solving, skill exercises, student presentations, and peer consultation.
- Provides support and motivation for student performance and learning.
- Provides seminar for faculty lectures, guest presentations, and other seminar content.

### Field Faculty/School of Social Work

- Work with practicum supervisor to develop learning opportunity and affiliation with agency/organization.
- Responsible for student selection and community placement.
- Develop and approve learning plan and supervisory arrangements with student and practicum supervisor.
- Develop syllabus and teach field unit seminar to provide relevant theoretical, practice and problem content.
- Share in ongoing practice supervision/consultation and help student integrate seminar content with placement experience.
- Provide good professional rolem odel.
- Maintain regular contact with practicum supervisor to monitor student performance, ensure learning opportunities, deal with performance problems, etc.
- Consult with student on professional growth and development.
- Help student integrate constructive criticism and responsible for evaluation and grading.
- Work with practicum supervisors on future planning.

### Field Practicum Supervisor/Community Setting

- Work with faculty to develop and maintain learning opportunities and affiliation with the University.
- Participate in student selection/placement process.
- Work with student and faculty in developing learning plans and supervisory arrangements.
- Orient student to agency, work unit, and practice area.
- Possible teamwork with student.
- Provide ongoing practice supervision and help student integrate seminar content with placement experience.
- Provide good professional model.
- Consult with student on professional growth and development.
- Provide student and faculty with ongoing constructive criticism and participate in the final evaluation.
- Work with field faculty on future planning for student placements.

# FIELD EDUCATION UNITS REVISITED: A MODEL FOR THE 1990'S

John J. Conklin and Mary C. Borecki, *University of Connecticut*

## INTRODUCTION

According to a recent article in "Social Casework", the diminishing resources of schools of social work "have resulted in the phasing out of faculty-headed field units and a growing dependency on agencies for field instruction with fewer faculty to support this undertaking". (Raphael and Rosenblum, 1987). This is not a new phenomenon since a number of field units which formerly were funded by federal training grants were indeed "phased out" during the late 1970's and 1980's. A major cause of their demise had to do with the fiscal support for both faculty and students. The issue remains that a valuable teaching resource for practicum learning was lost in the process primarily because of funding problems. The authors tested this hypothesis so as to determine whether renewed efforts should be made by professional schools to reinstate a valuable field education model.

From experiences one of the writers had in two field units in the late 1960's during both years of graduate school, it was recalled that field units represented an excellent model for the training of students for several major reasons. "Units" defined as three or more students placed in the same agency who worked closely together and shared resources, including supervision, provided: 1. the opportunity for "transferability of knowledge" between students (Bruner, 1968); 2. the opportunity for an entirely different structure for learning other than individual tutorial experiences with a mentor; 3. positive gains in terms of professional identity and a support group experience for students in the unit; 4. the opportunity to integrate classroom learning with field practicum experiences enhanced by relationships with other professionals from the larger agency in which the unit was housed.

The authors instituted several such units in a graduate school of social work over a four year period. This paper will focus on the experiences inherent in three of the units. One is located in a large public school system at the primary, middle and high school levels. The second is in a child protective agency, specifically in a children's psychiatric hospital, an adolescent residential facility and a district office. The third is located in a private agency, a YWCA which provides special services for adolescents and young women.

There is a wealth of opportunity for creative learning opportunities for students and to conduct a variety of research projects. Preliminary studies of the student interns have corroborated the significance of field unit learning models in providing enriched learning experiences through multi-tiered supervision and faculty collaboration. Peer group, individual supervision, group supervision and staff development programs enhance the opportunities for students to integrate both class and field learning more effectively.

This paper will provide an overview of previous experiences with field units, present program descriptions of the three units, and highlight a number of observations concerning the necessary place of field units in professional education. Preliminary research on student attitudinal changes will be given and final conclusions will be posited.

## OVERVIEW

When tracing the origins of what are called field "units" one must move farther and farther back in time until it is clear that units, in fact, pre-dated formal education in schools of Social Work! Out of the early charity, philanthropy and social reform movements of the late 1800's came training in the social agencies of the time by supervisors who worked with groups of volunteers and altruistic citizens. Perhaps the best-known example of a social agency is the Charity Organization Society which began in Buffalo in the year 1877. A founder of that society was the Reverend Guerteen who was impressed by the work of Thomas Chalmers of Edinburgh. The Reverend Chalmers recognized twenty "districts" in that city and organized his attack on poverty by training a <u>unit</u> of twenty "district visitors" who made weekly visits to identify and remedy a wide variety of social problems including mental health, mental retardation, poverty and public health problems.

A major responsibility of the District Secretary was to teach the "assistants" how to complete forms, how to do interviewing so as to provide assistance to those in need of community agencies such as hospitals (Feder, 1936). Prevention was a sought-after early focus of the work of these trained assistants.

An early reference to the desirability of formal education including field education was presented in 1883 by Anna Dawes at a charity conference in Chicago who proposed:

> some course of study where an intelligent young person. . . can be taught what is now the alphabet of charitable science . . . with the various devices employed for the upbuilding of the needy. Some more immediately practical experience of the work likely to be required should also be given, some laboratory practice in the science of charity, if we may so speak (Brown, 1942).

Shortly after that, the Columbia College and the Charity Organization Society of New York began efforts to "yoke together". By the early definition, field work was referred to as "systematic instruction with practice under direction" (COS, 1893). By 1906, five schools of social work had been established in New York, Chicago, Boston, Philadelphia and St. Louis (Proceedings, 1906).

If we move through time to the recent past, some landmark publications were produced by Tulane University School of Social Work in reference to an approach called "Social Work Training Centers". The work represents some very solid reporting on a method of teaching that was popular in the late 1950's and 1960's *vis-a-vis* student units or centers, usually involving a group of graduate students under the tutelage of a "unit supervisor" or adjunct faculty member from a school of social work. Funding came from a variety of sources including substantial training grants from the National Institute of Mental Health after World War II. As previously mentioned, much of this disappeared when the funding was no longer available, although no one seems to dispute that this was an excellent method of educating professional social work students. (Kindelsperger and Cassidy, 1966).

Out of this long historical train, the authors began to explore the options which still exist for such an educational opportunity. It is not implied that all student units ceased to be in the past twenty-five years. Some evolved into free-standing community learning centers supported by third-party payments. Others continued by assigning a faculty member who was charged with obtaining funding and acting as an educational business manager. In our case, we also sought funding and began the long process of starting units from scratch. Three models are presented which illustrate that there are indeed many roads which "all lead to Rome". Funding of academic projects such as these has become more difficult to obtain but this does not diminish the idea that "units" still offer a unique learning opportunity for students in a variety of graduate and undergraduate programs.

## THE PROGRAMS

In the following section, three models of field unit programs will be discussed. The first has been established in several units of a state agency which provides protective services and in-hospital treatment for children and adolescents. The second concerns a large unit which is housed within a public school system in a large metropolitan area. The third is being developed in a private social agency which provides a variety of services for women. Other units are in the planning stage at the present.

### The Clinical Internship Program

The initial unit was established in a psychiatric hospital for children which is under the auspices of the State Department of Children and Youth Services. The writers had obtained an NIMH Training Grant for the Education of Master of Social Work students who were entering the field of "Child Mental Health". Out of this process, we began discussions with the staff of the hospital and the Central Office staff, particularly the Deputy Commissioner, concerning opportunities which might be created for Social Work students who were taking practicum education.

Further in the discussion, it developed that the Department also wished to train some of their own employees so we provided a work-study opportunity in a program entitled the "Clinical Internship Program" (CIP). During the initial phase of planning and implementation, we sent graduate students to a psychiatric hospital for children where all patients were under the age of fourteen. An Advisory Committee was established, some initial policies were set and regular meetings were held during which we discussed an educational leave program for employees of the Department. It was envisioned that a two year program could be established wherein employees who were accepted in the MSW program might serve one year of clinical internship at the hospital and complete the second year at a district office. During both of these years, they would continue to receive their salaries. In return, they would pledge a specific amount of post-graduate service to the Department.

Over the next several years, this is exactly what transpired. A Coordinator for the program in the Central Office was designated who worked with the various operating units, field instructors from the Department, the Personnel section, various District directors and the authors. A Selection Committee was established which ultimately interviewed all candidates from the Department.

Over the past three years, the program was expanded to include three sites for field placements. In addition to the children's hospital, a psychiatric facility for adolescents over the age of fourteen was also included as a first year placement. The second year placement was established at a District Office. An MSW was hired by the Department to serve as a unit coordinator and to provide supervision for the second year students who were placed there. The School of Social Work provided consultation and advisement to all students plus participated actively in all planning and implementation phases of the CIP.

Discussions are currently underway to determine whether there is a place for indirect service majors to be included in the CIP. Also, while there are three first year students and three second year students in placement, we are looking into the possibility of offering more placements to the Department employees.

## The Hartford School System Program

During the initial years of the CIP, the feedback from the students was that if we really wished to practice "preventive" mental health with the children admitted to psychiatric facilities, we should make efforts to work with them **before** they required hospitalization, i.e., somewhere in the public school system.

In our case, the School of Social Work is located in a large metropolitan area which has a high percentage of public school social problems including teen pregnancy, infant mortality, school dropouts, substance abuse and a host of all too familiar community problems (Conklin, Borecki, 1987).

Through contacts in both the political and social work community of Hartford, we began a series of discussions with a high school principal, school specialists in the School Social Work Department of the City and the Superintendent's Office. These discussions were wide-ranging in nature as the school system was already addressing the various social problems listed in a variety of ways. After a number of meetings, we began by sending one student to a single high school during the initial year. Weekly consultation was provided by the graduate school so that we could assess carefully what the learning opportunities were.

During the first year, we were exposed to a panoply of complex social, emotional, biological, cultural and financial problems. Clients of the practicum student were not attending class because they were living in shelters for the homeless. Others were not attending because of threats to their lives, extreme poverty, illness and transportation problems. Many dramatic issues emerged. Many "child mental health" problems existed and we began to learn that even earlier intervention was a necessity. Seeing adolescents who were seniors in high school was very late in the game. A large number of "children" had left school in their sophomore year!

Accordingly, we "staffed" the unit with six students during the second year. The interns are assigned to a variety of primary, middle and high schools. The specific approach used is similar to the "Rochester Model" of a mental health unit in the public schools (Dworkin, 1985). In this case, the clinicians are MSW students rather than community volunteers as they were in the initial project.

In our program, regular unit meetings are held each week with the Unit Coordinator who is one of the administrators of the School of Social Work program of the school system. Those meetings provide the opportunity for in-service training, support and learning from one another. Community leaders and Faculty present various programs. Students are invited to attend numerous parents' functions, community dinners and specific ethnic "theme nights". All of this greatly enriches the learning of the graduate students.

The student interns receive stipends from an NIMH grant to assist them with their financial indebtedness. They work under the direction of MSW trained field instructors in a variety of public schools in collaboration with other specialists and administrators from the various schools.

During the third year, we now have nine student interns working in different schools in a number of specific programs. The school system is in the process of setting up a model "clinic" program which carries out many types of health care and intervention. The Social Workers are an integral part of that program. As we are in the last year of the Federal grant, we are in the process of applying for funding for intern stipends. The University has also been active in providing minority stipends and tuition remission.

We have enjoyed a great deal of cooperation from the public school system, the specialists in it, the Superintendent's office, the President's Office of the University and our Administration's support. The current plans are to expand the program somewhat and to link it with other professional programs of the university.

**The YWCA Prevention and Division Unit**

The third of these programs is currently in its first year. Planning began this summer for a small unit which will eventually be staffed by four University of Connecticut graduate students who will provide services in casework, groupwork and community organization. Once again, the focus is upon specific community problems, in this case, teen pregnancy and infant mortality. The YWCA, in which this program is housed, is in Springfield, Massachusetts, which has the "second highest teen pregnancy rate in Massachusetts" (Gareffa, 1987).

The unit proposed has been funded by the United Way of Springfield, which in turn, provides some of the stipend monies for the one student intern placed there this year. The unit will accept referrals from other YWCA Social Service programs concerning children and families who are not receiving services with other human service agencies on a continuing basis. Case managers in the unit will provide specific outreach services in public schools. They will also provide referral, ongoing support and counseling, plus provide parenting education within a prevention focus. Supervision will be provided by the Unit Coordinator, an employee of the YWCA and other MSW's who will serve as Field Instructors.

## Similarities Between Units

The previous description has noted a variety of similarities between the three types of units. All are professionally led by interested MSW's who coordinate the program and supervise other MSW's who are the Field Instructors. Different from the models of the 1970's the Unit Coordinators are not adjunct or "in-residence" faculty as they were when the Schools óf Social Work hired them to provide services to the agencies. In this case, they are all employees of the agencies who collaborate with the School toward the education of their employees, or interns who receive stipends from the School or agency.

This unique mix of collaboration works differently than the earlier focus of "unit supervisors" who are faculty since the practitioner working in his own system understands it differently than the "outsider" who comes into it anew. This obviously has good sides and not so good sides to the argument. In our case, its collaboration works very effectively as long as there is mutual respect and recognition given on both sides.

In the examples cited above, a large state agency, a large public school system and a private community agency have linked together with a school of social work to provide some unique learning experiences for sixteen graduate students. Presently, we have begun discussions with other agencies as to the opportunities which exist in a variety of settings.

## Differences Between the Units

Perhaps the similarities are only in the eyes of the authors. Indeed, in the first case, the state agency is paying a few of its employees their salaries while they attend graduate school. Also, the public school system is staffed by interns who receive stipends from the graduate school as well as minority fellowships and tuition reimbursement while they are in school. The third program provides the stipends for the students from private fundraising.

A pragmatic question might be: "So what's new about field units?" Perhaps the answer offered in the first part of this paper is that there is nothing at all new about units, they antedate graduate school. However, what is new to the 1990's is that they are an excellent source for students to learn from other students and a variety of staff people while in several host agencies. There is a major similarity between what students are learning in all of the above community settings. Their satisfaction with this learning opportunity, according to the initial research we have done, is extremely high. Staff satisfaction with the interns is very high. Client satisfaction with services provided is very high. The integration of classroom theory and practice is high, particularly when a great deal of time is donated by the School to the agencies and by the agency Field Instructors and Unit Coordinators to the education of the intern. In the next section, we will address some of the specific findings of preliminary research which was done concerning student attitudes. (Johnson, 1987)

## The Attitude Surveys

As part of the development of the three units, we have begun to design attitude surveys of the students which are administered on a pre-test and post-test basis. Other research is being designed to measure the actual effects of the student interns on their clientele. For our purposes, the most complete data is available on the public school unit. Portions will be reported here.

To understand the context in which the interns practice, certain facts about the City of Hartford School System need to be presented. Twenty-nine public schools provide the education for 23,590 students. Of that number, 80% are from minority groups, 56% come from single parent homes, 58% of the students are from homes which receive welfare, 45% speak a native language other than English, 18% of the students are in special education classes. Tied to these figures is the observation that "children from low-income families in our state are at greater risk of being developmentally disabled than are children in our state as a whole (Hartford School System, 1985). Many of the children served by the School Systems are from impoverished homes; come from single parent families and have serious emotional disorders which have a serious effect on their school attendance and classroom performance (Ward, 1984). In stark contrast to the fact that Hartford is one of the poorest of the large cities in the nation, the State of Connecticut is listed as having the highest per capita income.

In that school system, during the academic year 1986-87, six Social Work Interns provided services to fifty-four regular and special education students. The services included 390 interviews with public school students and their parents, 462 consultations with school personnel, 48 home visits, 181 collateral and miscellaneous contacts. Other services include the preparation of individual education plans, social work reports of various types and attendance at a variety of group and pupil team meetings.

The interns who provided these services were given a pre-test prior to entering the unit to determine the effectiveness of the unit in meeting their learning needs. The post-test given at the end of the scholastic year provided some interesting data. Among the findings, the interns now felt that they were much more aware of the needs and behaviors of the public school students with whom they worked. They remained enthusiastic about working with children and adolescents. They felt that they had learned a great deal about public school systems, the administration, the Board and staff, plus the resources of the community of Hartford.

A strong recommendation was offered that more prevention services be offered at lower grade levels in primary schools. After the internship, they all felt more comfortable dealing with the complex issues around teen pregnancy, behavioral problems, truancy and school dropout. Interestingly, the areas that they were less comfortable with concerned handicapped children and those adolescents who were actively involved with substance abuse, particularly with drugs.

All of the interns were comfortable in working with the parents of children-at-risk. They also felt that they were competent when making home visits.

In general, their expectations were met through the supervisory process and unit support format which provided them with multiple opportunities to share with one another and with instructional personnel. They were quite positive about the opportunity to have both individual and unit supervision as they felt that they had experienced several "styles" of supervision concurrently.

The interns also made a number of specific recommendations for the development of additional orientation tools, i.e., courses that should be taken at the School in preparation for the unit. In addition to the response from the students, the Coordinator noted that enthusiasm had grown within the social work staff of the school system which culminated in requests for still more student interns. Jokingly, the Assistant Superintendent of Schools once offered to training our entire second year class as he felt there were ample learning opportunities for all of our students.

Some school administrators, requested interns for the following year. The latest information is that the Hartford Board of Education is hiring more of our graduates (Johnson, 1987). It seems that this experience can be replicated by other schools of social work throughout the country with positive results.


## CONCLUSION

The foregoing paper has offered a number of observations about three types of field units and may be established by graduate and undergraduate schools of social work. Different in their funding sources and in their construction, they share a number of characteristics which were codified over twenty years ago by the Tulane University School of Social Work *vis-a-vis* the important opportunity that "units" offer for field learning at a different level than the familiar tutorial method.

In a publication entitled: "Social Work Training Centers: Tentative Analysis of the Structure and learning Environment" by Kindelsperger and Cassidy, a number of important observations were made which still apply today. A few of the "criteria for the general structure and environment of centers" will be summarized.

Geography is a factor in locating a center but the site need not be limited to one locale. The center should serve a variety of clients with various social problems for the students in the unit to address. All social work methods should be used. Home visiting should be performed as it provides a valuable learning experience for interns.

Multi-disciplinary collaboration is highly desirable since this provides the opportunity for students to observe the interventive methods of other professions in handling school and student problems. Lectures, in-service training and group discussions with authorities in the system enhance learning.

An opportunity exists for important support-group experiences to take place which provide self-teaching and the generalization of knowledge throughout the unit. The coordinator can also take this opportunity to train staff who are providing supervision to the students. this can be done on a group basis wherein the advanced field instructors can share their expertise with beginning instructors. (Kindelsperger and Cassidy, 1966).

"Real" changes can take place with the larger system because of the enthusiasm of the student interns. The students may learn to develop specializations with a large organization. In addition, we learned that continuity of social work service may be achieved throughout the "career" of a child, adolescent or client as the "case" is reassigned year after year to successive student interns. Major programmatic changes may be effected in the service delivery system by "staffing" programs with student interns. "Target populations" for intervention may be assigned to the interns so that they receive intensive services.

While we have adapted some of the language of the Tulane report somewhat to reflect the changes made in terminology over the past twenty years, the conceptualization is still sound. Unit instruction for practicum students offers many unique opportunities for enhanced learning. As we have shown, funding for such units is a goal which is well within our grasp. The answer is a function of our own creativity.

## BIBLIOGRAPHY

Brown, Esther (1906) SOCIAL WORK AS A PROFESSION, New York: New York: Russell Sage Foundation.

Bruner, Jerome S. (1966) TOWARD A THEORY OF INSTRUCTION, Cambridge: Harvard.

Conklin, John J. and Borecki, Mary (1987) "A State University-Public School Partnership: The Hartford Model Mental Health Service Component", presented at the NASW Conference "On the Leading Edge, Social Work '87", New Orleans, LA.

Dworkin, Paul H. (1985) LEARNING AND BEHAVIOR PROBLEMS OF SCHOOLCHILDREN, Philadelphia, Saunders, 151-164.

Feder, James (1936) UNEMPLOYMENT RELIEF IN PERIODS OF DEPRESSION, New York: Russell Sage Foundation.

Gareffa, Domenic, (1987) "Challenge Grant Proposal", Springfield YWCA, Springfield, Massachusetts.

Johnson, Winston. (1987) "Annual Report, Unit Coordinator". University of Connecticut/Hartford School System Field Unit, Hartford, CT. Hartford School System Annual Report, (1985), 75.

Kindelsperger, W.L. and Cassidy, Helen. (1966) "Social Work Training Centers: Tentative Analysis of the Structure and Learning Environment". New Orleans: Tulane University School of Social Work, 18-21.

McNeil, John and Litrio, John J. (1981) "Community Service Clinic: A Fieldwork Model at the University of Texas at Arlington", New York: Council on Social Work Education, JOURNAL OF EDUCATION FOR SOCIAL WORK, 17, 1, 111-118.

Proceedings of the National Conference of Charities and Corrections, 33rd Annual Session, (1906).

Raphael, Frances B. and Rosenblum, Amy Frank. (1987) "An Operational Guide to the Faculty Field Liaison Role", SOCIAL CASEWORK, 68, 3, 156-163.

Ward, H., Fletcher, C., Fuzeski, N., and Sayer, A.M. (1984) "Growing Up At Risk in Connecticut", Hartford: The Connecticut Association for Human Services and The Junior League of Hartford.

# EVALUATING A DELAYED ENTRY MODEL OF FIRST YEAR FIELD WORK

Bart Grossman and Richard P. Barth
*University of California at Berkeley*

The role and structure of M.S.W. field instruction has been one of the most discussed and debated curricular topics in schools of social work. Yet, field instruction may also be among the least researched areas of social work education. The extensive bibliography in Sheafor and Jenkins' QUALITY FIELD INSTRUCTION IN SOCIAL WORK EDUCATION (1982), lists only six publications that contain any empirical data. Until recently, only a few additional relevant articles have been published [Abbott (1986); Fortune et al. (1985); Hawthorne & Fleischer (1986); McRoy, Freeman, Logan & Blackmon (1986)]. A positive trend can be seen in the publication of Raskin's (1988) collection of research papers. However, we have identified only one study (Lewis, Howerton, & Kindelsperger (1962) comparing first year field work models: a conventional internship model was compared to an approach in which all students cycled through a similar set of tasks in various agencies. The evaluation showed little difference in outcome between the two designs.

A recent change in the structure of field education in the MSW program at the University of California at Berkeley provided an opportunity to investigate the effect of immediate vs. delayed entry into first year field instruction. Delayed entry into field placement is an often considered but rarely practiced idea. Gordon and Gordon (1982) assert: "If we take seriously the notion of knowing well before doing we would clearly not place students in the field immediately upon entering a professional social work program. We would indeed arm them with some social work knowledge and a social work value stance before sending them out to behave as professionals supposedly guided by professional knowledge and values" (p. 33). Despite this appealing argument, we have found, after discussion with a great many field coordinators and directors throughout the country, few graduate schools of social work that wait more than a week or two to start first year field placement.

In the delayed entry model, academic instruction prepares students to begin practice. This development is consistent with Rothman and Jones' (1971) suggestion that as a profession matures, the theoretical base for practice is increasingly transmitted in the academic rather than the professional arena. A delayed entry approach is also in agreement with Hale's (1969) contention that the role of the agency is to provide work opportunities, while it is the school's responsibility to teach a framework for practice. The ability of agency settings to teach students specific intervention knowledge and skills is the key reason that field work continues to be a major element of the curriculum in graduate schools of social work. Faculty are aware that most students enter school with great interest in practice particulars. They are sometimes concerned that agency placements may reinforce a narrow perspective at a time when students ought to acquire a broad, critical view of the field. The delayed entry model provides time for the transmission of a broad base of social work knowledge and values before students' sights are drawn to a specific professional role. This paper describes a delayed entry model and an analysis of its implementation and effects.

## THE DELAYED ENTRY MODEL

The delayed entry model described in this paper is designed to provide more timely academic preparation for field work. During the first eight weeks of the first semester students receive additional academic preparation prior to agency field practice. This preparation addresses: (1) the acquisition of a social work knowledge base; (2) exposure to the social work value base; (3) the acquisition of entry level practice skills; (4) an understanding of service delivery and policy structure of a particular field of practice (e.g., child welfare services); and (5) an approach to learning from practice. First year students begin their placement in the eighth week of the semester. The academic preparation is provided by organizing introductory courses so as to present an overview of all levels of intervention, the mission and values of the profession, the history and central issues in the development of social welfare and social service policies and institutions, and introductory knowledge about normal and abnormal human development before students begin field work.

In the first week of classes, students also begin a weekly field work seminar. These small seminars, organized by fields of practice (children and families, community mental health, health, and gerontology) introduce students to institutions, practices, and policy issues in each field. Seminar discussion is supplemented with presentations by community practitioners and visits to agencies. Entry level practice skills such as empathic responding are taught in laboratory format. Students prepare for field work in the seminars by identifying their learning goals and discussing the nature of field-based learning.

During the two months before students begin orientation in their assigned agency settings, students meet individually with their seminar leaders to discuss their interests and goals. The seminar leaders are members of the faculty whose primary role is as field work consultants. They establish and maintain relationships with agencies, arrange and oversee placements, and teach other courses in addition to field work seminars. In the traditional model, first year agency assignments are often based on student responses to a questionnaire and brief consultations. Delaying field work permits field consultants to become familiar with their students' strengths and learning needs before the field staff must select placements for them. The consultants view this opportunity as one of the most important positive effects of delayed entry.

These formal structures reinforce the effects of the time delay. Without the pressure for immediate professional performance, students have time to settle into the student role, to become familiar with basic social work knowledge and perspectives, and to become oriented to a field of practice. The field work seminars also become supportive groups in which students can share the stresses of confronting difficult client and organizational realities once field work begins.

During the first few weeks of placement, students receive a broad orientation to the setting, including its mission, policies, practices, and relations with the other agencies and institutions in its task environment. During this period the students share their learning goals (developed in the field work seminar) with their agency field instructors. With the support and direction of the field work consultant, the student and field instructor prepare a written learning agreement that describes the purposes, tasks, and responsibilities of each party in the field learning process. These learning agreements are used in the evaluation of student field performance.

Following the orientation period, first year students continue in placement for two days per week. The field seminar continues as a weekly meeting for the balance of the first semester. In the second semester it becomes a biweekly meeting in which students share, compare, and analyze field experiences. The seminar instructors aid students in examining the relationship between field and classroom learnings in the social work program.

In summary, then, the delayed entry model as contrasted with the traditional immediate entry approach, provides time for a broad introduction to key areas of social work knowledge. The curriculum may be organized to sensitize students to an overview of the profession and field without the pressure of specific application questions arising in agencies. There is also more time to plan and prepare for placement and to support students in their role transitions.

The assumption of increased responsibility by the schools for orienting students to the field is consistent with the reduction, in many agencies, of resources for student training. The more gradual transition to the professional student role in the delayed entry model is particularly appropriate for the increasing numbers of older, reentry students in most graduate schools of social work.

## EVALUATION

The delayed entry model of first year field instruction described in this paper was planned a year before implementation, providing an unusual opportunity to compare the experience of two similar groups of students exposed to different field work patterns within the same institution. Students and agency field work instructors completed questionnaires at the end of field placement. The delayed entry model was assessed in terms of its impact on students' practice experience and preparation, and the satisfaction of agency field instructors and student.

The first questionnaires were mailed to all (105) graduating students, all (100) students completing first year courses under the previous immediate entry model, and all of the field instructors of both groups. A late mail distribution contributed to a low return rate of 24 percent for graduating students. The return rate improved in the following two years (see Table 1). In the third year, first year students completed a pretest in September, permitting comparisons of program outcomes with student expectations.

### Table 1: Questionnaire Return Rates

| | YEAR I | | YEAR II | | YEAR III | | | |
| | Spring | | Spring | | Fall | | Spring | |
| | N | % | N | % | N | % | N | % |
|---|---|---|---|---|---|---|---|---|
| 1st Yr. Students | (40) | 41% | (47) | 53% | (63) | 58% | (65) | 60% |
| 2nd Yr. Students | (24) | 24% | (44) | 45% | | | (60) | 68% |
| 1st Yr. Supervisors | (31) | 34% | (52) | 47% | | | (65) | 81% |
| 2nd Yr. Supervisors | (34) | 40% | (37) | 49% | | | (55) | 55% |

A comparison of age, sex, ethnicity, experience and specialization choices across the three years of the study shows few differences between the cohorts. The cumulative sample was 75 percent female, 25 percent male, 75 percent White, 3 percent Black, 5 percent Latino, 3 percent Asian American, and 3 percent American Indian, and showed a mean age of 28. These findings closely match the total population with the exception that minority percentages in the sample appear higher than in the actual population. This phenomenon occurs because the number of minority students from each group in the total population is very small (about six of each ethnic group per year), magnifying the contribution of each minority member in the context of the sample. The only significant changes were in the characteristics of agency field instructors. Second year instructors were more likely to be from hospitals or mental health settings and there were few child welfare instructors in the second year group. These differences are consistent with the distribution of settings in the field program.

## Preparation

Student preparation for field work was assessed by asking students and their field instructors to rate students' readiness for specific practice tasks at the time they entered the field on a four-point scale from (1) very well prepared to (4) unprepared. The instrument included items about preparation for basic assessment, interviewing, case management, program planning, using of supervision, and engaging agency resources to help clients. Student reports of preparation for these activities were not significantly different in the delayed entry group from the conventional immediate entry group. Only the ability to do research was reported as higher by delayed entry students. (This appears largely attributable to a curriculum change moving the first research course forward into the first year.) Items could be rated "not relevant" if they did not fit the particular student's method of practice. Summary scores were computed by summing student and field instructor responses to each item.

Students and field instructors indicated how prepared students were when they began to deliver services in the agency. According to students and supervisors, first year students showed modest increases in preparation for undertaking program evaluation, research, and tasks related to social agency management. On the summary scores, there were no meaningful differences between years.

Other evidence suggests that students are at least as well prepared to complete agency tasks under the delayed entry model. A dependent t-test shows that students who completed measures before and after their first year reported an increase ($p<.01$) in their preparation to perform field tasks. To assess preparation for the more intensive second year field placement, second year students and second year field instructors were asked about their level of preparation to begin second year placements. They reported somewhat but not significantly higher ($p<.10$) rates of preparation for the delayed entry group.

**Field Tasks**

In any field instruction model there is a predictable delay between the beginning of placement and the time when students become functional members of the agency system. One concern with delayed entry is that such a time lag combined with a late start could mean significant reductions in field tasks in the first year. Although it was clear that delayed entry would mean a reduction in practice experience for first year students, the planners hoped that enhanced on-campus preparation would allow students to become quickly involved in significant practice activities. Students and instructors were, therefore, asked to indicate in what month after they started graduate school students: (1) observed a professional practitioner perform an intervention; (2) began to work with a client or to perform other significant practice tasks; and (3) felt like a contributing member of the agency. yielded only one dimension of satisfaction, therefore the items were also combined into a summary measure, with a respectable Cronbach's alpha of .76.

**Table 2: Commencement of Direct Practice Tasks for First Year Students**

(Months after School Begins)[a]

|  | YEAR I[a] | | YEAR II | | YEAR III | |
|---|---|---|---|---|---|---|
|  | Mean | S.D. | Mean | S.D. | Mean | S.D. |
| Student Report |  |  |  |  |  |  |
| Observe a Professional | 2.40 | 2.46 | 4.27 | 1.64 | 3.59 | 1.77 |
| Significant Work with Client | 2.25 | 1.04 | 5.62 | 1.70 | 4.37 | 1.17 |
| Contribute to Agency | 3.68 | 2.36 | 6.46 | 2.21 | 5.53 | 1.62 |
| Supervisor Report |  |  |  |  |  |  |
| Observe a Professional | 1.79 | 1.13 | 4.13 | 1.68 | 3.42 | 1.70 |
| Significant Work with Client | 4.13 | 1.68 | 5.05 | 1.71 | 4.59 | 1.64 |
| Contribute to Agency | 3.33 | 1.71 | 5.67 | 2.28 | 5.33 | 1.87 |

[a]All 1983 to 1984 to 1985 differences are significant at $p<.01$ level as indicated by overall ANOVA and all 1983 to 1984 comparisons are significant at $p<.01$ and
all 1983 to 1985 comparisons are significant at $p<.05$ level or higher.longer for students in the new

Table 2 shows that significant work with clients and contributing to the agency took longer--about 3 months--to commence in the delayed entry program. Thus, in the first year of operation, the additional 8-weeks of academic preparation did not seem to hasten student's integration into fieldwork.

The second year, following program refinements, shows a lag between beginning graduate school and beginning meaningful fieldwork practice that is slightly shorter (about two months) but still shows that practice tasks were begun significantly later in the school year than before the delayed entry model. It took program to assume significant roles in their agency. Typically, they began these in January rather than November.

### Satisfaction

Student and instructor satisfaction with the several aspects of the field practicum was assessed in terms of their degree of agreement on a four point scale from (1) strongly agree to (4) strongly disagree (see Table 3). The 7-items assessing satisfaction with the field were: (1) I am generally satisfied with the MSW program; (2) I am disappointed with the program; (3) the program was better than I expected; (4) I have been satisfied with my university-based field work consultant; (5) I am satisfied with my university-based field work practicum; and (6) I have been satisfied with my agency field work instructor. A factor analysis using a varimax rotation

---

**Table 3:  Student Satisfaction Item Means and Comparisons**

| Item | YEAR I N=40 Mean | S.D. | YEAR II N=44 Mean | S.D. | YEAR III N=60 Mean | S.D. |
|------|------|------|------|------|------|------|
| 1.  Summary | 2.9 | (.51) | 2.5* | (.82) | 2.8* | (1.3) |
| 2.  General Satisfaction with School | 3.0 | (.66) | 2.4 | (.62) | 2.9* | (1.3) |
| 3.  Disappointment with School | 2.9 | (.91) | 2.2* | (.68) | 2.5* | (.72) |
| 4.  School Better than Expected | 2.3 | (.74) | 1.8* | (.37) | 2.3* | (1.05) |
| 5.  Field Consultant | 2.9 | (.92) | 3.0 | (.77) | 3.0 | (.81) |
| 6.  Field Work Practicum | 3.2 | (.85) | 2.4* | (.97) | 3.0* | (1.06) |
| 7.  Field Work Instructor (Supervisor) | 3.4 | (.85) | 3.1 | (.89) | 3.3 | (.75) |
| 8.  Field-Class Learning Well-Related | 2.8 | (.70) | 2.2* | (.86) | 2.7* | (1.06) |

\* = $p<.01$ for ANOVA comparing YEARS I, II, and III and for Scheffe's test between YEARS II and III.

---

Satisfaction items were compared for the three entering classes. Student satisfaction declined in the first year of the new model compared to the last year of the immediate entry approach. On most measures, however, student response continued to score in the positive direction. Only in the case of "The program was better than I expected" is the mean on the disagree side. In the second year of delayed entry program satisfaction scores rebounded. A two-tailed independent t-test comparing first and third-year scores shows only one significant difference. On the whole, then, students in the second year of implementation were not significantly more likely to express disappointment with the school. Interestingly, students' positive reaction to key figures in field work, the field consultants and field instructors, did not decline in the first year of the new program and remained positive in the third year.

A backdrop to these findings comes from a comparison of second-year satisfaction scores for two cohorts of students who had immediate entry into field placement--that is, between the first-year cohort and students who entered in the prior year. Although both of these groups experienced the same immediate entry field work program, the latter group was somewhat more satisfied on items 3, 4, 7, and 8 (p<.05). The finding that the comparison immediate entry group was more satisfied than the previous year's cohort is somewhat surprising, as the faculty had believed that these students might be neglected in the transition period. In any case the comparison between this very satisfied immediate entry group and the first year of the new program may exaggerate the appearance of differences between programs.

There was an expectation of some negative reaction in the first year. A survey conducted a year prior to implementation in 33 so-called core agencies found that 26 would not accept the notion of delayed entry. The model advanced at that time, however, would have reduced first year field work to one semester of two days a week, significantly less than the schedule finally adopted by the school. Also, the "core" agencies included many that had not taken first year students in the then existing field work system. The reactions of field instructors were not greatly different under the two models (Table 4), except that somewhat less satisfaction with field arrangements was expressed in the first year of implementing the delayed entry model. This level of satisfaction also rebounded in the second year.

#### Table 4: Field Instructor Satisfaction Item Means

| Item | YEAR I N=32 Mean | S.D. | YEAR II N=55 Mean | S.D. | YEAR III N=65[a] Mean | S.D. |
|---|---|---|---|---|---|---|
| 1. Summary | 3.6 | (.47) | 3.4 | (.38) | 3.7 | (.77) |
| 2. General Satisfaction | 3.7 | (.54) | 3.5 | (.54) | 3.8 | (.81) |
| 3. Field Arrangements[a] | 3.4 | (.62) | 2.9* | (.52) | 3.4 | (1.19) |
| 4. Student Caliber | 3.6 | (.62) | 3.6 | (.57) | 3.8 | (1.06) |
| 5. Current Students | 3.7 | (.47) | 3.5 | (.63) | 3.7 | (.82) |
| 6. Field Consultant | 3.6 | (.57) | 3.4 | (.54) | 3.7 | (.85) |

[a]ANOVA comparing YEARS I, II and III and contrast between YEAR II and YEAR I and and YEAR III are significant at p<.01 on Scheffe's test.

## CONCLUSIONS

The limitations of the research design and data collection strategy demand acknowledgement. The sample was not large or random. Return rates were modest and the field instructors were not a constant group across the years. Because of the rather unique field work model under study, the generalization of results to other schools cannot be assumed. The data are, at best, suggestive and must be interpreted with the crude research design in mind. Finally, we did not measure student performance in the field or after graduation. Supervisor reports of preparation and student reports of satisfaction and accomplishment of field work tasks served as analogues for performance with clients. This is in keeping with much educational research, but certainly not ideal. Still, the available evidence provides more information about the delayed entry model than was heretofore available.

For now, we can say that the advantages of the delayed entry model are not so much in skill preparation as in providing students with an overarching perspective about the social welfare system and the complex service delivery systems (e.g., child welfare or community mental health) in which student's agencies and offices are embedded before they begin field practice. Of course, it is hoped that such a preparation will create more effective, flexible practitioners in the long run.

While it is too early to view the delayed entry model as a great success, it has certainly avoided the severe negative results predicted for it. Forecasts that student learning would be drastically damaged and that agencies would withdraw their placements in droves were unfounded. Neither of these predicted outcomes has occurred. The reasonably affirmative outcomes suggest that other schools can explore adaptations of the delayed entry given their local culture and program goals.

Although we did not thoroughly assess changes in student knowledge and understanding of the broader social welfare mission, we believe that the additional academic preparation boosted students' knowledge and broadened their conception of the field. Our data do indicate that students are reasonably satisfied with the model and seem, in the view of second year field instructors, to be at least as adequately prepared for second year placements as they were under the prior program and a bit stronger in the area of research and evaluation.

The delay in beginning field tasks has been a concern, however, because it results in fewer case contacts by direct practice students in the first year and delayed participation in other significant agency experiences. Our impression is that our faculty has achieved its goal of a more significant role in orientation for professional practice; moreover, students now have a view of the field and the profession that better reflects a range of practice roles. The cost has been a smaller number of opportunities to apply this knowledge in first year field instruction. In a time when the professional identity and commitment of social workers in many fields has become indistinct, blurring into an amorphous collection of human services workers and psychotherapists, attempts by social work faculty to help students develop a clearer view of the profession seems especially worthwhile.

Whereas the impact of delayed entry on agency relations has not been as negative as some had feared, there have been some problems. Difficulties with the delayed entry model has been cited by approximately 20 agencies that have withdrawn from first year field instruction in the last three years. It is not possible to separate the contribution of delayed entry from other factors affecting agency involvement in field instruction including budget reductions, the increasing severity of client problems, competition by other pre-professional and post-graduate interns, and reduced agency commitments to training.

Agencies that have students from other schools and disciplines have difficulty adding students who start later than the agencies' accustomed orientation time. Some agencies feel that the first year placement is too short to justify their investment in supervision. The losses in some fields (especially among private, nonprofit agencies) have been balanced by increased placement in public sector and contract agencies as our school implements a  mission of preparation for public service social work. Maintaining good first year settings is a continual difficulty that seems not to be lessening with time. We cannot tell how much the delayed entry model aggravates this problem, but we suspect that it does.

In agencies that accept first year students the challenge is to ensure that a rich experience is provided despite the shortened time.  One consequence of late or limited assignment is that students may be disadvantaged in seeking second year placements, since most local agencies insist on pre-placement interviews.  In many agencies, social work students compete for placement with other graduate and post-graduate internship candidates.  Although the evaluation findings show that field instructors were satisfied with the preparation of students when second year field work began, interviews for second year placements have occurred at a time when some first year students had just begun significant first year field tasks.  The shortened first year was cited by some agencies as a reason for rejecting students who appeared inexperienced when interviewed.

The original delayed entry model provided four weeks of one day per week orientation before students began two days per week of placement.  This design has been modified so that students now begin at the same time, but are placed two days a week from the start.  While this change has not been formally evaluated, preliminary reports suggest that it has further reduced the start up lag cited above.

For the present, the supply of quality placements is adequate for first year and ample for second year students.  The transition to delayed entry has been achieved without dire consequences.  Problems in implementing this, or any other field work model, are inevitable given the field practicum's position as the focal point at which educational goals and practice realities converge.  As the model undergoes refinement the school will continue to learn more about how to balance its educational responsibilities with student and agency needs and perspectives. Social work educators must balance between preparing students to fulfill existing practice roles that are shaped and shared by professionals from other disciplines and preparing students with a unique attachment and commitment to social work and social welfare. Delayed entry models offer a strategy for increasing the chance that students will understand the contribution that their practice, the agency, and the service system make to shaping the future of service programs, local and national policies, and the profession.

## BIBLIOGRAPHY

Abbott, A. A. (1986)  The field placement contract:  Its use in maintaining comparability between employment-related and traditional field placements. JOURNAL OF SOCIAL WORK EDUCATION, 22(1), 57-66.

Barth, R. P. & Gambrill, E. D. (1984) Learning to interview: The quality of training opportunities. THE CLINICAL SUPERVISOR, 2(1), 3-14.

Fortune, A. E., Feathus, C. E., Rook, S. R., Scrimenti, R. M., Smollen, P., Stemerman, B., & Tucker, E. L. (1985) Student satisfaction with field placement. JOURNAL OF SOCIAL WORK EDUCATION, 21(3), 92-104.

Gordon, W. E. & Gordon, M. S. (1982) The role of frames of reference in field instruction. In B. W. Sheafor and L. E. Jenkins (Eds.), QUALITY FIELD INSTRUCTION IN SOCIAL WORK. New York: Longman.

Grossman, B. (1987) Themes and variations: The political economy of field instruction. Plenary paper presented at the Field Work Symposium. Council on Social Work Education. Annual Program Meeting. March 1987. St. Louis, Missouri.

Hale, M. P. (1969) Curriculum models for social work education. In MODES OF PROFESSIONAL EDUCATION: FUNCTIONS OF FIELD LEARNING IN THE CURRICULUM, Tulane Studies in Social Welfare, Vol. 11, New Orleans: School of Social Work, Tulane University, 211-227.

Hawthorne, L., & Fleisher, D. (1986) A new look at laboratory training in first year field education. ARETE, 11(1), 44-53.

Lewis, M., Howerton, D., & Kindelsperger, W. (1962) AN EXPERIMENTAL DESIGN FOR FIRST YEAR FIELD INSTRUCTION, Tulane Studies in Social Welfare, Vol. 4, New Orleans: School of Social Work, Tulane University.

McRoy, R. G., Freeman, E. M., Logan, S. L., & Blackmon, B. (1986) Cross-cultural field supervision: Implications for social work education. JOURNAL OF SOCIAL WORK EDUCATION, 22(1), 50-56.

Raskin, Miriam, (ed.) (1988) EMPIRICAL STUDIES IN FIELD INSTRUCTION. Special double issue of THE CLINICAL SOCIAL WORKER, 6(3/4).

Rothman, J. & Jones, W. (1971) A NEW LOOK AT FIELD INSTRUCTION. New York: Association Press.

Sheafor, B. W. & Jenkins, L. E. (Eds.) (1982) QUALITY FIELD INSTRUCTION IN SOCIAL WORK. New York: Longman.

# A MODEL FOR GROUP SUPERVISION FOR SOCIAL WORK: IMPLICATIONS FOR THE PROFESSION

Theadora Kaplan, *Adelphi University*

This paper consists of three distinct, yet interrelated parts: concepts of individual and group supervision, social groupwork theory that informs the model and clinical illustrations that highlight specific concepts. The model presented is an outgrowth of a pilot project in group supervision of students at a university-based, multi-service social agency on Long Island, New York. A short description of the composition of the group is provided below and should serve as a springboard for the discussion as well as to ground the concepts of the model in practice.

Four female students, two first-year and two second year, were involved. Lynn, age 40, held a doctorate in a related field, was a first-time parent and worked as a high school teacher. Kelly, 32, a rehabilitation counselor in a hospital, was proficient in conducting groups with chronic patients. The first-year students were Helen, 53, who held an administrative position in a high school and Haylee, 28, who was doing personnel work. The group started in summer session and continued through to the end of the academic year. Because of their job commitments, all four students needed special hours for placement and field instruction. Their selection for the group served: 1) to accommodate their hours and 2) to provide an anchor and connection for them, since their part-time attendance left little time for interaction with fellow students and faculty or for socialization to the profession.

## HISTORICAL PERSPECTIVES

Evolving on the heels of the individual case method at the turn of the century (Munson, 1979; Getzel and Salmon, 1985), the tutorial focus in supervision, influenced by psychoanalytic theory, obtained through the forties. Relations between the social worker and supervisor often paralleled worker-client relationships; it was believed that the insights produced through addressing issues of transference and defenses produced competent practitioners. A shift in emphasis occurred in the late fifties and sixties when institutional, methodological, psychological and educational components of supervision were delineated (Berl, 1960). Concurrently, an interesting discussion ensued.

The Census Bureau questioned the professional status of social work, indicating that practitioners appeared never to be fully responsible for their practice (Kadushin, 1976, Salmon and Getzel, 1985). Leader (1957) discussed issues of dependency and the seeming endlessness of supervision and suggested, along with others, a three to six-year time limit. The reality that experienced social workers tended to utilize supervision for administrative purposes rather than to enhance their clinical acumen led to the proposal that dual supervision, i.e., administrative and clinical, be employed (Getzel and Salmon, 1985).

While group supervision was not defined as another form of supervision until the late 1950s when the advent of peer supervision was discussed by Fizdale (1956), Brackett, in 1902, offered a rudimentary definition as he talked of "a study group of six or less persons whose similarity of experience and educational background could engage with one another for the purpose of helping persons in distress" (Munson, p.14). Zelpha Smith made an effort to describe goals and Mary Richmond (1917) emphasized learning through engaging in discussion groups and attendance at conferences.

Fizdale (1958) helped to crystallize the idea as she asserted, in her paper on peer supervision, that more important than deciding whether or not peer group supervision falls within the definition of supervision is whether the peer group supervision process can enable workers to grow professionally and  become increasingly more productive. She further noted that there might be specific merit in this process and method that is not available through the tutorial model.

The seventies brought the notion of group supervision into even greater focus. It was viewed as useful in promoting opportunities for problem-solving, to generalize learning experiences, to deepen identification with the profession and to minimize issues to power and hierarchical status. It was perceived also as an educative system, a mutual aid system and a process and method in which the supervisor is helped to formulate his or her own tasks and responsibilities (Abels, 1970; Young, 1971). The issue of oversupervision and its corollary, the viability of autonomous practice was discussed. Epstein (1973) bemoaned, however, the lack of specific models to operationalize the method.

Discussion of disadvantages included concerns that competition between workers might arise, that new arrivals in already established groups would encounter difficulties, that discomfort around risk of practice and discussion of personally sensitive material would pose issues in resistance and that individuals could abdicate personal responsibility for decisions. In addition, the greater numbers would suggest that the group setting would allow for numerous sources of critical feedback, a situation that could be difficult for some individuals. Last, but not least, it was noted that in utilizing this format, the supervisor runs a greater risk of threat to his or her own self-esteem due to exposure of ineptitudes (Kadushin, 1976).

Kadushin (1976) offered his framework for group supervision, but since he perceived no clear advantages, he advocated for coexistence of individual and group in a planned, complementary program. Concurrently, however, he cited the 1970 research efforts of Sales and Navarre and those of Lanning in 1971. Their studies suggest that the individual method was not significantly different from the group method and that very similar outcomes were produced. Empirical work in the area is indeed, sparse. (One model, developed by the Wel-Met Camps and operationalized in 1967, is offered for consideration by Getzel, Goldberg and Salmon, 1971).

The theoretical underpinnings for group supervision stem from social groupwork theory. The concept of mutual aid (Shulman, 1982), i.e., that the sharing of data, the availability of lateral help, providing the arena in which sensitive issues may be raised, the support afforded through the awareness that members share similar concerns and the overall emotional support provided all auger well for use of this modality. Papell and Rothman (1980) highlight the central identity that emerges from the interplay of the group, the member in the group, the activities of the group and the worker with the group. In this interplay of mutuality of goals, mutual and real experiences are stressed as is the concept of externality, expanded to include the idea of the value of the group in its continued applicability of group experiences beyond the actual boundaries of the group experience.

Reid and Epstein (1972) and Fortune (1985) add the view that the focus on problem-solving inherent in task-centered groups fosters collaborative spirit and advocates the use of other systems to assist in the completion of tasks. Schwartz (1971) notion that group members are "concerned with their internal relationships . . . the interplay of . . . external authority and mutual interdependence" (p.9), is relevant. He follows by stating that this characterizes the manner in which individuals function in a group, that themes of authority and intimacy are played out and that the involvement mobilizes the human association and mutual aid component of the group process which, in turn, promotes growth of both the investment of group members in one another and in the learning process.

The concepts cited are intimately related to group supervision, for, as a group, supervisor and supervisees engage in mutual problem-solving, are involved in and concerned with their internal relationships, can work out issues of intimacy and risk and can, through the investment of group members in one another and in the process, grow both personally and educationally. Furthermore, the experiences and discussions can be internalized or, at least remembered and considered for later use.

## PRELIMINARY CONSIDERATIONS

Essential to the implementation of a model for group supervision is the enthusiastic sanctioning of the project by the agency involved. Concurrence between administrative and supervisory personnel does not suffice. Line staff and students must be apprised of the rationale and time must be allotted for discussion of inherent benefits and limitations. Additionally, a time lapse should be built in to permit the informal network to have opportunities to discuss the impending change in order to mediate the possibility that group supervision will be attributed only to cost-effectiveness; without this, a sense of deprivation and concurrent anger could become pervasive and subsequently counterproductive.

Of particular relevance is the selection of the supervisor; a respected member of the staff, one whose administrative, teaching and clinical skills are savored and sought, should be considered. When students are involved, it must be understood that their concerns about the cost of education are often coupled with feelings about getting their moneys' worth in various facets of the process. They feel easily short-changed or cheated, and being placed in a situation where they might consider themselves less fortunate that those receiving individual supervision can result in a less than optimal learning environment.

Equally important is the beginning phase of the group, for although task-centered, the supervision group is a group like any other in the sense that it needs to be nurtured in its development and that the phases of group development may be expected to emerge. (The Garland, Jones and Kolodny (1976) model of group development is seen by this author as relevant.) Pre-group preparation, both in physical and conceptual terms, is important. The model offered below was developed from the experiences derived from working with the students cited earlier. It was utilized as the primary method of field instruction with individual consultations available on an as-needed, emergency basis when client problems of a serious nature appeared emergent.

## THE MODEL

### Time, Setting and Participants
1. Four students, one field instructor.
2. Two-hour time framework, weekly.
3. Private room, not too large.
4. Regularly scheduled specific day and time.
5. Punctuality.

### Objectives and Practice Principles
1. Primary objective: education of students.
2. Secondary objective: better and more efficient services to clients.
3. Focus: the work as it pertains also to education administrative issues, accountability and the transmission of the agency mandate.
4. This is a structured, task-centered group with mutuality indicated by common concerns (agency and studentship) rather than by educational level and/or experience.
5. The sharing of experiences makes for generation of ideas and enriches sources for learning.
6. There is opportunity for lateral as well as hierarchical teaching.
7. Participation is promoted through the potential for allies within the peer grou
8. Viewing the work of others enhances reality testing.
9. The development of group norms and group cohesion encourages a professional identity.
10. Self-confidence, mutual respect and greater independence are fostered through the utilization of the specialized knowledge of participants.
11. The field instructor shares responsibility for teaching.
12. The field instructor shares power.
13. The field instructor can observe students' inter-actions and use of self.

### Techniques
Specificity is needed to ensure success. Throughout the first three sessions the field instructor must attend to the comfort of participants and provide clarity regarding what will transpire in relation to purpose, expectations and process. For this reason, the following specifics are offered.
1. Elicit level, experience, reasons for pursuing social work education and any personal information willingly shared by participants.
2. Clearly identify the purpose of the group. Stress structure and task.
3. Encourage discussion of students' expectations about what might occur in the experience.
4. Provide guidelines for oral and written requirments, i.e., case presentations, process records, active involvement in discussions and role-play.

5. Introduce the concept of mutual aid as well as accountability for agency reports and statistics.
6. Allocate specific time for dissemination of administrative information and discussion of specific individual problems or concerns.
7. Stress the transferability of knowledge by using practice situations presented by students or by offering personal illustrations.
8. Be open. Model a "real" practitioner, one who seeks knowledge and growth, one who is clearly identified with the profession. If the field instructor can present him or herself as a sometimes fallible human being, students will appreciate him or her as a person and will be better able to "risk" with field instructor and peers.
9. Introduce the subject of evaluation by the third session. It can be done as a group or with individuals. Clarify expectations for various levels of education and competency. Share school norms. Sharing will serve to reduce anxiety levels. Do acknowledge that students are anxious about the impending experience of being evaluated and indicate that the process is really ongoing.
10. Address each student during each session. Inquire about individual learning needs.
11. Give positive as well as carefully couched negative feedback. Always clarify purpose: learning and professional growth, particularly when students are feeling inept in relation to the complexity of the work. End sessions on a positive note.
12. Foster conceptualization from themes and techniques; encourage continual connection between theory and practice and between classroom learning and practical applications
13. End sessions on time. Student anxiety combined with the intensity of the learning experience must be curtailed before a saturation point is reached and before concerns about "getting more field instructor time" lengthens sessions and results in "private" time due to uneven endings.

The rudiments offered above were derived from the efforts of the authors cited earlier and the personal experience in the demonstration project conducted by this writer. At this time some highlights of the experience, the problems as well as elevating moments that occurred will be presented. Without these, the principles outlined above could not have been offered.

The group began with three students; a fourth was added three months later. Each approached the situation characteristically. Lynn, the most experienced, was the first to offer her work. Focus on client productions lessened anxiety and served to foster a more relaxed atmosphere for sharing. Helen, the only first-year student in the group at the time, was less open. When engaged around her thoughts about the group field instruction, she reserved her opinion, noting that this was a first for her and that she had nothing to use for comparison purposes. Kelly, an experienced practitioner, immediately allied herself with the field instructor, began commenting on alternative interventions by the second session and became a catalyst. Role-playing was facilitated when the field instructor undertook the role of worker and students were encouraged to "play" their clients. Questions about field instructor competency and willingness to share practice wisdom seemed satisfied and a commitment to learning became normative.

Approximately four weeks elapsed when students began to express a need for "closer" supervision and requested written comments on the process records that were not dealt with in the sessions. In an attempt to ameliorate their anxiety and provide some additional input, the request was granted, comments were provided for two weeks and then the group exploded. Kelly lashed out about field instructor insensitivity, the others complained about the number of comments and the color of the ink. Discussion ensued. It was agreed that process would still be required, comments would be kept to a minimum in the future, students would arrive on time and would take responsibility for introducing issues and cases as needed. Other discussions would be curtailed to accommodate emergencies. It was further determined that the field instructor retains responsibility for professional judgement and may curtail or postpone discussions; questions related to such decisions would be addressed at a future time and could be initiated by anyone. No further struggles of this nature occurred.

In September, Haylee joined the group. A pre-group interview was used to describe the situation and address some of her anxiety. She presented as quiet, almost withdrawn. "Be kind to me," she said, and the group appeared to understand her comment clearly. The following week she appeared with a bag of candy that she shared. (She continued to do this throughout the year.) In spite of her efforts, she was experienced as an intruder and a two-week regressive period occurred. The others took less risks and awaited more field instructor input. The intimacy that had begun to take hold was put on hold.

A second phenomenon occurred simultaneously. The other first-year student, Helen, requested individual supervision since the other students in the agency had it and she felt she "wasn't getting enough". When field instructor and students discussed the advantages of group, particularly the broadening aspects, Helen retreated. When asked if she felt cheated of her due, she declined comment, but shrugged her shoulders.

Kelly continued to be open with her practice and feelings; Lynn's seeming expertise was tempered by her acknowledgement of the urgency with which she tried to extract movement from clients, and her ability to act on suggestions provided, together with Kelly's inordinate openness, a lovely ambience for the process. The students became a cohesive group that relied on one another between sessions and kept in touch outside of field placement hours.

Helen's anxieties and neediness were felt as she stayed behind after sessions to address additional concerns. When assigned a women's group of overeaters, she informed the group that she was a compulsive overeater. Kelly shared her inclination to merge with clients and told of her efforts to maintain her psychological integrity, Lynn told of her concern about her husband's serious illness and Haylee shared that the personnel work she had said she was involved in was in fact, something quite different. She was a barmaid and was considered by her co-workers as their resident "shrink". Helen again requested individual supervision, was seen once by the associate director of the agency and when time conflicts ensued, gave up her quest and settled down in the group rather than lose the connection with her peers.

The project was scheduled to end in June. Concerns about the next year, or next milestone for those who were graduating, were addressed. Lynn called several times to ask for employment leads. Kelly, embroiled in concerns about transferring her clients, continued to call throughout the summer months. Helen joined a group field instruction for the summer and Haylee terminated easily after noting that she'd be returning for her second year. Six weeks after termination open-ended question- naires were completed by the students. They suggested a three-hour format with students all at one level. One student stated that only second year students should be in group supervision. However, they highlighted the intimacy and connection they had established with peers and school and the rich learning experience in which they had participated.

## IMPLICATIONS AND CONCLUSIONS

Group field instruction is a powerful and inclusive experience, an interlocking process, one in which supervisor, student, function, role and process are equally weighted. The key is balance and the result, the generation of more ideas, a richer source for learning and a more expanded viewpoint. Anxiety related to risk of self exposure and practice competence can be addressed. Reality testing is enhanced through the opportunity to view the work of others and make comparisons with ones own work.

Responsibility for teaching and learning is accepted. Safety in numbers mediates the conflict of closeness and distance, anxiety is diminished and growth is fostered as personal issues are examined in light of their impediments to client progress. Differences are respected and greater tolerance, encouraged.

Currently, agencies and schools of social work are wedded to the tutorial model with group supervision used as an ancillary method, if it is used at all. Schools of social work, when hard-pressed for placement for undergraduate students, sometimes consent to having them supervised in groups. The looseness with which the modality is used, i.e., without instruction and/or the opportunity for field instructors to refer to a model for guidance, is of concern. Professional educators and interested individuals from the practice community must combined forces in an effort to provide leadership in this area. Efforts must be made to ascertain the degree to which groups are used, information must be disseminated, curriculum development must be undertaken and research projects designed.

The advantages of group supervision and field instruction appear to outweigh disadvantages. Economics cannot be ignored since the cost of individual supervision of agency staff and field instructors is considerable. However, of utmost importance is the need to provide premium educational experiences for students as well as for agency staff. The dearth of exceptionally talented supervisors is often of concern to educators and agency personnel. Group supervision, when possible, could ensure a more even experience in that more students and/or workers could be exposed to well-qualified, knowledgeable supervisors. Training for the profession could take on new meaning and have greater impact on the professional community, students and service delivery.

Additional implications obtain in relation to student learning. Today's students often request a greater voice in the educational process. Within the context of the group, the process takes on particular significance in that it provides a model for action and for the acceptance of responsibility for learning. It gives credence to and illustrates the power of numbers, demands that people help one another and creates the ambience through which an in-vivo example of purposeful cooperation can promote understanding of the value of difference while increasing competence. The initial investment of time and resources needed to generate interest and launch the practice of group supervision seems well worth the effort.

## BIBLIOGRAPHY

Abels, P. (1970) "On the Nature of Supervision: The Medium is the Group." in Munson, C. (ed) (1979) SOCIAL WORK SUPERVISION. New York: The Free Press, 133-142.

Abels, P. (1978) "Group Supervision of Students and Staff" in Kaslow, F. (ed) (1978) SUPERVISION, CONSULTATION AND STAFF TRAINING IN THE HELPING PROFESSIONS. San Francisco: Jossey-Bass, 176.

Brackett, J. (1903) "Training for Work" in Munson, op.cit, 6-17.

Epstein, L. (1980) THE TASK-CENTERED APPROACH. St. Louis: C.V. Mosby.

Fortune, A. (1985) TASK-CENTERED PRACTICE WITH FAMILIES AND GROUPS. New York: Springer.

Getzel B. Goldberg, J. and Salmon, R. (1971) "Supervising in Groups as a Model for Today." SOCIAL CASEWORK. New York: Family Service, 154-163.

Kadushin, A. (1976) SUPERVISION IN SOCIAL WORK. New York: Columbia University Press.

Papell, C. and Rothman, B. (1980) "Relating the Mainstream Model of Social Work with Groups to Group Psychotherapy and the Structured Group Approach. SOCIAL WORK WITH GROUPS. 3, New York: Haworth.

Reid, W., and Epstein, L (1978) THE TASK-CENTERED SYSTEM. New York: Columbia University Press.

Richmond, M. (1965) SOCIAL DIAGNOSIS. New York: The Free Press.

Schwartz, W. (1976) Between Client and System: A Mediating Function. in Roberts, R., and Northern, H. (Eds). THEORIES OF SOCIAL WORK WITH GROUPS. New York: Columbia University Press, 171-197.

# THE PRACTICE RESEARCH CENTER: A FIELD/CLASS MODEL TO TEACH RESEARCH, PRACTICE AND VALUES

Ami Gantt, *Mt. Sinai Medical Center*
Sidney Pinsky, *Long Island Jewish Medical Center*
Ellen Rosenberg, *Adelphi University*
Barry Rock, *Long Island Jewish Medical Center*

A School of Social Work and the Department of Social Work Services at a large urban medical center have organized a Center for Social Work Practice Research.

The objective of the program is to stimulate research among students, faculty and hospital staff by increasing necessary skills, promoting interest through exposure to actual and potential projects, and providing opportunities for research through a combination of integrative teaching and the provision of a field laboratory setting.

By pooling the resources of both the School of Social Work and the Department of Social Work, it was expected that social work students and practitioners would be better able to critically evaluate theory and empirical data and develop the skills and attitudes necessary for evaluating one's own practice.

In addition to encouraging this way of thinking among students and staff, The Practice Research Center has developed more generalized "applied" studies based on aggregate data in areas vital to the operation of social work programs; i.e., needs assessments, program evaluation, client surveys and proposal development. Rather than imposing research agendas, The Practice Research Center raises research questions which flow out of the needs of the various settings; the Center provides service to its "clients". The questions are often of a social problem nature and lead to social action, as will be seen especially in the studies of hunger described below. The structure and mission of the Center make its sponsorship by social work administration most appealing.

Conducting research in such diversified settings (an entire medical center including a municipal hospital, a private psychiatric hospital, and three different units of a regional children's hospital) called for knowledge of both the structures of the institutions and content in the practice area to be studied. Working closely with hospital staff, under research faculty supervision, students were able to learn in all three domains -- i.e., organization, clinical and research, -- and become acquainted with the interactional nature of all three. A description of the process involved in two of these studies will illustrate this.

Twenty first- year graduate students assigned to The Practice Research Center were offered two courses on the hospital campus (taught by faculty) and concurrently offered field work assignments - clinical and research practicums. In their clinical field work assignments students were supervised by social work staff, while the classroom research instructor served as the field instructor for the field research assignment. This had several purposes and consequences. Perhaps the most important of these was the facilitation of communication between the School and the Medical Center. This occurred in many ways. For example, there were monthly Advisory Board Meetings, at which Educational Coordinators from the Medical

Center, School Faculty Advisors, the Director of Field Work and the two classroom instructors met to discuss both student performance and potential projects. There were also meetings at which field instructors met with the classroom teachers to discuss students, and with the research teacher to learn about The Practice Research Center. Thus, participants shared information with each other, so the wide range of issues, settings and research approaches was available to all through on site integration of practice and research courses and joint involvement of classroom and field faculty. Through these and a variety of other contacts, mutual trust, knowledge and understanding were promoted. Although time-consuming, the high level of comfort in working together that was achieved was necessary for the success of the undertaking. The faculty and hospital staff's commitment to the Center was tested early (and frequently) by students, whose anxiety and anger about the expectation that they be involved in research in the field was voiced loudly, and in unison. In the long run, the solidarity of the student group became one of the Center's real strengths.

The structure, activities and focus of The Practice Research Center have been used to convey to social work graduate students a value orientation and a conception of social work's role in society. Dilemmas and challenges facing the profession are identified for students as such. The Center, as a joint endeavor of a large medical complex and a school of social work, enables students, staff and faculty to share responsibility for the selection and implementation of research projects deemed necessary to accomplish social work tasks and fulfill a professional mission. Thus, the process of value orientation begins with the nature of the topics suggested by staff, affirmed by faculty and chosen by students as worthy of study. So, for example, studies undertaken in support of social work's commitment to meeting the social needs of the disadvantaged have included documenting the extent of hunger among patients served by a municipal hospital and a study of the impact of respite care for Alzheimer's patients upon the family members or caregivers.

The process of conducting research also serves to raise students' consciousness. They begin with the issue of informed consent and review by "Rights of Human Subjects" committees, learning of client/subject protections now in place and the past and potential abuses (particularly among the poor) that make these essential. They go on to a focused literature review in content areas such as hunger and the use of psychoeducation with the families of schizophrenics; thereby, becoming familiar with facts and issues in these areas.

Finally, findings are considered in terms of implications for practice, which might include social action, a change in interventive strategies with clients, and/or workers' use of self. Thus, students are taught the value of an empirically based, self-monitoring practice to fulfill social work goals.

## Two Projects

As noted earlier, topics are chosen through a collaborative effort on the part of agency personnel, students and faculty. Most frequently, staff initiates proposals, and those deemed educationally appropriate by faculty are then considered by students, who are given latitude in making their choices. It clearly reflects the shared value orientation of all these groups that an ongoing project for three cohorts of students has been the Hunger Survey. Concern for meeting the needs of the disadvantaged continues to be a social work priority--and students in The Practice Research Center have been able to relate to this value very well.

**Hunger Survey**

For several years now, the Social Services staff at the municipal hospital complex has been concerned about the impact of the reduction of Federal and local funds for health and welfare and the concomitant increase in homelessness on the ability of their patients to obtain food. Therefore, students and faculty of The Practice Research Center were enlisted by the Social Services Department to provide both research expertise and person-power to ascertain the nature and extent of the problem. Working closely with staff and faculty, students devised a study plan and a questionnaire which they administered, along with staff, in a one-day survey conducted in December, 1985.

The degree of cooperation, commitment and enthusiasm of all participants can only be conveyed by the positive reactions to the many small crises that assailed the project. These included the need for an "emergency" pick-up of forms; several situations which required last-minute typing and reproduction of materials; problems with the planned data analysis; and the need for full participation in data collection on all services while conducting "business as usual". **Someone** always came through--sometimes hospital staff, sometimes students and sometimes faculty--because the study was considered to be important enough to warrant the extra effort. For many students, this project was their first exposure to poverty, hunger and homelessness, and they reported that they learned a good deal more than research methodology.

Results of the 1985 survey, based on data from 383 subjects, indicated that almost one quarter (22 percent) of the sample was, in fact, experiencing hunger. Findings also indicated that 8 percent of the respondents were homeless, while more than 25 percent had experienced a reduction in, or cessation of, food stamps or other government assistance.

An update in information was sought in February, 1989, when a second one-day survey was conducted. Three hundred and thirty-two subjects participated. Again, almost one-quarter (23 percent) reported the experience of being hungry and unable to obtain food. The major change evident was in the percentage reporting that they were dependent on **institutional** settings for food (that is, 18 percent depending on meals on wheels, compared to 3.5 percent in 1985; and 13 percent depending on soup kitchens--up from 4.5 percent in 1985). In 1985, 13.4 percent of respondents depended on relatives for food. In 1989, this rose to 17 percent.

Demographically, the 1989 sample was slightly younger than the 1985 sample, with a slightly higher income and cost of housing. Reported number of persons in the household was higher, while the percentage of homeless or those living in hotels or shelters was somewhat reduced (from 3.5 percent living in a hotel or shelter in 1985 to 2 percent in 1989; from 7.9 percent homeless in 1985 to 6.9 percent homeless in 1989).

Data from this study is still in the process of being analyzed. Students have suggested ongoing updates. As a result of this first survey, steps were taken that included obtaining food vouchers for patients' use in the hospital cafeteria, and compiling local resources for food, with appropriate referrals, (which may account for the increased use of institutional settings among those surveyed). More wide-ranging social action, perhaps in conjunction with other groups, is contemplated, using the documentation of need provided by the second survey.

**Interpersonal Moral Choices**

Social work's concern with youth (which may be viewed as an "at risk" group), with human growth and development, with current social issues, and with values--all led to this second project which focused on the development of an interpersonal moral choice questionnaire to range adolescents along an egoism-altruism continuum. In recent years, there has been growing concern with morality, especially as it is developed in the young.

As William Damon notes in his book, **The Moral Child** (1988), "children's morality is no longer simply a question of conduct in the home and corner play-ground.... It is the focus of public scrutiny and debate, a recognized societal problem of the first magnitude." He relates this concern to events ranging from scandals involving prominent public figures (which raises questions about the moral education of our youth) to health and welfare dangers, to the children themselves (which stem from sources such as AIDS, teen pregnancy, substance abuse and the violence of peers). Morality is seen developmentally as arising out of social relationships. Such choices were also seen as highly relevant for adolescents, in terms of the importance of the peer group. Thus, the study also focused, as do more recent works on moral development in general, on "practical moral decision making" (Keller, 1984, p. 141) as opposed to the focus on the more abstract moral judgments that characterized the earlier works on this topic.

As in the Hunger Survey, students were responsible for a literature review, instrument construction, and administration of the questionnaire (in this case, for pilot testing).

The first draft questionnaire consisted of fifteen questions such as "You and your friend are competing for the lead role in the school play. You find out that auditions have changed to the fifth period. What would you do?"

A) Make an effort to find your friend and tell him/her.
B) If you happen to see your friend, tell him/her.
C) Do not mention it to your friend if you see him/her.

Scores were assigned to each answer from "1" for an altruistic choice to "3" for an egoistic choice, and the instrument administered twice to 52 high schoolers. Good reliability was obtained.

The researchers are in the process of obtaining additional data on the ques-tionnaire by re-administering it along with a **Self-Concept Scale** and an **Empathy Scale** to a new group of adolescents. In this way, information on the reliability and validity of the questionnaire will be obtained while looking at possible correlates of interpersonal choices. For example, one research question is whether a good self-concept is associated with more altruistic choices. The variable of self-concept has been found to increase "invulnerability" or "invincibility" among children exposed to stress--perhaps it is the wellspring of other positive outcomes. Thus far, this does not seem to be the case. In fact, preliminary (or perhaps we should call them exploratory) findings, based on only 16 male subjects (as measured by the **Piers-Harris Self-Concept Scale**) indicate that self-concept is negatively correlated with both empathy and interpersonal morality scores. In fact, the second draft of The Moral Choice questionnaire had a statistically significant (p=.05) correlation of -.48 with self-concept scores.

Empathy, defined as the "recognition of another's feeling... (and) the sharing of these feelings, at least at the gross affect level", was measured using the Mehrabian and Epstein (1972) Emotional Empathy Scale. Empathy was, as predicted, positively correlated with morality scores (.44), but not significantly (p=.08).

Much work remains to be done on this project. Three professional social workers have continued to work on the study long after their graduation from Social Work school. Their interest and enthusiasm speaks well for their commitment to research, to the topic of morality, and to their own personal and professional growth. This is the desired outcome of The Practice Research Center.

## Conclusion

As this article demonstrates, a tremendous level of commitment, trust and shared goals on the part of the agency and the school is necessary for an effort as demanding and complex as practice-based research. When this ideal can be achieved both students and staff are able to learn from it. And in research, learning, after all, is the overriding purpose. In the projects cited, learning specifically related to current social issues deemed to be of importance in the profession have been emphasized.

## BIBLIOGRAPHY

Casselman, Betsy-Lea (1972) "On the Practitioner's Orientation Toward Research." SMITH COLLEGE STUDIES IN SOCIAL WORK, 42(3), 212-233.

Damon, W. (1988) THE MORAL CHILD. New York: The Free Press.

Eaton, J., S.A. Kirk and Joel Fischer (Winter, 1976) "Do Social Workers Understand Research?" JOURNAL OF EDUCATION OF SOCIAL WORK, pp. 63-70.

Keller, M. (1984) Resolving conflicts in understanding in everyday life. In Kurtines, W.M. and Gerwirtz, J.L. (eds.), MORALITY, MORAL BEHAVIOR AND MORAL DEVELOPMENT. New York: John Wiley & Sons.

Kirk, S.A., Michael Osmalow and Joel Fischer (1976) "Social Workers' Involvement in Research?" SOCIAL WORK, 2(2), pp. 121-124.

Mehrabian, A. and N. Epstein (1972) "A measure of emotional empathy." JOURNAL OF PERSONALITY, 4, pp. 525-543.

Piers, E.V. (1984) PIERS-HARRIS CHILDREN'S SELF-CONCEPT SCALE: REVISED MANUAL. Los Angeles: Western Psychological Services.

Rosenblatt, Aaron and Stuart Kirk (March, 1977) "Barriers to Students Utilization of Research." Paper presented at the Annual Program Meeting of the C.S.W.E., Phoenix, Arizona.

Weiss, Carol H. (ed.) (1977) USING SOCIAL RESEARCH IN PUBLIC POLICY MAKING. New York: Lexington Books, pp. 1-22.

# OVERVIEW OF BACCALAUREATE FIELD EDUCATION: OBJECTIVES AND OUTCOMES

Ellen Sue Mesbur, *Ryerson Polytechnic Institute*

## INTRODUCTION

For many years, undergraduate social work education has had an ambivalent and sometimes tumultuous relationship with graduate schools of social work and the social work profession. This ambivalence stems from both the historical roots of BSW education and from the social and political conditions which helped shape the development of professional programs. A review of these historical and socio-- political roots provides important insights into the dilemmas faced by field education, as well as their potential solutions.

## HISTORICAL OVERVIEW OF BACCALAUREATE SOCIAL WORK EDUCATION

From the late 1890s through the early part of the 20th century, courses in social work evolved from both the volunteer (field-based) training of the Charity Organization Societies and from university and college programs. As late as 1931, social work education followed three separate paths: "agency-based training, undergraduate education within colleges and universities, and one or two years of post-baccalaureate education" (Lowe, 1985, p.53). Debates which centered on agency-based training vs. university-based training were the basis of the tensions still experienced between field educators and the academic world, i.e., the theory-practice dichotomy.

Today, both the field and academic sectors have acknowledged the necessity for social work education to be centered in the universities. The apprenticeship-only system has been replaced by a partnership between the school and the field, with agency-based training becoming an integral part of the social work curriculum through the field practicum.

Within the university sector itself, further divisions developed between proponents of undergraduate education as the foundation for professional preparation and proponents of graduate education as "the only appropriate professional education" (Lowe, 1985, p.53). These debates continue today in spite of the 1984 CSWE (Council on Social Work Education) guidelines which finally acknowledged the baccalaureate degree as a foundation for social work practice.

Historically, many of the undergraduate programs were centered in western and midwestern land-grant universities. The mission of these (largely) publicly-financed institutions was rooted in an egalitarian, populist view of education, with a strong rural outreach. The programs were often developed in response to employment needs, particularly in the public welfare sector.

Graduate schools, on the other hand, were centered primarily within private institutions in urban settings. Their missions were rooted in an 'eastern establishment' view of professional education, one oriented toward establishing professional standards and enhancing acceptance by other professions.

Our system of social work education has been framed by these two histories, rural and urban, land-grant and private, each with its own mission and values. These differences have colored the nature of professional education and their inherent tensions have had major implications for field education.

The period 1932-1939 saw the establishment of the first curriculum standards for social work education and, later, the mandating by the American Association of Schools of Social Work (AASSW) that approved schools of social work must offer a mandatory, two-year master's degree program. Thus, the "professionalization" of social work education was complete within a scant seven years.

This official position of a graduate-only route for certification and professional recognition prevailed from 1939 until 1974, when the Council on Social Work Education (CSWE) adopted accreditation standards for baccalaureate social work education. The graduate-only definition for professional education also denied professional social work control "over the character of the labor supply for what became the principal social work employment sector during the 1930s: public social welfare and services" (Lowe, 1985, p.54).

Despite this graduate-only emphasis, undergraduate programs did not disappear. In 1942, the National Association of Schools of Social Administration (NASSA) was created to represent institutions (mostly land-grant colleges) which were "identified with the tradition that tax-supported institutions have a responsibility for meeting the needs of the State for professional and quasi-professional personnel" (Lowe, 1985, p.51). Throughout the 1940s, NASSA addressed curriculum formats relevant to social welfare/skills employment, surveyed merit system supervisors, and "tried to work out an educational program that supported the graduate emphasis while it addressed the rapidly increasing need for trained and qualified social workers. . ." (Lowe, 1985, p.58).

By the 1950s, three separate regulatory organizations, NASSA, AASSW and the National Council of Social Work Education (NCSWE) operated in tandem, though often at cross purposes, thus creating "a three-headed monster" (Lowe, 1985). In an attempt to resolve the ongoing conflicts, the Hollis/Taylor Study (1951) "articulated a continuum concept between undergraduate and graduate education" (Lowe, 1985, p.59). This report "strongly implied that there was a place for professional social work degree programs at the undergraduate level, and that these programs were not to be viewed as threats to graduate degrees" (Lowe, 1985, p.59).

In 1952, the Council on Social Work Education replaced NASSA, AASSW and NCSWE and became the single body responsible for accrediting and monitoring social work education programs. Despite the new organizational structure, however, undergraduate education remained unrecognized by CSWE.

In 1959, CSWE's comprehensive curriculum study was published. The Bisno report, which focused on undergraduate education, contained three major recommendations relating to issues raised in earlier studies by Hagerty and Hollis/ Taylor. These recommendations implicitly acknowledged the dichotomy between liberal arts and professional education, the legitimacy of undergraduate preparation for employment in social work and preparation for graduate study in social work, and the desirability of a "continuum" between the undergraduate and graduate levels.

Ten years after the publication of Bisno's recommendations, BSW graduates were finally recognized as "professional" (Lowe, 1985, p.52). In 1969, the National Association of Social Workers (NASW) accorded professional recognition to baccalaureate social workers. Thus, by recognizing these graduates as eligible for membership in the professional organization, the practitioners took the lead in acknowledging the contributions of BSW practitioners in the field.

Five years later, in 1974, the CSWE adopted accreditation standards for undergraduate social work programs, thus bestowing its own stamp of legitimacy on baccalaureate education. Since that time, these standards have been given substance as educators have struggled with issues of criteria and content appropriate for the BSW.

## HISTORICAL OVERVIEW OF BACCALAUREATE FIELD EDUCATION

From its earliest days, the social work profession has been concerned with "doing". "Learning through doing" is the essence of field education -- a manifestation of experiential learning which has characterized professional education since the apprenticeship system developed by the Charity Organization Societies.

In 1932, field instruction was formally recognized as an essential part of social work education in the curriculum standards of the American Association of Schools of Social Work (AASSW). By this time, the locus of control for the educational process had shifted to the universities, and the long, rocky partnership of field education and academic preparation had begun (Skolnik, 1985).

Skolnik's (1985) study reviews 50 years of curriculum policy statements as they related to field education. She delineates the variations in field education standards and guidelines, giving a comprehensive picture of one of the most basic and critical elements in social work education.

From 1932 to 1984, the place of field education in social work curricula waxed and waned, fluctuating between being required (in 1932) to being viewed as an addendum to academic work (in 1944). The 1984 Curriculum Policy Statement of CSWE, which defined the field practicum as one of the professional foundation areas, was the most fully developed of all earlier policy statements and firmly grounded field education as an integral part of the curriculum.

## PROVOCATIVE DILEMMAS IN BSW EDUCATION

### The Educational Continuum

The continuum in social work education has been the focus of much debate. Hartman (1983) highlighted the continuum issue by looking at the task for educators: "The task is to differentiate between the preparation afforded in the BSW and MSW professional degree programs while developing a continuum in which one program is built on and linked with but does not repeat the other" (p.19).

If, as Anderson (1985) suggests, the objective of the BSW foundation is preparation for immediate practice, "the definition and model for practice in BSW programs must guide learning specific skills. . . In sum, BSW programs must balance the breadth of practice-theory learning with the depth of skill learning needed for competence in entry-level, direct service, generalist practice in the foundation practice sequence" (p.66).

The apparent lack of consensus around the educational continuum has manifested itself in a great variation of educational programs. Dinerman's (1982) study of baccalaureate and master's curricula suggests "that there is enormous diversity both within and across levels of social work programs, so much so that the degree level is not a predictor of the extent of exposure to any content or the focus of the content that a graduate will have had" (pp.89-90).

In an attempt to clarify perceptions of the professional foundation, Griffin and Eure (1985) surveyed program directors of accredited BSW programs. Considering the continuum debate, it is noteworthy that their study revealed a high level of agreement on what areas should be part of the curriculum for the professional foundation. In a follow-up study, Eure, Griffin and Atherton (1987) addressed the degree of consensus between undergraduate program directors and deans and directors of MSW programs on these same priorities. Their findings indicated a similar level of agreement on the priorities of content for both the BSW and MSW groups. While their findings do not spell out a complete foundation for field education, this general agreement among educators suggests that a core of unanimity exists within the social work profession.

## The Acceptance of the BSW as the First Professional Degree

Since 1974, when CSWE formally recognized baccalaureate programs as offering the first professional degree in social work, dissention, vagueness, and negative reactions have been inherent in the educational institutions' responses to the BSW program. Sherwood (1980) outlines several factors which seem to be inherent in the passive, reactive, and resistant response to the BSW as foundation for practice:

a)  Many educators have denigrated the value of accredited BSW programs, not appreciating their substantive nature.

b)  Some assume that professional undergraduate education will undermine the "liberal arts base" of traditional social work education.

c)  Questions regarding a possible lack of "equivalence" from one BSW program to another are seen as an assumed threat to the overall integrity of the MSW experience.

Thus, BSW education, while recognized by CASW and NASW, still encounters well-entrenched attitudes, manifested in a reluctance to accept wholeheartedly the BSW program as a professional, entry-level program. But history speaks for itself: despite its constant, uphill battle, BSW education has survived and flourished. It is time for the history and debates to be put to rest so that educators can get on with the task at hand.

## BRIDGING IDEALS AND REALITY IN BSW FIELD EDUCATION

The objectives and outcomes of both BSW field education and the BSW degree are inextricably intertwined. As we approach the centennial of social work as a profession, our accrediting body has developed and instituted a vision of social work education in which the baccalaureate degree is considered as a foundation for professional practice. Although some graduates may view the BSW as a direct stepping stone to an MSW, or may wish to practice in the field a few years before returning for an MSW, the curriculum must include the knowledge, values, processes and skills which are essential for a professional foundation.

The Curriculum Policy Statements in CSWE's 1984 Accreditation Manual support the view that the baccalaureate is the first level of professional education.

> The baccalaureate social worker should attain a beginning professional level of proficiency in the self-critical and accountable use of this social work knowledge and integrate this knowledge with the liberal arts perspective.

> Students who receive a baccalaureate degree from an accredited social work program should possess the professional judgment and proficiency to apply differentially, with supervision, the common professional foundation to service systems of various sizes and types. There should be special emphasis on direct services to clients which includes organizations and provision of resources on clients' behalf. Each program shall explicate the ways in which students are being prepared for generalist practice.

> The purpose of undergraduate social work education is to prepare students for a beginning professional level of practice. Although some BSW graduates will subsequently pursue additional social work education at the graduate level, **this consideration is independent of the primary objectives of the under-graduate curriculum.** (emphasis added)

The mandate of field education, under CSWE's guidelines, is that it:

> . . . shall assume responsibility for a field practicum that is a clearly designed educational experience and shall have clearly articulated standards for selecting agencies for the practicum, for selecting field instructors, and for evaluating student learning in the practicum.

While social work education and accreditation resides in our American and Canadian university systems, the Curriculum Policy Statements and Accreditation Guidelines are a reflection of the historical diversity within social work education, the ever-present tension between national and local concerns, and the necessity to reflect the views and needs of different regions and institutions. Policies and guidelines which are too specific may become restrictive and rigid. Thus, educational institutions have been reluctant to define specific objectives and knowledge.

They have often opted for diversification, as opposed to centralization, resulting in a global structure which lacks an infrastructure of essential content in each curriculum area. The result is a shell without substance.

Field education requires a curriculum which links the generic to the specific. It is the regional differences and specialized needs, coupled with a solid theory base, which comprise the richness of our practice. This same diversity simultaneously plays havoc with our ability to articulate and evaluate criteria for field education.

Given these guidelines and expectations, how then do we transform these ideals into realities? The following is a synthesis of practical alternatives designed to accomplish this.

## Selection of Agencies

While students may obtain good learning experiences in human service, though non-social work, settings, it must be remembered that we are sending into the field graduates who must have a strong identification with the profession. Therefore, where possible, all field agencies should be identified with the profession through their mandate, purpose, professional staff, and approach to helping.

Agencies must be committed to the education of the next professional generation, thereby affording staff resources and time for field instruction. Schools must enter into explicit contracts with agency administration to foster this commitment and to allow field instructors time within their daily workload to work with their students.

Agencies must manifest their commitment to education through their willingness to involve students in all aspects of the agency. Thus, students should have access to information about the organizational structure and funding, plus opportunities to work with staff other than their field instructor, to attend regular staff meetings and case conferences, to meet with agency administrators, and to represent the agency to the public.

Students should not be used as "free labour" for an agency. Students do provide a service to agencies and, in times of setbacks and financial restraints, certain services might not otherwise be available to clients were it not for student field placements. However, the primary purpose of the placement is professional education, not a quick and ready answer to labor shortages.

## Selection of Field Instructors

Field instructors are the role models by which many students develop their identification with the profession, their models for practice, and their orientation to continuing professional education. The field instructor should, therefore, be a person who strongly identifies with the profession and who is recognized professionally through a BSW or an MSW degree and membership in the professional associations. This is not to deny the excellent field instruction that has been offered by other helping professionals; it is to reaffirm the necessity for us to strengthen our profession through the educational process.

Field instructors should have a minimum of two to three years practice experience before accepting students for placement. In addition, they should have been employed with the field agency for at least eight months to a year prior to the assumption of field instruction responsibilities.

Beyond his/her formal qualifications, the field instructor should demonstrate:

a) a commitment to the learning-teaching transaction, involving a reciprocal relationship with the student;

b) an understanding that field instruction involves:

   i) specific task supervision and accountability;
   ii) sharing of knowledge specific to the population being served by the agency;
   iii) process supervision;
   iv) an agreement to participate in field instruction training programs offered by the school and a willingness to work **with**, not against, the school;
   v) commitment to a view of field instruction as encompassing a variety of goals including: development of professional identity, integration of theory and practice, training in practice skills, development of critical skills, development of a creative use of self, and development of a "reflective practitioner";
   vi) a willingness to share their practice wisdom both in word and in deed.

**Characteristics of Field Experiences**

It is crucial for BSW graduates to experience at least two different field placements in their professional education. These placements must be direct practice experiences with agency clients, in which the student has primary responsibility for interaction with the client system. Observations of other workers, co-facilitation situations with other workers, simulations, and role plays are all worthwhile adjuncts to the placement, but are not acceptable in lieu of direct practice experience.

Since we expect graduates to function as competent workers upon graduation, their field experiences should be framed within a generalist context. Students in a BSW program should have opportunities to work with individuals, families, groups, and communities; to engage in some aspect of administration; to experience research; to work on a staff team; to work with a variety of client populations in different settings; and to work in both the public and private sectors in primary and secondary settings.

Recognizing that not all agencies can provide all of these experiences in any given placement, it is suggested that the school needs to take an active role in working with agencies and field instructors to structure learning experiences within the constraints of the agency setting. A major role of faculty field consultants and practice faculty (if they are not one and the same) is to develop joint assignments between class and field to help field instructors in their task of integrating practice with theory, and to help field instructors and agencies develop creative ways to enhance field learning.

We cannot expect agencies and field instructors to take sole responsibility for structuring field assignments. It is necessary for the schools to enter into a mutual agreement with the agencies, whereby the needs of the agency and the client populations, the expectations of the schools, the learning needs of the student, and ultimately, the accountability to the profession itself will culminate in solid, varied and well integrated field experiences.

## Theoretical Component of Field Instruction

Is there theory beyond the classroom? If our goal is to help students integrate theory with practice, and to view theory as useful and relevant to their practice, then it is necessary to delineate the school's expectations for a theoretical component within the field setting. A curriculum could be outlined which would enhance the practice theory of the school (often a generalist model) by providing specialized knowledge tailored to the particular field setting and client population. The specification of curricula would ensure that knowledge gained in the field practicum will not be "by chance". A curriculum outline should contain:

a) Knowledge required to function in a specific field of practice (eg: mental retardation, alcoholic abuse, child welfare). This should include terminology and theories;

b) Models of intervention used by the agency;

c) Knowledge of the cultural and socio-economic characteristics of the client population.

## Training of Field Instructors

It is incumbent upon the schools to provide ongoing education and training for field instructors. If viewed as a reciprocal process, this could act as a catalyst in generating enthusiasm for and commitment to education in field instruction. By acting as a source of information and support for field instructors, the school is also committing itself to the field in a tangible way. Thus each side is increasing its stake in the process.

In areas with a number of schools of social work, cooperative ventures in field instruction training could contribute to knowledge-building among schools with a variety of orientations and missions. In rural or large areas where distance may prevent easy access to the schools, creative innovations for field instruction could include: weekend workshops in regional areas, teleconferencing, video training programs, interactive use of video material such as tapes of student/field instructor interactions. Special programs for experienced field instructors are necessary for schools to maintain a level of commitment and interest. These are the people who are often ignored or taken for granted. Advanced seminars could contribute to their professional development.

A particular need in field instruction is for research into the area of field instructor/student interaction. In order to translate educational goals into measurable behavioral interactions, much work must be done. In partnership, the schools and experienced field instructors could contribute to our knowledge building.

## Evaluation of Student Performance

The evaluation of student performance in field work has often been problematic. The requirements for evaluation as set out in the accreditation guidelines are not defined. Of the several evaluation models which have emerged, a competency-based model seems most helpful to the school, the student, and the field instructor.

Griffin and Eure (1985) have made a significant contribution to a comprehensive delineation of knowledge, values and skills deemed important in the field practicum by social work educators. The 64 curriculum items which they identify as priorities for field education constitute a solid basis for further research.

Dwyer and Urbanowski (1981) propose five major areas for practice criteria which, if used in conjunction with Griffin and Eure, have the potential for a powerful and universally applicable evaluative system.

Social work as a profession is struggling (as are other professions) to define the nature of its practice. As Schon (1983) notes:

> Professionals have been disturbed to find that they cannot account for the processes they have come to see as central to professional competence. It is difficult for them to imagine how to describe and teach what might be meant by making sense of uncertainty, performing artistically, setting problems, and choosing among competing professional paradigms, when these processes seem mysterious in the light of the prevailing model of professional knowledge (pp.19-20).

Schon suggests that professionals must focus interactively on the outcomes of their actions, on the action itself, and on the intuitive knowing implicit in the action. If we consider this in light of student performance evaluation, we must help students to become "reflective practitioners" by providing a variety of tools to assist them and to engage with them in a useful and comprehensive evaluation process. Some of the tools which may be considered for this process are:

a. The process recording;
b. The reflective daily log;
c. Video or audio tapes and analyses of student-client interactions;
d. Learning contracts;
e. Integration seminars with faculty, consultants and other students;
f. The progress review with the student, field consultant and field instructor;
g. Student written and oral self-evaluations; and
h. Field instructor written evaluations.

## CONCLUSION

The development of social work education over the last 100 years has been fraught with controversy, differences of orientation and tensions. Our modern world is characterized by social problems requiring practitioners with greater depth and breadth of both theory and practice experience than in earlier times. Thus there is no longer room for divisions between field and classroom; baccalaureate and master's; learning and doing. Each is appropriate to a need. And each needs to be appropriate, so that all social workers are equipped to provide professional, competent service to the community as a whole.

By making a commitment to quality education, we need to commit ourselves to understanding other perspectives and overcoming our differences; to developing consistency and a broad consensus in our attitudes and approaches; and to selecting the best options among a full spectrum of alternatives. This paper is one attempt at such a process.

Experience shows that BSW practitioners are often in the front line of work with the most deprived and needy client populations, from widely varied cultural and socio-economical backgrounds, within the most multi-faceted environmental conditions. It is these graduates and those who will follow them in baccalaureate social work programs to whom our educational efforts must be focused, if we are to truly achieve the goals of professionalism. It is for these BSW graduates that we must provide the very best in field education experience, for they are, indeed, the future professional generation.

## BIBLIOGRAPHY

Anderson, Joseph (Fall, 1985) "BSW Programs and the Continuum in Social Work" - JOURNAL OF SOCIAL WORK EDUCATION, Vol. 21, No. 3.

Arkava, Morton L. and Brennan, Clifford E. (Eds.) (1976) COMPETENCY-BASED EDUCATION FOR SOCIAL WORK. New York: Council on Social Work Education.

Baer, Betty L. and Federico, Ronald (1978) EDUCATING THE BACCALAUREATE SOCIAL WORKER: REPORT OF THE UNDERGRADUATE SOCIAL WORK CURRICULUM DEVELOPMENT PROJECT. Cambridge, Mass: Ballinger.

Barker, Robert and Briggs, Thomas (Eds.) (1971) MANPOWER RESEARCH ON THE UTILIZATION OF BACCALAUREATE SOCIAL WORKERS: IMPLICATIONS FOR EDUCATION. A Report of the Undergraduate Social Work Education Curriculum Building Project Conducted by Syracuse University School of Social Work Under Contract With the U.S. Veterans Administration.

Cohen, Jerome (Winter 1977) "Selected Constraints in the Relationship Between Social Work Education and Practice" - JOURNAL OF EDUCATION FOR SOCIAL WORK. Vol. 13, No. 1.

Commission on Accreditation (1984) HANDBOOK OF ACCREDITATION STANDARDS & PROCEDURES (Revised July, 1984). New York: Council on Social Work Education.

Constable, Robert (1976) "Preparing for Practice: Field Experience and Course Work in the Undergraduate Social Work Program" in TEACHING FOR COMPETENCE IN THE DELIVERY OF DIRECT SERVICES. New York: Council on Social Work Education.

Dwyer, Margaret and Urbanowski, Martha (Winter, 1981) "Field Practice Criteria: A Valuable Teaching/Learning Tool in Undergraduate Social Work Education" - JOURNAL OF EDUCATION FOR SOCIAL WORK, Vol. 17, No. 1.

Eure, Gerald K., Griffin, Jerry E. and Atherton, Charles R (Spring/Summer 1987) "Priorities for the Professional Foundation: Differences by Program Level" - JOURNAL OF SOCIAL WORK EDUCATION, Vol. 23, No. 2.

Ewalt, Patricia L. (1983) CURRICULUUM DESIGN AND DEVELOPMENT FOR GRADUATE SOCIAL WORK EDUCATION. New York: Council on Social Work Education.

Farley, William O., Oviatt, Boyd E., Skidmore, Rex A. and Thackery, Milton G. (April, 1977) "Social Work - Professional Mediocrity or Maturation" - SOCIAL CASEWORK, 58, No. 4.

Feldstein, Donald (1972) UNDERGRADUATE SOCIAL WORK EDUCATION: TODAY AND TOMORROW. New York: Council on Social Work Education.

Finestone, Samuel (Fall, 1967) "Selected Features of Professional Field Instruction" - JOURNAL OF EDUCATION FOR SOCIAL WORK, 3.

Frumkin, Michael L. (Spring, 1980) "Social Work Education and the Professional Commitment Fallacy: A Practical Guide to Field-School Relations" - JOURNAL OF EDUCATION FOR SOCIAL WORK, Vol. 16, No. 3.

George, Aase (1982) "A History of Social Work Field Instructon" in Bradford Sheafor & Lowell Jenkins (Eds.) QUALITY FIELD INSTRUCTION IN SOCIAL WORK. New York: Longman.

Glick, Lester (Ed.) (1971) UNDERGRADUATE SOCIAL WORK EDUCATION FOR PRACTICE: A REPORT ON CURRICULUM CONTENT AND ISSUES. Report of the Curriculum Building Project Conducted by the Syracuse University School of Social Work Under Contract With the U.S. Veterans Administration.

Griffin, Neil and Eure, Jerry (Fall, 1985) "Toward a Definition of the Professional Foundation in Social Work Education" - JOURNAL OF SOCIAL WORK EDUCATION, Vol. 21, No. 3.

Hartman, Ann (Spring, 1983) "Concentrations, Specializations and Curriculum Design in MSW and BSW Programs" - JOURNAL OF EDUCATION FOR SOCIAL WORK, Vol. 19, No. 2.

Jones, Earle F. (Fall, 1984) "Square Peg, Round Hole: The Dilemma of the Undergraduate Social Work Field Coordinator" - JOURNAL OF EDUCATION FOR SOCIAL WORK, Vol. 20, No. 3.

Kettner, Peter M. (Winter, 1979) "A Conceptual Framework for Developing Learning Modules for Field Education - JOURNAL OF EDUCATION FOR SOCIAL WORK, Vol. 15, No. 1.

Kimberley, Dennis and Watt, Susan (1982) "Trends and Issues in the Field Preparation of Social Work Manpower: Part III, Educational Policy, Accreditation Standards and Guidelines" - CANADIAN JOURNAL OF SOCIAL WORK EDUCATION, Vol. 8, No. 1.

Loewenberg, Frank M. (Ed.) (1969) ESSENTIALS FOR UNDERGRADUATE SOCIAL WELFARE TEACHING. New York: Council on Social Work Education.

Lowe, Gary (Fall, 1985) "The Graduate Only Debate in Social Work Education, 1931-1959, and Its Consequences for the Profession" - JOURNAL OF SOCIAL WORK EDUCATION, Vol. 21, No. 3, pp.52-62.

Matson, Margaret. "Field Experience for the Undergraduate Social Welfare Student" in Lester Glick (Ed.) (1971) UNDERGRADUATE'S SOCIAL WORK EDUCATION FOR PRACTICE: A REPORT ON CURRICULUM CONTENT AND ISSUES. Report of the Curriculum Building Project Conducted by the Syracuse University School of Social Work Under Contract With the U.S. Veterans Administration.

Mossman, Mereb E. "The Bachelor's Degree Program in the Social Work Continuum" in Lester Glick (Ed.) (1971) UNDERGRADUATE SOCIAL WORK EDUCATION FOR PRACTICE: A REPORT ON CURRICULUM CONTENT AND ISSUES. Report of the Curriculum Building Project Conducted by the Syracuse University School of Social Work Under Contract With the U.S. Veterans Administration.

Mullen, Edward J. (1976) BACCALAUREATE PROGRAMS AND THE COMMUNITY COLLEGE TRANSFER STUDENT. New York: Council on Social Work Education.

Rothman, Jack (June, 1977) "Development of a Profession: Field - Instruction Correlates" - SOCIAL SERVICE REVIEW, 51.

Schillen, John (1972) "The Current Status of Undergraduate Social Work Education" in Kristen Wenzel (Ed.), UNDERGRADUATE FIELD INSTRUCTION PROGRAMS: CURRENT ISSUES AND PREDICTIONS. New York: Council on Social Work Education.

Schon, Donald A. (1983) THE REFLECTIVE PRACTITIONER. New York: Basic Books.

Schwartz, Paul L. (1974) "On the Self-Directing Professional in Undergraduate Social Work Education" in APPROACHES TO INNOVATIONS IN SOCIAL WORK. New York: Council on Social Work Education.

Sheafor, Bradford W. and Jenkins, Lowell E. (Winter, 1981) "Issues That Affect the Development of a Field Instruction Curriculum" - JOURNAL OF EDUCATION FOR SOCIAL WORK, Vol. 17, No. 1.

Sheafor, Bradford W. and Jenkins, Lowell E. (1982) QUALITY FIELD INSTRUCTION IN SOCIAL WORK. New York: Longman.

Sherwood, David A. (Winter, 1980) "The MSW Curriculum: Advanced Standing or Advanced Work?" - JOURNAL OF EDUCATION FOR SOCIAL WORK, Vol. 16, No. 1.

Skolnik, Louise (1985) FIELD EDUCATION PROJECT (Final Report). Washington, D.C.: Council on Social Work Education.

Thomlison, Barbara and Watt, Susan (1980) "Trends and Issues in the Field Preparation of Social Work Manpower: A Summary Report" - CANADIAN JOURNAL OF SOCIAL WORK EDUCATION, Vol. 6, No. 2 & 3.

Watt, Susan and Kimberley, Dennis (1981) "Trends and Issues in the Field Preparation of Social Work Manpower: Part II, Policies and Recommendations" - CANADIAN JOURNAL OF SOCIAL WORK EDUCATION, Vol. 7, No. 1.

Wenzel, Kristen (Ed.) (1972) UNDERGRADUATE FIELD INSTRUCTION PROGRAMS: CURRENT ISSUES & PREDICTIONS. New York: Council on Social Work Education.

Wijnberg, Marion H. and Schwartz, Mary C. (Fall, 1977) "Models of Students Supervision: The Apprentice, Growth, and Role Systems Models" - JOURNAL OF EDUCATION FOR SOCIAL WORK, Vol. 13, No. 3.

Wilson, Suanna J. (1981) FIELD INSTRUCTION: TECHNIQUES FOR SUPERVISORS. New York: The Free Press.

# DIFFERENCES AND COMMONALITIES IN BSW AND MSW FIELD INSTRUCTION: IN SEARCH OF CONTINUITY

Allie C. Kilpatrick, *University of Georgia*

The recognition of the BSW as the first level of professional social work practice has produced some provocative dilemmas in social work education. Some educators recognize the BSW as equivalent to the first year of graduate study while others do not. Some hold that the differences in the level of student maturity at the two levels is a decisive factor in foundation outcomes. Some postulate that both years of MSW should be graduate work with the first year different from the BSW while others believe that the professional foundation is the same at any level. These and other differences in viewpoints have implications for field instruction programs at both BSW and MSW levels. Practical solutions are needed which promote continuity as well as consistency.

In order to place these dilemmas in context, this paper first presents some historical perspectives on field instruction. Current contexts within which schools are presently functioning are then discussed. Specific questions which compare BSW and MSW field instruction are formulated from this review. Results of two surveys of accredited schools of Social Work which have BSW and MSW programs are then reported and the data used to answer the specific questions that have been raised. Finally, issues and implications of the study are discussed.

## HISTORICAL PERSPECTIVES

Education for social work began in the late 1800s with apprenticeship training - the actual provision of services in the field under the direction of others who had learned the same way. In tracing the development of social work from these early beginnings to 1980, George (1982) chronicles the historical events into three time periods.

### Before 1940

This period is characterized first by the academic approach when field instruction became centered more in schools of social work than in agencies, and an increasing number of schools were established. The emphasis was on professional development with concern both for the poor as individuals and for social institutions and social justice.

In the 1920s and 1930s, the emphasis shifted to understanding the individual being helped through the psychoanalytic and psychiatric knowledge current at that time. This shift led to the therapeutic approach where the personal growth and development of the student through productive use of supervision was emphasized.

An important development came at the end of this period with the 1939 decision that professional social work education needed to be at the graduate level.

This decision relegated undergraduate programs to preprofessional status at a time when half the programs were at the undergraduate level (Bisno, 1959).

## From 1940-1960

During this period there were indications of beginning attention to undergraduate social work education (including field instruction). The CSWE curriculum study of 1959 reported that 92 percent of the students in social work departments or social science divisions of member schools offering a social work major were given field experience programs. Although both the 1951 Hollis-Taylor report and the 1959 Werner Boehm report advocated for considering undergraduate education as part of professional education, these recommendations were not accepted. It seems that lack of maturity was used as a basis for not involving undergraduates in a carefully supervised field experience which could be considered as professional education. However, the same students might be recommended for employment in public welfare three months later. These examples point out the areas of confusion and illogical thinking concerning undergraduate field experience and professional social work education.

During this same period there was an effort to strengthen the educational quality of field instruction at the graduate level. The 1940-41 report of the CSWE Subcommittee on Field Work, both the 1944 and the 1952 CSWE curriculum statements, and the 1951 and 1959 studies of social work education stressed educational standards for field instruction.

## From 1960 to 1980

These years were marked by experimentation and a concentrated effort to achieve educational quality in graduate field instruction. Articulation of planned learning activities between class and field to integrate cognitive and experiential learning was a goal (Jenkins and Sheafor, 1982).

Undergraduate social work education was recognized as the first level of professional practice and replaced the first year of graduate study. Two events in 1970 put new emphasis on the use of field experience to educate undergraduate social work students for beginning entry into the profession: the decision of NASW to admit BSW graduates of CSWE-accredited programs to full membership; and the establishment by the board of directors of CSWE of new standards for undergraduate social work programs. These standards included the requirement of "an appropriate directed field experience with direct engagement in service activities as an integral part of that program" (George, 1982, p. 51).

## CURRENT CONTEXTS

Since George's review, three important documents have been produced which have far-reaching implications for BSW and MSW field instruction. The contents of each of these three documents on the 1980s also have specific implications for the differences and commonalities in the varying levels of field instruction. Some of the contents pose provocative dilemmas for social work education when the ideal is presented for which practical solutions must be found in our current reality, or when some reality is presented which needs to be in alignment with the ideal. The content which is most relevant to our present study will now be elucidated in order to formulate some specific questions which will be addressed to the collected data.

## The 1982 CSWE Curriculum Policy Statement (CPS)

The 1982 CPS, which became effective on July 1, 1983, gives more specific guidelines for both graduate and undergraduate field instruction programs. It succeeds the 1969 statement of curriculum policy for MSW programs and provides the first statement of curriculum policy for BSW programs. It states that:

> The content area on which all programs are required to build their curriculum are intended to provide social work students with a professional foundation- the basic values, knowledge, and skills required for entry into the profession (p.1).

The 1982 CPS then goes on to state that "the purpose of undergraduate social work education is to prepare students for a beginning professional level of practice" or generalist practice (No. 6.9 and 6.10, p. 4)., and that "in the master's program, the content relating to the professional foundation is directed toward preparing the student for concentration" or advanced specialized practice (No. 6.11, p. 4).

Although both programs are required to provide "the basic values, knowledge and skills required for entry into the profession," as mentioned previously, the ambiguity in these statements leads one to question whether the foundation which prepares for "a beginning level of practice" or prepares for "concentration" would involve the same or different objectives, content and skills.

In regard to the difference in the two levels of education, the CPS states that they "differ in the level of knowledge and skill students are expected to synthesize in practice competence." This is a rather non-specific statement, but it is clear that a difference in level of practice competence achieved in the BSW and MSW programs is expected.

## NASW Standards for the Classification of Social Work Practice (1981)

These standards were accepted by the Board of Directors of NASW in September of 1981. The intent of the Standards was to identify the specific social work content of social service employment and to provide a basis for differentiation among levels of practice. The differentiation of the basic professional skill level (BSW) and the specialized professional skill level (MSW) has specific implications for field instruction at both levels.

The NASW Task Force on Labor Force Classification identified seven factors which are applicable to four levels of social work practice, each with its own specific educational base. These factors are knowledge, responsibility, skills. situational complexity, social consequences, client vulnerability and social function. They then described each of these factors in relation to the differences by basic (BSW), specialized (MSW), independent and advanced professional levels of practice. The differences in all levels on all factors are specifically explicated.

For purposes of our study, it is clear that NASW expected that there would be specific differences in the levels of knowledge and skills achieved by BSW and MSW graduates.

### American Association of State Social Work Boards (1983)

The American Association of State Social Work Boards conducted a content validity study and reported the results in 1983. The intent was to determine whether there is a common set of important job tasks associated with social work practice, and if there is a difference in the execution of these tasks by different levels of personnel. The implications of these findings for both levels of field instruction are clear.

The data obtained by the task analysis examination committee indicated that there were no differences in the relative importance of job tasks as judged by social workers from different levels of existing licensure. The knowledge and skills required to perform these tasks were also the same. However, it was determined that licenses at different levels need to have different cognitive abilities in the application of their knowledge and skills. For example, BSWs are expected to primarily recall and comprehend knowledge and skills while MSWs are expected to apply and analyze the same knowledge and skills. The advanced level of licensure requires candidates to synthesize and evaluate, again based on the same knowledge. In other words, examiners would be required to have the same knowledge base, but its application would be different at various licensure levels.

### MODEL FOR THE EXAMINATION OF DATA

Based upon the findings from the three documents previously discussed, some questions are now formulated which deal with outcome rather than structural issues. These questions will be answered by data gathered from Schools of Social Work which have accredited BSW and MSW programs.

1. Are the foundation programs for field instruction different or the same for the BSW which prepares for beginning professional level of practice, and for the MSW which prepares for concentration?
2. Are the objectives for the professional foundation in BSW and MSW field instruction programs different? How do these objectives differ from the MSW concentration objectives?
3. Are the knowledge/theoretical bases for professional foundation in BSW and MSW field instruction programs different? How do these bases differ from the MSW concentration?
4. Is the level of practice skills achieved in BSW and MSW foundation field instruction programs different? How does this level differ for the MSW concentration?

5.      Is the level of application/integration of knowledge and practice skills achieved in BSW and MSW foundation field instruction programs different? How does this level differ for the MSW concentration?

**Current Data**

Data from a natural study will be presented here in order to answer the foregoing questions. This study builds upon one done by Eure, Griffin and Atherton (1987), and addresses the degree of consensus between undergraduate program directors and dean and directors of master's degree programs on the priorities for content of the professional foundation courses in social work education. The authors used the Delphi technique in two phases. The first phase was designed to identify preferred curriculum content important to the professional foundation. The results revealed that there is a high degree of agreement among BSW program directors on what areas should be part of curriculum material for the professional foundation. The second phase of the study is more crucial to our subject.

With a response rate of 34.6 percent of the accredited undergraduate programs and 29.5 percent of the graduate programs, the findings suggest that there is remarkable agreement on the elements that should be included in the professional foundation by deans and directors of graduate and undergraduate programs (Eure, et al., 1987). The authors conclude that there is really only one foundation curriculum as far as the nature of the content is concerned. The study does not deal with the question of the degree of depth of coverage, but is limited to the question of priorities.

Study two was conducted by the author. In my study, the directors of field instruction at each of the 49 schools with both graduate and undergraduate programs were mailed a questionnaire concerning differences and similarities in BSW and MSW field instruction in that school of social work. There was a response rate of 27 percent.

**OVERVIEW OF DIFFERENCES AND SIMILARITIES**

The questions covered items which were from general to specific. The first question requested a brief general summary of over-all differences and similarities in BSW and MSW field instruction by three different comparisons. The first part concerned the differences in BSW and MSW foundation field instruction. There were 77 percent of the responding schools which said the foundation practica were the same or very similar as shown in Table 1. Two schools stated that their MSW and BSW programs had different administrative/academic units and they did not have the information to compare. The primary differences stated were differences in direct contact hours or format: BSW is basic beginning level while MSW is beginning graduate level, MSW is more intense and analytical, BSW is generic while MSW is foundation to concentration, and one respondent stated that BSW students become familiar with agency life while MSW students must carry cases and be effective in intervention. The specific similarities mentioned were that both learned community resources, case management, and micro-skills, had similar content, knowledge base, objectives, basic principles and skills, and used similar settings for field instruction. Some schools taught the foundation content of both BSW and MSW programs in the same classes.

The answers given for the two questions of differences and similarities in BSW and advanced level MSW field instruction, and in MSW foundation and advanced level MSW field instruction were that, for all responding schools, the answers to both questions were basically the same. Therefore, these two questions will be answered together. Besides differences in format, responses were that advanced MSW practica had: an advanced level of practice, a concentration or specialization, different content, assignments, and practice experiences, more complexity, a higher level of integration and level of learning outcomes, more sophistication, more depth and breadth, more capability for evolving autonomous practice, more clinical focus on therapeutic activities, depth, intensity, analytical integration, broadening and deepening of basic skills, and had more macro system practice than did the foundation programs. One school stated that no comparisons could meaningfully be made between the BSW and advanced level MSW field instruction. Most schools implied that the advanced MSW field instruction program builds on both foundation programs.

**Objectives, Knowledge Base, Practice Skills, Integration and Agencies in Foundation**

The answers to more specific questions regarding objectives, knowledge base, practice skills, integration and field instruction agencies are also given in Table 1.

**Table 1. BSW & MSW Foundation Field Instruction:  Comparisons**

| Overview Summary | Same | Similar | Different |
|---|---|---|---|
| | 39% | 38% | 23% |
| Components: | | | |
| Objectives | 31 | 31 | 38 |
| Knowledge Base | 31 | 46 | 23 |
| Practice Skills | 56 | 11 | 33 |
| Integration | 50 | 40 | 10 |
| Field Instruction Agencies | 67 | | 33 |

*Objectives.* As is readily seen from this table, 62 percent of the schools reported the same or similar objectives for the BSW and MSW foundation. The differences stated were that there is more preparation for specialization in the MSW foundation, the BSW is more specific, more skill oriented and was considered "terminal", and that the levels of expectation are significantly different for the two levels with the MSW foundation being broader, more in depth and with greater professional responsibility.

*Knowledge Base.* Seventy-seven percent reported the same or similar knowledge bases. The differences given were that the BSW is task-centered, not therapeutically oriented, different books, more sophisticated readings and assignments, and more analytic thinking were expected in the MSW foundation, and that there is more depth and intensity in the MSW foundation. One school specialized by service area in the first year of the MSW program and placed more emphasis on groups and families.

*Practice Skills.* Achievement of practice skills were regarded as the same or similar by 67 percent of respondents. Differences given were that BSWs are on a basic level with a focus on casework and community resources while MSWs are more advanced with a focus on counseling and community needs assessments, and MSWs are able to apply knowledge more rapidly and with less supervision.

*Application/Integration.* The level of application/integration of knowledge and practice skills was seen as the same or similar for 90 percent of the schools. One respondent states that the BSW foundation focused more on task accomplishment. In response to the question as to how the outcomes are measures, the majority of the schools reported that outcomes are measured by both subjective and objective measures on an individual basis, and in seminars.

*Field Instruction Agencies.* In regard to field instruction agencies, 67 percent used the same agencies for the practicum for both foundation programs.

## Differences in Foundation and Advanced Level

A description of differences between the foundation programs and advanced programs on the same variables were also requested.

*Objectives.* As for difference in objectives for the foundation levels and the advanced level, responses were that the advanced level builds upon the foundation, is specialized, in depth, at a higher skill level, more involved in outcome resolution, more focused on methods and fields of practice as specialization, greater integration of theory and practice, more skill in evaluation effectiveness, less intense supervision, more complex and varies cases, and students carry cases from beginning to end.

*Knowledge Base.* Differences in the knowledge/theoretical base for the foundation levels and for the advanced level were given as more specialized, at a higher level or integration, deepening of foundation skill development, advanced practice concepts and macro practice material at the advanced level.

*Practice Skills.* Respondents saw the practice skills of the advanced level students as more specialized, at a higher level, more consistent, needing less supervision, more able to articulate theory, predict outcomes, apply knowledge more rapidly, practice autonomously and with more therapeutic strategies, and have greater responsibility, level of influence and sophistication.

*Integration.* The application/integration of knowledge and practice skills were seen as being at a higher level, more complex, consistent, and with different learning objectives at the advanced level, and students could evaluate effectiveness, predict outcomes, modify interventions with a wider range of methods, utilize social knowledge without as much supervision, achieve greater autonomy, and focus on the conscious use of self in a specialized area with achieving readiness to function as a staff person.

*Field Instruction Agencies.* The BSW and advanced level of MSW students used the same field instruction agencies in 58 percent of the schools. MSW foundation and advanced level used the same agencies in 65 percent of the schools.

## SUMMARY AND IMPLICATIONS

With the data we have reported, let us now attempt to delineate the answers to the previously defined questions.

1.  The findings from the Eure, et al. study (1987) suggest that there is really only one foundation curriculum as far as the nature of the content is concerned as judged by the Deans and Directors. The findings from the author's study show that 77 percent of the Directors of Field Instruction also see the BSW and the MSW foundation as the same or very similar, not only in content but in other areas as well as they relate to field instruction.

2.  As we look more specifically at various areas, we find that in 62 percent of the schools reporting the objectives for both foundation programs are the same or similar for field instruction.

3.  In regard to knowledge base, we find that 77 percent of the Directors of Field Instruction reported that it was the same or similar for both foundation programs.

4.  There were 67 percent of the Directors who reported that the practice skills attained for both foundation programs were the same or similar.

5.  When asked about the level of application/integration, 90 percent of the Directors responded that the level was the same for both foundation programs.

Differences given in the BSW field instruction program and the advanced MSW field instruction program were generally the same as the differences given for the MSW foundation and advanced field instruction programs. These differences were that the advanced year was specialized with concentrations, it built on the foundation, went into more depth with more intensity, at a higher level of integration, application and evaluation of effectiveness, and with increasing autonomy.

Although we must be careful about generalizing these findings due to the 27 percent response rate, we are able to see some trends toward more continuity in the foundation programs upon which the concentrations build. There also seems to be a degree of continuity and consensus on objectives for the advanced level of field instruction. However, specificity regarding how we know when students have attained the expected level of practice skills and integration of knowledge and practice is much more illusive. Is this the kind of phenomena that we do not know quite how to explain but we know it when we see it? Is it similar to the response to the question "What is jazz?" which is "If you have to ask, you probably won't understand the answer." Can the differences in level attained be measured by the degree of consistency in the practice behavior of students as was adopted by the University of Georgia in 1973? This particular document was the result of a search for continuity 15 years ago. It began with the associate degree and went through the baccalaureate, the MSW and the doctoral levels with 13 different objectives. The associate and baccalaureate levels were expected to meet these objectives only occasionally or sometimes not at all while the doctoral level students were to meet them almost always. This is an interesting continuum and the idea has some merit when considering levels of practice.

It seems that our future work could well be in the area of defining "higher" levels of functioning in field instruction and then determining how we help our students to achieve them. In a study done by Kilpatrick and Turner (1983) of all MSW and BSW practica programs, the use of objective measurement of performance was ranked highly be all schools as a possible method to increase effectiveness. Thus objective measurement of levels is a recognized need and one that deserves attention.

Let us look again at what our current professional documents have to offer in this area. CSWE's Curriculum Policy Statement (1982) states that the difference in the two programs is "in the level of knowledge and skill students are expected to synthesize in practice competence." The American Association of State Social Work Boards (1983) states that the knowledge and skills of both levels are the same but BSWs are expected to primarily recall and comprehend knowledge and skills while MSWs are expected to apply and analyze the same knowledge and skills. The NASW Standards for Classification of Social Work Practice (1981) state specific guidelines for each of the two levels on seven factors with specifications for each factor including skill levels stated in behavioral terms.

It seems that this last classification from NASW is the most comprehensive and specific that we have at this point in time by which to model. It holds much promise. Additionally, in order to produce the most effective social workers possible, we must continue to refine our Curriculum Policy Statement and support consistency of standards within our diversity. Only then can we find continuity between BSW and MSW field instruction.

## BIBLIOGRAPHY

American Association of State Social Work Boards (1983) CONTENT VALIDITY STUDY IN SUPPORT OF THE LICENSURE EXAMINATION PROGRAM, SUMMARY REPORT. Vol. 1, No. 1, American Foundation for Research and Consumer Education on Social Work Regulation, 1-12.

Bisno, H. (1959) THE PLACE OF THE UNDERGRADUATE CURRICULUM IN SOCIAL WORK. A Project Report of the Curriculum Study, Vol. 2, NY: Council on Social Work Education.

Boehm, W. E. (1959) OBJECTIVES OF THE SOCIAL WORK CURRICULUM OF THE FUTURE. The Comprehensive Report of the Curriculum Study, Vol. 1, New York: Council on Social Work Education, pp. 175-178.

Council on Social Work Education (1982) Curriculum Policy for the Master's Degree and Baccalaureate Degree Programs in Social Work Education. New York: CSWE.

Eure, G. K., Griffin, J. E., & Atherton, C. R. (Spring/Summer, 1987) Priorities for the professional foundation: Differences by program level. JOURNAL OF SOCIAL WORK EDUCATION, No. 2, pp. 19-29.

George, A. (1982) A history of social work field instruction. In B. W. Sheafor & L. E. Jenkins, QUALITY FIELD INSTRUCTION IN SOCIAL WORK. New York: Longman, pp. 37-59.

Griffin, J. E. & Eure, G. K. (Fall 1985) Defining theprofessional foundation in Social Work Education. JOURNAL OF SOCIAL WORK EDUCATION, No. 3, 73-91.

Hollis, E. & Taylor, A. (1951) SOCIAL WORK EDUCATION IN THE UNITED STATES. New York: Columbia University Press.

Jenkins, L. L. & Sheafor, B. W. (1982) An overview of social work field instruction. In B. W. Sheafor and L. E. Jenkins, QUALITY FIELD INSTRUCTION IN SOCIAL WORK, New York: Longman, 3-20.

Kilpatrick, A. C. & Turner, J. B. (1983) Quality control: Monitoring students' practicum performance. Paper presented to the Council on Social Work Education Annual Program Meeting, Fort Worth, Texas, 1983.

National Association of Social Workers, (1981) NASW STANDARDS FOR THE CLASSIFICATION OF SOCIAL WORK PRACTICE, POLICY STATEMENT 4. Maryland: NASW.

University of Georgia (1973) School objectives. In SCHOOL OF SOCIAL WORK INFORMATION HANDBOOK FOR AGENCY INSTRUCTIONAL STAFF. Athens: School of Social Work, pp. 161-165.

# INNOVATION IN FIELD EDUCATION

Robert W. McClelland, *The Ohio State University*

The education of students through field instruction has a well established history in social work professional education.[1] Every school devotes a sizable number of credit hours to the integration of theory and practice through practicum opportunities. Bachelor of Social Work students are expected to complete at least 400 hours in the field, while MSW students complete at least 900 hours. Although the commitment of student time to field education has remained high, it is probably fair to say that the commitment of educational institutions in terms of faculty time and support resources has seen better times. What is interesting in field instruction is that innovation has flourished in both good times and bad.

Innovation in the field is driven by many forces. Certainly public financing helped stimulate professional interest in child welfare, mental health, aging, developmental disabilities, health and many other fields of practice. But the loss of public support has also stimulated interest in other areas such as industrial settings, private practice, and interdisciplinary or host agencies. Hopefully, form and function are driven by more than financing but the importance of resource availability in stimulating the context in which field innovation occurs is unmistakable. Innovations in structure, educational content and outcome have been consistently reported in the literature. This paper will attempt to identify and classify many of these changes, noting how some of the major trends have changed our expectations in field education.

## STRUCTURE OF FIELD EDUCATION INNOVATIONS

It is helpful to examine some of the literature of the 1960's to establish a context in which traditional and innovative may be compared. Mark Hale (1969) identified the elements of traditional placements. They include the following:

1.  The focus is on development of practice skill in some one method of practice.
2.  Field learning and class learning proceed concurrently with relatively early introduction of the student to case-carrying, service-giving responsibilities and learning experiences. Some schools intersperse the

---

[1]See, for instance, Sheafor and Jenkins, **Quality Field Instruction in Social Work** (1982); Council on Social Work Education, **The Dynamics of Field Instruction: Learning Through Doing** (1975); Rothman and Jones, **A New Look at Field Instruction** (1971); Betty Lacy Jones, ed., **Current Patterns in Field Instruction** (1969); Council on Social Work Education, **Field Instruction in Graduate School Social Work Education: Old Problems and New Proposals** (1966); Schubert, **Field Instruction in Social Casework** (1963).

class and field learning at regular intervals, using a system of "bloc" placement in agencies.

3.    The field learning experiences are based primarily in the agency where the student is placed.

4.    The learning experiences are organized and directed by the agency's function and the service needs of the clients included in the student's caseload.

5.    The primary teaching-learning method is the tutorial or individual conference based on the relationship and role identification with the chief mentor - the field instructor.

6.    Work components in the experience are high, inasmuch as the student is expected to perform the work role of an employee in accord with the agency's policies and procedures.

Hale also noted a number of innovative trends which contrasted with the traditional model. First, he identified movement toward multi-method autonomous practice. Second, he pointed to an expansion of learning experiences and a reduction in reliance on case-carrying as the primary field experience. Third, he cited variations in teaching methods, ranging from personalized instruction to use of closed circuit television and fourth, he noted innovation in the application of learning principles and practice theory plus movement away from reliance on agencies as practicum settings. Since then, many of these themes have been extended and refined, generating new demonstrations in the field.

Yet, it is interesting to note that the traditional model remains common today in spite of over 20 years of change. Never-the-less, the number of variations reported at conferences and in the literature are testimony to the inherent flexibility in field education and the creative spirit of those who have provided leadership in this area. More recent innovations have been stimulated by several forces influencing social work education. Some are familiar, others are new. These forces include: 1) changing educational philosophy and technology, 2) changing student needs and interests, and 3) a dramatic period of institutional retrenchment and change.

## CHANGING EDUCATIONAL PHILOSOPHY AND TECHNOLOGY

Educational consensus about the appropriate method of practice for social workers at undergraduate and graduate levels has continued to shift over the years. Where single methods (casework, groupwork, community organization) were once the areas of practice offered, multi-method generalist practice has grown in acceptance, particularly for rural oriented programs (Doelker and Bedics, 1983). The literature is filled with field demonstration of the efficacy of both generalist (Henry, 1975; Koegler, Williamson, and Grossman, 1976; Hermandez, et. al., 1985) and specialized (Carroll, 1975; Barbaro, 1979) approaches to social work practice as well as analysis of the emerging consensus. The current consensus views the BSW as generalist in nature (Anderson, 1985) while MSW education builds on a generalist foundation (Griffin and Eure, 1985) which leads to more specialized advanced practice. Ann

Hartman (1983) has noted that this consensus is an uneasy one with individual schools creating their own unique interpretations. This tension is the force behind much of the innovation in field education during the late 1970's and early 1980's.

Thus, innovation in this context consists of 1) finding new ways to respond to the current trend or 2) demonstrating the continued value of less favored methods. Invariably, evaluations of these innovations conclude that the value of the approach used was confirmed. An independent observer might arrive at a slightly different conclusion. The essence of successful field demonstrations is that they are well planned. The importance of this is noted by a number of authors. Akabas (1978), in her article on the use of industrial settings, stressed the importance of assessing organizational readiness along with careful selection of students and clarity of social work function at the practicum site. Abbott (1986) stressed the value of a field placement contract in maintaining comparability of employment related and traditional placements. Larson and Hepworth (1982) noted the value of three planning principles: 1) specifying educational objectives in core skills that are observable and measurable, 2) assessing progress on an ongoing basis and 3) accurately evaluating achievements. Essentially, systematic detailed attention pays off.

What is often unstated in many of these field demonstrations is that the students note that they are being treated differently, and they respond to being "special." Whether field coordinators can provide the same level of attention to the majority of the students is debatable considering the time constraints and limited resources available to most field programs today.

In addition to shifts in educational principles, there have been a number of efforts to improve technology through simulated field experiences. Because of the increase in severity and complexity of clients' presenting problems, laboratory training prior to, as well as concurrent with, the practicum was reported by Hawthorne and Fleisher (1986), as a method of strengthening the capacity of students to perform successfully in the practice setting. Indeed, students can help design these supplements to the field. Austin and Sodec (1978) have described a process where students designed management simulations, combining knowledge and skills acquired in both classroom and practicum experience. The growing concern over school, agency and student liability undoubtedly make preparation prior to student-client contact increasingly desirable.

## CHANGING STUDENT NEEDS AND INTERESTS

In addition to the young inexperienced students noted above, schools of social work have reported an increase in the proportion of older students. These students present different needs because they are mature, experienced, highly self-directed individuals who are managing multiple priorities such as work, family, school and personal interests. Pursuit of an education proves to be very difficult for this group, and schools of social work have had to reexamine some long cherished beliefs about how education should be structured. Twenty years ago, students wanting to attend on a part-time basis were discouraged. They ran into barriers in the form of the one year residency requirement, course sequencing, separation of employment and fieldwork, and timeliness that made it impossible to complete the program without abandoning the family.

Today they have much less difficulty. Programs like the part-time work-study option at Hunter provide the flexibility needed (Haffey, 1985). Hunter and many other colleges have actively sought to attract the non-traditional student through a combination of variations in the timing and delivery of courses plus the use of work-study placements (Haffey, Marshack and Starr, 1984).

When student financial support was plentiful, being employed was viewed as an unacceptable conflict of interest. Now we have learned to negotiate learning contracts that protect educational objectives while acknowledging the value of existing employment in human service agencies.

It is worth noting that these extended programs are not without costs. They create added administrative responsibilities for field coordinators who must negotiate these arrangements, and faculty often resist the inconvenience inherent in outreach efforts. Faculty increasingly complain that they feel fragmented and torn between the demands of day, evening, part-time and community based programs. Schools wanting to pursue these options must recognize the impact on workload and provide incentives to make them attractive.

In terms of program flexibility, one of the most innovative schools reported in the literature is located in Canada. The University of Regina program, as reported by Emilia E. Martinez-Brawley, involved three major curricular innovations: curricular inversion, non-sequencing of courses and credit-for-competency (Martinez-Brawley, 1986). Curricular inversion involves taking BSW social work courses prior to the liberal or general education courses. Consequently, these students do not have a liberal arts prerequisite. Regina's program asserts that mature students may have gained this perspective independent of specific course instruction, and that it is not always possible or even desirable to offer general education courses in remote locations or to employed, task-motivated students prior to more practical content. Non-sequencing basically asserts that courses should be taken in the order that the students find useful. This allows for easy access to all courses for part-time students. Field instruction does require prior course work, but it is also possible to get credit for prior learning. The student submits a portfolio outlining his/her previous experience, demonstrating competence in a chosen area. Credits are awarded after a committee review of the portfolio.

The Regina School of Social Work has challenged some of the most prized educational dogma in our field. Whether this represents the next phase of innovation or a unique program that has "gone too far" is not clear, but it is well worth watching. Under current CSWE accreditation standards, a program such as this would not be possible in the United States.

The most active area of innovation in social work education probably goes largely unreported. This involves student initiated or designed placement opportunities that are uniquely suited to particular students' interests. Field coordinators would be wise to monitor and record these seemingly unique situations. It may be possible to identify trends and extract commonalities that would be useful in program planning and worth sharing at national meetings. Often emerging areas of practice are signaled by student requests for non-traditional settings.

## RESPONDING TO INSTITUTIONAL RETRENCHMENT AND CHANGE

Implicit in the reports on innovation in the 1960's and early 1970's is the assumption that human services would continue to expand and that money for educational demonstration projects would remain. These assumptions proved false, and yet innovation has grown out of adversity. Ernest Gullerud has noted that the declining enrollment of 18-year-old freshmen and decreases in student financial aid have generated interest in off-campus programs designed for the employed practitioner (Gullerud, 1981). Retrenchment in agencies has added to the pressure to negotiate work-study practicum options. Employers are now reluctant to provide educational leave and staff need to maintain an income. This shift has moved us back to a greater reliance on the agency as the focal point for field instruction.

There was a time when most schools had a large number of faculty based field instructors who maintained educational responsibility for a small group of students as a major part of their workload. There also were agency based field instructors who were fully designated to student instruction. This has changed dramatically. With the loss of Federal and State support for demonstration grants, field instruction has often been consolidated into the hands of one or two field instructors. To be sure, some schools have maintained a sizable faculty workload commitment to field instruction, but this alternative is viewed as expensive, and it is safe to say that there has been a dramatic reduction in the involvement of faculty in field instruction at most schools. The MSW practitioner-educator has largely been replaced by the Ph.D. researcher-educator who carries liaison responsibilities. Field coordinators have creatively responded to these circumstances by working to clarify the role and function of the faculty liaison (Rosenblum and Raphael, 1983) and to provide guidance in educational expectations for agency field instructors (Bogo, 1982). Yet, field education concerns have grown increasingly remote from the daily lives of regular faculty.

It appears that the management responsibilities of the field coordinator have expanded as the proportion of faculty workload devoted to field instruction has shrunk. This puts the coordinator in a central, but difficult, position. Even though responsibilities increase, fewer people in the organization understand and appreciate the contribution. Earle Jones (1984) has captured the dilemma in his article, "Square Peg, Round Hole." He notes the conflict between the demands of practice teaching and expectations of scholarly productivity, arriving at the following conclusion:

> Thus, the conventional criteria for job performance when applied to full-time field coordination, is built-in assurance that one will fail to achieve promotion and tenure. (p. 48)

It is essential that schools recognize the division of labor which is required in an effective educational organization and apply evaluative criteria that accurately assess competence in the position held. This is an area where many schools of social work have resisted what is common practice and good administration in most organizations.

As frustrating as the field educator role may be at times, it includes opportunities that can make the position unusually rewarding as well. The innovative capacity of field instructors in social work education may actually be a function of their marginal status, and boundary spanning role. Segal and Austin (1974, put it this way,

> Innovative professionals are frequently marginal persons - not in the sense of deviant, but in the sense that a large number of innovations seem to come from quasi-outsiders, persons occupying positions in two or more institutional realms. (p. 79)

Field faculty tend to resent their status, but love their work. Being marginal, perhaps even deviant, may be an important aspect of the innovation that is characteristic of the field component of social work education.

## CONCLUSION

Field education has shown the capacity to creatively respond to shifts in educational philosophy, to student needs and to periods of retrenchment. The field component has provided leadership in 1) applying new approaches of social work practice for existing settings and 2) developing new settings in which social workers can practice. Reports of innovation have been extensive, yet traditional models of instruction have maintained their credibility as well. Indeed, in some areas we have come full circle. Field activities designed to confront or change the system appear to have faded as schools have returned to dependence on agency settings for placement opportunities. The extent to which we have sacrificed the commitment to systems change because of the practical consideration of needing agencies to "house" students is worth further research and perhaps some soul searching. If we are to do more than respond to environmental influences on social work education, we will need to once again provide leadership in the creation and demonstration of new practice approaches for the profession of social work.

## BIBLIOGRAPHY

Abbott, Ann A. (Winter, 1986) "The Field Placement Contract: Its Use in Maintaining Comparability between Employment-related and Traditional Field Placements." JOURNAL OF SOCIAL WORK EDUCATION, 22/1, pp. 57-66.

Akabas, Sheila H. (Spring, 1978) "Fieldwork in Industrial Settings: Opportunities, Rewards, and Dilemmas," JOURNAL OF EDUCATION FOR SOCIAL WORK, 14/3, pp. 13-20.

Anderson, Joseph (Fall, 1985) "BSW Program and the Continuum in Social Work," JOURNAL OF SOCIAL WORK EDUCATION, 21, pp. 63-72.

Austin, Michael J. and Sodec, Beth (Winter, 1978) "Students as Management Simulation Designers: Guidelines for Integrating Classroom and Practicum Experiences," JOURNAL OF EDUCATION FOR SOCIAL WORK, 14, pp. 3-9.

Barbaro, Fred (Winter, 1979) "The Field Instruction Component in the Administration Concentration: Some Problems and Suggested Remedies," JOURNAL OF EDUCATION FOR SOCIAL WORK, 15, pp. 5-11.

Bogo, Marion (Fall, 1982) "An Educationally Focused Faculty/Field Liaison Program for First-Time Field Instructors," JOURNAL OF EDUCATION FOR SOCIAL WORK, 17, pp. 59-65.

Carroll, Nancy K. (Spring, 1975) "Areas of Concentration in the Graduate Curriculum: A Three-Dimensional Model," JOURNAL OF EDUCATION FOR SOCIAL WORK, 11, pp. 3-10.

Council on Social Work Education (1966) FIELD INSTRUCTION IN GRADUATE SCHOOL SOCIAL WORK EDUCATION: OLD PROBLEMS AND NEW PROPOSALS. New York: Council on Social Work Education.

Council on Social Work Education (1975) THE DYNAMICS OF FIELD INSTRUCTION: LEARNING THROUGH DOING. New York: Council on Social Work Education.

Doelker, Jr. Richard E. and Bedics, Bonnie C. (Winter, 1983) "An Approach to Curriculum Design for Rural Practice," JOURNAL OF EDUCATION FOR SOCIAL WORK, 19, pp. 39-46.

Griffin, Jerry and Eure, Gerald E. (Fall, 1985) "Defining the Professional Foundation," Journal of Social Work Education, 21, pp. 73-91.

Gullerud, Ernest (Winter, 1981) "From the Ivory Tower to the Practice Community: Three Approaches for Off-Campus Social Work Educational Programs," JOURNAL OF CONTINUING SOCIAL WORK EDUCATION, 1, pp. 9-26.

Haffey, Martha Freed (Winter, 1985) "The Work-Study Field Practicum in Social Work Education: A Theoretical and Structural Perspective," JOURNAL OF CONTINUING SOCIAL WORK EDUCATION, 3, pp. 17-21.

Haffey, Martha; Marshack, Elaine and Starr, Rose (Fall, 1984) "Costs and Benefits of Work Study vs. Traditional Field Placement Models," ARETE', 9, pp. 41-53.

Hale, Mark P. "Innovations in Field Learning and Teaching." In CURRENT PATTERNS IN FIELD INSTRUCTION IN GRADUATE SOCIAL WORK EDUCATION (1969), edited by Betty Lacy Jones, New York: Council on Social Work Education.

Hartman, Ann (Spring, 1983) "Concentrations, Specializations, and Curriculum Design in MSW and BSW Programs," JOURNAL OF EDUCATION FOR SOCIAL WORK, 19, pp. 16-25.

Hawthorne, Lillian and Fleisher, Dorothy (Spring, 1986) "A New Look at Laboratory Training in Field Year Field Education," ARETE', 11, pp. 44-53.

Henry, Cecil St. George (Fall, 1975) "An Examination of Field Models at Adelphi University School of Social Work," JOURNAL OF EDUCATION FOR SOCIAL WORK, 11, pp. 62-68.

Hermandez, Santos H.; Jorgensen, James D.; Judd, Peter; Gould, Marsha S. and Parsons, Ruth J. (Fall, 1985) "Integrated Practice: An Advanced Generalist Curriculum to Prepare Social Problem Specialists," JOURNAL OF SOCIAL WORK EDUCATION, 21, pp. 28-35.

Jones, Betty Lacy (1969) CURRENT PATTERNS IN FIELD INSTRUCTION. New York: Council on Social Work Education.

Jones, Earle F. (Fall, 1984) "Square Peg, Round Hole:  The Dilemma of the Undergraduate Social Work Field Coordinator," JOURNAL OF EDUCATION FOR SOCIAL WORK, 20, pp. 45-50.

Koegler, Ronald P.; Grossman, Coragon and Reyes Williamson, Emery (Spring, 1976) "Individualized Educational Approach to Fieldwork in a Community Mental Health Center," JOURNAL OF EDUCATION FOR SOCIAL WORK, 12, pp. 28-35.

Larson, Jo Ann and Hepworth, Dean H. (Spring, 1982)  "Enhancing the Effectiveness of Practicum Instruction:  An Empirical Study," JOURNAL OF EDUCATION FOR SOCIAL WORK, 18, pp. 50-58.

Martinez-Brawley, Emilia E. (Spring, 1986) "Issues in Alternative Social Work Education:  Observations From a Canadian Program With a Rural Mandate," ARETE', 11, pp. 54-62.

Rosenblum, Amy Frank and Raphael, Frances B. (Winter, 1983) "The Role and Function of the Faculty Field Liaison," JOURNAL OF EDUCATION FOR SOCIAL WORK, 19, pp. 67-73.

Rothman, Jack and Jones, Wyatt C. (1971)  A NEW LOOK AT FIELD INSTRUCTION.  New York: Association Press.

Segal, Brian and Austin, Michael J. (Winter, 1974) "Innovation in Field Instruction: Community College Teaching and Staff Development," JOURNAL OF EDUCATION FOR SOCIAL WORK, 10, pp. 79.

Schubert, Margaret (1963)  FIELD INSTRUCTION IN SOCIAL CASEWORK.  Chicago:  University of Chicago Press.

Sheafor, Bradford W. and Jenkins, Lowell E. (1982)  QUALITY FIELD INSTRUCTION IN SOCIAL WORK.  NEW YORK: LONGMAN, Inc.

# PART III: FIELD INSTRUCTION ROLES AND PROCESSES

## INTRODUCTION

Contemporary conceptions about the processes in field education and the roles assumed by all players--students, agency staff, and faculty--have been built upon theories derived from the adult education movement, humanistic education, and experiential learning, and consequently have offered an alternative framework to the clinical model of field instruction. The center of field education is the student's ability to develop the professional ego necessary to assume the professional role.

Field education revolves around the student's productive activities which enable the development of roles and skills, and the integration of values and knowledge in action. The student is required to synchronize principles learned in class with the practice situation. The student is called upon to develop self-awareness and the emotional integrity to work with clients whose issues often are bound to raise intense affect in the student, no matter how emotionally integrated he or she may be. Based on observation and a relationship of mutuality, the field instructor provides support for this undertaking by guiding the student, providing feedback to the student and setting the pace for learning. Moreover, the field instructor is a model for practice behavior with clients as well as a model for professional behavior with a spectrum of colleagues. The neophyte field instructor must learn about principles of adult education and andragogy. The field instructor is required to translate the practice skills of establishing contracts, mutuality, and assessment into the educational skills of developing learning contracts, establishing mutuality in educational planning, and delineating an educational assessment. Field instructors have to provide support to students in practice situations where they are overwhelmed, frustrated, or ineffective, not only helping the student marshall skill and understanding, but dealing with students' intense emotional reactions as well.

Furthermore, agency policy and staff must demonstrate adherence to social work values, respect for the social work profession, and a desire to serve as a forum for student education. This translates into a willingness to have their practices and policies scrutinized and reviewed, however indirectly as it may seem, by the school. By becoming accessible to the school, the agency is vulnerable to criticism for a range of its practices and policies. Along with the willingness to expose its functioning, the agency is required to provide release time and resources to the field instructor and student so that their respective roles are adequately assumed. Affiliated agency staff will have to attend meetings at the school, serve on advisory boards, and handle difficult student problems, which may be seen as inconveniences to agencies.

It is the school's responsibility to nurture and support the agency's investment in field education not only through its liaison efforts, but through its broader school policies and practices. Detachment from the exigencies faced by community agencies does not foster a fine tuning of educational process in the field. Rather, it brings about the perception by the agency that the student is in fact an apprentice at the agency and there is little relevant input the school can give about the realities of the trenches. The school's detachment appears in many insidious forms: the rewards to faculty for conducting research that is essentially irrelevant to the practice community; the effort by some faculty to be released from the liaison role; and the paucity of model programs conducted in partnership with agencies as alternative approaches to service delivery.

The paper by Lemberger and Marshack provides an overview of the process of educational assessment, offering a perspective on the mutuality between student and field instructor, and delineates guidelines for arriving at an educational assessment along with a set of future learning tasks. The research by Johnston, Reitmeir and Rooney addresses the interaction between student and field instructor. The paper examines the issue of power and supplies data on the use of feedback forms to help the student offer direct reactions to the field instructor.

Inherent in the student role is the susceptibility to a myriad of emotional intensities stimulated by a range of clients and problem areas. Developing students' abilities to handle these affects must be facilitated by the nonjudgmental stance of the field instructor who appreciates the students' intense reactions. The paper by Grossman, Levine-Jordano and Shearer describes the relationship between stages in field education and students' emotional reactions within the stages, offering teaching approaches for each stage.

Schools have developed various formalized orientation and educational programs for field instructors. The rate of turnover among field instructors is alarming (see Marshack and Glassman, Part II, p. 84) pointing to the urgency of identifying what they need for longevity in the role. In their research, Lacerte and Ray present data on incentives and rewards for field instructors. Through their survey, they discover which university affiliations such as tuition credit and library privileges are important before and after field instructors assume the role, and recommend inclusion of field instructors as classroom presenters.

The course for beginning field instructors required by some schools has often served as an incentive. This points to the necessity for providing continuous educational opportunities to this constituency. Fishbein and Glassman present the curriculum and process of an advanced seminar for experienced field instructors. They identify the participants' need for the course as a desire to re-connect to the school and learn about current trends in practice and education. They discuss as well the videotaping of one session of the seminar.

The faculty role in field education should not be narrowly focused on the monitoring of student progress. Rather, it should encompass efforts with students and agencies to instigate change in the community of the student's placement. Schneck presents a paradigm for considering the faculty member's educative role as arbiter of change who mediates among three representative groups--school, community, and students--taking initiative in each area. Brownstein, Faria, and Smith describe the third part of an extensive study of the faculty field liaison role, noting in particular the liaison's view of the role as mediator and consultant. They present the important aspects of the role as satisfaction and include the views of liaison faculty that the students' and agencies' valuations of the role is higher than that of the schools. All the papers in this section highlight important aspects of the educational process in the field placement setting.

# EDUCATIONAL ASSESSMENT IN THE FIELD:
# AN OPPORTUNITY FOR TEACHER-LEARNER MUTUALITY

Judith Lemberger, *New York University*
Elaine F. Marshack, *Hunter College of the City University of New York*

Educational assessment is a critical and ongoing component of field teaching. Educators have long recognized that learning is most effective when the student's uniqueness as a learner is taken into consideration (Austin 1952; Kadushin, 1976; Towle, 1954; and Webb, 1988). Mutuality between the teacher and learner underlies a productive assessment of the learning needs, styles, and resources of an individual student in the context of the learning opportunities available in an agency.

Three major approaches have characterized teaching of social work students in the field. Two of them, the apprenticeship model which emphasizes content and skills to be taught through doing and the growth model which focusses on the student's self-development, view the learner as the target of field instruction efforts. The third approach, the more recent role systems model, emphasizes transactions between field instructor and student in which both contribute to and grow through the educational process (Wijnberg and Schwartz, 1977). The focus is expanded to include all aspects of the learning situation and specifically considers the option of changing the system, not just having the learner adapt.

Mutuality in the teaching-learning situation has taken on new significance as the profile of social work students and the educational culture itself are changing. The average age of students has risen past 30 (Hidalgo and Spaulding, 1986), and older students have been less willing to view themselves in a dependent and subordinate role. There is more variation among students in current life circumstances, some of which is related to age. While the younger student may continue to struggle with issues of late adolescence, older students often have complex family responsibilities. Financial situations may be complicated. Older students are more likely to have experienced such life cycle issues as death and divorce, as well as temporary losses related to their educational choice (career change, loss of income, family role change). Many students in full-time programs are working part-time and some nearly full-time. The increase in part-time students is well known.

Social work educators also note that students seem more self-revealing about their personal lives, not only in application essays but also in pre-placement material submitted to agencies. Some students quickly reveal such information as recovery from alcoholism, abuse as a child, past or current therapy experiences.

Field instructors may be discomfited by students openly questioning authority and expressing dissatisfaction, options which may not have seemed available to them when they were students. They may experience students' demands as "entitlement," referring to the sense of being entitled to attention, care taking, or other benefits without having to give in return. Entitlement may also appear as a form of dependency, with students expecting to be stimulated or "spoon-fed" by the field instructor (Matorin, 1979). Field instructors must keep in mind that "there is a difference...between the responsible wish to have an effect on one's education and the entitled expectation that anything that makes learning difficult is an unfair imposition" (Dubovsky, 1986).

There is also a changing agency culture and climate in which we are educating social work students today. Agency practice occurs in an increasingly complex context and under greater time pressures. Agency staff rightly point out that there are no uncomplicated assignments or protected experiences for the beginning student. In addition, "practice has changed in the direction of increasing client involvement and participation in planning. Clinical practitioners seek to develop contracts with clients to ensure mutually agreed upon goals and then work to support clients' strengths and empower them in the active pursuit of change" (Livingston, Davidson, and Marshack, 1989). The agency situation in certain respects parallels the student situation: times seem more difficult and stressful; and there is more involvement, more mutuality, more recognition of the "consumer" of service.

## ASSESSMENT DEFINED

A number of terms are used in the literature--and in daily practice - to refer to the theme of this paper. The most commonly used terms--assessment, evaluation, and educational diagnosis--may appear interchangeably. The terms carry strong connotations and thus easily lend themselves to political disagreements. The authors use the term "assessment" to denote an ongoing process with educational objectives; reserve the term "evaluation" for the written instrument which serves as a "formal communication and accountability document between the agency and the school" (Gitterman and Gitterman, 1979) and recommend the abandonment of the expression "educational diagnosis."

"Diagnosis" is a problematic term, both in clinical and educational contexts because of its connotative values. The term diagnosis is deservedly in disrepute among social workers because of its association with conceptions of causality, with labeling, with sociocultural bias and with social control (Goldstein, 1984). The term "assessment" has replaced "diagnosis" in regard to clients just as the term "intervention" has replaced "treatment" reflecting a broader view of the helping process. For similar reasons, the authors support the abandonment of the term "educational diagnosis" in favor of "educational assessment."

In field work, assessment is a dynamic, shared process leading to an educational plan which is negotiated, adopted, implemented, and refined. The assessment process includes markers--events and instruments which differ from school to school (such as mid-semester oral or written statements, formal educational plans, and end-of-semester evaluations). The process inevitably involves a formal judgment and a decision (a grade) at some point.

In social work practice, there is (or should be) a direct relationship between assessment and a plan for intervention. The authors suggest that this is analogous to the direct relationship between educational assessment and educational planning. There is, however, a crucial difference related to purpose. In social work practice (whatever the theoretical framework determining the nature of the assessment process and subsequently the range of interventions considered), the purpose of intervention is related to solving problems. The purpose of assessment, underlying intervention, is to uncover the nature (and sometimes the cause) of the problem. Educational assessment departs from the analogy at this point.

Educational assessment involves the determination of a student's learning needs and the development of an individualized plan to help the student with those learning needs in relation to a common core of school and agency expectations. Educational needs are not considered problems in learning. If the student's performance is within an acceptable range, teaching addresses the gap between current knowledge and skills and objectives for learning. Problems, in this context, are pervasive patterns of behavior that interfere with students being able to learn.

## MUTUALITY

The ideal model of mutuality between teacher and learner assumes that both field instructor and student are mature individuals, open to learning. The mutuality of the assessment process depends on identifying and establishing a common language within the teaching-learning relationship and negotiating for a consensus on perceptions.

Mutuality in the assessment process also relies on a climate conducive to learning in which the student senses "mutual trust and respect, mutual helpfulness, freedom of expression, and acceptance of differences" (Morton and Kurtz, 1980). Mutuality involves the assessment of performance conditions as well as performance. It means that the unit of attention is not solely the student. At the same time, it is critical to acknowledge that the relationship is not symmetric. "Inevitably, the supervisor must take primary responsibility for the process in that he initiates it, explains its values and how to go about it..." (Miner, 1948). It is unavoidable that the issues of judgment and grading loom over the supervisory process. Despite field instructors' sincere intentions to be democratic and receptive teachers to their students, supervisees may still see them as feared and powerful judges (Doehrman 1976).

Given the reality of the power differential, how can the process of assessment involve open participation and self-scrutiny rather than superficial--or guarded -- involvement? First, the field instructor must be sensitive to the impact of the supervisory relationship in which "every compliment, suggestion, or criticism may be experienced as an evaluation of the supervisee's work" (Finch, 1977). The student inevitably feels tested, although that is not the spirit of the process. The fact of the field instructor's inherent power is unavoidable, although field instructors and students find ways to try to avoid it. Hawthorne (1975) described the games supervisors play as they struggle with their authority. Supervisors may play games of abdication, relinquishment of authority, or games of power. Another frustrating game might be called "pseudo-mutuality."

Rosenblatt and Mayer (1975) found that students coped with objectionable supervisory styles by deliberately conveying the impression of compliance. The norms of communication in social work education demand that students be open in supervision; however, "as they see it, it is always possible that the information revealed will be used against them. In other words, for a student to reveal his problems, although consistent with norms of communication, is to risk a negative evaluation." Field instructors have to be sensitive to the student condition and find creative ways to invite, stimulate, and support active participation. This difficult prescription requires a field instructor's readiness to hear whatever a student has to say and to deal with critical feedback without becoming defensive.

The context of the agency will also affect the relationship between student and field instructor. The presence and behavior of other staff, the hierarchical arrangement including the field instructor's position in it, and the general organizational climate all impact on the development of the process.

## THE ASSESSMENT PROCESS

The assessment process begins when a field instructor receives information about a student from the school. Field instructors are entitled to receive full and accurate information about the students they are asked to teach. For example, if a student had specific problems in first year, it is useful for a field instructor to be aware of still unresolved difficulties as well as successful struggles. What constitutes appropriate information is an area of possible conflict between school and agency, since schools are reluctant to "prejudice" a student's entry into a new agency. The pragmatics of the placement process must be faced: it is difficult to find an agency willing or able to accommodate an identified "problem student." The question of how much a school should (or even can legally) share with the placement agency may be problematic in relation to such data as handicapping or underlying health conditions, life style, or personal histories.

Assessment continues when field instructor and student first meet, an excellent time to discuss what the student brings in personal attributes and skills and hopes to accomplish in this new learning experience. Both field instructor and student come with subjective priorities and standards which influence the kind of data each values and how they will present themselves to each other. When both are aware of their own expectations, issues arising from discrepancies with reality (and discrepancies between their expectations) can be recognized.

Assessment is ongoing during supervisory conferences when a specific learning task of a student or aspect of the learning opportunity is discussed. These relatively informal exchanges usually pave the way for a formal stock-taking during which field instructor and student review the early learning situation and project plans for the remainder of the experience. This review should occur when the student has had enough assignments and has submitted sufficient recording to permit identification of learning patterns, personal resources, and tasks to be accomplished. A point between the sixth and eighth weeks of placement generally meets these criteria.

Some schools mandate written educational plans for all students to be submitted at or near mid-first semester of an academic year. These are usually brief documents primarily intended to insure that a planful educational assessment is underway and that the school is alerted to any potential problem in either the learning opportunities or student performance. First-time field instructors are sometimes required to prepare written educational plans with the intention of fostering a thoughtful and structured approach to the process. Other schools expect oral mid-semester evaluations to take place to insure that field instructor and student assess early student performance and the total learning situation.

Formal learning contracts between students and field instructors have received increased attention in social work. Contracts generally include detailed breakdowns of behavioral objectives, specification of activities to be carried out by student and field instructor, time frames for their achievement, and mechanisms for evaluation (Fox, 1983; Granvold, 1978; Hamilton and Else, 1983; Wilson, 1981).

While field instructor and student are the primary participants in the assessment process, the inclusion of others may be indicated. If secondary or task supervisors are also teaching the student, their observations are important to the process. The participation of a liaison or advisor from the school may be appropriate if a student's performance is problematic or if the learning opportunities, including teaching, may be inadequate.

Data to be reviewed in preparation for an assessment discussion should include the agendas submitted by a student for supervisory conferences as well as the field instructor's notes of the same conferences. Both may be especially helpful in identifying the early focus of teaching and learning, patterns in the student's use of field instruction, and the tempo of a student's learning. Student recording is a major resource for identifying student skills and learning needs.

The format which follows was developed especially for use by new field instructors to help them make their educational assessments explicit in the process of learning to develop educational plans. Many field instructors have used their plans as bases for mid-first semester oral evaluations with their students.

## OUTLINE FOR EDUCATIONAL ASSESSMENT AND PLAN

1. Life experience of student, including educational, employment, and volunteer activities
2. Student's resources in skills and personal attributes
3. Student's characteristic learning patterns
4. Learning tasks to be accomplished
5. Range and nature of learning opportunities in agency
6. Cultural, class, age, and gender characteristics of student, field instructor, and clientele
7. Educational plan

The review of students' relevant life experiences should help to clarify why they chose social work and what they expect of the educational experience, the level of their entry skills, and the potential impact of current life circumstances. Histories of employment and volunteer activities, as well as related education, are of primary significance. It is important that field instructors acknowledge students' prior experiences and help them build on applicable skills. If students discuss experience in close relationships, such as marriage or parenting, or with problems, such as serious illness or substance abuse, this knowledge may be a resource for them in dealing with similar client issues. Conversely, close identification with clients' experiences may make the achievement of objectivity and/or empathy more difficult. In either case, the data are relevant to a clearer understanding of a learner. Some people are attracted to social work for its expected therapeutic value in their own lives (Vigilante, 1983) or because of personal problems they have experienced, and such issues may intrude in the learning agenda at some point.

An identification of a student's relevant skills and personal attributes is basic to understanding the resources an individual can mobilize for learning. Attributes include such qualities as the direction and intensity of motivation for learning social work, ways of relating, quality of caring about others, objectivity, openness and enthusiasm for learning, initiative and self-direction, discipline, capacity for self-observation and awareness, responsibility, integrity, and judgment.

Skills include areas of knowledge as well as the ability to apply concepts and theory in practice. This category also includes a student's ability to conceptualize and articulate both orally and in writing.

Identification of a student's characteristic learning patterns and abilities is central to the formulation of a dynamic educational plan. Kadushin notes that a supervisor observes over time "the supervisee's use of supervision, the level of motivation manifested, the balance of rigidity and flexibility in learning, the level of preparation for and participation in conferences, the general attitude toward the content to be learned and toward the learning situation" (Kadushin, 1976). He further suggests attention to the procedures which elicit the learner's best response: does the student learn most readily through one-to-one teaching, in exchange with peers, from classroom instruction, from reading or listening, or from action in a practice situation? The student's participation in field instruction also points to learning patterns: what kinds of content does a student emphasize in discussion? Most students focus on the practice situation and the agency context for provision of service. Intermittent attention to personal issues or the supervisory relationship is expectable but, if either remains the main focus of the student's concern, availability for learning may be in question (Towle, 1954).

Identification of the types of problems, clients, and interventive modalities with which the student works most comfortably and effectively, in contrast to those which present the greatest challenge, provides another avenue to understanding the learner. The tempo of a student's learning, including both rate and consistency, is also to be considered.

There have been two major approaches to understanding how social work students learn: stage theories and learning style typologies. Stage theories emphasize the typical progression or benchmarks of students as they struggle to learn over time (Reynolds, 1942; Saari, 1987). Learning style typologies categorize individuals' preferred ways of processing information and experience (Berengarten, 1957; Kolb, 1981; Lee, 1980; Papell, 1978). Stage theories are helpful in normalizing educational struggles. Learning style typologies are useful in developing teaching approaches which are responsive to the ways in which individual students learn most effectively. Without this knowledge, field instructors are likely to use as models their own preferred styles of learning or the ways they were taught as students. If stimulated to think about learning styles, field instructors can be both flexible and creative in trying to adapt their teaching to ways in which their students learn best.

The specification of learning tasks to be accomplished should integrate a student's individual learning focus, the school's expectations at a given point in the program, and the agency's service focus. It is important to distinguish a student's learning tasks or needs from "problems" or "deficits." It is assumed that there is content to be mastered in every learning process. A degree of anxiety is expectable in situations in which students are called upon to acknowledge what they do not know and address themselves to changing their behaviors. In addition to such situational anxiety, unresolved personal issues may also be "touched off by the close contact with other human beings in trouble" (Austin, 1952). When assessment reveals that a student has difficulty working with particular client populations or problems, the focus of field instruction should be on performance rather than on the performer. Students should be encouraged to share only those facts and feelings that are useful in learning. When these problems persist and impede learning, the field instructor has a responsibility to identify the patterned response. It is the student's responsibility to deal with the issue, perhaps in consultation with a faculty liaison or advisor. The school can take some of the burden off the field instructor because the faculty advisor generally gives the grade for field work. The school should also have an independent student review structure beyond the faculty advisor and field work department. Many schools have mechanisms for referring students when treatment is indicated.

A focus on learning tasks leads logically into consideration of the range and nature of opportunities for learning in the agency. These include available assignments as well as resources for individual and group teaching. Plans for task or secondary supervision should be included.

Specification of demographic characteristics is intended to sensitize both teacher and student to the potential impact of similarities and differences on the learning situation. For example, if the student is older than the field instructor, there may be issues in accepting the field instructor's authority or in maintaining a clear distinction between the two participants. Differences in ethnicity may contribute to discomfort in communication or provoke stereotypical expectations (Gladstein and Mailick, 1986). Some research has suggested that same sex combinations are generally more positive than unlike combinations in field education so that gender differences might help to account for a lack of ease in the teaching-learning situation (Behling, Curtis, and Foster, 1982). Field instructors may fear that direct discussion of personal characteristics may make students uncomfortable or aggravate problems in the teaching relationship. On the contrary, frank acknowledgement of differences or similarities has often been experienced by field instructors and students as providing a welcome opportunity for exploration of potentially significant data. Beyond its value for assessment, the openness of the field instructor models desirable behavior with clients.

The six areas of assessment outlined here underpin development of an educational plan. The plan should include both short and long-range objectives, the major teaching focus and methods, and types of learning opportunities intended to advance student learning.

**SAMPLE EDUCATIONAL PLAN**

1. *Life Experience of Student*

A 24 year old Asian woman, the student, received a Bachelor's degree in mathematics from the state university and worked for three years in customer service for a corporation. She had volunteered as a camp counselor and receptionist in her church during adolescence. She is now a direct practice major in her second year of an MSW program. Her placement agency is a multi-service center with a strong child guidance component.

2. *Student's Resources in Skills and Personal Attributes*

Personal attributes include analytic intelligence, respect for others, supportive and receptive qualities, and a non-threatening demeanor. The student has demonstrated an ability to engage clients in a positive, accepting manner but at this time is much more comfortable with children than adults. She has a basic understanding of the dynamics of human behavior and is beginning to recognize the salience of cultural and individual developmental factors for a dynamic assessment. She has a conceptual grasp of the relationship between assessment and interventive planning. The student demonstrates a beginning understanding of the functions and organization of the agency and presents herself to clients in a professional manner. She is willing to learn and makes an effort to risk herself both with clients and in field instruction. She has a beginning ability to be self-reflective. She struggles to produce process recording but makes good use of it for learning when she succeeds in writing it.

3. *Student's Characteristic Learning Patterns*

The student expresses a preference for a didactic style of teaching with minimal participation on her part but is responding to efforts to engage her more actively. While she learns from discussion of concepts, experiential methods such as review of case examples, observation of practice, and role playing seem more effective. She makes an apparent effort to apply learning from field instruction in her work with clients but needs frequent reminders to complete her charting, statistics, and other administrative responsibilities.

The student's focus in conferences is primarily on deepening her understanding of clients and their problems. She rarely initiates discussion about her own feelings and responses to clients. The student tends to make assumptions and form hypotheses on the basis of limited data. Her tempo of learning has been generally slow as she struggles with new assignments and learning content.

4. *Learning Tasks to be Addressed*

The student is supportive and protective in her manner with clients and tends to respond with solutions or reassurance on the basis of limited data. She now needs to become more focused and specific in her exploration and more objective and penetrating in her understanding of problem situations as a basis for interventive planning. Psychopathology is a new area of learning, and she is struggling to grasp and accept it. The relationships between feeling and action and between manifest and latent content also need deepened understanding. Increased facility in written and oral communication is a task made more difficult by the fact that English is her second language. Greater initiative and assertiveness in mobilizing agency and community resources in her clients' behalf are further objectives for her learning.

## 5. *Range and Nature of Learning Opportunities in the Agency*

The student's case assignments provide opportunities for crisis intervention and ongoing services to families, couples, and individuals of varied ages and ethnic backgrounds. Referrals come from schools, hospitals, and other agencies; many clients are seen on a walk-in basis.

The student has weekly conferences with the field instructor. She takes part in weekly student meetings and staff case conferences. She also participates in selected disposition meetings and psychiatric consultations.

## 6. *Demographic Characteristics*

The student is an unmarried member of an Asian family which emigrated during her childhood. The field instructor is a 27 year old, unmarried white woman of middle class background. The agency clientele is composed predominantly of Hispanic, Greek, and other white ethnic groups of poor and working class backgrounds and ranges in age from latency through older adulthood.

## 7. *Educational Plan*

In preparing this educational assessment, the field instructor has increasingly recognized that cultural factors may play a large role in this student's approach to social work practice and need to be understood as they enter into the learning situation. Her expectation that the field instructor would impart knowledge didactically to a relatively passive recipient, her orientation to task and problem solution rather than social processes, and her discomfort in exploring personal information with clients may all have a cultural component (Ryan, 1981). It will be important, therefore, to be sensitive to instances in which the student may be experiencing conflict around learning on this basis and provide an opportunity for her to discuss these issues. At the same time, the field instructor will attempt to call on her strong analytic skills in sorting out and assessing problem situations. It would also be helpful for the field instructor to be more specific about the basis for use of experiential teaching methods which may initially be uncomfortable for the student. A short-term goal, therefore, will be to enhance the student's comfort in the learning situation by making cultural issues more explicit and by continuing to model the open and direct communication which remains challenging for her. Her difficulty in recording may relate to use of English as a second language and needs to be further explored.

Longer-range goals for the student include greater autonomy in thinking and increased assertiveness in both practice and learning. The submission of agendas with her specific questions for discussion in conferences and periodic review with her of the scope of her learning assignments should help toward this objective. In an effort to help her deepen her exploratory and assessment skills, the student will be given some intake assignments. She will also add assignments with elderly clients and work with a task supervisor in this area. This assignment will include visits to senior centers and collaboration with other professionals.

## BIBLIOGRAPHY

Austin, L. (1952) Basic principles of supervision. SOCIAL CASEWORK 33:10, 411-419.

Behling, J.; Curtis, C. and Foster, S.A. (1982) Impact of sex-role combinations on student performance in field instruction. JOURNAL OF EDUCATION FOR SOCIAL WORK 18:2, 93-97.

Berengarten, S. (1957) Identifying learning patterns of individual students: an exploratory study. SOCIAL SERVICE REVIEW 31:4, 407-417.

Bogo, M. and Vayda, E. (1987) THE PRACTICE OF FIELD INSTRUCTION IN SOCIAL WORK: THEORY AND PROCESS. Toronto: University of Toronto.

Dewey, J. (1938) EXPERIENCE AND EDUCATION. New York: Macmillan.

Doehrman, M.S.G. (1976) Parallel process in supervision and psychotherapy. BULLETIN OF THE MENNINGER CLINIC 40, 9-20.

Dubovsky, S.L. (1986) Coping with entitlement in medical education. THE NEW ENGLAND JOURNAL OF MEDICINE 315:26, 1672-1674.

Finch, W.A. (1977) The role of the organization. In Kaslow, F.W. et al. (Eds.) SUPERVISION, CONSULTATION AND STAFF TRAINING IN THE HELPING PROFESSIONS. San Francisco: Jossey-Bass.

Fox, R. (1983) Contracting in supervision: a goal oriented process. THE CLINICAL SUPERVISOR 1:2, 137-149.

Gitterman, A. and Gitterman, N.P. (1979) Social work student evaluation: format and method. JOURNAL OF EDUCATION FOR SOCIAL WORK 15:3, 103-108.

Gladstein, M. and Mailick, M. (1986) An affirmative approach to ethnic diversity in field work. JOURNAL OF SOCIAL WORK EDUCATION 22:1, 41-49.

Goldmeier, J. (1983) Educational assessment, teaching style, and case assignment in clinical field work. ARETE 8, 1-12.

Goldstein, E. (1984) EGO PSYCHOLOGY AND SOCIAL WORK PRACTICE. New York: The Free Press.

Granvold, D. (1978) Training social work supervisors to meet organizational and worker objectives. JOURNAL OF EDUCATION IN SOCIAL WORK 14:2, 38-45.

Hamilton, N. and Else, J.F. (1983) DESIGNING FIELD EDUCATION: PHILOSOPHY, STRUCTURE AND PROCESS. Springfield, IL: Thomas.

Hawthorne, L. (1975) Games supervisors play. SOCIAL WORK 29:3, 179-183.

Hidalgo, J. and Spaulding, E. (1986) STATISTICS OF SOCIAL WORK EDUCATION IN THE UNITED STATES. 1986. Washington, D.C.: Council on Social Work Education.

Kadushin, A. (1976) SUPERVISION IN SOCIAL WORK. New York: Columbia.

Kolb, D. (1981) Learning styles and disciplinary differences. In Chickering, A.W. and Associates (Eds.) MODERN AMERICAN COLLEGE. San Francisco: Jossey-Bass.

Kruzich, J.M.; Friesen, B.J.; and Van Soest, D. Assessment of student and faculty learning styles: research and application. JOURNAL OF SOCIAL WORK EDUCATION 22:3, 22-30.

Lee, J.A.B. (1980) A study of teaching behaviors for perceived relevance. Mimeographed.

Livingston, D.; Davidson, K.; and Marshack, E. (1989) Education for autonomous practice: a challenge for field instructors. JOURNAL OF INDEPENDENT SOCIAL WORK 4:1.

Matorin, S. (1979) Dimensions of student supervision: a point of view. SOCIAL CASEWORK 60:3, 150-156.

Miner, G.F. (1948) Techniques of mutual evaluation. JOURNAL OF SOCIAL CASEWORK 29:10, 400-403.

Morton, T.D. and Kurtz, P.D. (1980) Educational supervision: a learning theory approach. SOCIAL CASEWORK 61:4, 240-246.

Papell, C. (1978) A study of styles of learning for direct social work practice. Unpublished D.S.W. dissertation, Yeshiva University.

Reynolds, B. (1942) LEARNING AND TEACHING IN THE PRACTICE OF SOCIAL WORK. New York: Farrar and Rinehart.

Rosenblatt, A. and Mayer, J. (1975) Objectionable supervisory styles: students' views. SOCIAL WORK 20:3, 184-189.

Saari, C. (1987) The process of learning in clinical social work. Paper read before the Fifth Annual Symposium for Field Instructors, New York Area Schools of Social Work, New York, N.Y.

Towle, C. (1954) THE LEARNER IN EDUCATION FOR THE PROFESSIONS. Chicago, IL: University of Chicago Press.

Vigilante, F.W. (1983) Students' narcissism and academic performance. SOCIAL CASEWORK 64:10, 602-608.

Webb, N.B. (1988) The role of the field instructor in the socialization of students. SOCIAL CASEWORK 69:1, 35-40.

Wijnberg, M.H. and Schwartz, M.C. (1977) Models of student supervision: the apprenticeship, growth, and role system models. JOURNAL OF EDUCATION FOR SOCIAL WORK 13:3, 107-113.

Wilson, S. (1981) FIELD INSTRUCTION: TECHNIQUES FOR SUPERVISORS. New York: The Free Press.

# SHARING POWER:  STUDENT FEEDBACK TO FIELD SUPERVISORS

Nancy Johnston, Ron Rooney, *University of Minnesota*
Mary Ann Reitmeir, *Bemidji State University, Minnesota*

Field practice is the primary arena for the integration of theory and knowledge and the context in which students test that integration in the practice of professional skills.  The agency social worker as field instructor plays a critical role in that development, acting as supervisor, skill teacher and professional role model. Prior to beginning their study in social work, most students have not experienced supervision which emphasizes learning practice skills and provides consistent feedback on role performance (Shulman, 1981).  The evidence that work with clients parallels the dynamics established in the supervisor/supervisee relationship emphasizes the need for good professional role models to enhance professional practice (Kahn, 1979; Doehrman, 1982).  The student-supervisor relationship can then provide a model for student sharing of feedback, support and power. While precise formats for evaluating student performance have been developed, formats for evaluating supervisory performance have not been developed.  This article reports the development and initial testing of a form designed to provide feedback from students to supervisors in order to enhance professional practiced.

## REVIEW OF THE LITERATURE

Field practice is a "consciously planned set of experiences, occurring in a practice setting, designed to move students from their initial levels of understanding, skill, and attitude to levels associated with autonomous social work practice" (Hamilton & Else, 1983, p.11).  While a requirement of all accredited social work programs, the field component varies widely in required credits and time spent in the field, and in whether the field experience occurs in a block placement or concurrently with classroom course work. In addition, programs differ in viewing field as a course, with a syllabus, lectures, and assignments, or as a practice entity, apart from the academic environment. (Hamilton & Else, 1983; Simon, 1966) These differences in program philosophies shape individual placements, the role of the field instructor and the supervisory relationship itself.

The transition from practitioner to teacher is difficult for some field instructors.  Not only does this shift challenge practitioners "to rethink practice, and then teach and share the gift of experience" (Matorin, 1979, p.150), but it also requires supervisory knowledge and skills, tested for the first time in their role as field instructor.  The field instructor is the theoretical link between the student's academic experiences and the world of practice.  Thus, it is important for the social work faculty to provide access to new knowledge in the field.  For if practice is the priority of the field faculty, knowledge development and distribution is the priority of the social work faculty (Fellin, Thomas & Freud, 1968).  According to Fellin,

Thomas, and Freud a "a common type of mal-coordination arises from the introduction of new knowledge in the classroom before that information has been transmitted to field instructors." (1968, p.5)

The field instructor must develop a supervisory teaching role that will facilitate a challenging learning experience for the student. A supervisory relationship that helps "students discipline their thinking and exercise their problem-solving abilities" (Matorin, p.152) better prepares them for the "demands of autonomous practice" (Matorin, p.152).

This relationship can be supportive without being constrictive, yet providing sufficient direction and nurturance so that the student experiences acceptance and clarity of expectations (Matorin, 1979; Fortune et al, 1985). While students and supervisors don't always agree on what is important to the field experience, studies indicate that a balance between directedness and autonomy contributes to higher student satisfaction (Rosenblatt, Welter, & Wojciechowski, 1976 ) and an unspoken, but similar approach to the relationship results in less reported strain between supervisor and student (Nelsen, 1974). The development of a feedback form was based on the assumption that an open relationship in which each understands their own responsibility and authority will be a more positive relationship.

## THE DEVELOPMENT OF THE FEEDBACK FORM

The idea to develop a form came from two sources. While developing a revised form for evaluating students, students on the Field Advisory Committee suggested that a more formal way to evaluate supervisory experience was needed. Secondly, field practice seminar facilitators suggested that practice of feedback skills could be enhanced by use of a supervisory feedback form. These biweekly practice seminars are forums in which students discuss field issues, integrate class and field learning, and emphasize skills in giving and receiving feedback.

The feedback form was adopted by the Field Advisory Committee in the spring of 1985 from a form piloted by the third author at the University of Wisconsin, Madison. This form identified eight supervisory skills and provided a narrative description of low, expected and high level performance for each skill.[1] Students were requested to complete the feedback form before the end of their first quarter of placement. This early date was selected as part of an effort to provide feedback early enough in the relationship that an opportunity to modify some areas while still in the relationship would be possible. The purpose of the form was described in an accompanying memo as providing a guide to facilitate optimum learning situations for students and to point out areas to which field instructors might want to direct more attention. Students were informed that most field instructors were likely to fall in the middle range on most skills, with few instructors rated at the high end of the continuum on all skills. Students were advised to give honest and considered ratings and that field instructors would view student feedback as a way to strengthen the supervisory relationship and field learning. Students were also

---

[1] The feedback form was influenced also by models provided in Wilson (1981).

informed that information on the form was considered private and would not be shared with persons other than the school's field liaison after it was received by the Director of Field Instruction.

---

This information is confidential

**SCHOOL OF SOCIAL WORK**
**STUDENT FEEDBACK FORM**

Signature of Instructor_____ Signature of student_____
Date completed_____

Please check one:  first year_____  second year_____

(please circle one number for each skill area)

---

| SKILL AREAS | Least helpful | | | | Most helpful |
|---|---|---|---|---|---|
| | 1 | 2  3 | 4 | 5 | 6 |
| Student Orientation | Provides minimal information needed to begin placement or information which is not helpful. | Arranges a variety of observational experiences, appropriate readings and policy guidelines. | | Information and experiences form a coherent whole. Steps are shaped to lead from simple to more complex. | |
| | 1 | 2  3 | 4 | 5 | 6 |
| Modeling job skills | Model is unsatisfactory: poor or unprofessional job skills and values. Limited ability to teach skills. | Modeling is satisfactory to good. Demonstrates ability, judgment, commitment to professional values, ability to teach or conceptualize. Skill may be limited. | | Provides excellent model of skills, judgment, values. Skilled in teaching those skills and fitting them to student level. | |
| | 1 | 2  3 | 4 | 5 | 6 |
| Consulting, supervising | Not regularly available for consultation and supervision; does not provide useful guidelines for improving practice. | Usually available at regularly scheduled time plus some drop-in consultation. Consultation is often useful. | | Highly available for consultation. Consultation often adds new insights to improve practice. | |
| | 1 | 2  3 | 4 | 5 | 6 |
| Giving feedback, evaluation | Gives sporadic or no feedback or feedback provided is not useful; may be overly negative or overly positive, tends not to be constructive or applicable. | Gives regular feedback which is often useful; feedback is is balanced and constructive, sometimes based on specific incident. | | Provides frequent useful feedback. Pinpoints specific positive work and areas for improvement; helps student improve own problem-solving. Provides challenge to greater skill development. | |

---

[NOTE: Feedback form is continued on the next page.]

| | 1 | 2 | 3 | 4 | 5 | 6 |
|---|---|---|---|---|---|---|
| Commitment broader issues in student education, | Narrowly concerned with functioning of particular job; not interested or discourages broader concerns and questions about social work issues; pessimistic about integration of course material with field skills. | | Occasional referencing to broader issues and support of student integration; sometimes encourages questioning the system. Encourages students to become familiar with other roles in the agency such as administrator, support staff encouraging. | | Frequently leads student or supports questioning of larger issues; actively models systems perspective, questioning, use of other data sources. Helps students envision the agency as a whole, representing broad exposure to roles and objective assessment of agency strengths and weaknesses. | |

| | 1 | 2 | 3 | 4 | 5 | 6 |
|---|---|---|---|---|---|---|
| Provision of support | Generally unsympathetic or does not convey interest, concern with student learning or block learning. | | Provides periodic support for student learning or blocks to to learning. | | Frequently communicates genuine concern with students progress and learning. Students feel supported. | |

| | 1 | 2 | 3 | 4 | 5 | 6 |
|---|---|---|---|---|---|---|
| Provision of theoretical perspectives | Provides minimal information on theoretical models or perspectives; seldom discusses integration of theory and practice. | | Periodically discusses theoretical models and perspectives; sometimes concerned with integration of theory and practice. | | Frequently calls attention to theoretical models and perspectives as they relate to students' work; initiates discussion of theory as it specifically relates to student's practice. | |

| | 1 | 2 | 3 | 4 | 5 | 6 |
|---|---|---|---|---|---|---|
| Creating a learning environment | Frequently discourages students from asking questions or giving negative feedback; discourages interaction with other staff. | | Periodically encourages questions and feedback from student and interaction with other staff. | | Consistently creates an open, helpful environment, including honest feedback and encouragement to interact with other staff. | |

## METHODOLOGY

While considering the feedback form to be based on sound principles, an evaluation was planned to discover how students and supervisors in fact used it and responded to its use. For example, concerns began to be raised that too much candor might be expected of low power field students to provide written feedback to their supervisor early in their relationship, and before, in fact, the student would have received his or her own first written performance evaluation from the instructor.

The Field Advisory Committee hence decided to pretest the form and educate both students and field instructors about its use before requiring its use. Several students and willing instructors then pretested the form near the end of the school year, and their comments were incorporated before the form was used the following fall. The form was introduced at a fall meeting and two faculty role-played a student giving feedback to her field instructor. The form was introduced to first year students in the practice seminars, in which they were encouraged to be aware of the content areas of supervision and to discuss the difficulties inherent in giving feedback to a supervisor.

## RESULTS

It was decided to ask students to complete the form a second time at the end of placement. The results reported here compare ratings provided by students early in their placement with a second use during the last month of their placement. An evaluation of how both students and supervisors responded to use of the form is also reported. 70% of the 110 MSW students completed the form in the fall and 64.5% completed the form in the spring.

When the form was first administered in the fall, students mean ratings for their supervisors were in the high middle range of the continuum on all skill areas. Particularly high ratings were provided for "creating a learning environment" (5.15) and "provision of support" (4.92), while lower ratings were provided for "provision of theoretical perspectives" (4.14) and "providing feedback" (4.28). Mean scores were **higher** on all skill areas when the form was readminstered in the spring, near the end of placement. The rank ordering of skill levels was similar, with "creating a learning environment" and "provision of support" rated highest and "provision of theoretical perspectives" rated lowest (see table 1). The largest gains in student scores were in the areas of "providing feedback" (+.56) and "modelling job skills" (+.41).

**TABLE 1: Mean Scores on Supervisory Skills**

| | Fall Score | N | Sd | Spring Score | N | Sd | Change in mean |
|---|---|---|---|---|---|---|---|
| 1. Providing student orientation | 4.39 | 77 | .77 | 4.56 | 67 | .88 | +.17 |
| 2. Modelling job skills | 4.75 | 66 | .99 | 5.16 | 71 | .79 | +.41 |
| 3. Consulting, supervising | 4.84 | 77 | .86 | 5.04 | 77 | .77 | +.20 |
| 4. Providing feedback and evaluation | 4.28 | 77 | .76 | 4.84 | 70 | .77 | +.56 |
| 5. Commitment to broader issues in student education | 4.52 | 76 | .88 | 4.80 | 71 | .69 | +.28 |
| 6. Provision of support | 4.92 | 77 | .90 | 5.27 | 70 | .83 | +.35 |
| 7. Creating a learning environment | 5.15 | 76 | .90 | 5.38 | 70 | .77 | +.23 |
| 8. Provision of theoretical perspective | 4.14 | 76 | 1.0 | 4.45 | 68 | .94 | +.31 |

Students and field instructors were also asked at the end of the spring quarter to evaluate the feedback process itself. 55 students and 64 supervisors responded to this request, about half of the students and supervisors involved in placements. The process of giving feedback to supervisors was rated by student respondents as at least somewhat helpful by 87% and very helpful by 42%. Supervisors were somewhat less favorable, with 78% rating the process somewhat helpful and 7% as very helpful. Conversely, 53% of the students reported that the process of providing feedback was at least somewhat anxiety producing, while 75% of the field instructors reported little or no anxiety in receiving feedback. As there had been concern that asking students to complete the form in their first quarter might provoke anxiety, both students and supervisors were asked about the timing of the process. 75% or more of both the students and supervisors reported the timing to be "about right". Similarly, 82% of the students and 75% of the field instructors thought the criteria provided on the form were useful in providing feedback.

## DISCUSSION

Since about 30% of the students did not complete the feedback form in either the first or second administration, the results reported here may not be representative of those who did not submit the form. For example, it is possible that students who were more anxious about their supervisory relationship might have decided not to use the form. Hence, the fact that about half of those using the form reported at least some anxiety may underrepresent the actual anxiety among students choosing not to complete the form.

## USE OF RESULTS

The data provided by students were analyzed for guidance in ways that the school might provide better service to students and supervisors. For example, when the lowest mean score reported in the fall was on "provision of a theoretical perspective", this was not entirely unexpected as Fellin, Thomas and Freud (1968) suggest that this role falls primarily to classroom faculty. However, to facilitate greater coordination of theoretical perspectives, a packet of syllabi of core and concentration courses was distributed in spring and fall 1987. Further, in the winter of 1988, field instructors were invited to a meeting in which faculty met with supervisors in small groups and discussed the content of their courses. In addition, while supervisory skills were generally rated at a high level by students, the School began to require new field instructors to complete a 15 hour field instruction training program.[2]

Since the criteria "Giving feedback and evaluation" had received the second lowest rating by students in the first use of the feedback form, the course emphasizes the "parallel process" in teaching skills in giving and receiving feedback.

Finally, the student's use of the rating form was also utilized by faculty liaison as a means of monitoring student satisfaction with supervisory experience. In cases of particularly low ratings ways to improve supervision were discussed with students and supervisor.

---

[2]videotapes and the booklet TEACHING THE HELPING SKILLS: A GUIDE FOR FIELD INSTRUCTORS by Lawrence Shulman are used as a theoretical base for this training.

Based on the evaluation of both the content and process of using the feedback form, the School of Social Work plans to continue to use the form to teach the skills of giving feedback and relationship building as well as the knowledge of what is expected in field supervision. The formal process by which students provide feedback to their field instructors provides a helpful lesson in responsibly sharing power.

## BIBLIOGRAPHY

Doehrman, M. (1976) Parallel processes in supervision and psychotherapy. BULLETIN OF THE MENNINGER CLINIC, 40, 9-20.

Fellin, P., Thomas, E. J., and Freud, C. (1968) Institutes in behavioral science knowledge for field instructors. JOURNAL OF EDUCATION FOR SOCIAL WORK, 4(1), 5-13.

Fortune, A. E., Feathers, C. E., and Rook, S. R., Scrimenti, R., Smollen, O., Stemerman, B., Tucker, E. (1985) Student satisfaction with field placement. JOURNAL OF SOCIAL WORK EDUCATION, 21(3), 92-104.

Hamilton, N. and Else, J. F. (1983) DESIGNING FIELD EDUCATION: PHILOSOPHY, STRUCTURE, AND PROCESS. Springfield, Ill.: Thomas.

Kahn, E. M. (1979) The parallel process in social work treatment. SOCIAL CASEWORK, 60 (9), 520-28.

Matorin, S. (1979) Dimensions of student supervision: A point of view. SOCIAL CASEWORK, 60(3), 150-56.

Nelsen, J. C. (1974) Relationship communication in early field work conferences. SOCIAL CASEWORK, 55(4), 237-43.

Rosenblatt, A., Welter, M., and Wojciechowski, S. (1976) THE ADELPHI EXPERIMENT: ACCELE-RATING SOCIAL WORK EDUCATION. New York: CSWE.

Shulman, L. (1981) IDENTIFYING, MEASURING, AND TEACHING HELPING SKILLS. Ottawa: Canadian Association of Schools of Social Work.

Simon, B. K. (1966) Design of learning experiences in field instruction. SOCIAL SERVICE REVIEW, 40(4), 397-409.

Wilson, S. (1981) FIELD INSTRUCTION TECHNIQUES FOR SUPERVISORS. New York: The Free Press.

# WORKING WITH STUDENTS' EMOTIONAL REACTIONS IN THE FIELD: AN EDUCATION FRAMEWORK[1]

Bart Grossman, Nancy Levine-Jordano, and Paul Shearer
*University of California at Berkeley*

## PROFESSIONAL AND EDUCATIONAL VIEWS OF WORKERS' EMOTIONAL REACTIONS TO CLIENTS

Although our profession is deeply concerned with validating the emotional reactions of clients, we have been less comfortable addressing the emotional reactions of workers and students. There was a time when somewhat more attention was devoted to this topic in social work training, but the view of worker's emotional responses was often negative. Strong reactions to clients were labeled countertransference and countertransference was generally seen as a "problem." Sugarman (1981) says that, in the classical view, countertransference was, " . . . a hindrance to the psychoanalytic process, an interference reflective of the analyst's own psychopathology which needed modification through the analyst's own analysis."

Charlotte Towle (1954) sought to reframe professional training in a developmental perspective. "Our task is education," she said, "not therapy; and these two cannot profitably be mixed or performed at the same time by the same person. We should deal with the student's emotional difficulties only in so far as they interfere with his learning. If he needs more therapeutic help, then we should refer him elsewhere for therapy" (p. 89).

Towle didn't intend that we ignore emotional issues in education, but rather "focus on personality conflicts in the current reality" (p. 89), not probe the student's past. Towle pointed out that emotional reactions to the assumption of professional responsibility are inevitable because the sources of anxiety for the student are powerful. These include:

1. fear of helplessness due to lack of knowledge and skill;
2. fear of the new by reason of its nature and meaning, because in a social work context the new implies substantial personal change and reconsideration of past issues;
3. experiences which threaten self-dependency;
4. the demand for understanding experiences beyond one's own; and
5. the responsibility to sustain consciousness of self and to use the concept of the unconscious.

---

[1]A version of this paper was published in THE CLINICAL SUPERVISOR, vol. 8, No. 1, Spring 1990. It is printed here with permission.

All these sources of anxiety are confronted by students within the high stakes situation of proving their ability to function in their chosen lifework. Given such pressures Towle directed Social Work educators:

> . . . Whenever possible, we should accept the individual's way of learning until we get some idea of its import and probable outcome. This implies that we do not react to negative responses as necessarily problematic. If they operate for the integration of learning they will subside (p. 129).

Today, emotional responses to clients are more often seen by practitioners as normal, inevitable, and even useful. Such reactions can enable a worker to better understand a client's communications in terms of the worker's affective reactions to the client's messages and behaviors. Wile (1972) attempts to reconcile the two views of countertransference by distinguishing between practitioner-related counter-transference; a response which is a product of the practitioner's own history, and client-induced countertransference (or objective countertransference); a reflection of the client's behavior which can be used to follow the progression of client's moods and reactions.

## STUDENT EMOTIONAL REACTIONS AND SOCIAL WORK EDUCATION

While the practice literature has become more comfortable with social workers' emotional reactions to clients, social work education continues to be uncomfortable with this area. Several factors have influenced the hesitant attitude of educators. The recent and important emphasis on empirically based and scientifically verifiable methods of practice has, perhaps, drawn attention away from more subjective and personalistic aspects of practice. In addition, concern with student rights of privacy as adult learners and fears of litigation have discouraged educators from attending to aspects of student behavior and personality.

It is a serious mistake, however, to ignore worker subjectivity as an educational issue. The importance of self-understanding in professional practice is underlined repeatedly by such work as Witkin's (1982) article on cognitive processes in clinical practice. Witkin discusses the frequency with which workers make clinical judgments based on negative, personality-focused attributions about their clients. These attributions are often confirmed even when erroneous, because interviewers tend to ask questions that support their personal hypotheses. Practitioner judgments are also relatively impervious to change even when, as has been shown experimentally, no real evidence exists for them. Obviously, social workers in training must become conscious of their assumptions, biases, and of the influence of past events on their judgments.

It is inevitable that many social work students will experience strong positive or negative identification with clients. In a study by Finkelhor (1984) of a random sample of college students, 20 percent of the women and 9 percent of the men reported having been sexually abused as children. Kinsey, Pomeroy, Martin, and Gebhard (1953) reported 25 percent of adult women in their study had been sexually abused. There is no evidence that the prevalence of sexual abuse is lower among social work students. Similar bases for identification and strong reactions exist in many other practice contexts.

Traumatic experiences, when worked through and integrated, can be the source of enormous motivation, empathy and positive contributions on the part of the worker. The very motivation to help others is rooted in subjectivity. As Helen Harris Perlman (1979) points out, " . . . many of us who are drawn to the human service professions have known enough of hurts and sorrows to resonate to them in others and thence to want to ease or heal them in others as if once again to heal them in ourselves" (p. 205).

## AN EDUCATIONAL FRAMEWORK FOR THE FIELD

Field educators are the segment of the social work education community most likely to be confronted with student emotional reactions to clients. It is, therefore, important that field work faculty and field instructors are prepared to recognize and assist students in coping productively with such occurrences. Furthermore, field educators need to address students within an educational framework that:

1.  "normalizes" subjective reactions;
2.  prepares students to anticipate areas of particular emotional sensitivity; and
3.  teaches students how to use personal and professional resources, including the support of field instructors, faculty members, professional colleagues, and, when appropriate, personal therapy, to deal with these reactions in a manner that is useful to, or at least does not harm, clients.

Accordingly, we offer a framework related to the stages of field instruction. Siporin (1982) had developed a five-stage model of the process of field instruction, including stages of engagement and orientation, assessment, planning, implementation, and termination. Our framework suggests that at each stage in this process there are particular appropriate activities related to the issue of student emotional response to clients. Moreover, successful coping and learning from emotional reactions in later stages, such as implementation, is more likely if preparatory discussions occur in the stages of engagement, assessment, and planning.

In the final section of the paper we offer two case examples drawn from different fields of practice illustrating the application of the framework in field instruction.

### Stage 1 - Engagement and Orientation

This stage of the field instruction process is marked by the student's initial contacts with the setting and the beginning of the student-field instructor relationship. The field instructor may begin to form some initial impressions of the student's strengths and vulnerabilities from the student's style of engagement. Is the student eager or reluctant, focused on learning or on proving himself or herself?

**Dealing with students' associations to the setting.** For some students initial contact with the agency and its clients may engender old personal associations. It is probably premature to probe such reactions at this stage but they should be noted by the field instructor. An accepting, "normalizing" response by the field instructor at this stage is important to the establishment of a relationship in which later reactions that impact on the student's performance can be discussed.

## Stage 2 - Assessment

**Assessing students' vulnerabilities to countertransference.** Assessing student vulnerabilities to practitioner-based countertransference while respecting students' privacy and the educational rather than therapeutic nature of the relationship can be a delicate process.

Students may be under the impression that a "good" social worker never has strong personal reactions, and certainly never has negative reactions to clients. Students are occasionally upset when they experience strong reactions related to personal issues that they believed they had "worked through" on their own or in therapy. It is helpful to indicate that "working through" an issue enough to achieve personal comfort is different than being comfortable with the issue as a practitioner helping others.

Schools ought to prepare students with basic theoretical knowledge about the impact of subjective reactions on practitioners. The field instructor may build on this base by discussing specific issues in the given field of practice that may engender strong reactions. In the case of work with AIDS patients, for example, Dunkel and Hatfield (1986) identify various possible positive as well as negative sources of countertransference including fear of the unknown, fear of contagion, fear of dying and death, denial of helplessness, homophobia, overidentification, anger, and the need for professional omnipotence.

The field instructor can share examples from his or her own experience and the experience of colleagues, illustrating the way in which workers become aware of, work through, and use subjective reactions. Such a presentation can be followed by a suggestion to the students that they identify for themselves particularly sensitive areas that may engender strong reactions. Students should be invited, but not required, to share this information as it becomes relevant to their work in the agency.

## Stage 3 - Planning

In the planning phase, as the student, field instructor, and faculty liaison work to develop the student's particular task assignments, several questions arise that touch on students' emotional reactions. Students who have identified particular types of cases that represent areas of emotional vulnerability may wish to avoid such situations or may seek to plunge, counterphobically, into these areas to overcome their problems. Either extreme can be counterproductive.

**Choosing task assignments in vulnerable areas.** The field instructor should help the student to be realistic about the consequences of avoiding particular types of cases. Can they really be avoided in the long run? How much may the student be limiting himself or herself? What specific aspects of this type of situation are particularly problematic? Are there aspects of work with such clients that would be less threatening as a place to start? With both avoidant and counterphobic students it is probably best to think about gradual and limited exposure in the area of sensitivity, beginning with assignments that involve the least intensity. If the student can achieve comfort with this level, he or she may move on to a more central role.

The sort of exploration entailed in this type of planning requires that the field instructor have a clear sense of the boundaries of his or her educational role. The field instructor may help students to identify personal issues but should avoid probing into their origin and broader personal significance. If a student is closed to exploration the field instructor should not persist, but may need at times to point out to the student the importance of dealing with the issue in another context, for example in personal therapy.

## Stage 4 - Implementation

**Preparing students to recognize and handle emotional reactions with clients.** An important area of implementation involves discussing with students what they should do if personal reactions arise in the course of working with a client. Field instructors should talk with the students about the kinds of indicators that suggest practitioner countertransference. Wile (1972) says these include:

> premature termination or referral, affective withdrawal (plodding, low energy practice), entering into personal relationships with clients for self-validation, adoption of fads or overactivity, or, on the other hand, regression to theoretical orthodoxy, criticizing clients (especially for things for which clients already blame themselves), labeling clients "poor candidates," for treatment, adoption of limited goals, an undercurrent of pessimism, and/or practitioner self-punitiveness (p. 39).

Students should be encouraged to discuss such manifestations and any strong emotional reaction to a client with the field instructor.

**The structure of field instruction meetings.** A key factor in helping students to cope with and learn from identifications and other emotional reactions to clients rests in the structure of meetings between the student and the field instructor. The field instruction meetings should have an agenda that flows from the learning goals of the student. Discussion of particular cases should deal with practical questions (i.e., What should I do next?) and also with educational questions (i.e., What am I learning from the case about this type of client, effective intervention strategies, and my own strengths and limitations as a worker?).

Process recordings that include personal reactions or assessment of worker-client interactions are valuable in helping students to evaluate their responses, in relation to the goals of the intervention (see Kagel, 1984). Audio or video tape, and direct observation of the student's work by the field instructor are important sources of data for field instruction. These devices, because they bring uncensored material into the field instruction meetings, may initially be quite threatening to the student. The field instructor will need to prepare the student well by discussing the purpose of these activities, describing how they will be used, and, perhaps, sharing critically some examples of his or her own work.

Initially, the student should select the segments of a tape that he or she wishes to discuss. These should include some interventions of which the student is particularly proud as well as critical incidents, moments of confusion, and occasions of strong emotional reaction to the client. In time, the field instructor may begin to suggest types of segments to discuss that reflect the student's current learning needs and difficulties.

**Working with student reactions**. The field instructor who detects indications of practitioner countertransference of which the student seems not to be conscious faces what Havighurst (Perlman,1979, p. 92) calls a "teachable moment." The first step is to bring the issue to the student's awareness. A remark like, "You seem to be angry at Mrs. Smith," may be enough to begin the student reflecting on his or her reactions to the client.

Beyond this initial exchange the field instructor might ask the student to consider whether s/he can identify any other person(s) or situation(s) in his or her past or present life of which s/he is reminded by the current case. If such an association can be made the student might be asked to think for a moment about ways in which the case is similar and, especially, ways it is different from the life situation of which s/he is reminded.

When students experience negative identification with clients, role playing can be an excellent way of deepening their empathy. Field instructors may play social worker to the role play client or students may be asked to play both roles and then discuss their feelings in each position.

Once the student's reactions have been brought to awareness and discussed, the field instructor should quickly move the focus of discussion to how the situation should be handled with the client. If the student needs to explore the source of the reaction at greater length, the field instructor should suggest personal counseling or other appropriate supports.

Questions to be considered would include:

1. Is the student able to regain sufficient objectivity in order to continue with the client?
2. Does the student's reaction provide some information about how other persons may react to the client that is useful to the the treatment?
3. Would sharing any aspects of the student's response with the client be of value to the client in relation to the goals of the treatment?
4. If the response is to be shared, when and how should it be done?
5. How can the student monitor himself or herself in order to maintain awareness of his or her reactions in this case?

### Stage 5 - Termination

As the termination of placement approaches, it is extremely helpful to recall with the student times when s/he experienced strong reactions and was able to develop perspective and continue effectively with the client. The field instructor can help the student to integrate the personal and professional learning from these events into his or her repertoire of skills.

Once in a while, however, a student's emotional reactions may be so strong, so pervasive, so dangerous to clients, or so threatening to the student, that the field instructor may need to reconsider the appropriateness of the placement. If such a possibility exists, it is important that the field instructor and field liaison work closely and meet together with the student as soon as possible.

A student may even be relieved by such an assessment if it is not experienced as a personal failure. To avoid this negative outcome, the student should be given the first opportunity to reconsider the placement, be supported and encouraged to deal with the personal issues in a safer context, and be given appropriate reassurance that s/he has a worthwhile contribution to make, albeit in another type of practice as a social worker, in another field, or when the personal issue has been worked through, in the current social work milieu. If the student is not appropriate for the profession, our responsibility as social work educators includes helping the student to find resource in order to deal with the loss involved and redirect his or her career plans.

## TWO CASE EXAMPLES

The following examples illustrate the work of field instructors helping students to deal with strong reactions to clients based on personal issues. In the first instance, a hospital pediatric unit, the difficulty stemmed from the student's negative identification with victims of sexual abuse as a result of her denial of having been sexually abused as a child. In the second example, an in-hospital AIDS program, the student began with strong positive identification with clients based on a variety of factors including his experience as a gay man. However, the student needed to learn to balance his personal identification with a professional perspective in order to be self-observant and helpful to his clients.

### The Sexually Abused Social Work Intern

**Stage I - Orientation.** Judy entered social work school immediately following her graduation from a local college. Her first placement was in the pediatric social work unit of a busy inner city hospital. When discussing her interests with her field instructor, Judy stressed the warmth of her family and the positive model provided by her concerned and loving parents as her chief impetus for wanting to help children. As a minority student Judy felt she had a special commitment to and understanding of the minority patients and families in the hospital.

On her first day in the hospital Judy was dressed in a full skirt, a puffy-sleeved, ruffled blouse, and flat shoes. On the second day she wore a tightly fitting skirt, a sweater, and high heels. Although she made no comment at the time, the field instructor wondered if this contrast in dress might be a signal that Judy was experiencing some confusion about herself in the role of social work intern.

**Stage II - Assessment.** As Judy discussed her initial reactions to the hospital she seemed to assume a "we" against "they" attitude, identifying strongly with patients and dismissing staff's understanding of many patient problems as "cultural misinterpretations." The field instructor supported Judy where there was validity to her reactions, but also saw some of her behavior as overidentification and projection typical of first year students.

**Stage III - Planning.** Judy was particularly interested in practicing play therapy with children and in working with minority families and children. The plan involved a gradual development of such a case load, beginning with intake and assessment assignments. The student was taught to do extensive process recording using a verbatim record followed by the student's commentary about her reactions at key points in the interviews.

**Stage IV - Implementation.** As the process recordings were shared and discussed the field instructor noticed and pointed out a few patterns. Judy seemed to focus immediately and narrowly on the most concrete problems presented, for example housing issues. She frequently failed to get a full picture of clients' needs or, even with regard to the focal problem, to explore the client's previous coping attempts and other background information.

Her first case assignment of a sexually abused child signaled more significant difficulties. The field instructor observed Judy's attempts to undo the child's upset and report of abuse and, at the same time, to rationalize the father's actions by suggesting that it was merely "loving behavior." In a subsequent review of the case Judy stated that her father had similarly touched her, but denied that such fondling was abusive or traumatic. Judy volunteered that she had felt very attached to her father in her early years, but he had moved away and cut off regular contact with Judy.

Other problems began to emerge in Judy's handling of assigned cases. The field instructor noted that Judy consistently avoided material involving separation issues. She was critical of children's behavior, judging them as unappreciative or provocative, while attempting to normalize questionable behavior of parents. Judy curtailed interviews in which clients began to explore angry feelings. Techniques such as role playing and modeling seemed to heighten Judy's anxiety and increase her resistance to exploring emotional material.

Judy showed herself to be extremely hard working and diligent, especially in following through on resource finding. However, her reaction to the sexual abuse case, her resistance to exploring patient's feelings, and her need to rationalize and deny clear evidence of parental abuse indicated problems beyond the scope of field instruction interventions.

The field instructor maintained close contact with the student's field advisor at the school. The advisor, a member of the same minority group as the student, could provide some additional reality testing with regard to the student's assertions of cultural issues. The field instructor and advisor agreed that Judy's development as a professional seemed to be blocked by a need to defend against early traumatic experiences.

Judy's progress in field work was discussed in a three-way meeting prior to the Thanksgiving break. By this time Judy was experiencing a good deal of anxiety and depression. While she did not agree that her difficulties might be related to countertransferential feelings, she did accept a referral for individual counseling.

During the weeks that followed the conference and therapy referral, Judy's assignment was restructured to emphasize contacts with clients regarding material and concrete assistance. Cases were carefully screened to avoid sexual abuse and other potentially charged issues. Several initial interviews were held with the field instructor present as an observer.

Judy began to become more able to express her discomfort around case issues and to discuss these issues in field instruction meetings. Gradually Judy began to connect some of these case issues with desire to avoid and deny negative feelings and experiences. By the spring, Judy was able to conduct initial interviews, explore emotionally charged issues with clients, and develop effective treatment plans based on clients' strengths and deficits. However, by mutual agreement, Judy was not assigned child protection cases in the Emergency Room nor did she carry ongoing cases if sexual abuse was an identified issue.

**Stage V - Termination.** In her final field conferences Judy expressed the feeling that the placement had been difficult but extremely productive. She felt that getting into therapy was "the best thing that happened." In discussing her second year placement she expressed a need to "go slow," take time to plan, and to seek a less intense, more structured setting. The field instructor praised Judy for her hard work and determination and the significant personal and professional progress she had been able to make that year.

## The Experience of an AIDS Social Work Intern: A Reflection on Youth, Death, and Homosexuality

**Stage I - Engagement and orientation.** Barry initiated discussion of his second year field placement several weeks before the formal start of the placement process because, as he put it, "I want the position very much and I can do it well." He had chosen to change his primary field of practice from gerontology to medical social work, explaining that he needed to respond to the AIDS epidemic in some way meaningful to him. "I need to get off the sidelines," he emphasized.

At his initial interview with the field instructor Barry explained that his first internship had been with an inpatient geropsychiatric service at a major metropolitan hospital. During that affiliation one of Barry's mentors had been struck down by AIDS and Barry had witnessed the young doctor's life transform and vanish. He recalled the experience with a great deal of pain. "He was my age," Barry offered. "I just assumed our friendship would grow over the years. Worst of all, I realized for the first time in my life that I, too, am going to die someday."

During that first placement Barry had also witnessed a significant increase in the number of people being hospitalized for AIDS-related dementia, a malady which, at that time, could not be treated effectively. Barry was clear that patients who were cognitively disabled presented the greatest challenge to him. Most of them, like the young psychiatrist, were close to Barry's age. And most of them, like Barry, were gay.

Barry was happily settled into a long-term primary relationship as well as in close relationships with his parents and siblings. He was bright, well educated, and sociable. He was, then, very much like the majority of people with AIDS at that point in the epidemic: young, gay, and presumably in control of his destiny.

**Stage II - Assessment.** The possibilities for projective identification between Barry and his clients were great and each seemed to carry potential for both negative and positive consequences. First among these possibilities was that of a strong peer identification with his clients based on a shared developmental stage and many social commonalities. Although frank discussion of personal experiences and support required a certain degree of self-disclosure, the field instructor felt, under the circumstances, that it was essential for Barry to demonstrate an understanding of the issues confronting his clientele, specifically loss and surviving loss.

In the discovery phase of the interview, Barry was asked to talk about his personal experience with death and dying. He had lost an older brother to leukemia when they were both teenagers, and the recounting of his grief process showed a sense of healthy resolution. He had also grieved the deaths of several elderly relatives. And what about his present-day emotional support? Who took care of him and how did he take care of himself when he was vulnerable? Was he afraid of getting AIDS through his work? What did death mean to him? What was responsible for the epidemic? Was he angry about it? Barry was candid at every turn. He presented as a well-grounded young man who, despite all the potential for over-identification with his clients, demonstrated the experience and understanding he needed for this demanding placement.

As Barry and his field instructor developed a long-term plan for the placement, Barry was assigned an initial client. Two weeks into this assignment Barry hit a snag.

He initially described it in supervision as "something uncomfortable" about a particular client. He couldn't put his finger on it, but the situation clearly puzzled him. But as he talked, he grew furious at the man. "I can't stand that arrogant bastard," he fumed. "Nothing I do is good enough, nothing I do is done right. He says I'm incompetent, he yells at me, and he always gets the last word by throwing me out of his room!" Barry paced and steamed and eventually reached deep inside and recognized the anger and grief he still felt toward his brother's death. "I thought this was all over with and now this guy brings it back like it happened yesterday. He treats me like my brother did and as much as I hate that I still don't want him to die. But he's going to die and there's nothing I can do . . . " And then he sat down and grieved for the man and for his brother and, finally, for himself.

**Stage III - Planning.** Barry had expressed concern during early interviews about working with patients afflicted with dementia. In the process of designing his learning goals, he suggested two specific tasks that would help him achieve the goal of "identifying effective psychosocial interventions with demented patients." The first task was to develop a model that would translate his experience with Alzheimer's patients for use with the AIDS population. He would then apply and evaluate the model.

Another goal Barry had developed but which he did not formally include among those in his learning agreement was to explore the current meaning of his brother's death. He felt that he was capable of working with patients who provoked his brother's memory, but he felt, also, that he had uncovered an unhealed wound that needed personal resolution. He chose to do that work in private counseling.

**Stage IV - Implementation.** Barry's goal of developing a model of treatment for dementia provided him with a cognitive structure allaying his discomfort with the illness. The goal was a focus of many supervisory sessions, a process that allowed him to progressively work toward a psychosocial intervention where no other guides existed in the literature. The implementation phase was punctuated with feelings of helplessness, anger, hope, and, ultimately, success as his interventions paid off.

**Stage V - Termination.** As Barry moved through the final phase of training, he integrated his early, intuitive urge to "get off the sidelines" with professional strategies that allowed him to respond to the epidemic in ways that were meaningful to him and to his clients. And he did it with joy and with tears.

## CONCLUSIONS

Social work education, and particularly field education, cannot and should not divorce itself from concern with the subjective reactions and emotional responses of students to their clients. Such reactions should be dealt with as normal and potentially valuable. Field educators should consider student emotional reactions within a framework that prepares students to recognize, cope with, and use their responses in meeting the needs of clients and the students' goals as learners.

## BIBLIOGRAPHY

Dunkel, J., & Hatfield, S. (1986). Countertransference issues in working with persons with AIDS. SOCIAL WORK, 31(2), 114-119.

Finkelhor, D. (1984). CHILD SEXUAL ABUSE: NEW THEORY AND RESEARCH. New York: Free Press.

Kagel, J. D. (1984). SOCIAL WORK RECORDS (Chapter 3). Homewood, IL: Dorsey Press.

Kinsey, A. C., Pomeroy, W. B., Martin, C. E., & Gebhard, P. (1953). SEXUAL BEHAVIOR IN THE HUMAN BEHAVIOR. Philadelphia: Saunders.

Perlman, H. H. (1979). RELATIONSHIP: THE HEART OF HELPING PEOPLE. Chicago: Univ. of Chicago Press.

Siporin, M. (1982). The process of field instruction. In B. W. Sheafor & L. E. Jenkins, QUALITY FIELD INSTRUCTION IN SOCIAL WORK (pp. 175-198). New York: Longman.

Sugarman, A. (1981). The diagnostic use of countertransference reactions in psychological testing. BULLETIN OF THE MENNINGER CLINIC, 45(6). The Menninger Foundation.

Towle, C. (1954). THE LEARNER IN EDUCATION FOR THE PROFESSIONS. Chicago: Univ. of Chicago Press.

Wile, D. (1972). Negative countertransference and therapist discouragement. INTERNATIONAL JOURNAL OF PSYCHOANALYTIC PSYCHOTHERAPY, 1(3), 36-67.

Witkin, S. L. (1982). Cognitive processes in clinical practice. SOCIAL WORK, 27(5), 389-395.

# RECOGNIZING THE EDUCATIONAL CONTRIBUTIONS OF FIELD INSTRUCTORS[1]

Judith Lacerte and JoAnn Ray, *Eastern Washington University*

## INTRODUCTION

The practicum has offered a creative and efficient way for a school of social work to expand its teaching resources by enlisting the unpaid assistance of agency-based practitioners to supervise students in their field learning settings. Qualified agency supervisors are especially important today when educational resources are declining. Considering the large amount of time students spend in an agency setting, it is surprising that the Council on Social Work Education does not require schools to provide training for agency supervisors.

Historically, agency personnel who work with students have been referred to as supervisors. Today, many schools are using the designation of instructor to emphasize the educational expectations of the field experience. The two titles will be used interchangeably in this paper with the understanding that the authors view the practicum as an educational experience, not as on-the-job training.

There is a wealth of social work literature on field instruction. Excellent bibliographies can be found in two recent books, QUALITY FIELD INSTRUCTION IN SOCIAL WORK (Sheafor & Jenkins, 1982), and FIELD INSTRUCTION: TECHNIQUES FOR SUPERVISORS (Wilson, 1981). Subject headings are numerous and include performance evaluations, student learning, techniques of supervision, and field instruction in specific practice settings. Supervision of students doing practicum in the workplace and the role of faculty in field coordination are two of the most popular topics presented at practicum workshops.

A subject area that has been largely overlooked is how a school of social work can effectively reward and train agency supervisors. Questions needing answers include: Do schools do enough to express appreciation to their field instructors? Is what the schools do to show their appreciation what the supervisors really want? Do supervisors need special training to perform their function in a skilled manner, and if so, what should that training include?

The desire to compile nationwide data about what other schools are doing to recognize, reward, and train agency supervisors was the primary motivation for this research. The secondary purpose was to contrast what practicum directors said they did, or wished they could do, with what field instructors reported was most important to them.

---

[1]A version of this article, co-authored with Lois Irwin, has been published in the JOURNAL OF TEACHING IN SOCIAL WORK, Vol. 3(2), 1989, and is printed here with their permission.

## METHODOLOGY

Two databases were required for this research: 1) a survey of graduate schools' practicum directors, and 2) a survey of agency supervisors.

The ninety-plus graduate schools of social work listed in the CSWE directory were mailed a survey questionnaire requesting information from their practicum directors. (By mistake, some undergraduate programs were also mailed a questionnaire.) The questionnaire contained questions regarding the amount, type, and content of training provided to agency supervisors, and what types of recognition the schools gave to their field instructors. The practicum directors' opinions regarding the adequacy of training and recognition were also elicited.

The second questionnaire was mailed to eighty-nine campus-based agency supervisors who had provided practicum placements during the past three years for the graduate students from the School of Social Work and Human Services at Eastern Washington University. This questionnaire requested information regarding why they initially became practicum instructors and why they continue to do so. They were asked which incentives they most appreciated.

## FINDINGS

### Practicum Coordinators' Questionnaire

One hundred eight completed questionnaires from schools of social work were returned, and the ten clearly noted as relating to undergraduate programs were eliminated. Four questionnaires were returned by the post office as undeliverable.

Nearly 100% of the practicum directors believe that agency supervisors need special training. Slightly more than three-fourths (79%) of the practicum directors reported that they provide an orientation for field instructors. A majority (58.8%) of the schools have been doing this for over five years. Although only half of them require instructors to attend, over 70% of the schools report that between 50% and 100% of their agency supervisors have completed an orientation program.

The primary purposes for an orientation session(s) are to acquaint the agency instructors with the school's expectations, practicum policies, and procedures, and to review the field manual and the curriculum. The secondary goal focused on helping the supervisor to make the transition from practitioner to teacher. Other goals mentioned less frequently included: to help supervisors network with each other, to provide information on the generalist perspective, to explain characteristics of adult learners, and to develop and use student learning contracts, learning assessments, and evaluations. Most of the schools that provide training use a similar curriculum, as indicated by Table 1.

### Table 1: Content of Training Programs
#### (N=74)

| | |
|---|---|
| Evaluating student performance | 94.6% |
| Developing learning contracts | 89.2% |
| Teaching learning styles | 89.2% |
| School's curriculum needs | 87.8% |
| How to teach specific skills | 73.0% |

Curriculum areas that were added via handwritten comments centered in three areas of concentration: working with problem learners and/or working within problem situations; using process recording and other educational tools; and providing special interest seminars (i.e., cultural diversity, computer awareness, and Alzheimer's disease).

Nearly 100% of the practicum directors believe that field instructors need special training that goes beyond what is offered in an orientation session (or sessions) although only 60% offer it.

Nearly 70% of the schools report that between 75% and 100% of their supervisors have completed a training program that goes beyond orientation. Nearly half the schools (48.5%) have offered training for five years or more. Only 5.8% report that less than 25% of their supervisors have completed a training curriculum. Schools which have been offering training for five years or longer tend to have a greater percentage of trained supervisors.

Most social work programs provide recognition for their agency instructors; most frequently this recognition is a university library card or free workshop attendance. Least likely is monetary compensation.

### Table 2: Recognition for Agency Supervisors
#### (N=92)

| | |
|---|---|
| University library card | 71.7% |
| Free workshop attendance | 65.2% |
| Adjunct professor status | 50.0% |
| Certificate for being an agency supervisor | 48.9% |
| Recognition ceremony | 38.0% |
| Certificate for completing training | 23.9% |
| Certificate for completing orientation | 9.8% |
| Monetary compensation | 1.1% |

Almost 70% of the practicum directors stated that they felt their school did not do enough for their agency supervisors. Table 3 presents a comprehensive list of the recognition methods, privileges, and training/educational opportunities that schools of social work are using to reward field instructors. This table demonstrates that, as a profession, social work education offers multiple rewards to field instructors.

### Table 3: Comprehensive List of Recognitions, Privileges, Training/Educational Opportunities Provided by Schools of Social Work to Reward Field Instructors

**Recognition:**
- Send thank you letters
- Host recognition breakfast, lunch, dinner, party, reception
- Provide a yearly recognition ceremony
- List supervisors' names in departmental and/or university publications
- Publish a newsletter on practicum events and activities
- Take photographs of supervisors in action
- Invite the supervisors to be guest lecturers in the classroom
- Invite the supervisors to help train new supervisors
- Provide supervisors with professional articles on a subject of interest from a journal to which they are not likely to have easy access
- Invite supervisors to the Practicum Fair to meet students and to present their agencies

**Privileges:**
- Provide supervisors the opportunity to influence the school's curriculum--by meetings with faculty and administrators and by sitting on school committees
- Recruit first among supervisors when hiring for part-time employment to teach electives
- Offer a reduced cost to college events: sports, plays, etc.
- Offer free university parking
- Award clinical instructor status
- Award adjunct professor status
- Award the title of preceptor to those who have supervised for more than two years
- Award state certification
- Offer error and omission malpractice insurance
- Pay honorarium and/or mileage to training events

**Training/Educational Opportunities:**
- Offer reduced tuition for supervisors (and/or spouse) for up to 6 credits a year
- Offer free tuition for 3 credits per year
- Give a 10% discount at the university bookstore
- Provide a free textbook
- Reduce fees for university-sponsored workshops for the supervisors or an employee of the same agency
- Provide other educational opportunities
- Offer advanced supervisory training

## Agency Supervisors' Questionnaire

### Description of Sample

Sixty-six of the graduate agency supervisors completed the supervisors' questionnaire for a 74.2% return rate. Sixty-eight percent of the respondents have a Master's in Social Work, and approximately 18% have a master's degree in another discipline. Just over one-third of the respondents have attended Eastern Washington University for their graduate education. Fifty-five percent of the agency supervisors are female, and over one-half are between the ages of 36 and 45. Approximately 45% of the respondents have been student supervisors for one to two years; however, 8% have served as agency instructors for over seven years. Approximately 12% have been granted adjunct professor status, although this opportunity has been available for only two years. Eighty-four percent of the supervisors rated their relationship with the school as good or better, and most felt they were valued by the school for their role as field supervisor.

Our social work program is in a position of having many more well-qualified agency instructors available than can be matched with students. While there are several other schools in the area, competition for agencies is not an issue.

## Description of Findings

Supervisors were asked to give the reasons they first started to supervise and why they continued to supervise. The checklist of suggested reasons was basically the same for both questions, except that two options were added to the second question. These were: "Like to influence another's professional development," and "Sense of achievement."

The agency supervisors stated that the reasons for first taking graduate practicum students were a feeling of professional duty, a desire to teach, a new challenge, and extra help for the agency. Less often given as reason for supervising are prestige and the agency's request. Reasons most frequently given by the supervisors as to why they continue to take students include wanting to influence another's professional development, the desire to teach, and a feeling of professional duty.

**Table 4: Reasons for First Supervising and Continuing to Supervise**

|  | Reasons First Supervise (N=65) | Reasons Continue Supervise (N=61) |
|---|---|---|
| Influence another's professional development | not included | 60.7% |
| Desire to teach | 54.8% | 57.4% |
| Professional duty | 56.9% | 55.7% |
| Extra help for the agency | 44.6% | 45.9% |
| Sense of achievement | not included | 45.9% |
| Keep up with latest knowledge | 40.0% | 39.3% |
| New challenge | 47.7% | 37.7% |
| University connection | 33.8% | 29.5% |
| Agency wanted me to supervise | 27.7% | 29.5% |
| Prestige | 6.2% | 6.6% |

When asked about disincentives to supervising, the extra paperwork is the most frequently mentioned disadvantage with approximately 58% of the supervisors checking this item. Lack of time is the second most frequently mentioned disincentive, noted by 24% of the group.

Almost two-thirds of the supervisors rated their ability to supervise in the very good area. None rated themselves less than good. When asked how they learned to supervise, almost all the supervisors stated that they learned on the job. Supervisors' workshops and training at a university were mentioned by the majority. Approximately 15% of the respondents stated that they had received no special training.

### Table 5: How Supervisors Learned to Supervise Students
(N=66)

| | |
|---|---|
| On the job | 92.4% |
| Special supervisors' training | 59.1% |
| Workshops | 56.1% |
| Read books on supervision | 28.8% |
| No special training | 15.2% |

Many of the recognitions offered by the program are important to the supervisors. Most often mentioned were the free workshop, the orientation, adjunct professor status, and the networking with other supervisors.

### Table 6: Rewards Valued by Supervisors
(N=53)

| | |
|---|---|
| Free workshop | 64.2% |
| Orientation | 58.5% |
| Adjunct professor status | 56.6% |
| Networking with other supervisors | 52.8% |
| Certification program | 41.5% |
| Invitation to Practicum Fairs | 37.7% |
| Supervisor forum | 30.2% |
| Other training on specific topic | 22.6% |
| Photo gift | 1.9% |
| Name in newsletter | 1.9% |

A group discussion with approximately 20 supervisors further clarified the value of recognitions and rewards. Most valued rewards included the free workshop, recognition letters to the supervisor's superior, guest lecturing in the classroom, preferential hiring for electives, certification, and adjunct faculty status.

## DISCUSSION

### Comparison of Why Supervisors Start and Why They Continue to Supervise

There are striking similarities between why professionals begin to supervise and why they continue. Two of the top three reasons for supervision, professional duty and desire to teach, show up in the top three in both columns. Desire to teach holds second place both times.

The first initial motivator, professional duty, drops from first to third place with experience, yet there is only .8% overall point difference (56.9% vs. 55.7%). Professional duty continues to be a strong motivating factor for the supervision, but it is not as meaningful as the personal rewards that have been discovered while first supervising: those of teaching and influencing others.

The desire to teach appears to increase with experience. Is it possible that those who supervise in an agency have self-selected themselves to do so because of an accurate self-assessment that they would like to teach? In addition, the initial desire to teach is viewed as a positive new challenge, causing that to be the third motivating factor for why professionals seek to supervise.

Because wanting to influence another's professional development is not given as an option for the first question, it cannot be entirely ruled out as an initial motivating factor. This variable is like desiring to teach: both come directly from an individual's need to invest in a personal relationship with a student. It might be assumed that the desire to influence another's professional career is more a product of actually doing it than of thinking about it. The new role of mentor brings satisfactions not previously envisioned.

The need for extra help was the fourth reason given for both initial and continuing reasons to supervise. Apparently the need for extra help is being met by taking on a student, in spite of the extra work involved in student orientation, training, and supervision. The field instructors still believe that they are getting their "money's worth". The addition of a sense of achievement, also in fourth place as a continuing reason to supervise, is perhaps one reason why the extra work involved in having a student is seen as worth the effort. Not only do agency projects get done by the student, but the supervisor also receives a sense of accomplishment in the process. Such a feeling of accomplishment, like influencing another's professional development, is difficult to imagine and may require the experience of having it happen to give it life.

Reason number five, keeping up with the latest knowledge, is in the same place in both columns. New challenge, initially in third place, drops to number six as a reason to continue supervision. Apparently, new challenge is replaced by sense of achievement.

A major concern of practicum directors, however, is how they (the university) can increase their expression of gratitude to unpaid field instructors. Accordingly, it is of interest to note that the supervisor's desire to be connected with the university actually dropped from sixth place to seventh (33.8% vs. 29.5%) after this association had become a reality. How is this explained? Did the supervisors expect something from the university connection that did not materialize? Although the amount of decrease might not be viewed by some as important, the fact that it dropped during a time of increased recognition and benefits is a puzzle and maybe a concern. Why isn't a university affiliation more highly valued? Does its value decrease with exposure?

The pressure from the agency to supervise remained in seventh place in both columns. Apparently there is neither decreased nor increased pressure from agency executives to get student placements once the practicum process is in place. Along this same line, it is intriguing to notice that prestige often assumed by faculty to accompany a university connection was, in fact, the eighth or last reason given by supervisors for both why they start or continue to supervise graduate students.

It is also interesting to note that keeping up with the latest knowledge does not appear to be associated with a university connection. Is there a need to reconnect university affiliation with new knowledge and challenges? If so, how is this done, and by whom? If this happened, what would be the effect on the prestige of being a supervisor?

In conclusion, what has changed is that the supervisor's motivation, although always somewhat personally motivated, has become even more so with experience. As the motivation becomes more personally based, it becomes correspondingly less professionally or agency grounded. This factor is significant because, although the reasons to supervise are strongly personal, they are not tied to either financial gain or prestige, but to the desire for personal and professional growth and service. This speaks well of our profession.

## Supervisor Rewards

When the supervisors were asked to rank a list of rewards and recognitions devised by the authors, they chose free workshops, the certification program, and the adjunct professor status. When asked the open-ended questions about what they saw as the rewards of supervision, what they liked best about supervising students from our program, and what other contacts with the school they valued, the responses centered around distinctly different areas than those from the ready-made list. Write-in comments strongly suggest that supervisors like working with students and faculty in a teaching and collegial fashion, respectively, and the opportunities that supervision provides for their own personal and professional growth.

The free workshop is a strong attractor. While free workshops are clearly the most valuable reward for the supervisors, only 65% of the schools offer free workshops to practicum supervisors.

Other rewards which were no listed on the survey or identified by the other schools (see Table 3) were requested by the supervisors' discussion group referred to earlier. These include recognition letters to the supervisor's immediate superior, guest lecturing, and preferential hiring. A letter to the superior appears to be much more valuable than a thank you letter sent to the supervisors themselves.

Guest lecturing, which is consistent with the high ranking of "desire to teach" as a reason for becoming an agency supervisor, was rated highly as a reward. Similarly, preferential hiring for teaching electives was another item rated very highly. Preferential hiring again relates to the supervisor's desire to teach.

It is important for practicum directors to develop rewards in the agency setting, also. There needs to be a distinction made between rewards/recognitions to the individual supervisor and the sponsoring agency. Examples of agency-related rewards include inviting agency directors to a banquet to thank them and to educate them about the school's curriculum; offering free meeting space and university facilities for agency use; and making both core and elective social work classes available to agency personnel on an auditing basis. This is consistent with the fact that almost one-half of the supervisors choose to initially supervise and continue to supervise students to help their agencies.

Mentoring is a highly motivating factor for practicum supervisors. Ways to enhance the mentoring process, therefore, need to be developed. Field supervisors requested that they receive evaluative feedback from the students and the faculty after they conclude the practicum.

This information has implications for training. It would appear the supervisors will be attracted to training that they believe will provide them with new knowledge, increase their ability to influence the students' professional development, and make them better teachers. Practicum directors can piggyback onto this desire to influence students by being sure to design such supervisory training in a way that is commensurate with the mission of the curriculum.

## CONCLUSION

Agency supervisors have proved to be a successful solution to the need for agency-based student education. In an era of declining resources and greater demands, this free service is highly valued by practicum directors, as demonstrated by the numerous and multiple forms of recognition, rewards, and training opportunities given to supervisors by schools of social work. The belief held by practicum directors that schools should do even more leads to the provocative question: what do field instructors want--university privileges, or opportunities for personal and professional growth?

If our local group of supervisors can be assumed to be somewhat representative of other field instructors across the country, practicum directors may do well not to spend a lot of time and effort trying to negotiate with their university powers to provide reduced course tuition or stipends for field instructors. Instead, new opportunities for supervisors to teach in the classroom as occasional guest lecturers or as instructors for elective offerings may be more appreciated. Supervisors' training that is perceived as increasing teaching skill and knowledge, as well as the ability to influence students' professional growth, should both attract participants and receive rave reviews. Such a curriculum also meets a desire repeatedly voiced by practicum directors to encourage and assist supervisors into moving toward a more educationally based practicum model of student instruction. This is not to suggest that recognition ceremonies and special privileges should not be given, but that they are not the mainstays behind why supervisors either begin to supervise or continue to do so. This should not come as a surprise if Maslow's hierarchy and Erikson's developmental phases are reviewed. Supervisors are meeting their survival requirements through agency employment. Now they are seeking new opportunities to meet affiliation needs, new ways to give to the next generation, and new avenues for self-realization. By helping supervisors meet these needs, practicum directors will better serve the students and, thus, the profession of social work eduction will better serve the community.

## BIBLIOGRAPHY

Sheafor, B. W., & Jenkins, L. E. (1982). QUALITY FIELD INSTRUCTION IN SOCIAL WORK. New York: Longman Press. 262-282.

Wilson, S. J. (1981). FIELD INSTRUCTION: TECHNIQUES FOR SUPERVISORS. New York: The Free Press. 327-339.

# THE ADVANCED SEMINAR FOR FIELD INSTRUCTORS: CONTENT AND PROCESS

Helene Fishbein and Urania Glassman, *Adelphi University*

## PURPOSE OF THE PAPER

This paper will describe the varied aspects of an eight session Advanced Seminar for Experienced Field Instructors. It will: a) identify the need for the seminar, b) outline the underlying assumptions that guide its design, c) describe participants, and d) look at the educational tools used. It will e) discuss the whole curriculum and the theme for each session,f) describe the growth of the seminar as a learning group, and g) delineate the roles of the co-instructors. (Excerpts from a videotape of one session were presented to demonstrate aspects of the process.)

## NEED FOR THE SEMINAR

By agreement of a consortium of schools in the New York area, all beginning field instructors are required to attend a twelve week course on field instruction. Within that context one school decided to pursue a mutual desire of the consortium to create a seminar for experienced field instructors in that school. It was felt than an experienced group of field instructors could benefit further from a current look at their teaching, as well as the contextual arena of their part in social work field education. The assumption was made that field instructors would benefit from re-connecting with the school's resources in field education, particularly those that focused on differential approaches with students. The beginning seminar taken by participants concurrently with their first field instruction experience is often conducted in a trial by fire context. This process may parallel (Shulman, 1984) the perils of a first semester student in the field. Thus, the current seminar was constructed to provide experienced field instructors an arena for raising issues more thoughtfully, where the need for mastery is not an overwhelming issue.

## ASSUMPTIONS GUIDING DESIGN OF SEMINAR

Field instruction is an educational process in which the field instructor develops the conscious use of self as a teacher by making a shift from the role of practitioner to the role of educator. In this process of becoming an educator, the field instructor learns to meet the varied needs of students by developing a range of skills in educational assessment and teaching. As an educator, the field instructor centers primarily upon teaching a student, not managing a case. The partnership between the field instructor as agency representative and the school is further supported and enhanced through the development of this seminar for experienced field instructors. Furthermore, for experienced field instructors, the seminar may serve as a model for them in developing educational programs for their students.

## PARTICIPANTS

Six field instructors from a range of agencies, several with more than fifteen years experience, took part in the entire process. The agencies represented included a child welfare program, nursing home, community center, community health center,community mental health center, and a senior center. When asked in the first meeting what they hoped to gain from these meetings,many expressed the desire "...to get back to basics", "...identify new trends in education", and to solidify a connection to the school.

## STRUCTURE AND PROCESS

The seminar met weekly for two hours for four consecutive weeks in the late afternoon, so as to interfere with agency imperatives as little as possible. Then, after a four week hiatus, four sessions followed. It was felt that this break in time could help over-extended practitioners space out the time away from the agency. In addition four consecutive weeks prevented the discontinuity in process that bi-weekly seminars might have created. Returning after time to reflect on the learning and experiment with new strategies was another advantage the hiatus created. Participants were required to submit a process record of a field instruction conference.

The seminars took on a patterned form. A structured presentation by one of the instructors often began the seminar. Aspects of a topic were discussed as the field instructors described their work with specific students. Different educational tools were used in each session and varied depending on appropriateness.

The cohesion of the class as a group (Schmuck and Schmuck, 1975) was rapid due to size, commonality, and emphasis on the group itself as a cooperative learning unit in which the atmosphere of sharing and mutual respect for one another's learning mattered.

## EDUCATIONAL TOOLS

These ranged from cognitively to experientially-oriented strategies to include lecturettes, presentation of members' process recordings of a field instruction conference, role plays,readings, and a videotape of the seminar itself. Conceptual material was drawn from the literature in education and field instruction. It was used to connect members to their experiences as illustrative of concepts. Process recording, primarily a cognitive tool (Hartford, 1967; Papell, 1984) designed to help the learner reflect upon prior behavior through broader lenses,was used. Its use in a class or seminar stimulates interaction and discussion. Role play (Sharan and Sharan, 1976; Milroy,1982) is an experiential tool used to help participants and observers put themselves in someone else's shoes (Klein, 1956). It enables examination of simulated interaction in an arena that allows comfort because real persons are not at stake. The videotape from participants supervisory conferences or the seminar group itself is a rich medium offering great opportunity to extend the more cognitive and traditional process recording. By allowing a view, in this case of oneself in process, it helps people scrutinize and reflect on their's and others' participation and input in a new way. Viewing enables an acute here and now awareness of interaction through whatever lens viewers choose or are directed to use. It is most useful as an experiential tool when not viewed in total, but interrupted in brief intervals for viewers reactions, input and critiques (be it of practice or teaching).

The thrust of this seminar was to mix the use of these tools with a clear mind towards developing the group process and sharing necessary for a successful learning experience. The seminar was to be a participatory enterprise so that tools used not only had to be synchronized with the content taught, but with the process as it evolved. More experientially oriented tools centering directly on the members' own work were used later on in the process as participants felt more comfortable with one another.

## CURRICULUM

The development of the curriculum was guided by the participants expressed needs, the view of education as a partnership of adults (Knowles, 1972), the desire to offer a framework for educating social workers in the field, and the instructors' commitment to the creation of experiential opportunities (Reynolds, 1965) as a way to help field instructors maintain connectedness to students' issues, and to understand the deeply affective component of the field instruction experience.

In the first meeting members were asked to respond to the question, "What do you hope to gain from this seminar?" As participants offered ideas and wishes, these were written on newsprint taped to the wall to be saved by the instructors for the group's future reference. Responses included "linking administration back to supervision", "taking time out to reflect," and "connecting to the school." Important too was the feeling of isolation from peers and the resultant possibility that a new trend in practice or education had been missed, that there was "something in the air that has not yet been formally captured." Other issues included working with "the problem student," and using process recordings in innovative ways.

The instructors put forth topic areas they had prepared and a tentative topic outline for the weeks ahead. These included educational assessment, differential use of strategies in the field instruction conference, and approaches for field instructing discreet social work methods. Use of process recordings and other educational tools was included. The outline was modified to include the participants suggestions. It was obvious to the participants that the instructors were prepared with a suggested curriculum, and it was apparent that members' needs could be met through much of it.

## CONTENT AND DESIGN

The first session had three facets. The initial one included an introduction and goal setting in which the participants and seminar leaders developed mutuality on the nature of the course. This was followed by a lecturette to refresh their memories on andragogical (Knowles, 1972) approaches to education. A role play followed, designed by the instructors to set the norm for the inclusion of experiential formats and point to beginning issues of mutuality, support, and trust infield instruction. The enactment presented a young student with anxiety and reluctance regarding her placement in a nursing home, and two field instruction approaches. This led to a discussion of differential approaches to anxiety, the student's need for support, ways of offering support, and orienting the student to the agency and population. The field instructors drew from their prior experiences with students. Connections were made to andragogical concepts requiring the student to be treated as an adult learner.

The second session revolved around the use of process recording as an educational tool, and educational assessment. A lecture on the stages of learning (Reynolds, 1965) began. This helped members re-connect to last week's role play and share examples of students in different stages of learning. A member presented a process recording of a field instruction conference. Participants raised questions and shared similar experiences so as to embellish the field instructor's educational assessment in two areas--the student's practice,and the student's learning style. This was a student with several practice gaps and a know-it-all defensive quality.

The third seminar focused on differential educational planning and the field instructor's use of self. A lecturette on theories of instruction and developing steps in the educational process to allow for sequential learning opened the seminar. The characteristics of growth were reviewed as well as the educational process in the field experience (Siporin, 1982),from engagement, assessment, planning, executing, and evaluating an educational program to planing the next steps. A member's process recording of a field instruction conference along with the student's recording of a group were discussed, enabling the field instructor to develop an educational assessment of the student and a teaching strategy. This was an example of a student who had difficulty taking risks in the group and other practice situations.

The fourth seminar focused on problems with students. Members were asked to consider problem areas they had experienced with students. The instructors did the same. A lecturette on typologies of students in the field and strategies for working with these was presented. These included the following student types: "Know-it-all," "Fraidy cat", "Non-affective thinker", "Doer," "Feeler," "I-am-not-a-student," "Starkly different student", "I don't trust authority", and "Me? I'm only-a-student!" Experiences were discussed and strategies for each were identified. For instance, staying with the work and setting limits is important for the "Know it all"; and partializing and moving away from trivia helps the "Fraidy cat."

Participants were then asked to reflect silently for a few moments on the question of how each of them best learns. For many, this was the first time they had ever addressed this question so directly. Examples from work with students followed to show the communication gaps that occur if the field instructor expects the student to learn in one way but the student learns differently.

In anticipation of the four week break in the seminar,members were asked how they wanted the last four sessions to proceed. They encouraged instructors to continue with what was being planned, interjecting several request which were subsequently incorporated (i.e. working with a nonsupportive agency administration to develop student education).

The fifth session included a review of prior sessions and identification of themes for the next meetings. The request for the group's permission to allow the next meeting to be videotaped was presented and discussed along with the rationale for doing it and plans for its use as an educational tool for future field instruction seminars. Members and instructors shared anxieties, including the embarrassment of how they would look. They agreed to do the videotape and to view it during the seventh session. The meeting continued by looking at highlights from the criteria for field performance for each educational level. This was followed by a presentation of a process recording of a student. The recording was used to make an educational assessment drawing from the criteria for student performance, and the material from the last session on typologies of student learners.

The sixth seminar was videotaped (by one student in the communications department). It began with a lecture on the field instruction of group work (Glassman and Kates, 1988) and moved into a discussion of when to assign groups to students. The view of some members that the group is "too precious" to be assigned to a student at the outset was challenged. A brief process recording of a student's practice with a group was presented and two members volunteered to role play the field instruction conference. A discussion of the role played conference followed. An educational assessment of the student and strategies for field instructing this student's group practice in a generic context were discussed. Group work content necessary for the student to learn was discussed and a chart describing strategies of field instruction that could be used to teach particular groupwork practice principles was distributed and reviewed. When the camera was turned off, the instructors shared positive and enthusiastic feedback with the group. Members also talked about their own stage fright.

In the interim the instructors saw the tape, locating and numbering important sequences so as to edit out portions for their viewing (being sure to include significant views and behaviors of everyone).

The seventh seminar was devoted to viewing the video and reflecting on the seminar's process and the educational issues that emerged. One member brought candy and nuts to the "theatre party" and everyone ate in the dark engrossed in the TV and commenting with ease. The tape was stopped at various points for discussion. Faith in the group's effort and process were discussed along with pleasure at having agreed to the taping. In this session in particular, newer conclusions about field instruction were drawn, old learning was deepened for each member according to personal learning agendas as well as serendipitous phenomena. The instructors emphasized the level of group interaction reflected on the tape -- the ability to listen to each other's content and process and to identify one another's presentations of educational themes. It was emphasized that the collective spirit of discovery brought about the group's consensual validation of important principles of field instruction.

The eighth session, while devoted to summarizing, addressed several themes. The role of agency administrators in helping or hindering the educational program, and strategies for educating agency directors to the importance field instruction plays in worker morale and the upgrading of learning for the field instructors, were discussed. Suggestions were also made for future seminars: One suggestion for future seminars was that each could be centered on one theme. For instance, a series on using the process recording which included several efforts by participants to role play supervising a student from a process submitted, could be offered. Another suggestion was to emphasize and include more on the teaching of specific skills. Participants and instructors identified what they gained from the seminar. Several felt doing the video tape was a high point which opened up newer options for them around use of this medium.

## ROLE OF INSTRUCTORS

The Advanced Seminar was taught by two faculty members who were also the Director and Assistant Director of Field Instruction. They shared equal responsibility for the seminar throughout (SOCIAL WORK WITH GROUPS, 1980) in its design and teaching, taking turns doing a lecturette or conducting a section of each seminar. Their roles and statuses in the school were a latent part of the process. For instance, at the start, members tended to direct their comments to the Director of Field Instruction, as if expecting she was in charge. As it became clear that both had equal input into the seminar by their behavior in it though different statuses in the school, members responded to both instructors.

The literature on co-leadership in groups (SOCIAL WORK WITH GROUPS, 1980) does not generally recommend its widespread usage. It does support the use of co-leadership when statuses are equal and mutual respect and relationship exist. In this case, unequal status outside the group was counteracted by equal status in the group which was the result of respect and relationship. Additionally the instructors guided the process bringing the discussion back to its conceptual meaning or generalized conclusions that connected to a particular theory or construct.

## CONCLUSION

Such opportunities to take part in exploring the nuances of field instruction are meaningful for field instructors. Most importantly seminars for field instructors require a design, a curriculum that includes a content for each session, and clear purposeful plans that include the prepared use of educational tools such as role play or video for each session. When carefully constructed these seminars become a "gift" to the field instructors who need to feel the time commitment they made paid off. When carefully constructed, educational experiences for field instructors reflect a proper interface of town and gown. Free floating, content free, and purely process focused seminars are discouraged. They send a distorted message that there is little substantive theory of education underpinning the school's requirements of field instructors.

# BIBLIOGRAPHY

Glassman, Urania and Kates, Len (1988) "Strategies for the Field Instruction of Group Work." SOCIAL WORK WITH GROUPS, 11:1/2, pp. 111-124. This paper was first presented at the APM, Wash, D.C. 1985.

Hartford, Margaret (1967) "The Preparation of Social Workers". JOURNAL OF EDUCATION FOR SOCIAL WORK. 3:2, pp. 49-60. The author discusses the need to go beyond using only process recording as an educational tool and suggests use of more experiential strategies.

Klein, Alan (1956) ROLE PLAYING IN LEADERSHIP TRAINING AND GROUP PROBLEM SOLVING. N.Y.: Association Press.

Knowles, Malcolm S. (1972) "Innovations in Teaching Styles and Approaches Based Upon Adult Learning." JOURNAL OF EDUCATION FOR SOCIAL WORK, 8:2, pp. 32-39.

Milroy, Elice (1982) ROLE PLAY: A PRACTICAL GUIDE. Great Britain: Aberdeen Univ. Press of Pergamon.

Papell, Catherine. "The Process Recording Re-visited: An Educational Artifact or a Cognitive Exercize". (Unpublished paper).

Reynolds, Bertha (1965) LEARNING AND TEACHING IN THE PRACTICE OF SOCIAL WORK. Russell and Russell.

Rothman, Beulah (1973) "Perspectives on Learning and Teaching" JOURNAL OF EDUCATION FOR SOCIAL WORK. 9:2, pp. 39-51.

Schmuck, Richard A. and Schmuck, Patricia A. (1975) GROUP PROCESS IN THE CLASSROOM, 2nd Ed. Dubuque, Iowa: Wm. Brown.

Sharan, Shlomo and Sharan, Yael (1976) SMALL GROUP TEACHING. Englewood Cliffs, N.J.: Educational Technological Publications.

Shulman, Lawrence (1984) SKILLS OF FIELD INSTRUCTION AND STAFF MANAGEMENT. Itasca, Il: F.E. Peacock. He refers to the parallel process between field instructor and student, and student and client.

Siporin, Max (1982) "The Process of Field Instruction" in B.W. Sheafer and L. Jenkins. QUALITY FIELD INSTRUCTION IN SOCIAL WORK. N.Y.: Longman.

SOCIAL WORK WITH GROUPS (1980) 3:4. The entire issue is devoted to Co-leadership in groups.

# ARBITER OF CHANGE IN FIELD EDUCATION: THE CRITICAL ROLE FOR FACULTY

Dean Schneck, *University of Wisconsin-Madison*

An arbiter is one who has the responsibility and the power to judge and decide a disputed issue. Utilizing a political economy framework for analyzing field program decisions, one can readily perceive the inevitable and sometimes unreconcilable role for field directors and educators as we strive to actualize our faculty and student potential and expectations vis-a-vis indigenous community resources, needs and pressures.

The faculty or field director can be portrayed in the arbiter role using the interactive depiction below:

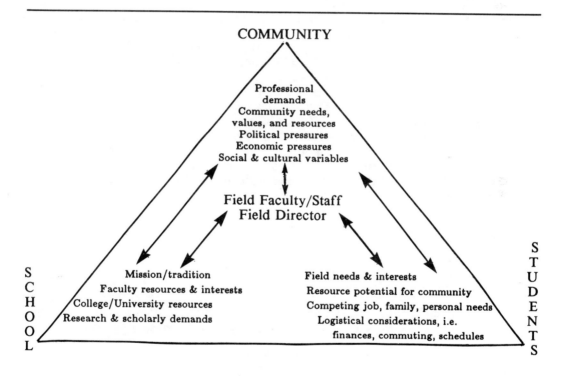

Field education staff (whether titled faculty, field liaisons, field consultants) must make judgments and decisions sometimes with incomplete information and often at a frightening pace on the practice issues and needs of field students and

233

their clients. He or she must be a master problem solver in mediating these forces, much less trying to satisfy everyone. Given the changing and continuing needs of clients, the new policies, methodologies, and program structures, we are constantly evaluating choices and strategies for merit and viability as well as congruence with our traditional values and commitments. It is at once an awesome and an exhilarating responsibility.

Looking more closely, we are compelled to examine evolving treatment methods and techniques for their relevance and effectiveness. We must bring our intuition and analytic skills to bear upon the task of naming new problems, redefining old ones, and judging among various policy responses. Finally, we are expected to be vigilant toward the rapidly changing delivery structures and auspices (e.g., privatization). Perceiving the important questions which derive from client experiences and services, organizational effectiveness and efficiency, funding methods and sources, deployment of staff, and community support requires diligence and incisive oversight.

In the role of faculty arbiter, we should ideally be able to see beyond the superficial dynamics to the essence of each situation--a tall order for those of us with feet of clay. Yet, this is precisely what most field educators and directors do every day--not with every student or in all areas--but some part of it virtually every day.[1] At the Field Education Institute in 1985, it was noted:

> Models of field education represent an idealized and integrated mosaic of educational and practice philosophy, delivery structure and learning process, external demands and referents, faculty and community resources, and local practice opportunities and needs.
>
> . . . The interaction of opportunities to practice, learn, and grow, to influence and contribute to our communities to wrestle with resource, logistical and attitudinal constraints, to manage the synergistic dynamics between class and field are but a few examples. . . . They rightfully reflect the diversity of client populations, particularized regional needs, as well as demographic and university resources and constraints. (Schneck, 1985)

It seems be clear that a conscious and articulated model of field education synthesizing educational process components with community practice opportunities requires a multiplicity of roles for faculty and continual judgments and balances. Seeking not only balance, but harmony and congruence from disparate and potentially competing needs among students, the school, and the community, represents a nexus of influence clearly evocative of our finest problem-solving and negotiation skills.

Often, situational constructs can be helpful in fulfilling the arbiter role. For example, the notion of a resource exchange, formal or informal, between the school and the community often proves fruitful. In such an arrangement, students with faculty and community guidance can often move beyond traditional assignments to

---

[1]Whenever we reflect on such things, we find ourselves on the razor's edge between hyperbole and understatement.

extend new services and resources or develop a demonstration project or innovative model for approaching client problems. Learning opportunities in such a project, both the conceptual and interactional, can be very rich and exciting. Occasionally, structural variations, purposively designed, such as teams of students within a particular agency or interagency teams focused upon common clientele or new initiatives, can offer fine potential.

Similarly, field learning centers situated in a school or sponsored by a school and located in an agency or multi-service center have an interesting history and impressive potential in field education.[2] The proximity of field staff and students to agency staff and programs in the learning center format often allows for timely and reciprocal management of these dynamics. Moreover, field staff involvement in the agencies for regular student business can occasion opportunities for consultation to the agency, or identification of needed research and evaluation projects. I have encouraged faculty:

> . . . to recognize the long-range collaborative possibilities between staff professionals and field faculty which transcend individual students and yearly projects. Many kinds of program and resource development projects, joint research, as well as policy/advocacy efforts are possible. . . . the development of these feeds back into potential for student projects. (Schneck, 1990. p. 39)

In the working of such a resource exchange, the primary skills are networking and problem-solving toward a mutual benefit circumstance in which agencies enhance their service capability and students accrue timely practice lessons. This task/process awareness and facilitation has ample precedent in social work practice. Yet, whenever one employs a variation from a normative pattern, it is imperative to demonstrate adherence to the highest standards of performance and accountability as a *quid pro quo* for flexibility and creative liberty.

An important source of support in working with field agencies is a system of reward and recognition for their instructional and supervisory contributions. Certainly the *sine qua non* is the altruistic commitment of community social workers to contribute to the education of the next generation of practitioners. One frequently hears student supervisors affirm the intangible yet very real benefits of having students in their agencies. They speak of their enthusiasm, their tough questions and new ideas with delight and regard. We have affirmed that,

> Rewards in field teaching occur naturally as we fulfill our commitment to students, educational ideals and quality practice. The personal and professional rewards which accrue from working with students over the course of a year, seeing them develop and do well with clients, following the advance of their careers remain one of the more gratifying sources of

---

[2]For discussion of teaching-learning centers, see MODES OF PROFESSIONAL EDUCATION: FUNCTIONS OF FIELD LEARNING IN THE CURRICULUM (1969), particularly contributions by Kenneth W. Kindelsperger, Scott Briar, Herbert H. Aptekar, and Donald Brieland.

satisfaction. Students represent the future and our involvement with them often does us as much good as we hope it does them. (Schneck, 1990, p. 26)

It is not incompatible with this commitment, however, to recognize educational contributions and to extend such university titles, rewards and privileges as are available and appropriate. Many schools award adjunct faculty titles, free tuition, library and recreational privileges, course credit for workshops, and professional recognition within the community. It seems only fair and logical that community practitioners will identify with the mission of the school, particularly in the day-to-day expectations and demands, to the extent they feel involved, appreciated, and recognized. Some schools also have elected advisory or consultative committees which participate actively and represent community and professional opinion in curriculum, admission, and field program matters. The ongoing participation of a representative professional group in vested and meaningful ways within the organizational infrastructure of a school goes a long way to assure practice relevance and agency support of educational programs as well to prevent unnecessary and gratuitous struggles.

The faculty arbiter, therefore, earns and develops various kinds of influence which are judiciously traded or expended in the pursuit of educational goals. Students are the future of social work. The quality of our involvement with them will be evident in their successes and their strength. The realization of such an endeavor is certainly worthy of our finest negotiation skills and our wisest judgments.

## BIBLIOGRAPHY

MODES OF PROFESSIONAL EDUCATION: FUNCTIONS OF FIELD LEARNING IN THE CURRICULUM. (1969) Tulane Studies in Social Welfare, Vol. XI New Orleans: School of Social Work, Tulane University.

Schneck, Dean (1985) "On Field Education Models: Living with the Loose Ends while Weaving the tapestry." Presented at Models of Field Education: Examining the Common Elements, Post-Conference Institute, Annual program Meeting, Council on Social Work Education.

Schneck, Dean. (1990) "Field Placement Guidelines and Expectations," University of Wisconsin School of Social Work FIELD EDUCATION HANDBOOK.

# THE LIAISON ROLE: A THREE PHASE STUDY
# OF THE SCHOOLS, THE FIELD, THE FACULTY

Cynthia Brownstein, *Bryn Mawr College*
Harrison Y. Smith, *University of Kansas*
Geraldine Faria, *University of Akron*

Social work students are required to spend an extensive amount of time in the practicum. In some schools fully half the students' time is spent in practicum settings (Brownstein, 1981). This heavy emphasis on practical training, in part, reflects the deep practice roots of the social work profession. Social work employs a concurrent model of education which engages students simultaneously in the practicum of the field and the academic work of the classroom. In this model, the schools and programs of social work are accountable and responsible for the entire educational program, including both the field and classroom components.[1] This is different from other professional training. For example, in medicine and psychology, an internship in the field follows the completion of academic requirements.

In social work the duties of monitoring the practicum and evaluating the students' practicum work are assigned to the faculty liaison. The faculty liaison is responsible for linking the field agency to the school. This is to ensure that the agency placement provides a quality educational experience to the students. Social work students are paying for their placements. The academic credits for field work usually total about five academic credits per semester. Social work students are considered to be learners, and are not viewed as assistants to the workers, or as apprentices. They are learning in the natural settings where social work gets practiced in order to be able to acquire and develop their skills of practice. Both the field and the class are necessary conditions for the development of a social work practitioner. The practicum and academic components of the curriculum are dependent on each other to accomplish the purpose of training and educating persons for the practice of social work. The faculty liaison provides the link between the practicum and the academic, and monitors the quality of the practicum.

In addition to linking and monitoring the practicum, the faculty liaison is responsible for evaluating the students' performance. Social work is a practice profession; the BSW and MSW are practice degrees. Students have to do more than cognitively deal with the material covered in the classroom. They have to be able to address real problems and live people in situations that often defy the rules and

---

[1]In addition to presenting the third phase of the liaison study, this article will be summarizing the first two phases, and will be citing frequently from the following two articles: 1. "Utilization of Social Work Faculty in the Role of Liaison: A Field Study" (Fall 1986) 22:3 and 2. "A Survey of Field Instructors' Perceptions of the Liaison Role" (Spring 1988) 24:2 JOURNAL OF SOCIAL WORK EDUCATION, co-authors, Geraldine Faria and Harrison Smith.

prescriptions found in books and covered in lectures. The liaison faculty assigns the students' practicum grades, which are based on the students' capacities to practice.

These primary liaison functions of linking the practicum and the classroom components of the curriculum, monitoring the practicum, and evaluating the students' work in the practicum are central to the education of social work students. The lack of definitional clarity about the faculty liaison role and a scarcity of information about the importance of this role relative to other faculty duties prompted these authors to launch a study of the faculty liaison. This paper reports on three phases of the study. The first phase examined the liaison role as perceived and described by schools and programs of social work. The second phase presented the perceptions of the field agencies about the faculty liaison role. These two phases have been published (see footnote, p. 237) and will here only be summarized. The third phase explored how the liaison faculty themselves perceive and define their role. This final phase of the liaison study will be reported here in more detail.

## THE ROLE OF LIAISON: A LITERATURE REVIEW

Despite the critical importance of the liaison in social work education, there has been scant research attention to the practicum in social work education, and only a few studies have focused on the liaison role.

Rosenblum and Raphael (1983), comment on the complexity of the liaison role. They pose three major functions to define the role. "...(1) facilitating field teaching, students' learning, and integration of theory and practice, (2) monitoring educational opportunities offered by the agency and students' progress...and (3) evaluating field instructors' efforts and students' achievement."

Gladstein and Mailick (1986) discuss the liaison as an advisor having "...responsibility to alert the field instructor and agency to the unique qualities of each student and the particular impact of ethnic issues... ." McCroy, Freeman, Logan and Blackman (1986) consider the liaison important in resolving difficulties in cross-cultural supervision. In Fortune's study about students' satisfaction with field placements the "school-agency" relationship is identified as one of the four critical links associated with student satisfaction (Fortune, Feathers, Rook, Scrimenti, Smollen, Stemerman, Tucker, 1985). The faculty liaison person is central to this relationship.

## THE FIRST PHASE: THE SCHOOLS[2]

This three phase study began with eighty-eight schools and programs of social work. These were the accredited MSW degree granting programs at the start of this study, which included a number of BSW programs. A total of fifty-four schools responded, a response rate of sixty-one percent.

The Practicum Directors at each of these schools were sent questionnaires eliciting information about assignment of faculty as liaisons; title, academic degrees

---

[2]See Smith et.al. (1986) for fuller discussion

and training of liaisons; evaluation of liaisons; and liaison responsibilities. The questions were specifically open-ended, to capture some of the breadth and diversity of the liaison role. It was hoped that this phase could build some structure for defining the work of the liaison.

### Assignment of faculty as liaisons

At most schools, not all faculty were given liaison assignments. The criteria on which these decisions were based are not easy to categorize. The most frequently cited reason for excusing faculty from liaison activity was "other work assignments". The major finding was that liaison duties are not assigned equally to all faculty. It is not clear how much attention is given to the needs of the practicum when assignments are made, and how practicum assignments are balanced with academic assignments to meet the needs of the entire school.

The criteria for weighting liaison assignments as part of the total work load was also unclear. Over half the schools indicated they used a formula in balancing total workload. These formulas varied greatly, from counting the number of students, to not counting students and treating liaison as one unit out of a total number of units. Schools which had no formula indicated they considered certain factors in balancing workload such as: administrative duties, community service, advisement, grants and research projects. It appears that the assignment of faculty to liaison duties takes place without clear guidelines, and at some schools, may be arbitrary.

### Liaison title, degree and training

The lack of uniformity about the liaison role became immediately evident when schools identified sixteen different titles to designate this position. Fifty-nine percent did use the designation "liaison". Some schools used the title "faculty advisor" which incorporated academic advising and the practicum duties. Other titles included "educational consultant", "educational liaison", "contact person", and "school practicum instructor".

A majority of schools, seventy-six percent, indicated that only faculty members with MSW degrees were assigned as liaisons. Some schools assigned non-MSW faculty to the Program Planning or Administration areas.

Fifty-four percent of the schools provided training for faculty new to liaison work. Again there was great variation in the type of training, ranging from optional meetings with the Practicum Director to required bi-weekly meetings.

### Evaluation of liaisons

The variation among schools continued to be evident in evaluating the work of the liaison and how that evaluation was considered in merit pay, promotion and tenure decisions. Most schools indicated that they did evaluate the work of the liaison, but there was a range from informal meetings with the practicum director to specific forms handed out by the Dean's office.

Fifty-two percent of the schools reported that evaluation of the liaison was taken into account in faculty merit pay decisions. The actual weight of these evaluations varied among the institutions. The quality of the liaison activity performed by the faculty member is not evaluated or rewarded on a consistent basis by schools of social work.

## Liaison responsibilities

One of the major outcomes of this phase of the study was a categorization of liaison duties. Sixty-five percent of the schools participating in the study sent their formal listing of liaison responsibilities. Through a content analysis, the following ten categories of liaison activity were identified:

(1) Linkage: The bridge between the school, the agency and the community; interprets school policies, procedures, and expectations to agencies; assesses the fit between school curriculum and educational experiences provided by the agency.
(2) Mediator: Assists in resolving problems between student and field instructor and/or other agency personnel; may involve re-assignment of student and/or termination of agency as placement.
(3) Monitor: Carries out ongoing assessment of agency, field instructor and assignments provided for student, to ensure the quality of the educational experience.
(4) Evaluation: Evaluates students, field instructor and agency; assigns students' grades; makes recommendations for continued use of agency and field instructors.
(5) Consultant: Assists field instructor in developing teaching and supervisory skills, in making the transition from practitioner to teacher.
(6) Teacher: Assists students with the integration of coursework and practicum.
(7) Advisor: Assists students in planning for practicum, including identifying learning needs and possible practicum sites.
(8) Advocate: Provides relevant information when student is under academic review.
(9) Practicum Placement: Selects agencies and field instructors and matches them with student learning needs.
(10) Administration: Ensures completion of placement forms, letters to agencies, evaluations of agency; writes final summary of student.

## THE SECOND PHASE: THE FIELD[3]

The second phase of the study focused on the agency field instructors, the persons having contact with the liaisons. A selection of ten schools participating in the first study, representing programmatic and geographic diversity, were asked to provide lists of field instructors. Fifteen field instructors were randomly chosen from each of the eight lists which were returned. Sixty-four field instructors participated in the study, a response rate of fifty-three percent.

The field instructors were asked for their descriptions of the liaison role and their perceptions about which roles the liaison actually performed.

### Field instructors' descriptions of liaison role

The field instructors were asked to describe in their own words what they perceived to be the role of the liaison. This was to obtain the field instructors' perceptions about the duties of the liaison. Using content analysis, the responses were grouped according to the categories identified in the first phase. The liaison role most frequently described by the field instructors was linkage (58%), followed by mediator (38%) and monitor (36%). Surprisingly, missing from most of the narrative descriptions were the responsibilities of grading or evaluation, completing paper work and forms included in administration duties, and the duties of teacher and consultant.

### Field instructors' perceptions about liaison performance

The field instructors were presented with the ten categories of liaison functions which had been identified in the first study phase and asked to indicate which functions the liaison actually performed. Again, the functions most frequently reported were linkage (86%), mediator (78%) and monitor (70%). However, administration and evaluation received 69% and 59%, respectively. In other words, though the field instructors narrative descriptions about liaison duties did not include the completion of practicum forms and grading, when presented with a list of these duties, the field instructors did acknowledge that the liaisons did carry out administration and evaluation duties. Consultant and teacher continued to be low. Only 44% of the field instructors identified that the liaisons functioned as consultant and 31% acknowledged the liaisons as teachers.

## THE THIRD PHASE: THE LIAISONS

The final area of investigation for the authors was how the responses from the social work schools and practicum agencies compared with the responses from the liaisons themselves. Was there any agreement between how the schools defined the

---

[3]See Faria et al. (1988) for fuller discussion

role of liaison, what the field agencies expected from the liaisons, and how the liaison faculty defined their role?

A selected sample of twelve schools participating in the first study were asked to distribute questionnaires to their liaison faculty. These schools were representative of program size, geographic location and a mixture of public/private. A total of ninety-five responses were received from the 161 liaison faculty contacted, a response rate of fifty-nine percent. The average number of liaisons responding from each school was eight, with a range from four to fifteen.

### Liaisons' descriptions of liaison role

Liaison faculty were asked to describe, in their own words, what they perceived to be the role of the liaison. The narrative descriptions offered by the liaisons provided support for the two previous phases of the study. Again, the most frequently cited functions were linkage, monitor, and mediator. Some of the responses were:

"A linkage for student and field instructor to interpret field placement policy, resolve agency/instructor/student issues and determine ultimate quality of student placement arrangements."

"Provide a bridge between the University and the field. Interpret school expectations for the field. Maintain current information on field developments to update curriculum. Monitor quality and consistency of field."

"Maintain, monitor and support the connection between school and agency about student progress and assignments, and school curriculum, be a mediator."

#### Table 1: Descriptions of Liaison Activity
1= Most important   10= Least important

| Liaison functions | Percentage of liaisons performing | Average ranking of importance |
|---|---|---|
| Linkage | 96 | 3.17 (2) |
| Monitor | 93 | 3.06 (1) |
| Mediator | 89 | 4.39 (5) |
| Evaluation | 84 | 4.89 (6) |
| Advocate | 81 | 5.73 (8) |
| Advisor | 79 | 4.03 (3) |
| Teacher | 67 | 5.40 (7) |
| Administration | 64 | 7.73 (10) |
| Consultant | 57 | 4.12 (4) |
| Practicum Placement | 30 | 5.90 (9) |

Liaisons were provided with the categories of liaison functions identified earlier, and asked to indicate whether they actually performed them, and to rate their relative importance. The results are listed in Table 1. Again the functions of liaison, monitor and mediator were listed as the most frequently performed. Ninety-six percent of the liaisons indicated they functioned as a linkage, while monitor was listed by 93% and 89% of the liaisons indicated they functioned in the role of mediator.

When considering the ranked importance of these functions, there were discrepancies. The liaisons ranked monitor as the most important function, with linkage and advisor as next most important. Consultant was considered the fourth most important and mediator, just behind as fifth most important.

It appears that the advisor function, which includes helping students to identify their learning needs, is considered very important by the liaisons, even though only 79% of the liaisons report themselves performing in that role. The function of consultant was viewed similarly. The liaisons considered it an important function for them to help the practitioner transition into the role of educator, ranking it fourth in importance. However, only 57% of the liaisons reported being used in that capacity.

### Relative importance of liaison role

In order to determine the importance liaison faculty assign to the liaison role, the liaisons were asked to rate in importance the faculty duties of teaching, scholarship-/research, school service, liaison, academic advising, university service and community service. Table 2 presents the averages of the rankings for each item, in decreasing order of importance.

---

**Table 2:\* Importance of Liaison Duties Relative to Other Faculty Duties**

1= Most Important   10= Least Important

| Duties | Average Ranking |
|---|---|
| Teaching | 1.32 |
| Scholarship | 2.40 |
| Liaison | 3.91 |
| School Service | 4.09 |
| Academic Advising | 4.30 |
| Community Service | 5.05 |
| University Service | 5.96 |

\* Persons with liaison as only assignment not included in figures

---

"Teaching" was assigned a "1" as most important (1 = most important, 10 = least important) by 80% of the liaisons, for an average score of 1.32. "Scholarship/research" was assigned a "2" as most important by 60% of the liaisons, with an average score of 2.40. There was no further majority clustering of rankings among the remaining faculty duties. The "liaison" duties averaged 3.91, making it the third most important faculty duty, putting it slightly ahead of "school service", which received an average ranking of 4.09.

### Descriptions of helpful and unhelpful liaison activity

To provide knowledge about the liaison's perceptions of their role they were asked to present examples of helpful and unhelpful liaison activity. The liaison functions are evident in the examples and are marked in parentheses following each example. The liaison descriptions of helpful liaison activity show a decisive use of position and authority, a commitment to maintain high standards, and a willingness to devote time to the role:

"I helped the field instructor in moving from a caseworker role with her student to one of educator, and helped develop appropriate assignments." (consultant and linkage)

"I supported the student through intra-agency disputes, teaching her how not to get caught in the middle and to develop a reasonable set of options. The agency chaos did not settle down and I recommended not using this agency again." (monitor and evaluation)

"I helped the student 'stick through' the placement, though she was very anxious. She came in with training in another discipline, and needed help in re-framing into a social work perspective." (teacher)

"I interpreted to the agency executive the importance of community-based experience, gave examples of what other agencies are doing, and helped the student and agency develop a meaningful project." (linkage)

"I backed up the field instructor in her assessment of difficulties the student had in working with minority clients. I supported the field instructor in developing different teaching approaches and had talks with the student to help her examine her values." (evaluation, consultant, teacher)

Examples offered by liaisons in which they were unhelpful often involved lack of role clarity, lack of time and a laziness about carrying out the responsibilities of the role:

"I didn't confront disagreements between the field instructor and student and the situation got worse." (did not function as mediator)

"The field instructor evaluated early on that the student might have difficulty completing the work satisfactorally. I didn't stay closely enough connected and recognized too late that the student should have been counselled out." (did not do evaluation)

"I supported the field instructor's wish to continue to teach the student who showed no capacity for engaging clients. I should have moved earlier to an educational review process." (did not do evaluation and did not advocate)

The breadth and complexity of the liaison role is evident in the above examples. The faculty liaison is continually having to make judgements, moving in and out of the different functions of the position.

**Who are the liaison persons?**

The degrees and teaching assignments of the liaisons are listed in Table 3. An overwhelming number, ninety-eight percent, possessed the MSW degree. Only nine percent had a doctoral degree, with no MSW. Eight percent were doctoral students. Most were full time, eighty-eight percent, forty-eight percent were tenured faculty, and thirty percent were not on a tenure line. Two of the programs represented in this data do have separate field faculty, which explains the high number, almost a third of the faculty liaison, who are not on a tenure line. This might prove a fruitful area for further research. Is there any difference in the work performed by liaisons who are not educators? Is this a trend in the profession, and, if so, is it a welcome trend?

### Table 3  Academic Characteristics of Liaisons

| Characteristic | Percentage |
|---|---|
| M.S.W. Degree | 98 |
| Doctoral Degree | 63 |
| Part Time | 16 |
| Full Time | 78 |
| Tenure Line | 70 |
| Tenured | 48 |
| Practice Faculty | 58 |
| HBSE Faculty | 28 |
| Research Faculty | 26 |
| Policy Faculty | 20 |
| Doctoral Faculty | 19 |
| Doctoral Student | 8 |

Liaison assignments appeared to be spread over teaching content areas. Over half, fifty-eight percent, of the liaisons were practice faculty. twenty-eight percent taught HBSE, twenty-six percent were research faculty, while twenty percent taught in the policy sequence.

## DISCUSSION

In examining the importance of the liaison role in social work education, it does not appear that liaison activity is considered an integral part of the academic role and rewarded on that basis. Liaisons report feeling more appreciated by their agencies and students than by their schools. Two-thirds feel appreciated in their liaison role by their school, while ninety-five percent feel appreciated by the agencies and ninety-five percent feel appreciated by the students.

Seventy-two percent of the liaisons indicate that liaison roles and functions are not considered in tenure decisions. Less than half think that liaison duties should be considered in these decisions due to their lack of definitional clarity and unacknowledged importance in an academic setting.

These responses are supported by the liaison narratives discussing the match of their expectations with the school and agencies. Liaisons were asked to describe how their school's expectations for the liaison role matched their own expectations. The comments were poignant and indicate how the liaisons feel caught in a system that doesn't value the work they do:

"There is a feeling of malaise. Many faculty do not take field liaison very seriously. Often, the role itself is not understood very well."

"Does the social work profession take field instruction as seriously as it did twenty years ago?"

"There's a basic problem--the liaison assigns a grade--yet is not seeing the student perform."

"Other faculty are not really informed about what we do."

"School prefers more involvement. However, faculty rewards system is based on research and publications. The liaison and advisement load is too large to allow devotion of much time to it."

"The school views it as necessary, not crucial or essential."

Liaisons were also asked to describe how their agencies' expectations of liaisons matched their own expectations for the position. Again, the responses indicate lack of clarity about the role.

"Some agencies see liaison as a formality and don't really see the liaison having anything to offer."

"Very few have a clear idea-- they think our job is only to evaluate the student."

"Some field instructors expect the liaison to do direct supervision."

One senses the liaisons feel in a real paradox. They perceive themselves to be separate from the non-liaison faculty, and that among their faculty peers, they have to defend what they do as liaisons. Though they may feel acknowledged and appreciated by the field, they still have to clarify for the field what they can offer in their role of liaison. They also know, from their own MSW education, the critical impact of the field in shaping their own professional careers. It is almost as if they are doing the "dirty work" of social work education, work that needs to be done, but has little respectability (Emerson and Pollner, 1982).

## CONCLUSIONS

These three phases of study into the liaison role were exploratory, initiated to develop some definitional clarity about the duties and functions of the faculty liaison. Categories of duties were identified in the first study phase, which surveyed schools of social work about the duties assigned to the liaison. These categories were validated in the next two study phases, with the field instructors and with the faculty liaisons. However, the responsibilities included in these categories have some overlap, and are not all relevant to all programs. For example, in some schools the advisor function is handled by a different faculty member, and in many schools placement is handled only by Practicum Administration.

A great deal of diversity exists among the schools in regard to the liaison's responsibilities, assignment of faculty as liaisons, their title and training, and the evaluation of their work. Diversity also exists in the field, where the liaison's actual performance did not always match what the field was expecting from the liaison. Central to the liaison role is evaluation, yet this function was missing from most field descriptions of the liaison role.

For the liaison faculty, there was also the diversity, and as well frustration. The liaisons were often not functioning in roles they considered important, such as advisor and consultant. Yet, they were spending time in the role of mediator, which they did not consider an important function.

Though the categories identified in this research probably do support a core set of liaison responsibilities, the current categories may be too global. They may need to be further separated into specific behaviors or activities. The current state of affairs makes it difficult to conduct research on the performance of the liaison role, and consequently, to ensure quality practicum education.

The real issue is the role and importance of the practicum in social work education. Further inquiry into the liaison role could help the profession examine this critical, but unstudied, partnership between the schools and the field agencies. This type of review might be undertaken by the Council on Social Work Education.

As long as Schools of Social Work are granting the degree based on both course and field work, the Schools are responsible and accountable for the quality of both classroom and field activity. About one-third of the students' credit hours are generated by the practicum, yet the criteria and process by which the practicum gets monitored are not clear. The liaison is currently the profession's structure for conducting education in the field, and for maintaining the importance of the practicum in social work education. The thrust of social work education is the integration of practice and theory. The practicum is where the practice gets taught. The profession can no longer be irresponsible in monitoring the practicum.

# BIBLIOGRAPHY

Brownstein, C. (Fall, 1981) "Practicum Issues: A Placement Planning Model." JOURNAL OF EDUCA-TION FOR SOCIAL WORK. 17:3.

Emerson, R. and Pollner, M. (1982) "Dirty Work Designations: Their Features and Consequences in a Psychiatric Setting." in THINGS THAT MATTER: INFLUENCES ON HELPING RELATIONSHIPS. H. Rubenstein and M. Bloch, eds. N.Y.: MacMillan Publishing.

Faria, G, Smith, H., Brownstein, C. (Spring, 1988) "A Survey of Field Instructor's Perceptions of the Liaison Role." JOURNAL OF SOCIAL WORK EDUCATION. 24:2.

Fortune, A., Feathers, C., Rook, S., Scrimenti, R., Smollen, O., Stemerman, B., Tucker, E. (Fall, 1985) "Student Satisfaction with Field Placement." JOURNAL OF SOCIAL WORK EDUCATION. 21:3.

Gladstein, M., Mailick, M. (Winter, 1986) "An Affirmative Action Approach to Ethnic Diversity in Field Work." JOURNAL OF SOCIAL WORK EDUCATION. 22:1.

McCroy, R., Freeman, E., Logan, S., Blackman, B. (Winter, 1986) "Cross-Cultural Field Supervision: Implications for Social Work Education." JOURNAL OF SOCIAL WORK EDUCATION. 22:1.

Rosenblum, A., Raphael, F. (Winter, 1983) "The Role and Function of the Faculty Field Liaison." JOURNAL OF EDUCATION FOR SOCIAL WORK. 19:1.

Smith, H., Faria, G., Brownstein, C. (Fall, 1986) "Utilization of Social Work Faculty in the Role of Liaison: A Field Study." JOURNAL OF SOCIAL WORK EDUCATION. 22:3.

# PART IV: EDUCATIONAL ISSUES

## INTRODUCTION

The converging of conditions in two separate fronts--the worlds of practice and the university--has created a crisis in field instruction. In the practice arena, contemporary social crises coupled with inadequate resources to deal with them, let alone to teach students about them, place students in what are often stressful field instruction environments. The resultant responses by students to placement in child welfare, family violence, chronic mental illness, homelessness, corrections, AIDS, and poverty are not without hopelessness and frustration, and even refusal to be placed in the setting altogether. Furthermore, on the academic front, the lag between curricula and communities' service needs, and the pressure on faculty to publish and do research rather than to develop service delivery models for the education of skilled practice professionals, contribute to the students' frustrations, narrow perspectives, avoidant attitudes, and skepticism about the school's credibility. The lack of substantial scholarship aid for a student body in debt, further affects the student's skepticism about the school's responsiveness.

Students are older, having more family responsibilities than their younger counterparts of prior years. For these students, a job is a must, if not full time, at least part time. Even with an assistantship, younger students cannot support themselves as they did twenty-five years ago. It has been necessary for the school to respond flexibly by moving away from traditional views of the student as a full time member of the professional/academic community. Models of social work education have changed to meet these changing needs of students, with many part-time programs flourishing in the U.S. and Canada. Furthermore, schools have found that by holding to outdated views of full time studentship, they would eliminate from the pool students without independent financial resources, creating an elitist profession due to structures and institutions that close out people who must work. In many schools, this group represents a large proportion of minority populations. This is contrary to all social work values centered upon equal access to opportunity. The school of social work is the first place where an adherence to social work values can be demonstrated. After all, the teaching of values begins at home.

Starr and Haffey discuss the current effort to develop non-elitist structures in social work education that provide access to agency personnel with bachelor's degrees, many of whom are working in the public sector. In the context of a comprehensive plan for part time programs, they identify the issues in developing and monitoring quality work-study field placements. Experienced personnel in human services can develop the skills to function as professional social workers, which often may result in the professionalization of underserviced areas. Along similar lines in a highly provocative paper, Reeser, Wertkin, and Davis call attention to the stunning fact that BSW student placements are different from MSW level ones in that the former are assigned to work with poor minority populations in significantly higher numbers. The implications are startling. Elitism in the field placement process emerges as the key issue as the most skilled students are being socialized away from the highest risk clients who actually need them the most. Schools have to accept responsibility for correcting this type of institutional elitism and racism.

This commitment to provide education to students who must work by using the employment site for field placement, has required the schools to develop educational structures and criteria for designing assignments and monitoring agencies, rather than the regressive alternative of ignoring the inequity. Navari examines the relationship of learning styles and field models, suggesting newer approaches to the design of part-time programs are needed. Martin focuses attention to the specific structures and guidelines the field instruction department can use in developing opportunities for students to use their place of employment for their field instruction. Marshack, in describing the older student as a new constituency, delineates their characteristics which emanate from rich life experiences, and suggests the types of educational approaches and programs most suitable for adult learners.

As schools have become larger, with more complex routes to the baccalaureate and masters degrees, and practice so diversified it is hard to keep up with developing standards for each practice domain, concerns about gatekeeping have been uppermost. The gatekeeping function of the field instruction setting has to be monitored and supported by clear policies and standards and skilled faculty. In their research, Hartman and Wills gather data about the degree of difficulty field instructors experience in their efforts to fail a student, and the school's and agency's track records in failing students. They identify key criteria used to evaluate student failure, and discuss the essential roles the school must provide for the field instructor to support this agency/school function.

Larger schools will be accompanied by bureaucratization which may bring about a social work technocrat rather than a creative, energetic, professional. The study by Rosenthal and Raphael shows that most field instructors do, indeed, expect their students to express differences with them early on in the educational process. Moreover, in a majority of student-field instructor relationships, both parties report being able to express and deal with their differences--most of which revolve around practice approaches. It would seem then, that to further build upon those processes that reinforce the expression of difference, the school must assume major responsibility for structuring opportunities for enabling students to become assertively creative and to take risks in their field experience.

Another point of interest is the field director and his or her views about the educational and administrative process. In their study of field directors, Hawthorne and Holtzman examine the views and expectations about the field practicum, and satisfactions and dissatisfaction with the role and the role set of two cohorts of field directors--east coast and west coast. The study's findings show that there is more convergence in the views and expectations of the two cohorts than there is divergence.

The papers in this section all direct the reader towards views of contemporary issues through newer lenses.

# THE ACCESS VS. QUALITY DILEMMA IN MSW WORK-STUDY PROGRAMS

Rose Starr and Martha Haffey, *Hunter College of the City University of New York*

Despite the growing need for MSW practitioners in both public and voluntary services, workers with such training are often reluctant to commit themselves to the demands of these settings. They correctly perceive that intense practice demands are not adequately counterbalanced by financial rewards, career advancement, or professional stimulation. The social welfare economy in the decade of the 80's has limited the ability of many social agencies to attract MSWs and to retain its core personnel. As a result, an ever-changing pool of BA-level workers carry the responsibility for the provision of "front line" services.

Even with the frustrating conditions of their work environment, many of these workers have demonstrated commitment to client populations with limited access to professional service-the substance abuser, the homeless, victims of violence, the frail elderly, the physically disabled, the chronically mentally ill, aids victims, and children in care. Providing BA-level workers--many of whom are minorities--with access to professional education can help upgrade and thus create equity in services for underserved, socially-stigmatized populations. The community service and affirmative action missions of the profession can also be strengthened by assuring more adequate representation of these workers within the ranks of the professionally trained.

At present the design of master of social work programs and the scarcity of scholarship aid limits schools' ability to meet the personnel needs of the field and provide access to underrepresented minority populations. Agencies can no longer rely on schools--struggling to maintain enrollment in an environment of scarcity and low status for the profession--to develop a diverse group of professionals with interests and commitments consistent with agency service needs. These same factors also exclude those social service workers who must remain in full time employment and cannot leave the work place to meet all degree requirements. As a result, agencies and workers have few options. Traditional social work education programs fail to facilitate a mechanism through which agencies can identify and develop valued pre-professional personnel, and BA-level workers can achieve professional aspirations.

The lack of trained minority professionals is a case in point. Council on Social Work Education data show that the numbers of minority students in social work education are small and decreasing in both part-time and full-time programs.[1] The work-study field work design allowing students to retain employment provides

---

[1] Statistics on Social Work Education in the United States: 1984

schools one way to create access to under- represented students constituencies.[2] It also provides a mechanism for agencies with few resources and serving the most deprived populations to retain and upgrade non-professional staff and improve the quality of service. From this perspective, the work-study structure may be viewed as an innovative instrument for equity and access.

Nevertheless, many educators and practitioners fear that work-study benefits represent trade-offs with educational quality. Underlying this concern is the assumption that masters programs that deviate from the normative full-time, two-year model are inferior and camouflage a primary interest in organizational survival rather than quality education or service to the community.

It appears certain that both work-study and part-time models of social work education will continue to grow to meet the economic requirements of new, mainly older and working student populations. Thus, the question to be addressed by the profession is not **if** but **how** such alternatives can be incorporated without diminishing the quality of the educational process and its outcome.

Until recently, CSWE Accreditation Standards assumed that quality in alternative educational models can be maintained by using the same program structures and procedures as those developed for the traditional full-time model. Our research and that of others in the field suggests otherwise. From our perspective, differentiation in program design and administration is essential for quality assurance. For example, adaptations in the structure of faculty advising, admissions procedures and field work planning are necessary to respond to the particular needs and characteristics of work--study students. Furthermore, it is important to recognize that when an innovative program is introduced, the change is not isolated but will "ripple" through all aspects of the organization.

This paper will provide a conceptual framework for understanding the agency-school dialectic that differentiates the work-study innovation from traditional educational models. We will also present specific guidelines for quality assurance that recognize the comprehensive impact of work-study arrangements on a school's educational and administrative processes. Central to this conception is the emergence of new forms of school-agency collaboration and the opportunities created for the profession and its community service mission.

---

[2]In a prior study by the authors, data on the percentage of minority students enrolled in the part-time phases of the Hunter College School of Social Work One Year Residence Program, a work- study, employment-based program, were compared to national figures on minority enrollment in part-time programs. The data demonstrate that in each of the years for which statistics were compared, Hunter's program reflects substantially higher percentages of minority students than do part-time programs nationally. These data support the contention that differences in program structure, in particular the design of the field work component, can have a markedly different impact on minority enrollment. These data contribute to the authors' hypothesis on the connection between employment and access to professional education for minority students. see Martha Haffey, Elaine Marshack, Rose Starr, "Costs and Benefits of Work Study vs. Traditional Field Placement Models," Arete, Vol. 9, Fall 1984, p. 41-52 and Martha Haffey and Rose Starr, Designing a Work-Study Program: Where Social Service Employment Meets Professional Education (New York: The Lois and Samuel Silberman Fund, 1988), chapter 3.

## ISSUES IN THE WORK-STUDY OPTION: A FRAMEWORK

Work-study as an educational program at the MSW level refers primarily to the structure of field placement arrangement. In a work-study plan, the student carries both student and employee roles at the social welfare agency or organization in which s/he is employed as a full-time worker. As a result, the student maintains wage earning capacity and on-going work responsibilities while earning MSW degree credits during the required field work practicum. In this model, work assignments in their totality serve both educational and organizational goals. While schools may have different eligibility requirements for work-study applicants (such as prior work experience in the field or the agency), the central feature of this alternative is the employing agency's sponsorship of their employee's field work training as a masters social work student. In our perspective, the variables of role, control and goal provide a framework for conceptualizing the unique aspects of the work-study alternative and for understanding the necessary educational and organizational modifications that are required to make it work.

## GOAL

The identification of social work as a profession, as opposed to an occupation, assumes a body of knowledge, values and interests broader than the boundaries of a single agency. Professional education in the context of the university, although utilizing practice for learning and valuing the service goals for which it educates, emphasizes the independence of the learning process as much as performance and service outcomes. The ideal of professional education, reflected in what will be termed the "educational" or "professional development" goal, seeks academic and practice experience through which the student may identify practice principles and generalize knowledge and skills. To achieve this goal, the learning needs of the individual student require primary focus and protection. In contrast, the social agency places greater emphasis on the performance of service to meet client and organizational interests. Student learning is supported as it is instrumental, in the long if not short run, in meeting these goals. Educational institutions and social agencies share client service as an ultimate goal, but achieve it through differing intermediate or instrumental goals - professional development/education and agency service, respectively.

Although different emphases are evident and potentially in conflict in traditional models of social work education, the educational goal can be primary when the student is independent of the agency providing the learning experience. A clash of goals, i.e., educational versus service, is almost inevitable when the student is a full member of both school and agency. This is the reality of the work-study model, as the student-employee is expected (and wishes) to meet both the learning goals of the school and the service goals of the agency.

## CONTROL

The "control" variable relates to the locus of decision-making in educational planning. In the transition from "town to gown," the determination of what constitutes professional education in class and field has become the domain of the university. While continuing to use and value social agency settings for experiential and applied aspects of learning, schools have claimed the expertise to match agency practice and student learning needs. By maintaining control over whether and how social agencies may become MSW field placement sites, professional schools exert strong influence over the educational experience and the primacy of the educational goal.

In the traditional two year model of social work education, there are constraints that influence this ideal. Highly-sought training agencies, for example, as well as those providing student stipends may have a significant say in the planning and delivery of the educational experience. The increasing scarcity of agency resources for both service and training also has an impact on the purity of the educational rationale for student internships and the way agencies deploy resources for student training. Not only are students looked to to fill service gaps irrespective of their educational potential, but also the increased demand for service also exerts influence on the willingness of agency personnel to devote time to students' educational goals.

The conditions fostering an increase in agency clout with respect to educational decisions are further accentuated in the work-study model. The agency has a claim on the employee-students' use of time and work assignments. To the extent that learning and service needs are complementary, a mutually-agreed upon educational plan can emerge. The field placement planning process for the work- study student involves a negotiation between two systems with equal interest in and claim over the social work student. This process differs substantially from that engaged in for full-time two year students, even though service pressures on the implementation of the field placement experience are increasingly similar.

## ROLE

The variable "role" refers to the expected behavior of the work-study learner in the dual status of employee and student. Traditionally the school has been considered the primary institution through which exposure of the novice to professional role models, values and principles is controlled. The student as learner is expected to adhere to the values of the profession which may at times appear to conflict with agency practice and priorities. Independence and objectivity of the student from the locus of the field placement experience are considered essential for clarity in fulfilling the student role. Although goal conflicts and control issues may have an impact on student role expectations in traditional programs, the school can more readily identify and intervene in situations that threaten the maintenance of role clarity.

In contrast such clarity is rare for the student-employee in work- study programs who must meet multiple role expectations. Even when school and agency support and protect the employee-student's educational goals, the student-employee is always responding to the expectations of the work place. Furthermore, s/he is ever-aware that the preservation of employment ultimately ensures continued access to education.

In sum, what distinguishes work-study from traditional models of MSW education is the duality in goals (service and education), control (school and agency) and role (student and employee). These dualities are intrinsic to the work-study structure and create a more complex educational environment for all parties involved in the learning contract. Some educators in acknowledging these complexities have chosen not to provide work-study arrangements as an educational option. Others in an attempt to maintain quality and control have relied on the application of traditional standards and structures. As we will suggest, however, there is an imperfect fit between the work-study innovation and the program structures traditionally utilized to maintain quality in graduate social work education. When alternative programs are offered to increase educational access, "doing business as usual" may be counter-productive. Modifications in educational designs and delivery may in fact enhance educational quality. It is crucial furthermore that the broader spin off effects resulting from these structural adaptations and different needs be recognized and dealt with. Focusing on the variables goal, control and role as the factors differentiating work-study from other program structures, we will analyze their impact on admission and recruitment, curriculum and teaching, and school--agency relations.

## ADMISSION/RECRUITMENT

Schools and agencies differ in their missions but ultimately share the goal of quality service to clients. It is important for schools to work with agencies to utilize advanced education to improve client service. A goal conflict engendered by the work- study structure can occur if the desire of the student-employee for professional education, and subsequent individual application to a school's work-study program, is not perceived by the employing agency as beneficial to the organization. If, however, at the point of admissions, agencies have an investment in the employee who is a work-study applicant, the quality of the educational arrangement provided by the agency will benefit. When agencies view an investment in the professional development of their employees as instrumental towards organizational maintenance and mission, there is goal congruence between student-employee and agency. This mutuality fosters a positive educational climate. Indicators of such a climate include the agency's willingness to meet individual leaning needs through the manipulation of formal and informal structures. The deployment of extra time and specialized personnel as well as adjustments in caseloads and case coverage are often necessary to bolster the student-employee's freedom to pursue educational goals.

Practically, what this goal-sharing suggests is that schools need to take the initiative in communicating to the agency community the organizational benefits of work-study education. This implies a direct effort by schools to recruit agencies located in specific fields of practice rather than recruit individual students alone. To do this schools need to be aware of the manifest and latent interests of diverse types of agencies in supporting professional education for their employees. Viewed in this light, school-agency relationships in work-study programs move toward a continuing education model in which organizational and community needs motivate educational efforts. This conception has been integral to the emergence of many part-time programs and merits further exploration in the work-study arena.

We have found that agencies may exert considerable control over the admissions process for work-study students. Thus, it is important that schools identify the way that agency influence would be most useful in admissions decision-making. For example the agency reference form may be revised to better utilize the information and perspective that agencies have on the professional potential of employee--applicants. The type of information elicited may also help schools clarify the stake agencies have in the education of specific employees. At bottom, it will help schools identify when agencies have little or no stake and thus may not be counted on to provide the resources required for quality education during the residence year.

Agency influence at admissions creates the potential for wide diversity in students' academic abilities. The employees with agency support for advanced education may be valued for qualities that meet a variety of agency and client needs. Such employees may relate well to clients and staff, handle caseloads responsibly, have strong advocacy and networking capabilities, and have characteristics useful in providing service to special needs populations. At the same time some of these applicants may have relatively marginal academic credentials. The School's willingness to risk acceptance of such students can lead to less homogeneity in level of academic skill or the perception of classes as comprised of the "most" and the "least" able. This situation will of necessity create increased costs in faculty time and effort. Additional advising support to coordinate remedial resources and plan extended, slower paced individualized programs will also be necessary.

Finally, the complexities of the dual roles carried by work-study students become apparent during the admissions process. It is at this point that employees desiring agency support for a work-study plan and seeking the agency reference required by the school must begin to negotiate the agency resources for completion of degree requirements. In order to help applicants understand the nature and importance of negotiating a student role, we have found it useful to provide group orientation sessions that apprise workers of the dual roles in a work-study program. This orientation can be done in information sessions for perspective applicants prior to formal application as well as during the group interviews conducted for admissions. At Hunter, the linkage of the orientation with the admissions process has been useful in alerting workers to incipient role issues. This process also clarifies for interested applicants the nature of the flexibility and support that they may expect from their agencies in accommodating the student role before a personal commitment to an employment-based model of professional education is made.

## CURRICULUM AND TEACHING

The education of work-study students requires modifications in classroom teaching, field instruction and faculty advising to maintain an educational focus among competing goals. What educators can expect is anxiety and reaction from both student and agency when the risk-taking and new perspectives required for professional development press the student to challenge her own thinking and the agency's performance. Whereas an educational objective for students who are guests in the agency is to become a part of and learn its system, the process of education for the work-study student may require broadening of the agency's specific approaches so that professional development can be achieved. The reality or perception of both disengagement from and disloyalty to agency views resulting from these goal conflicts have an impact on student learning and agency service. These dynamics require attention in the content and process of field instruction, classroom teaching and faculty advising so that both employment and learning can be maintained with integrity.

Overload in work responsibilities and assignments is a specific indicator of the encroachment of service priorities over educational goals. It is often a struggle for students, pressed by agency concerns to build in quality educational time. Given the destructiveness of work overload, identified by both students and faculty in our preliminary research, it is crucial that those responsible for planning and monitoring the work-study field placement be especially sensitive to this problem.

To alleviate goal-conflicts a proactive stance by the educational institution is necessary. Field instructors and faculty advisors need to take the initiative in making early assessments of the educational integrity of all work-study placement, followed by preventive intervention. The faculty advising system may need to adjust its routines and expectations so that early contact with all parties is assured. It is also important that the school help bolster the educational role of the field instructor through such educational mechanisms as, field instruction seminars, work-study focused meetings and orientations, and increased contact by the faculty and field work department.

Tensions between school and agency emerging from the struggle over control of the student-employee's time are a central concern in planning the work-study field practicum. School guidelines based on rules for structural changes or on learning contracts often fail to prepare faculty for the flexibility required in putting together an educational plan that takes into account the total environment of the employing agency and its constraints and possibilities. Negotiations that focus only on the agency's ability to provide changed assignments and supervision unwittingly become enmeshed in the "underbelly" of the planning process-ownership of the student-employee's time. Solutions to this control dilemma often result in an attempt at maintaining separate spheres for education and employment within the same agency. (This type of work-study plan is favored by the Council on Social Work Education accreditation standards.) At best, these arrangements result in the agency relinquishing its claim on the employee's time during the practicum. More often, however, failure to work out shared control leads to a student's simultaneously carrying two different workloads that are equally demanding.

With control as a central theme in the planning process, faculty involved in developing an educational plan are often faced with the difficult task of balancing and weighing a variety of needs. Our explorations suggest that flexibility is required by both parties in the negotiation. More importantly, the school's open consideration of the learning potential in employment assignments and the agency's reduction of a portion of the employee's workload present areas of flexibility in both systems.

Another type of control issue focuses on the relevance of the curriculum to agency or professional practice. Although it is clear that professional social work education must prepare practitioners beyond specific jobs, once the degree is earned and work-study students return full-time to the employing agency, their changed perspective can create conflict. Precisely because professional education has encouraged questioning of specific methods and has broadened students' capacities for organizational practice, the graduating employees may feel increasing dissatisfaction with agency practices. They may also perceive little opportunity, given job or role restrictions, to implement what they have learned. Conversely agencies may feel that professional education is limited and not relevant to the current demands of practice. Although it is not possible to resolve the curriculum questions generated by these tensions, work-study programs increase the potential for mutual influence of professional education on agency practice and vice versa.

As may be expected, role conflicts are most apparent in class and field teaching. Because of identification with the agency and the role of employee, the student may perceive the service demands of the agency as legitimate. S/he may be reluctant to look to the school for support in righting the educational balance even when there is awareness of the negative impact of role tension and overload on professional education. S/he may also fear that the school's intervention may threaten the employment contract, cause the agency to withdraw from supporting the field placement, or both. This dilemma may result in the student's collusion with the agency to mask the minimal attention paid to educational requirements.

Dual role and status have several implications for schools seeking quality education for work-study students. First, not only may the student respond to multiple identifications and demands, s/he may also appear to shun the identification of student (with its "know- nothing, novice" connotation) in favor of that of the experienced, knowledgeable employee. Schools should not interpret this identification as necessarily indicative of resistance to learning. Rather, approaches to teaching the work-study student need to acknowledge the existence and value of both roles for professional development. Second, advisors should be aware that role tension is the norm in the work-study situation and not necessarily indicative of negative learning conditions. However, they need to be able to assess the point at which normal tensions associated with the performance of dual roles may become destructive of the student learning experience.

Third, given the potential dangers resulting from role overload and the loyalty of the student to the employing agency, faculty advisors of work-study students need to recognize that advisors and the school are outsiders to the employee-agency system. Special sensitivity to organizational as well as educational issues is required for the advisor to gain the student-employee's trust. Only then will advisors be able to intervene purposefully and knowledgeably in behalf of the work-study student's educational needs. Modifications in the structure of advising may be required to ensure the advisor's availability to students with different schedules and time constraints. In addition, it is important that the advising curriculum for both part-time and residence phases provide opportunities for the timely discussion of expected role issues.

Fourth, in light of the special needs and characteristics of work- study students, schools should pay special attention to the assignment of faculty for classroom instruction. Some may argue that a separate cadre of faculty with in-dept knowledge of and interest in these students should carry the primary responsibility for instruction. Although it would be useful to explore this direction, we can speculate that separation is inherently unequal and thus presents many potential dangers. In our view, the dual roles of work-study students require that they be exposed to the range of a school's full-time faculty so that such students' incorporation into the educational program can be assured by those most familiar and identified with it. Conversely we would question the use of a preponderance of adjunct faculty due to the likelihood of their relative unfamiliarity with relevant role and system tensions. Exposure to the range of a school's faculty does not settle the question of the integration of work-study with full-time students in the classroom. Differences in program structures and course sequencing as well as geographic location may necessitate the separation of work-study and full-time students at various points in the educational process. In such periods, administrators should be aware that limitations in course offerings and other educational resources may be necessary and will constrain work-study students' choices of specializations. In order to gain the numbers of students necessary to offer certain specializations, integration of work-study and full-time students may be necessary. There is little data on the educational impact of such integration. Our own beginning exploration suggests that there can be advantages and disadvantages - a sharing of common strengths (idealism and realism) or a resentment at being the "teacher's helper." Thus we suggest that further research be conducted on who benefits and who may lose if integration is required.

Field instructors should be encouraged to see themselves as agency-based advocates for the student's professional development. Specifically, they may be in a position to make adjustments in workload allocation and case coverage that may ease role overload. More generally, the field instructor in a work-study placement may need to take responsibility for maximizing the learning potential of all aspects of the employment experience, regardless of how work and learning assignments are differentiated.

Should the field instructor be unable to fulfill this pivotal function, we recommend that the faculty advisor supplement the student's learning as much as possible. This may require the early anticipation of problem situations and the weighting of faculty advising assignments accordingly. To our knowledge such differentiation of advising workloads according to projected degree of difficulty or need is not common in social work education in general. We recommend innovation and experimentation in this area while recognizing potential ethical dilemmas. Even if it were possible to supplement the agencies' educational efforts, schools will need to develop principles for the inequitable distribution of their resources.

Finally, schools need to be aware of the implications of educational failure for social work students who carry dual roles. Theoretically, one might assume that "flunking" substantial academic or field work requirements would be detrimental to the student's employment situation-that is, that agencies would terminate employment of those who do not succeed in school. Such has not been our experience, as agencies have retained but not necessarily promoted these employees. The failure of the practicum by work-study students, however, does appear to limit their options for degree completion. The agency rarely provides a second chance to repeat field work within the agency context. Thus, should the school be willing to allow students to repeat the field work year, they may be required to leave the job and complete degree requirements as unpaid, full-time students.

The firing of the work-study student from the job while in field placement clearly presents an obstacle to degree completion. Because agencies tend to view firing as an employment rather than an educational matter, the reasons for the firing and its implications for professional development may remain unclear to the school and inhibit realistic educational assessment and planning. As was true at admissions, agencies often perceive education and employment as separate domains. Thus, at the evaluation end of the continuum, they remain unwilling to jeopardize the student-employee's opportunity for professional advancement. Should increased mutuality develop between school and agency, judgements made in one sphere are likely to have considerable impact in the other.

## SCHOOL-AGENCY RELATIONS

We cannot overemphasize the centrality of the agency in the development of quality work-study education. The agency is the hidden applicant at admissions and has major ongoing influence in all phases of the student's education. Thus, the major prescription for action is to re-orient schools toward interacting with agency systems rather than individual students. Specifically our work on goal, control and role issues suggests that schools must actively engage agencies on their interests and investment in professional education for their employees. This approach ensures the mutuality and longevity that can be a solid foundation for educational partnership. The development of an advisory board composed of the leadership of key work-study affiliates in various fields of practice can institutionalize this type of relationship. Such a board can help the school keep abreast of emerging community needs and remain responsive. It can also help agencies planfully utilize masters education for both personnel and service improvement. One outcome of this collaboration can be, as in the Hunter example, the development of contracts with agencies for staff professionalization. This collaboration may also generate joint grant proposals utilizing the work-study model for the development of new programs and qualified professionals in a variety of fields of practice. In this way, schools may effect an ongoing presence in specific agency settings and influence the quality of service to clients.

We believe that there are many routes to the achievement of a professional level of social work practice. However, schools should be cognizant of the relationship between educational design and institutional mission. If the advancement of the life chances of underserved students and client populations is perceived as a central value, the work-study design should be recognized for the potentials it can generate.

# DIFFERENCES IN UNDERGRADUATE AND GRADUATE PRACTICUMS: ELITISM, RACISM, AND CLASSISM?

Linda Cherrey Reeser and Robert A. Wertkin, *Western Michigan University*
Eddie Davis, *Wayne State University*

Social work has an established tradition of advocating for the oppressed and disenfranchised in society. There is concern that this tradition will be lost with the efforts of social work to become more professionalized. Bisno (1956) stated:

> There is rather general agreement within the profession that it is desirable for social work to acquire greater prestige...what we are concerned about though is that assuming the rightness and naturalness of this trend we have tended to ignore the question of the price to be paid for the higher status and whether it is worth it. Does it imply a weakening of the social in social work?

Social work's apprehension about the loss of commitment to social activism and to service to oppressed populations is explained in part by devotion to: "acquiring the status symbols of the old-line professions" (Benthrup, 1964) and "abandonment of the poor" to gain the prestige of being affiliated with middle-class clients (Cloward and Epstein, 1965).

Much of the social work literature in the '60s expresses these concerns about the effects of professionalism. The '60s were a time of widespread social activism and of assault on the professions for their irrelevancy. Such social movements as welfare rights, women's rights, and civil rights forced the social work profession to examine its elitism, racism, sexism, commitment to the poor and to social change. Since then, the socio-political climate has grown much more conservative. The 1980s have seen massive cutbacks in social services, economic crises, and the federal government's retreat from its commitment to provide for the social welfare of its citizens. Some of the consequences for social work of this attack on the social services are job insecurity, concentration on cutback management, and defending existing services and increasing numbers of social workers entering private practice. These changes and social work's increasing efforts to become professionalized suggest that social workers today may be less committed to the poor and oppressed.

Howe suggested that the 1979 revision of the social work code of ethics may have signified a return to the "private medical-type model" for social work in its efforts to attain professional status. She argued that the greater number of references in the code to the social workers' primary obligation being to individuals rather than to social change, may be "heralding a new era of disengagement from the poor" (Howe, 1980).

Reeser and Epstein surveyed social workers in 1968 and 1984 and found that in 1968, they approved the professional goals of emphasis on societal change and social work devoting most of its attention and resources to the problems of the poor, whereas social workers in 1984 endorsed the goals of adapting individuals to their environment and social work devoting attention and resources equally to all classes (Reeser and Epstein, 1987).

This shift in goal orientation for the profession in 1984 may possibly be attributed to the ascendancy of clinical practice in social work. Clinical practice is assumed to be important to the professionalization of social work because it is based on a systematic body of knowledge. The majority of social work students concentrate in social treatment rather than policy, planning, administration, or community organization. Clinical social work practice has received criticism for its goals of adapting individuals to the environment rather than engaging in broader processes of change (Rein, 1975) and for developing technologies that discriminate against the poor (Cloward and Epstein, 1965).

There are trends in social work that are assumed to signal increased professionalization and status. Within the last decade, social work has become increasingly privatized. The majority of the members of the National Association of Social Workers are employed in private agencies. With the increasing purchase of social services from private agencies, many social workers have left the public sector and sought the more "professional" responsibilities in the private sector. In response to this decline, a recent National Association of Social Workers' conference addressed the problems of recruitment and retention of professionally trained social workers in public child welfare service (NASW News, 1986) Another manifestation of this trend is the growth of private practice. "According to an idealized model, the epitome of the professional is the autonomous individual practitioner" (Alexander, 1980). The establishment of the Register of Clinical Social Work and the Society for Clinical Social Workers is evidence of the aforementioned trend toward clinical practice in social work.

The trends toward private practice and clinical practice in private agencies may also mean that social workers are serving more middle and upper-income clients. Identification with poor clients may be regarded as detrimental to social work moving up in the hierarchy of professions (Cloward and Epstein, 1965). Walsh and Elling (1972) demonstrated that members of occupational groups striving to increase their power and prestige are more negative in their orientation toward lower-income clients than are members of occupations less actively striving.

Reeser and Epstein (1987) found that social workers in the '60s were more likely to serve predominately low-income clients and more likely to prefer to do so than their colleagues in the '80s. The majority of respondents in both samples preferred an equal representation of all income groups as their client preference. The expressed preference for serving all social class groups may indicate a more socially acceptable way of expressing a preference for middle class clients. The decline in commitment to serving the poor is likely to reflect the greater emphasis on clinical practice in the private sector and the fewer social workers employed in the public sector serving low-income clients.

Another sign of efforts to professionalize social work is the high status awarded to psychotherapy as a social work method. Case management and casework seem to have low status. Thus, clients such as the elderly and chronically disabled who may need advocacy and linkage with resources may be defined as undesirable by social workers. Johnson and Rubin (1983) state that "social work clinicians seem to pay scant attention to intervention into social systems..., workers seem to have abdicated the distinctive dual focus of social work...in favor of a psychological focus (p. 53)." This is not a new development in social work history. In the quest for professionalization in the early twentieth century, social work aligned itself with psychiatry to gain a scientific knowledge base and affiliation with an established profession (Lubove, 1965, p. 56).

Johnson and Rubin (1983, p. 52) found that social workers in community mental health centers had only a modest commitment to case management activities and placed more emphasis on psychodynamics than did other workers. A mental health curriculum study conducted in 1975-78 by the Council on Social Work Education found that many MSW mental health practicums regarded brokerage and advocacy and work with the chronically mentally ill as menial tasks. Students were encouraged to focus on psychopathology and most students aspired to be psychotherapists (Rubin, 1979, pp. 24, 48). Rubin and Johnson assessed the practice interests of students entering MSW programs. They found that the majority of entering direct practice students want to get an MSW so that they can become psychotherapists in private practice. They found that students "do not want to perform brokerage, linkage, advocacy, or case management functions..." and they do not want to work with clients who need that approach (Rubin and Johnson, 1984, p. 51)." Rubin, Johnson, and DeWeaver did a follow-up study of these MSW students to assess whether their interests and aspirations change from entry to graduation. The findings indicate that commitment to a dual practice perspective appears to be slightly greater at graduation than at entry and there is some decline in the appeal of therapy and private practice. However, the majority of students still aspire to be psychotherapists (Rubin, Johnson, and DeWeaver, 1986, p. 98).

As a profession, we need to decide if we want to emulate the traditional professions and whether such trends as clinical practice, practice under private auspices, emphasis on psychotherapy, service to all income groups equally, and service primarily to clients with acute problems are the directions in which we want to move. It is important to assess whether these trends are reflected in schools of social work. The kinds of field practicums utilized send a message to students about the goals of social work, the nature of professional practice, and which client groups have priority.

Field work offers students an opportunity to verify whether the values and ethics espoused in the classroom have meaning in the real world. Is there a hierarchical notion of professionalism implied in the assignment of students at different levels of social work education to certain types of agencies and client groups for field placement? Are there patterns of elitism, racism, and classism in field practicums? Are the assignments based on the differential levels of practice expected for students at different educational levels? It is necessary to examine if schools of social work and agencies are promoting social responsibility through their policies and practices.

This paper reports on a comparative analysis of undergraduate and graduate social work field placements in a midwestern, regional university. An exploratory-descriptive research design was used to answer the following questions:

1.	Are there differences in the clients served by students at different levels of social work education?  Specific client study variables include populations served, acuteness/chronicity, degree of functioning, focus of intervention, duration of cases assigned, socioeconomic status, gender, race, and involuntary versus voluntary status.

2.	Are there differences in the agencies in which undergraduate, first-year, and second-year students are placed?  This includes fields of service and methods of practice.

## METHODOLOGY

A 13 item self-administered questionnaire was developed for collecting data on differences among BSW, first- and second-year MSW field placements. Instrument items sought information about the type of student and agency, methods of practice used by the student in the field placement, and characteristics of the client population.

Enclosed with the questionnaire was a cover letter that explained the purpose of the study, how long it would take to complete the items, and how confidentiality would be maintained.  A self-addressed, stamped envelope was also included with the questionnaire.

Questionnaires were coded to simplify a second mailing to those that did not return the completed questionnaire.  Code numbers were then removed from the instruments in order to protect the confidentiality of the respondents.

A total of 285 questionnaires were mailed.  Ten were returned as non-deliverable and 3 were returned non-usable.  There were 224 completed questionnaires returned which is 81 percent of the total number of field placements used by the School within the two year study period.

The sample population consisted of all field instructors that participated in the field education program of a regional, midwestern social work program between 1984 and 1986.  This included field instructors that took BSW, first-year MSW or second-year Social Treatment MSW students.  Second-year Policy, Planning, and Administration students and field agencies were not included in this study.

Data were converted to mark sense sheets and analyzed on a VAX-8600 computer using the Statistical Package for the Social Sciences (SPSSX).

## FINDINGS

Completed questionnaires were returned with placement information about 63 BSW students, 81 first-year and 80 second-year MSW students.  Sixteen of the first-year and 17 of the second-year students were in the part-time program.

Field instructors were asked to indicate the "field of service" that their agency fits from 31 categories. Distinct differences were found in the types of agencies in which students at various educational levels were placed. There were numerous similarities in the type of placements that the BSW and first-year MSW students had compared to the second-year social treatment students. There were also some similarities in the first- and second-year placements compared to the BSW student's placements.

It was found that no second-year students were placed in adult or child protective services, child care institutions, adult or juvenile corrections or courts, emergency crisis services, foster care and adoptions, non-hospital health services, neighborhood centers and organizations, public welfare agencies, or women's services. In addition, only one of eight students placed in the field of aging was a second-year student.

Some placements were heavily second-year or primarily second- and first-year with very few BSW students. Seventy-three percent of the family and children's services placements were second-year and another 20 percent were first-year students. Fifty-nine percent of the medical social work placements were second-year and another 24 percent first-year. Seventy-one percent of the mental health institutional and 65 percent of the mental health outpatient were second-year placements. School social work was evenly divided between first- and second-year with only 1 BSW student placed in the schools. Child guidance outpatient was used exclusively as a second-year placement.

Furthermore, there were some placements that included only undergraduates such as information and referral services, political service offices, emergency hot lines, and nursing homes. Some fields of service did not take any BSW students. These included: industrial social work, mental health institutional, and substance abuse (both inpatient and outpatient).

Field instructors were asked to indicate the primary and secondary method of practice used by the student in the field placement. As with field of service, clear distinctions were found between BSW and MSW first-and second-year students. No social treatment student's primary or secondary method of practice was advocacy, investigation, recreation or support groups. No primary method of intervention was indicated for second-year students in rehabilitation.

BSW students dominated three categories, advocacy, case management, and resource referral and development. BSW and first-year MSW students accounted for 81 percent of the crisis intervention and 94 percent of the intake/assessment categories.

Treatment with individuals, families or groups was dominated by second-year students as both primary and secondary functions of their placements. Eighty-three percent of the second-year students had these areas indicated as their primary method of practice and another 50 percent as their secondary method. Forty-six percent of the first-year students had treatment as their primary method of practice and another 23 percent had it as their secondary method.

Findings presented so far are neither surprising nor remarkable. It would be expected that second-year social treatment students would be placed in social treatment agencies. It would also be expected that these students would be designated in these agencies as social treaters.

An analysis of variables regarding client characteristics, however, pointed to some disturbing differences between students in different agencies and at different educational levels. This data also raised some serious concerns about the client populations served by students in certain agencies and the compliance of the School of Social work in reinforcing some institutionalized patterns of ageism, racism, classism, and elitism.

Field instructors were asked to indicate the primary and secondary client population served by the student placed in their supervision. Significant differences were found between the second-year students compared to the first-year and BSW students regarding the primary population served ($X^2$ = 7.83, d.f. = 3, p = .04). The second-year students were more likely to serve adults or families as their primary client population. The BSW and first-year students were more likely to serve children, adolescents or elderly clients.

Another variable analyzed was the acuteness/chronicity of the client problems served by the student. Significant differences were found between groups. The BSW students were least likely to treat clients with acute problems ($X^2$ = 13.21, d.f. = 4, p = .01) and most likely to treat clients with chronic problems ($X^2$ = 9.26, d.f. = 4, p = .05). Second-year students were opposite the BSW group in that they were most likely to treat acute clients and least likely to treat chronic clients. The first-year students fit somewhere between the two other groups.

Field instructors were asked to estimate the percentage of clients that students served that were high, middle, and low functioning. No significant differences were found between student groups for this variable.

Focus of client interventions was trichotomized as focusing on internal processes, external situational factors or dual focused. The second-year students were more likely to focus on internal processes but the difference was not statistically significant. The BSW students were more likely to focus on external situational factors than the other two groups ($X^2$ = 29.39, d.f. = 6, p = .0001).

Another variable analyzed was the duration of cases assigned to students. No significant differences were found between groups regarding the case duration of clients assigned to students by the agency.

Field instructors were asked to indicate the financial status of clients served by students in percentages. Three categories were used--low, middle, and high income. Significant differences were found between the second-year students compared to the BSW and first-year students regarding the income status of clients served ($X^2$ = 6.72, d.f. = 2, p = .03). The BSW and first-year were more likely to serve low-income clients than the second-year students. No students were serving a substantial number of high income clients.

Field instructors were asked to indicate the percentage of males and females served by their students. No significant differences were found between the gender of the clients served by the three groups.

Significant differences were found regarding the race of clients served by the three student groups. The BSW served fewer percentages of white clients compared to the first-year students who in turn served fewer whites than the second-year students ($X^2$ = 15.36, d.f. - 4, p = .004). The same pattern in reverse was true for Black clients. The BSW students served a greater percentage of Black clients, followed by first-year and then second-year clients ($X^2$ = 12.44, d.f. = 6, p = .05)

Finally, the voluntary/involuntary status of the clients served by the students was analyzed. The BSW and first-year students were more likely to treat involuntary clients than second-year students and less likely to treat voluntary clients ($X^2$ = 9.11, d.f. = 4, p = .05)

## DISCUSSION AND IMPLICATIONS

It is important to remember that this was an exploratory study. Thus, the findings should be interpreted with caution until a larger, more representative sample can be attained and a more refined instrument is developed. However, the findings in this study suggest consistent differences in the agencies and clients served by undergraduates, first-year, and second-year students. These differences support the authors' concerns about the effects of professionalism and the meta-messages that the profession is giving to students. More specifically, important differences were found in fields of service, methods of practice, populations served, acuteness/chronicity, client focus, income, race, and client status. Also, differences in the agency auspices may be inferred from fields of service.

Second-year social treatment students were found primarily in settings that were under private auspices such as family and children's services, child guidance clinics, and private hospitals. They were not to be found in such public settings as the courts or public welfare or in such private advocacy-type organizations as women's services or neighborhood centers. BSW and first-year graduate students were concentrated in these public and private settings in which social treatment students were not placed. BSWs were rarely found in agencies that take second-year students, whereas first-year students were more likely to be found there. BSWs were also placed in some unique settings that have never taken first or second-year students, e.g., congressional offices, information and referral. Many of these practicums offer students phone contact with clients rather than face-to-face contact.

It appears that there is a private/public split in placements for second-year graduates versus first-year students and BSWs. It may be that the differentiation is a result of the kinds of learning opportunities found in these settings. We would expect that social treatment students would be placed in agencies in which they would learn clinical skills and that BSW and first-year graduate practicums would provide for the learning of generic skills. However, those first-year graduate students who come into the program with social work experience may have the opportunity to be placed in a primarily second-year graduate field agency.

Is there a message being given to students when we assign more advanced students to private agencies, that private is superior to public? We may be reinforcing the distrust that exists in this society toward public agencies and the notion that private agencies are more quality-oriented, innovative, flexible, and responsive to changing community needs. Government funding priorities to purchase social services from private agencies certainly have contributed to an exodus of social workers from the public sector. Ostrander found in her study (1985) of voluntary agencies that reductions in federal support have led to decline in services to the poor, minorities, and women. She argues that the present quality vs. quantity, service to the non-poor vs. service to the poor, distinctions between the voluntary sector and the public sector are "damaging the support for welfare state services."

What are the implications of placing BSW students in some settings in which we would never place MSW students and defining certain fields such as substance abuse and family and children's services as basically off limits to them? It may be a reflection of elitism within the profession. There continues to be a debate over the level of professional achievement of the BSW (Specht, Britt, and Frost, 1984; Dyer, 1977). It may possibly reflect the differences in competencies expected of BSWs and MSWs. However, a substantial number of BSWs are placed in the same agencies as first-year students. In an employment survey of MSWs and BSWs it was found that the MSW group was concentrated in mental health settings while BSWs were more highly represented in public social service settings (Kolevzon and Biggerstaff, 1983). Is this the kind of differentiation we want to encourage?

The patterns that emerged in regard to method of practice were not unexpected. Second-year students were doing treatment and they were not doing advocacy or running support groups as a primary or secondary method. Few were primarily utilizing case management and resource referral and development as methods of practice. BSWs primarily performed the resource provision, advocacy, and case management functions. First-year students overlapped with the functions of both BSWs and second-year students.

The patterns may possibly be attributed to the educational continuum defining the BSW as the entry-level professional social work degree with differential competencies expected at each level of the curriculum. Thus, MSW and BSW field practicums would reflect the substantive differences. However, many first-year students were performing the same functions as BSWs. In 1983, Kolevzon and Biggerstaff, in their study of the functional differentiation in job responsibilities between BSWs and MSWs, found BSWs spent more time on case management and MSWs on direct practice. However, the most frequently performed task for both the BSW and the MSW was that of individual therapy. The researchers stated that:

> Functional differentiation along the social work education continuum may express a reality that is very different from the functional differentiation operating in the employment arena...The expansion of undergraduate social work education and the attendant growth in the pool of BSW graduates entering the job market may serve to heighten demand that social work educators become more sensitive to employment contexts and settings in which the career expectations espoused by BSW education fail to be actualized...It should be noted that differentiation in the work activities of BSWs and MSWs did not present overwhelming evidence of the legitimization of the social work education continuum by the employment arena...agency setting played a more powerful role in differentiating work activities than did degree level (Kolevzon and Biggerstaff, 1983, pp. 27, 31).

Social work educators must assess the educational continuum for its congruence with the employment situation for BSWs and MSWs. We must decide whether to prepare social workers to function in the employment arena as it exists or prepare them to change it. Are we equipping BSWs and MSWs with the knowledge and skills they need to practice effectively? Do we want the seemingly sharp division of labor in field practicums between BSWs and second-year clinical graduate students?

The pattern discovered in this study of placing second-year social treatment students in private agencies to primarily do treatment with the advocacy and case management primarily being done by BSWs in public and private agencies may be cause for concern. Second-year students' interventions were more likely to focus on clients' internal processes, rather than a dual person-in-environment focus. To what extent are we socializing graduate students to the social work perspective? Rubin and Johnson found that eighty-six percent of entering MSW students wanted to become private practitioners. They equated private practice with psychotherapy. However, minority students and students who majored in social work as undergraduates were more interested in resource provision functions than in doing psychotherapy (Rubin and Johnson, p. 56). It may be that social work students' practice orientation predates their entry into graduate school. Thus, recruiting more BSWs and majority students may be one solution to having students who are committed to the unique mission of the profession.

Changing our policies and practices of field assignment may be another way to reaffirm our commitment to the person-in-environment perspective. Practicum assignments may be an important factor in socializing students to the distinctive functions of social work. Are the specialized clinical courses and practicums an effort by the School of Social Work to convey to students the high professional status awarded to social workers who become clinical therapists as compared to case managers or case workers? Is it a response to consumer demand or acquiescence to agency demands?

The findings in this study in regard to characteristics of the clients served by students seem to imply a hierarchy of client desirability. Second-year students were more likely to serve middle class clients; whites; adults, or families; those with acute problems; or those who sought services voluntarily. BSWs and first-year students were more likely to serve low-income clients; Blacks; children, adolescents, or the elderly; those with chronic problems or those with involuntary status. It may be that the differential assignment of clients to students at different educational levels is a reflection of placement in private clinical agencies versus public agencies. Private clinical agencies tend to serve primarily middle-income clients and clients with acute problems who are motivated to have psychotherapy. Data on clients seen in private agencies suggests that cuts in government support have resulted in services being denied to the neediest clients (Ostrander, p. 441).

The different agency assignments and client populations served by our students may be explained by the structure and functions of field agencies. However, it is the view of these authors that the School of Social Work is sending dangerous meta-messages to its students about the most professional agencies and appealing clients. It is the least advanced students--undergraduates and first-year-

-who practice their skills with the most dependent and vulnerable clients. The more advanced social treatment students work with clients who are likely to be more articulate and responsive to therapy and who give status to the profession. We are reinforcing institutionalized patterns of ageism, racism, classism, and elitism in our field assignments. What is our commitment to work in the public sector with client populations who need care and resources more than curing interventions. Morris (1978) states that:

> Social work, in its search for a professional foundation, has lost sight of its original social purpose, the need to take care of the weak and helpless groups in a new industrializing society: the severely disabled, neglected children, mentally ill, developmentally disabled, and the enfeebled aged. No other profession is qualified to, or seeks to satisfy this need...We now need to consider whether our historic contribution lies in a restoration of the caring function, while relegating the search for a cure to social problems to the exploratory and experimental frontier (pp.82-83).

## BIBLIOGRAPHY

Alexander, Leslie B. (November 1980) "Professionalization and Unionization: Compatible After All," SOCIAL WORK, 25 pp. 474-484.

Benthrup, Walter C. (April 1964) "The Professions and the Means Test," SOCIAL WORK, pp. 10-17.

Bisno, Herbert (April 1956) "How Social Will Social Work Be?," SOCIAL WORK, 1, pp. 12-18.

Cloward, Richard A. and Epstein, Irwin (1965) "Private Social Welfare's Disengagement From the Poor: The Case of Private Family Adjustment Agencies," PROCEEDINGS OF THE ANNUAL SOCIAL WORK DAY INSTITUTE, Buffalo: State University of Buffalo.

Dyer, Preston M. (November 1977) "How Professional is the BSW Worker?," SOCIAL WORK, 22, pp. 487-492.

Galper, Jeffry (1975) THE POLITICS OF SOCIAL SERVICES. Englewood Cliffs, NJ: Prentice-Hall Inc.

Howe, Elizabeth (May 1980) "Public Professions and the Private Model of Professionalism," SOCIAL WORK, 25, pp. 174-190.

Johnson, Peter J. and Rubin, Allen (Jan.-Feb. 1983) "Case Management in Mental Health: A Social Work Domain?," SOCIAL WORK, 28, pp. 49-55.

Kolevzon, Michael S. and Biggerstaff, Marilyn A. (Spring 1983) "Functional Differentiation of Job Demands: Dilemmas Confronting the Continuum in Social Work Education," JOURNAL OF EDUCATION FOR SOCIAL WORK, 19, pp. 26-34.

Lubove, Roy (1965) THE PROFESSIONAL ALTRUIST. Cambridge, MA: Harvard University Press.

Morris, Robert (Spring 1978) "Social Work Function in a Caring Society: Abstract Value, Professional Preference, and the Real World," JOURNAL OF EDUCATION FOR SOCIAL WORK, 14, pp. 82-89.

Ostrander, Susan A. (September 1985) "Voluntary Social Services in the United States," SOCIAL SERVICE REVIEW, 59, pp. 435-454.

"Public Child Welfare's Crisis Under Scrutiny," (May 1986) NASW NEWS, 31, pp. 30-31.

Reeser, Linda C. and Epstein, Irwin (December, 1987) "Social Workers' Attitudes Toward Poverty and Social Action: 1968-1984," SOCIAL SERVICE REVIEW, 61, pp. 610-622.

Rein, Martin (April 1970) "Social Work in Search of a Radical Profession," SOCIAL WORK, 15, pp. 13-28.

Rubin, Allen (1979) COMMUNITY MENTAL HEALTH IN THE SOCIAL WORK CURRICULUM. New York: Council on Social Work Education.

Rubin, Allen and Johnson, Peter J. (Spring 1984) "Direct Practice Interests of Entering MSW Students," JOURNAL OF EDUCATION FOR SOCIAL WORK, 20, pp. 5-16.

Rubin, Allen, Johnson, Peter J. and DeWeaver, Kevin L. (Spring/Summer 1986) "Direct Practice Interests of MSW Students: Changes From Entry to Graduation," JOURNAL OF SOCIAL WORK EDUCATION, 22, PP. 98-108.

Specht, Harry, Britt, Doris, and Frost, Charles (May-June 1984) "Undergraduate Education and Professional Achievement of MSWs," SOCIAL WORK, 29, pp. 219-224.

Walsh, James Leo and Elling, Ray H. (1972) "Professionalism and the Poor -- Structural Effects and Professional Behavior," in MEDICAL MEN AND THEIR WORK, eds. Eliot Freidson and Judith Lorber Chicago: Aldine Atherton, Inc., pp. 267-283.

# THE IMPLICATIONS OF PART-TIME PROGRAMS FOR FIELD WORK MODELS: PROVOCATIVE DILEMMAS AND CONCEPTUAL FRAMEWORKS

Sylvia Navari, *California State University, Sacramento*

## INTRODUCTION

The marrying of part-time programming and field education models gives rise to a series of provocative dilemmas. This paper identifies several of those dilemmas and offers conceptual frameworks that may be used to address the dilemmas.

The marriage is framed by two distinct contexts: 1) the goal of social work education and 2) theories of learning. The dilemmas derive when we attempt to integrate field education and part-time programming **within** the contextual frameworks. This concept is depicted below:

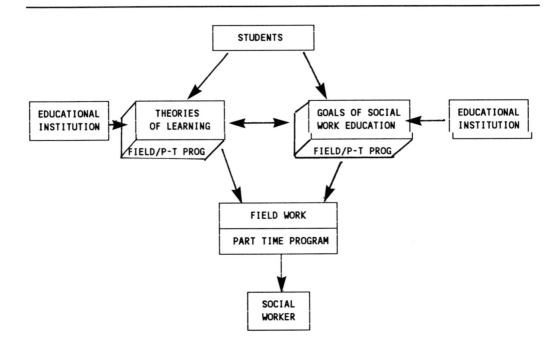

## THE CONTEXTS

As educators, we teach within contextual parameters which we often ignore or take for granted. Two such parameters are **how people learn** and the **educational goal** we set for students choosing our particular degree. As educators, we must always keep these two parameters in view and teach from within them, otherwise we fail our students and ourselves.

### The Goal of Social Work Education

The goal of social work education is an ideal type best epitomized by the phrase, "Inventor of Interventions" (Rosenfeld, 1983, p. 186). The goal is the development of a particular type of professional who learns a particular set of skills, values, and knowledge. The ideal social worker is both scientist and artist (Reynolds, p. 5), founded upon a humanistic ethic tempered with a bit of rational science. She can think critically and is willing and able to generalize without treating individuals or systems as interchangeable parts. We, as social work educators, attempt to educate and train students in this ideal; and this is done this through the study of five core content areas.

In their efforts to develop "Inventors of Interventions", educators are faced with certain realities. One reality is the mixing of an apple and an orange--part-time programming and field work. As never before, while our core content areas, teaching methods, and scheduling remain the same, those who would be social workers are more complex and different than their predecessors.

As educators, we are must deal with more students representing a wider range of difference. And we do this because we are faced with other realities, like full-time equivalents, maintaining enrollments, etc. Thus, we attempt to mix apples and oranges in pursuit of our elusive goal.

## THEORIES OF LEARNING

How one learns is a question without one simple answer. This question and the responses to it form the second context of social work education. Education cannot occur without seriously thinking about how people learn and taught.

Historically, traditional education and non-professional degree programs have assumed a primarily cognitive approach to learning. This approach to learning tends to be teacher-centered. It derives from the cognitive theorists who assume that information and knowledge comes to us in the form of ideas, concepts, and mental images: hence the lecture method. This theory of learning lays at one end of a continuum of grand theories (see Figure 1).

Professional education, on the other hand, by virtue of the fact that it tends to be grounded in its environment, utilizes the associationist and behaviorist approaches to learning. Charlotte Towle (1954) informed us that one objective of professional education is "that students be oriented to the place of their profession in the society in which it operates" (p. 16). Professions cannot exist outside their environments; they respond, as do living organisms, to their environments. And, more importantly, most professional degree programs require their students to do some form of field practicum--practicing the tools of their trade in the environment in which they operate. This suggests that professional education, at least in part, operates in a passive mode, i.e., that students learn by responding in the environments of their practicum.

## FIGURE 1

| COMPONENTS OF LEARNING | GRAND THEORIES OF LEARNING | | |
|---|---|---|---|
| | COGNITIVISTS | ASSOCIATIONISTS | BEHAVIORISTS |
| What is learned (form of info) | Mental Images | Associations/ connections | Response to environment |
| How it's learned (acquisition) | Insight/"AHA" Syndrome | By sensing | Through Reinforcement |
| From whence does learning come | Nature--Innate developmental learner is active and passive | Biological **and** environmental learner is primarily passive | **Nurture--** learner is passive and learning comes from environment |

By its very nature, field education assumes at least an associationist, if not behaviorist, approach to learning. However, field education is only one part of a whole; the other parts of social work education tend towards the more traditional cognitive approach. These differences are emphasized by Rothman: "The practice-oriented person tends to lean toward development of skill and technique; the educated-oriented person toward enhancement of theory and knowledge (Jones, p. 111). Rothman's statement epitomizes the dichotomy of, and the consequent challenge for social work educators. We must both **train** and **educate**.

Thus, it seems that social work education incorporates all three grand theories of learning by virtue of its content. What this means for educators and for students is best explained by actually applying the theories, in an integrated way, to our programs. To do this we must look to mid-range theories of learning.

## THE RELATIONSHIP BETWEEN CORE CONTENT AND LEARNING

The mid-range learning theory used as the analytical framework herein is Kolb's (1984) "Experiential Learning Theory." While many of us in field education claim experiential learning theory as the foundation of field learning, I offer experiential learning theory as the foundation for social work education as a whole. By viewing social work education through this lens we can see the complexity of learning required to become a social worker.

Kolb's experiential theory "emphasizes the integration of the abstract concepts of social knowledge with the concrete, subjective experiences of personal knowledge" (p. 22). His model establishes a competency circle of four (4) stages of learning which blend in combinations to establish four (4) styles of learning. The theory maintains that every individual has a learning style that dominates the way in which one learns. These learning styles are graphically depicted in Figure 2:

## FIGURE 2

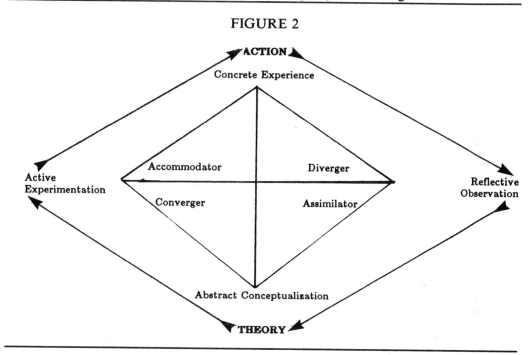

The *accommodator style* combines the concrete experience and active experimentation stages of learning as the basis of learning. Essentially, the accommodator learns from hands-on experience. The *diverger style* combines the concrete experience and reflective observation stages. The diverger learns by observing concrete situations, assessing, judging, and brainstorming. The *assimilator style* combines reflective observation and abstract conceptualization. The assimilator learns by using logic, understanding theory, conceptualizing, and observing. The *converger style* combines abstract conceptualization and active experimentation. Convergers learn by searching for problems to fit theories and ideas; they conceptualize and plan, then try out their ideas.

These four styles represent the various ways in which people learn. Where one is located in the circle depends on the individual and the content to be learned. One's ability to utilize all styles is dependent upon the extent to which one is fully individuated, i.e., the extent to which one has developed his/her cognitive and behavioral skills.

If the core content areas are placed on the circle in accordance with the generally practiced ways the core subjects are taught, it becomes evident that social work education requires the simultaneous use of all four learning styles (Figure 3).

## FIGURE 3

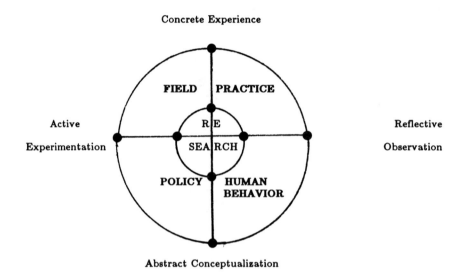

When field education is combined with practice and the other core content of social work education, as is the case in a full-time concurrency program, students are required to incorporate all theories of learning simultaneously. This is at best difficult for some and, at worst, impossible for others because not all people learn in the same ways. Some people are geared towards concrete experience and behavior modeling while others are conceptual and reflective. Further, social work education is rife with the phrase "knowledge guided practice." This phrase assumes a cognitive approach to learning, i.e., that theory guides practice. But we also know that often this particular relationship between theory and practice is only partially accurate because practice, largely environmentally determined, also informs theory.

Thus, social work education requires the full range of learning capacities as well as an action-theory perspective. Our students are expected to accommodate these various methods by moving from theory to action and action to theory; and by moving from cognition to behavior/practice and from practice to theory. This is a monumental undertaking.

## PART-TIME PROGRAMS

Within the contextual frameworks previously discussed, we must grapple with the concept of part-time education. This concept elicits different meanings from different people. It seems, however, that the majority of part-time programs in social work education are really full-time programs, wrapped in a different package.

Of the 83 part-time programs listed in the Directory of Schools of Social Work, CSWE 1987, 78 simply take their regular program and extend it our over 3 or 4 years (or longer depending on the student). While some schools alter time frames, i.e., 13% of the schools offer weekend programs and 30% offer evening programs (different than simply holding classes in the evening), all but one school have structured programs. Only one school was identified as offering unstructured programming wherein a program is structured to fit the life and social service experience of a student. At best the task of finding a field site that fits the student falls on the field education coordinator.

The data below describe the part-time programs currently in existence by structural options and academic format.

## FIGURE 4: PART TIME PROGRAMS

ACADEMIC PROGRAM: N = 83

| FORMAT | | RESIDENCY | |
|---|---|---|---|
| Weekend | 11 | Full | 79 |
| Evenings | 24 | Reduced | 3 |
| Regular program extended | 78 | **STANDING** | |
| Individual content | 4 | | |
| Combination | 24 | Regular | 20 |
| | | Advanced | 62 |

**FIELD WORK MODELS**

| Concurrent | | Block | |
|---|---|---|---|
| Traditional | 42 | Traditional | 7 |
| Job site | 21 | Job site | 3 |
| Combination | 25 | | |
| Choice | 6 | | |

## Role and Purpose of Part-time Programs

In 1982, 29% of all MSW students nationally were part-time. Today, fully one-third of the entering MSW class at my institution has entered the part-time program. The increasing number of part-time students exists for several reasons. Clearly economics and family responsibilities force students to forego full-time student status in the pursuit of educational and career goals. Being a full-time student is a luxury, particularly for those students entering the field of social work.

In a recent survey, 48% of our part-time students cited financial responsibilities as the reason for choosing the part-time program. 30% cited both financial and family responsibilities, while 9% cited solely family responsibilities as the reason for choosing part-time rather than full time status. These reasons are further supported by the fact that 71% of our part-time students work, as compared to 46%

of the full time students. And, of the part-time students who do work, 80% work 21 hours per week or more, while only 35% of the working full time students work 21 hours per week or more. Roughly 2/3 of both working groups maintain jobs in the social service arena. Thus, part-time programs accommodate a particular type of student, who, if we did not have part-time programs, would probably not enter or complete the MSW degree. This statement is supported by the fact that of the full-time students who receive financial assistance (61%), 41% of these students would not have entered the program without the assistance while 30% would have entered on a part-time basis. Of the part-time students who receive financial assistance, 41% would not have entered the MSW program.

Social work educators have attempted to accommodate these students, but often in spite of our educational goals and theories of learning. While there may be institutional or professional advantages to operating part-time programs as the majority exist today, such programs generally require more resources, are less efficient, and raise questions about the quality of learning. Siporin states, "one can question what actually is lost with regards to learning, personal development, and socialization into the profession, if adult learners shift... to part-time patterns of study" (Dinerman and Geismar, 1984, p. 242). He goes on to state that this trend challenges schools to find ways to maintain student quality, performance, learning, and effective socialization patterns. Siporin's statements are quite reasonable in direct relationship to traditional social work education and the traditional social work student. However, they seem rather unreasonable in light of present day students, keeping in mind that 2/3 of both working groups (53% of the total student population) currently work in either the public or private social service arena. Maybe these older, adult learners **can learn** on a part-time basis **if we develop programs that fit them** rather than simply repackage what has always been.

### Implications for Learning

The description of part-time programs and part time students suggests that we are attempting to wrap a non-traditional student in a traditional package. Full time students are different than part-time students. This dictates the need for two substantively different programs--lest we succumb to the nature of bureaucratic leveling (See Max Weber on bureaucracy for discussion on leveling.) In addition to the social and economic demographics noted above, 27% of the part-time students indicated they will remain in their current job as compared with 9% of the full time students. More significant are the age differences:

### FIGURE 5

| AGE | PART-TIME | FULL-TIME |
|-----|-----------|-----------|
| 22-30 | 27% | 46% |
| 31-40 | 52% | 36% |
| 41- | 21% | 18% |

Part-time students are generally older, with more life and social work experience. Today's full-time students are beginning to reflect what was the full-time student of yesteryear: young. This younger student population is a subtle change and cannot yet be classified as a trend. However, discussions with other field coordinators leads me to believe that the younger student is not peculiar to just my institution. This subtle change poses a range of dilemmas for part-time programming, field work, and social work education in general.

First and foremost, students without life or social service experience are very difficult to place. Agency resource constraints hinder the acquisition of pure field instruction which is generally required for young inexperienced students. Secondly, essentially the same content/skills are taught to both experienced and inexperienced students. The impact on learning is formidable for both types of students. The older student may be bored while the younger student is overwhelmed. This latter occurrence is reflected in a statement made in reference to full-time students by a part-time student whose life and social work experience was limited, "How can you absorb everything in two years?" Her statement ironically suggests that students without life and social service experience should be required to enter part-time extended programs (minimum 3 years), and the older more experienced students should have a reduced but more intensive learning experience such that they could enter and exit the MSW program in a maximum of two years. This latter suggestion would require some alternative unstructured programing.

The above suggestion is an example of a program concept that would be driven by our student populations. Currently, both full and part-time programs (excepting those with reduced residency--only 3), are driven by institutional concerns. In essence, the implications for learning in the part-time programs is not a function of the structure of part-time, but is a function of the individual student and what is taught. The problem is that one single program generally does not fit the range of students.

## FIELD EDUCATION MODELS AND METHODS

### The Concept

The purpose of field education boggles the mind. But it must be this way; for the field setting is the nexus wherein the values, knowledge, and skills of social work become integrated to form that unique professional we call a social worker. The uniqueness of social work is not in its individual parts predominantly espoused in a classroom; rather it exists only in the field, when the social worker is called upon to integrate the disparate parts into a meaningful whole in order to assist the individual, group or community.

How we learn **to be** a social worker in the field is complex. Clearly field education is grounded in experimentation--either active, which draws on some abstract conceptualization, or concrete, which draws predominantly on feelings. (see Figure 2, p. 275). Field education and becoming a social worker are predicated, in the final analysis, on learning by doing. The models and methods employed to implement field work ought to reflect this portion of experiential learning theory upon which field work is predicated.

### Models

Unfortunately we again find ourselves confronted with institutionally driven models and methods, rather than ones clearly grounded in consumer need and learning, and theory. Neither the concurrent nor block field work models--the two traditionally used in social work education--started from a solid theoretical position. On the block model Alice Seylan comments (Jones, 1969, p. 88):

> Any discussion of the block plan may begin with the frank admission that a primary reason for its adoption has been as much one of expediency as of its considered merits.

And Margaret Schutz comments on both the concurrent and block models (Jones p. 99):

> I suspect that both plans, in many instances, began not as a result of evidence gained from empirical study or even as the result of a strong educational theoretical position; also I suspect that both will probably continue, as a result of historical or geographical accident regardless of the specific merits of either.

Fortunately, the fact that we adopted these models out of expediency does not mean each is void of any theoretical base. The implications, characteristics, and presumed relationship to Kolb's experiential learning theory will be identified for each model of field education. The descriptive elements of each model have been juxtaposed for the sake of comparison (see Figure 6).

---

### FIGURE 6: Descriptive Elements of Field Models

| | BLOCK | CONCURRENT |
|---|---|---|
| 1) Derived from | 1) increased enrollment, expanding programs, lack of adequate placements in vicinity of schools | 1) Historical model--allowed for scientific based social work--reaction against apprenticeship training |
| 2) Student role | 2) Full-time student-professional | 2) Alternates student and student-professional role |
| 3) Learning style | 3a) Concrete experimentation<br>b) Immersion<br>c) Gestaltist | 3a) Active experimentation<br>b) Gradual learning<br>c) Incrementalist |
| 4) Learning is function of | 4) Relationship with Instructor (mentee-like) | 4) Integration of material by learner (student-like) |

| 5) Learning principles | 5) Intense doing, trial/error | 5) Reinforcement/feedback |
|---|---|---|
| 6) Instructor role | 6a) Great emphasis on relationship (mentor-like)<br>b) must be more attuned to learner/worker role conflict | 6) Less emphasis on relationship (teacher-like)<br>b) less attuned to learner/worker role conflict |
| 7) Advantages/disadvantages | 7a) Wider array of learning opportunities<br>b) learning-growing process more sustained | 7a) Learning opportunities limited<br>b) growth process periodic unless precision exists between class and field |
| 8) Theory/practice relationship | 8a) Action - theory<br>b) less concern with scientifically based social work | 8a) Theory-action<br>b) Presupposes social work is scientifically based |

## Comparison of Elements and Perspectives of Models

Each of the models represents a different perspective in relation to six critical elements in field instruction identified by this author:

* student-instructor relationship
* clarity of student role
* exposure to diverse learning opportunities
* integration of theory and practice
* specificity of learning objectives/ordered sequencing
  of learning experiences

These elements were garnered from the responses students gave to why they would choose a particular field work model. A quality field experience seems dependent upon the first two elements, relationship and role. The good field experience requires that a student be exposed to diverse learning opportunities and different ways of doing. Lastly, the experience ought to allow for the integration of theory and practice and sequencing of learning. These last two critical elements were identified by students, but also are necessary if field work is to be minimally in accord with the objectives of social work education. Each of these elements is discussed below from the perspective of each model and in relation to Kolb's learning theory.

## Student-Instructor Relationship

Under the block model this critical element is reflective of a mentor-mentee relationship. Such relationships are usually intense and difficult to formulate. Further, a mentee role requires one to have assimilated a significant amount of information, and then be able to move into experimentation.

The student-instructor relationship under a concurrent model is more teacher-student than mentor-mentee. It is less intensive and may require less individuation

on the part of the student. It does, however, require a student to draw upon different learning styles simultaneously unless movement
between styles is automatic (a function of the degree of individuation). If students are not adept at the various learning styles the tendency is to emphasize one to the exclusion of the others, thus the relationship between field and course work becomes muddled. This is often true of the less mature student.

### Clarity of Student Role

Very simply, there is much less student role conflict in a block than in a concurrent model. In the block placement, the learner is a student-professional most of the time, while under the concurrent model the student alternates from being a student to being a student-professional. This switching bothers some students and not others. The point is that the roles must be kept clear; and, depending on the student, one model might be better than the other.

### Diversification and Different Ways

These two critical elements are easier to achieve under a block model simply because the student is always available to undertake diverse assignments and to attempt varied approaches. Because the student is one with the agency, as crises arise or as planned services progress the student will be accessible and immersed. Under a concurrent model these two critical elements require more attention. Each can be accomplished under the concurrent model, but the field instructor and student must actively identify diverse situations rather than assume, as in a block model, that diversification will occur.

Each field model clearly emphasizes the opposite ends of the theory/action continuum. The block model operates from an action-theory perspective while the concurrent model operates from a theory-action perspective. These differences ideally should be reflected in the student assignments. Thus, the concurrent model requires students who can move readily between reflective observation, abstract conceptualization, and concrete/or active experimentation; while the block model requires the student to be predominately in the active experimentation mode of learning.

### Integration of Theory and Practice, Sequential Learning and Specificity of Objectives

Sequential learning is more easily achieved under the concurrent model because the learning environment is more controlled. Under the block model, learning tends to be more random because the learner tends to respond primarily to the environment. Lastly, the congruency between practice course content and the field experience may be more easily maintained under concurrency given the incremental nature of most course syllabi and the element of controlled learning.

## Models

The last piece of our puzzle includes the methods used to actuate a field work model. By methods I mean the structure of the placement itself:

* the traditional agency/school agreement
* the use of job site
* the use of one's actual job
* inter-agency/school agreements--"person-swapping"

Each of these methods appears to be more or less conducive to each field model. Figure 7 identifies the consequence of each method under the different models.

### FIGURE 7

| PLACEMENT | PROBLEM | CONCURRENT | BLOCK |
|---|---|---|---|
| Traditional Agency/School Agreement | Agency resource constraints preclude pure field instruction | *Learner role emphasized<br>*Requires 2-4 learning styles | *Learner role<br>*Requires 1 learning style |
| Use of job site | Role confusion between learner/worker | *Helps to lessen role confusion<br>*Requires 2-4 learning styles | *Hazardous to learning<br>*Requires 1 learning style |
| Use of job | Congruency between field and practice | *Reinforces learner<br>*Requires 2-4 learning styles | *Mentor/mentee relationship very important<br>*Requires 1 learning style |
| Person swapping | Unique circumstance required | Not readily feasible due to time factor --too much stress | *Requires more mature, individuated student |

## Traditional Agency/School Agreements

In general this method, under either model, emphasizes the learning role regardless of style. The student is placed in the agency to learn. The student is more likely to be perceived as a learner under the concurrent than the block model because the student is only present in the agency 2 or 3 days each week. When a student is in an agency everyday, the tendency is to perceive the student as a worker. On the other hand, some students learn better being totally immersed. However, in either case, because of the nature of the agreement, there is a built in framework for learning.

## Use of Job Site

Both this method and the next, use of actual job, came into existence with the changing economic conditions of students. As part-time programs expanded, so too did variations on field work methods. This method is subject to role confusion and the possibility of no new learning taking place. These hazards are reduced under the concurrent model: because the basic problem with this method is role and task conflict, it seems reasonable to suggest that clarity of roles is more easily maintained when one is attending classes and thus is constantly reminded of one's student role.

Under the block model, use of job site can produce significant role conflict and strain unless the student can isolate physically and mentally his/her learning tasks from regular job location and tasks. Even then, the lack of connection to course work might still push the student towards more of an apprenticeship model or no model at all. In any case, learning under this method is difficult because the environment-person relationship has been previously fixed. In the final analysis, the more one is fully individuated the less hazardous this method might be, but, theoretically, this method poses problems for learning under either model.

## Use of Actual Job

This method exists only in conjunction with civil service organizations that use a job classification of "Social Work Trainee." These positions are time limited and truly trainee positions. Normally they are available only to regular employees who enter an MSW program. This method works equally well under both models, though under the concurrent model the learner role is emphasized. Closer attention to the congruency between practice course content and field is of import here because the trainee tasks and duties are usually pre-determined and may not clearly be aligned with the curriculum sequencing.

## Interagency Agreements/Person Swapping

This method is not known to exist anywhere. However, it is a method that lends itself (in theory) to the block model. Essentially person swapping would occur between the places of employment of two students. For example, student A works in Glenn County Social Services and Student B works in Butte County Social Service. The field experience would be fulfilled if student A went to work in Butte and student B went to work in Glenn. This would provide a completely new environment, supervisor/instructor, different ways of doing and allow the student to continue working.

Such an arrangement would not readily work under a concurrent model. This arrangement requires total immersion so that the individual can become a competent learner and fulfill the shoes of the old employee to 80% capacity. This requires a mature student who can incorporate various learning styles.

## THE PROVOCATIVE DILEMMAS AND CONCEPTUAL FRAMEWORKS

Now that we have examined the various parts, it is time to look at the implications. The major implication, unfortunately, is rather negative; for what we have done by repackaging a traditional program--overlaying part-time programs onto field work models--is to raise the spectre of chaos and incompatible elements. We are at the point where we are confronting ourselves with contradictions. We are required to make some choices and the choices are our provocative dilemmas. They arise by mixing and matching what essentially are the six variables discussed in this paper:

1) the goal of social work education, inclusive of content
2) experiential learning theory
3) field work models
4) field work methods
5) part-time programs, including program formats
6) students, the input

The possible combinations are obviously infinite because no two students are exactly alike. This latter problem--our first provocative dilemma--may be dealt with in one of at least three ways. Schools can 1) limit the type of student accepted, 2) offer unstructured programs--thus providing the flexibility to create a type of program that best fits the particular student, or 3) offer both a structured program that fits a general type of student and risk bureaucratic leveling and an unstructured one to handle the opposite kind of student.

A second dilemma arises when we attempt to combine experiential learning theory, part-time program formats, and field models. The dilemma revolves around the learning styles required for the various combinations. In essence, a full-time concurrent model requires students be capable of the simultaneous use of all four learning styles; while a part-time concurrent model requires at least two styles but usually three. A block model, under either a full-time or part-time format, requires one predominate style--preferably active experimentation--during the field practicum. Students then are required to use at least two other styles pre and post block placements. Given this range of combinations, where students are in their learning cycle or how well developed is their capacity to learn ought to dictate the program format and model.

A third dilemma derives from the student population and changing economic conditions. It is, perhaps, time to rethink our programs in light of these situations. The situation includes the population from which our students come, our own particular institutional constraints, and the economic situation around us. Some of us are in communities more lush than others. Thus, the availability of field sites and possible field methods varies significantly. We need to try to match our students, programs, and community resources.

There are a myriad other provocative dilemmas, but I think the above three are enough to ponder for now. They are fairly specific. They do, however, fall within the ultimate dilemma we all face:

What kind of programs do we set up which will turn **a given** -- the student with a particular learning style -- into that which we call a social worker, when we know that to be an inventor of interventions requires the capacity to learn using four different styles?

Lastly, it is clear that no one solution fits all, and that no solution is a solution forever. We must conceptualize for ourselves the meaning and implications of part-time models, for this concept can be implemented in a variety of ways. We might decide to limit our student population to a particular profile, which in turn will dictate a particular type of program content and format; or we might decide to have unstructured programs to accommodate a variety of student types. Either way, we must be attuned to the congruency between learning styles and teaching methods. We must, not ironically, all be social workers--inventing interventions so we might serve well both our students and our profession.

## BIBLIOGRAPHY

Campbell, T.F. (1967) FIFTY YEARS OF SOCIAL WORK EDUCATION. Cleveland, Ohio. The Press of Case Western.

Dinerman, M. & Geimar, L. (1984) A QUARTER CENTURY OF SOCIAL WORK EDUCATION. Washington, D.C.: NASW-CSWE.

Gerth and Mills. (1946) FROM MAX WEBER: ESSAYS IN SOCIOLOGY. New York: Oxford University Press.

Jones, B.L. (1969) CURRENT PATTERNS IN FIELD INSTRUCTION. Washington, D.C.: CSWE.

Kendall, Katherine. (1986) PATHFINDER FOR THE PROFESSION. Silver Spring, Md: NASW

Kolb, David. (1984) EXPERIENTIAL LEARNING. Englewood Cliffs, N.J.: Prentice Hall.

Reynolds, B.C. (1985) LEARNING AND TEACHING IN THE PRACTICE OF SOCIAL WORK. Silver Spring, Md.: NASW.

Rosenfeld, J. (1983) "The Dominion and Expertise of Social Work". SOCIAL WORK 28:3, 186-191.

Towle, C. (1954) THE LEARNER IN EDUCATION FOR THE PROFESSIONS. Chicago, Ill: University of Chicago Press.

**ADDENDUM: "Individualized Fast Tract"**

This addendum describes one possible programmatic solution to the major provocative dilemma identified in the conclusion. The program model described herein is entitled "Individualized Fast Tract."

The intent of the model is as follows:

A) Give part-time students, who are generally older with social service experience, an opportunity to complete the MSW degree within two years of start date
B) Give each student a learning experience that is congruent with his/her learning style and level of knowledge and experience
C) Alter the leveling effect of social work education by altering the program format

The model calls for the following:

1) Individualized programs
   A. Course work
      *assess learning styles of each student
      *assess teaching styles of all faculty
      *match learning styles and teaching styles (faculty would be called upon to teach all phases of social work education)
      *one faculty member (or a team) would be responsible for teaching/mentoring a group of students through all elements of social work education
   B. Field Work
      *learning style of student matched with complementary style of field instructor
      *required field hours--dependent upon social services work experience (evaluation to be made based on standard criteria; i.e., 5 years as an eligibility worker might be equivalent to first year field and 5 years as a CPS worker might be equivalent to 2nd year field. A student with extensive experience may require minimal field experience--particularly if s/he intends to remain in her/his current place of employment
      *field offered either as block or concurrently (best fit for student)

2) Intensive Program Format
      *all courses offered as intensives--some combination of 8-hour days. For example, a 3-unit course normally equals 45 class hours spread out over 15 weeks: an intensive program might schedule six 8-hour days as 3 consecutive weekends or spread out, or one 4-day weekend (Fri., Sat., Sun. and Mon.) followed by one 2-day weekend
      *intensives facilitate completion of an MSW degree in two years or less
      *year-round programming is required (a program catering to part-time must utilize the entire calendar year)

# EMPLOYMENT SETTING AS PRACTICUM SITE: A FIELD INSTRUCTION DILEMMA

Marcia L. Martin, *Bryn Mawr College*

Directors of field instruction at schools of social work are faced a with a dilemma about student's concurrent use of agencies as both employment and practicum settings. An increasing number of Master's program applicants are inquiring as to whether or not they may use a current employment setting as a practicum site. The request is often related to the rise in the cost of education and the decrease in the availability of financial aid, the desire to continue at an agency where one perceives a professional future, and the growing number of older, more established, bachelor level social workers seeking graduate education. Schools often accede to these requests because of a desire to attract these mature students who have already made a commitment to social work, an intent to attract a diverse student population, and in some instance a need to establish a larger applicant pool.

As we began to review this issue at Bryn Mawr Graduate School of Social Work and Social Research, we wanted to consider the experiences of other graduate schools of social work. For this purpose, a questionnaire was sent to directors of field instruction at the eighty-seven accredited Master's on Social Work programs listed in the July, 1985, Council on Social Work Education brochure. These directors were queried about the number of students using their employment setting as a practicum site, the criteria used to determine the appropriateness of an employment setting for practica, the factors about a student's experience, career interests, and educational background that were considered, the methods used to monitor employment related settings, the nature of contracts signed between school and agency, the distinctions made between job and practicum work assignments, and the general experience with employment settings used as practicum sites. A copy of the questionnaire is attached as Appendix A.

Sixty-three of the eighty-seven questionnaires which were sent, were completed and returned by January, 1987. Overall, nine percent of the students enrolled in these Master's programs are using employment sites as practicum settings, however, the range is primarily from zero to twenty-seven percent, with one school at fifty-two percent and another at one hundred percent. Some schools specifically prohibit such a practice, many have developed policies and procedures for students using paid employment sites as placements, and some have established special programs for employed students who elect to remain at their work setting. Numerous criteria are used and specific factors are considered by schools in determining the appropriateness of an employment setting as a practicum site. In addition, schools have developed a variety of contracting and monitoring strategies to cope with the potential conflicts between work and school tasks and expectations. While a majority of schools rate their general experience with employment settings used as practicum sites as positive, the number of students participating in this type of arrangement is small. Many schools seem reluctant, or at least cautious, about using employment settings.

The material gathered from the questionnaire has been quantitatively and qualitatively summarized and evaluated. The primary purpose of undertaking this survey was to aid us in establishing criteria for the use of current employment settings as practicum sites. Our Field Instruction Committee is developing a set of criteria to be applied to students, agencies, and field instructors who are involved in work/practicum arrangements. These criteria emerged from our consideration of the experiences and concerns of other social work programs.

**Table 1: Number of Graduate Schools with Specific Percentage of Students Using Employment Sites  (n=63)**

| Numbers of Schools | Percentage of Students |
|---|---|
| 5 | 0% |
| 37 | 1-10% |
| 15 | 11-20% |
| 4 | 21-30% |
| 1 | 51-60% |
| 1 | 100% |

Table 1 shows the quantative picture. In general, the large schools (250-550 students) placed 10-20% or less of their field students in employment settings. Medium-sized schools (150-250 students) also placed 10-20% or less (with one exception in which more than 50% of the students were placed in employment settings); while the percentage of small schools placing students in employment settings ranged from 5% to 25% with one notable exception in which all 20 students were so placed. Five of the responding sixty-three schools do not permit their students to use a work site as a practicum setting, and thirty-seven schools, or almost fifty-nine percent, have ten percent or fewer of their students participating in employment/practicum arrangements. While almost all of the responding schools have developed guidelines for employment/practicum settings, the students involved in these placements matriculate in the regular school curriculum. Some schools have developed entire programs for students wishing or needing to use their work sites for field instruction. As examples, Portland State University Graduate School of Social Work has instituted an "Employed Social Worker Option" to incorporate field instruction into the employment setting;  Hunter College School of Social Work has undertaken the "One Year Resident Program" as a part-time work-study option for experienced bachelor level social workers, the State University of New York at Stony Brook School of Social Work has planned "Pathway Options" for students using paid employment for field instruction;  Atlanta University School of Social Work has established a "Night Program" with the employed student particularly in mind. Schools of social work are increasingly recognizing the needs of employed bachelor level social workers who wish to obtain an advanced social work degree but who are not in a position to give up their employment in a social service agency. This category of student has long existed, but in the nineteen sixties and early seventies they were often granted leave from their agencies (particularly those in the public service sector) with a work commitment following graduation, or in more recent years as "exceptions" to the general field placement requirements.

Schools show a remarkable similarity in the criteria used to determine the appropriateness of an employment setting as practica. First and foremost, agencies must meet the normal standards established by the school, and field instructors must also adhere to the normal educational and experiential standards established by the school. In addition, the vast majority of schools demand that a student's field work tasks be distinctly different form his/her work tasks, take place in a different department, service, or division, meet the educational goals of the student and school, and represent a significant reduction in work load when compared with assignments made to regular staff members. The majority of schools also require that the field instructor be someone other than the employment supervisor. The emphasis here is clearly on facilitating a distinction between the work experience and enriching the student's activities to enhance skill development and reflect the student's status as a student and not simply an employee. Several schools indicate that a student's employment agency may serve as a practicum setting for only one year; the second field placement must represent a totally new experience in a non-work related setting.

A general concern about compromising a student's learning is apparent in responses to the questionnaire. Special factors are carefully considered in allowing a student to use a work site for a practicum experience. Included among these factors is the financial need of the student, the student's prior social work experience, and the compatibility between the agency's service, organization, and values, and the school's social work curriculum and orientation. In general, opportunities to use an employment site for a practicum setting are reserved for students with prior social work experience who evidence financial need and are employed in social service agencies which offer diverse experiences to their staff.

While approximately fifty percent of the responding schools note no differences in the monitoring of employment related settings, other schools have established specific procedures. For example, at several schools liaisons visit employment related settings more frequently in order to assure the educational integrity of the setting and the continued distinction between job and practicum. While seventy-nine percent of the responding schools sign a formal contract with all of their practicum settings, several schools have established agreements with work sites that vary from the usual contracts. These agreements are designed to clearly distinguish practicum tasks from work assignments, specify days and times designated for practicum as opposed to job, identify the field instructor and the specific time for educational supervision, and confirm agency administrative support for the practicum/work arrangement.

The clear distinction between job and practicum assignments is obviously crucial to the success of the student's experience. Eighty-three percent of the responding schools which permit students to use work sites, "require" that job and practicum assignments be distinctly different; another ten percent "prefer" that they be different. Ninety-three percent of these schools also require that the field instructor be different from the job supervisor and that the field instruction days and hours be separate and distinct from job time. A significant number of these same schools also emphasize the importance of separating the student evaluation process from employee status evaluations.

As mentioned earlier, the majority of schools rate their experience with employment settings used as practicum sites as positive. Ten percent indicated that their experiences are "very positive, they are almost always successful"; fifty-nine percent suggest that their experiences as "not very positive, they have on occasion been problematic"; nineteen percent rate their experiences as "not positive at all, they are frequently problematic". Schools attribute success -- positive experiences -- to good contracting, careful monitoring, the diversified nature of the agency, and the agency's commitment to education, staff advancement, and the development of professional skills. Schools attribute problems -- mixed or negative experiences -- to confusion between student status and employee role, difficulty in providing "protected" educational time for a student at his/her agency, and abuses by agencies more concerned with task completion than with a student's learning needs.

Our experience at Bryn Mawr with employment/practicum settings reflects that of other schools. Like many new or "irregular" undertakings, the use of employment settings for field sites has resulted in mixed outcomes. Some students and agencies are very successful in balancing work and practicum demands; learning tasks are not sacrificed for job responsibilities. In other instances, a tension exists between school expectations and work requirements; the student is caught, needing to keep his/her job for financial reasons and/or future professional considerations, but wanting to learn new skills.

In discussing practicum planning with the eleven students who requested permission to use an employment site as a practicum setting during the 1987-88 academic year, it became apparent that five students wished that they could explore other options. Financial considerations were among the primary reasons each gave in explaining the need to continue at a work site. In each instance the work site is an appropriate practicum setting; each could provide an acceptable field instructor and a set of new tasks in a different department or service that would meet the learning expectation of the school. In each case, however, the student felt that he/she would not be stretched to the fullest, and viewed the decision to remain at an employment site as a compromise -- not the best road but the only road to an advanced degree. Five other students who described their work/practicum assignment in more positive terms are each employed by a large, public, child welfare agency where a shift to a new department represents a significant change in assignments and collegial associations, and where future opportunities for promotions to supervisory level positions and salary increases are great. The remaining student works at a relatively small agency but has completed a first year placement at a dramatically different setting. She is committed to beginning her professional career at her current employment site and because she elected to enter the "Management" track has been given a totally new set of responsibilities. She views the opportunity to use her work site in very positive terms.

Employment/practicum experiences obviously vary. At Bryn Mawr we decided that we could not develop a rigid set of policies or procedures to direct the use of these settings, but rather we developed a set of guidelines. These guidelines have emerged from a careful consideration of the responses to the previously discussed questionnaire and from our own limited experiences. These guidelines reflect the potential problems and cautions expressed by many directors of field instruction. (They are included here as Appendix B.) They are designed to set the parameters for decision making regarding the use of employment sites as practicum settings. As with all guidelines, they are designed to suggest a direction but not a single narrow path. We say we are confident that a different department or service is better and a different supervisor is essential. But is this "always" true or is it only "generally" the case? Is it more true for someone who has been at an agency for four years than it is for someone who has worked at an agency for only one year? We say that a student must have been employed at an agency for at least eighteen months before he/she could consider it for a practicum. But would a newer employee experience greater learning opportunities than a three or more year "veteran"? The questions and concerns revolving around the employment/practicum issue persist far beyond any guidelines, and the answers simply are not definitive.

As requests for employment/practicum experiences increase, we cannot rely on the arbitrariness of a case by case consideration, but neither can we turn over the decision making to a rigid set of rules. We not only need to learn what works but why it works and under what circumstances it works. We know that the student can make a difference, the agency and its personnel and services can make a difference, contracting can make a difference, monitoring can make a difference. These factors are no different than those which impact on the success or failure of any field placement. Ultimately the crucial issue may not revolve around the means by which we select, monitor, and evaluate employment/practicum sites, but rather whether we use them at all. They often do result in certain compromises in the experiences of the students involved, and as gatekeepers of the profession can we allow these compromises to exist? Yet, as gatekeepers, are we guarding only one gate through which access to an advanced degree in social work can be obtained? The employment/practicum dilemma challenges us to consider other routes of entry, routes which are different but which pass through the important checkpoints along the way. Like any true dilemma, the employment/practicum problem seems to defy a totally satisfactory solution.

## APPENDIX A

### FIELD INSTRUCTION SURVEY

NAME:                    TITLE:
SCHOOL OF SOCIAL WORK:ADDRESS:
TELEPHONE: (    )
        AREA CODE
Under what auspices does your agency operate? _____ Public  _____ Private
Do you have a BSW program? _____ yes      _____ no

Questions 1 to 8 refer to the 1986-87 academic program at the masters level.
1. How many students are in field placement? _____
2. How many field placement settings do you use? _____
3. a. How many agencies offer student stipends? _____
   b. How many of these are private? _____
4. What is the range of stipends offered (dollar amount)? (WRITE IN)
       From a high of $_____ to a low of $_____
5. How many of the stipends carry a post graduate work commitment? _____
6. What is the nature and extent of such commitments? (WRITE IN)
7. What type of agencies currently offer stipends? (CHECK ALL THAT APPLY)
    _____ a. Aging/Gerontology       _____ i. Health
    _____ b. Alcohol/Drug or Substance   _____ j. Industrial Social Work
    _____ c. Child Welfare           _____ k. Mental Health or
    _____ d. Community Planning     _____ l. Mental Retardation
    _____ e. Corrections/Justice      _____ m. Public Welfare/Assistance
    _____ f. Family Services        _____ n. Rehabilitation
    _____ g. Group Services        _____ o. School Social Work
    _____ h. Governmental/Legislative   _____ Other _____
If you currently or have in the past used an employment settings as a practicum site please answer
questions 9-16. If not, please skip to question 17.

8. How many students use their employment settings as a practicum site? _____
9. What criteria are used to determine the appropriateness of an employment setting for practica?
(WRITE IN)
10. What special factors about the student's experience, career interests, etc. are considered? (WRITE IN)
11. Are employment related settings monitored differently from non employment related settings? If so,
how? (WRITE IN) _____ yes _____ no
12. Are formal contracts signed between the School and the agency? (CHECK ONE) _____ yes _____ no
13. How is the field instructor selected? (WRITE IN)
14. How are job/practicum assignments distinguished? (WRITE IN)
15. How is job/practicum time arranged? (WRITE IN)
16. Is the evaluation of student and field instructor effected by the employment status? If so, how?
(WRITE IN) _____ yes _____ no

17. a. How would you rate your general experience with employment settings used as practicum sites?
      _____ very positive, they are almost always successful
      _____ positive, they are usually successful
      _____ not very positive, they have on occasion been problematic
      _____ not positive at all, they are frequently problematic
  b. Why do you think this is the case? (WRITE IN)
18. What other programs have you developed through the field instruction office to meet financial aid
requests?  (PLEASE DESCRIBE)

    _____ Please share any general findings with me.

Thank you for your cooperation. Please return this questionnaire in the enclosed envelope.

**APPENDIX B**

GUIDELINES FOR
EMPLOYMENT SITE AS PRACTICUM SETTING

I. Student Guidelines

    A.    Student must have been employed by agency for at least eighteen months.

    B.    If student's employment experience is limited to this one agency, student may use this agency as a practicum for only one academic year.

    C.    Student's employment performance evaluations must be at a satisfactory level and the student should provide us with the most recent evaluation.

II. Agency Guidelines

    A.    Agency must offer diverse opportunities appropriate to the track the student has selected
    B.    Agency must have an internal employee evaluation system in place.
    C.    There must be a clear termination of the student's previous work assignment or a clear split between the practicum and work assignments. The practicum assignment must be in a different department or service from the previous work assignments. All should be specified in a written contract between the agency, school, and student.
    D.    The agency must provide in writing a current employment description and a proposed practicum description.
    E.    The time for practicum and employment assignments must be specified in a written contract between the agency, school, and student.
    F.    In addition to the two evaluations completed by the field instructor, an evaluation of the student's work assignment should also be submitted at the end of each semester.

III. Field Instructor Guidelines

    A.    The field instructor must meet the criteria set by the school for all field instructors.
    B.    The field instructor must be different from the current employment supervisor.
    C.    The field instructor must attend field instruction seminars.

IV. School Guidelines

    A.    The school will provide the agency with a Field Instruction Manual and other pertinent information.
    B.    A member of the Field Instruction staff will conduct an evaluation of the agency prior to use as a practicum site. Emphasis should be placed on determining the     ability to distinguish employment tasks from practicum assignments.
    C.    A faculty liaison will visit the agency and talk with the student, field instructor, and agency contact person at least two times during the academic year.

# THE OLDER STUDENT: SOCIAL WORK'S NEW MAJORITY

Elaine F. Marshack, *Hunter College School of Social Work*

For most M.S.W. graduates, the field practicum had particular significance as the place where their growing knowledge and skills found expression in the provision of social services. Their effectiveness as helpers derived, in large part, from the astuteness with which they were able to assess the complex range of variables shaping human need at any one time in our society. Similarly, our effectiveness as educators depends, in large part, on our dynamic understanding of the changing characteristics and needs of students.

"Whom are we educating?" Arnulf Pins (1964) asked in his landmark study of first year M.S.W. students in 1960. Among other characteristics he noted a slight decrease in median age over the previous decade. In 1960 less than one-third of first year M.S.W. students were over 30. Twenty-six years later 54% of M.S.W. students were over 30 and 20% were over 40 (Hidalgo and Spaulding, 1986, p. 36). Since the trend toward an older student population in M.S.W. education is likely to continue, this paper examines the salient characteristics of older learners and their implications for field teaching.

As the pool of younger applicants to M.S.W. programs has shrunk in recent years, schools have increasingly directed recruitment efforts toward older students. Social work is not alone in this effort; by 1985 a majority of those attending community colleges and increasing proportions in senior colleges and post-secondary institutions were older or non-traditional students.[1]

Older students in social work are drawn from three major constituencies. Women returning to education after some years of remaining at home with children have long been represented among social work students. Pre-professional employees of social agencies have increasingly been recruited to reduced residence and other part-time or advanced standing programs in social work. A third and rapidly growing constituency is composed of men and women making career changes. As life expectancy and occupational mobility have increased in the United States, it is becoming the norm for individuals to make at least one career change in a lifetime (Sontag, 1986). Often the change is prompted by dissatisfaction with an earlier career choice or changing values and aspirations as one grows older. At other times it involves preparation for a new career after retirement from an earlier one.

A comparison of mid-life female students with their younger counterparts suggested similarity in their reported objectives for M.S.W. education. Both groups sought personal fulfillment and a knowledge base for practice. "The unique themes of the mid-life women (were) the importance they (gave) to changing careers" and their awareness of aging which lent urgency to the achievement of their goals

---

[1] House higher education bill provides for older students. (Dec. 5, 1985). AGING SERVICE NEWS, p. 170.

(Rappaport, 1983, pp. 99, 101).    In contrast, the younger group placed more emphasis on their earning power and chances for advancement.

The transition to a student role is likely to be more difficult for older students.  They often experience losses in status, money, power, and autonomy in returning to school (Sarnat, 1952).  Their stake in succeeding in this new venture may be exacerbated by a sense of risk in relinquishing a job in which they were successful or trying again to build a rewarding career after failing in an earlier effort.

Many older students struggle to maintain a balance between multiple and often conflicting roles, not only as students in classroom and field but also as partners in intimate relationships, parents, and often employees.  Role overload or situations in which the totality of demands exceeds students' capacities to meet them can occur (Sales, Shore and Bolitho, 1980, p. 61).

One study of students 35 years and older found that lack of time to meet the conflicting demands of home, school, placement, and often workplace was perceived by respondents as their major non-academic difficulty. Accompanying this dilemma were feelings of guilt about neglecting children and spouses (Rappaport, 1983, p. 93)

In a study of working mothers, four major facilitators in reducing role conflicts and preventing role overload were identified (Hoffman, and Nye, 1974). They included (1) the absence of preschool children; (2) the extent to which a partner helps with household and child care chores; (3) the availability of extended family resources; and (4) the use of paid houseworkers.  In contrast, often represented among social work students are single parents of young children whose financial resources are too limited to hire household help.

Adaptation to the intensity and intimacy of tutorial learning in the field practicum can present particular challenge to older students. An informal survey by one older student of her peers suggested that those who had worked within bureaucratic organizations, such as hospitals, public services, or large businesses, adapted more readily to the role of supervisee than those who had been entrepreneurs or "whose work histories identified them as non-conformists" (Sondheim, 1986. p. 12).

Significant age differences between an older student and younger field instructor can cause initial discomfort for both.  The broader life experience of an older student can be intimidating to a younger field instructor.  Each may wonder what the field instructor has to teach that the student doesn't already know.  Older students may also fear being found wanting by field instructors many years their junior, perhaps even age peers of their children.

Older students often experience authority and dependency conflicts in tutorial learning.  They may more readily identify with agency staff than younger students and be more comfortably assertive and challenging. At the same time, they often find it harder to expose their learning needs and take risks. Accepting help can be very difficult for older students after years of more self-reliant functioning. In their field work practice many older students are initially more reserved and reticent about sharing of themselves with clients than their younger peers, behavior which may be felt by clients as lack of caring or interest.

Generally less malleable than their younger classmates, older students often feel that their knowledge or habits are being devalued in the process of transition to social work. They have developed methods for performing other adult roles which they are likely to carry over to social work education, sometimes appropriately and other times less so. If their earlier work emphasized production or outcomes, it may be difficult for them to understand the close attention to process and the emphasis on self-reflection and awareness which characterize social work education. Those who were successful pre-professionals in social work may find the expectation of a new level of performance especially challenging.

At the same time, older students are often intensely motivated to succeed in social work education. Their approach to this new learning is frequently characterized by steadiness and resiliency. Having coped with difficult experiences before, they can usually mobilize resources to meet the challenge of M.S.W. education.

The aging of the M.S.W. student population challenges field educators to reexamine their teaching approaches. Assumptions about the art and science of helping adults to learn can be a useful starting point in this effort. While the principles and techniques of andragogy are relevant to all social work students, they have particular meaning for older students. Adults are assumed to be self-directing, to bring a reservoir of experience, to learn most readily content which is directly relevant to their performance of evolving social roles, and to have a problem-centered orientation to learning (Knowles, 1972).

Respect for the self-direction of adult learners implies a climate which is not only accepting and supportive but also open, informal, and collaborative (Clancy, 1985, p. 76). Greater reciprocity between teacher and student places emphasis on a field instructor's serving primarily as a facilitator and resource person rather than a leader and transmitter of knowledge (Foeckler and Boynton, 1976, p. 40). A student role as active initiator rather than passive recipient of learning is implied.

Given the range of transitional issues typically presented by older students, the process of their induction into the placement experience is of critical importance. One woman, self-described as used to running her own show, reported that her adaptation to the practicum had been greatly facilitated by her first field instructor's "(sitting) me down and explaining what the field process was about. She identified where I might anticipate problems and how to deal with them" (Sondheim, 1986, p. 12).

The typical motivation of older students to acquire skills within a problem-centered orientation suggests that formulation of goals for the practicum should be a joint effort between student and field instructor from the start. Integral to such a plan is field instructors' readiness to help older students begin to identify the potential relevance of their earlier learning and roles to social work practice. Specific identification of skills a student possesses but may not accredit as useful can help to reduce feelings of incompetence. An administrative secretary, for example, may not regard her strong organizational and writing skills as valued assets for social work practice.

Often, of course, the value of prior experiences cannot be anticipated until a specific situation elicits it. In one instance, a widowed student in her 40's was working with a family when the father was murdered. The student moved immediately to help the widow deal with her anguish and, at the same time, include her children in mourning and initiate funeral plans. The field instructor, a neophyte in her mid-twenties, had never experienced a death firsthand and had not considered many of the issues the student immediately recognized as important. It was a valuable lesson for the field instructor in developing comfort with areas in which the knowledge of her supervisees exceeded her own. Reciprocity in learning is a hallmark of andragogy but requires, first, that teachers be secure with what they do and do not know.

The ways older students learn most comfortably and productively are important to consider in educational planning for them. For some students, the intensity of a single instructional relationship can interfere with rather than facilitate their learning. Field instruction in M.S.W. education has been historically characterized by its reliance on a single tutorial relationship between supervisor and student. Deriving from its apprenticeship origins, this model was sustained during the period when long-term clinical practice predominated and the intensive teaching relationship modeled the practice with clients (Berkman and Carlton, 1985).

Changes in both students and practice mandate reexamination of dependence on a single tutorial relationship for field teaching. Practice has moved increasingly toward flexible use of varied methods of intervention within short time frames. M.S.W. graduates need to be prepared to exercise thoughtful judgment without the close supervision which once characterized early professional practice. One approach to educating self-initiating, accountable social workers is to use task or ancillary field teachers to supervise student practice in specific modalities or programs. With a primary field instructor integrating the educational experiences, a student is exposed to a range of models for identification and a variety of learning opportunities. The challenge of integrating varied perspectives is highly appropriate for older learners.

The pragmatic orientation of many older students makes observational experiences especially valuable. Opportunities to critique the work of others can also help them to begin review of their own practice. Peer exchange in group supervision or student and staff meetings is often more comfortable than concentrated teaching by an authority. Help to students in formulating questions and exploring them independently encourages self-directed learning. Specification of theoretical frames of reference is especially important in working with students who begin with skills in pragmatically-based practice.

Students who have been away from school for many years may struggle with expectations for written work, extensive reading, or even changes in the culture of education. They may also express difficulty in managing their multiple roles. Field instructors can help free students' energies for learning by acknowledging these issues and providing help in prioritizing or compartmentalizing while, at the same time, holding them to clear expectations for performance.

Older students often bring unrealistic expectations of themselves or fear that more will be expected of them than of their younger peers. And it can happen that field instructors, intimidated by the knowledge or experience of older students, may be overdemanding. On the other hand, intimidation can lead field instructors to abrogate their authority by modifying expectations or reducing their critical appraisal of students' work. It often requires the intervention of another person, perhaps the school liaison, agency supervisor, or seminar leader, to identify such interactions and help a field instructor to establish and maintain reasonable expectations.

Older students who have been pre-professionals in social work or a related field often experience a rude shock in finding they must replace much of what they took for granted as useful accomplishment. Charlotte Towle (1954) observed that "Sometimes old adaptive responses and learnings become problematic because they are not conscious ... when the learning has much recall of the old in it, the learner may stop at partial mastery and fall back on the old when he can 'make do' with it ... He may struggle to regain the old competence and thus ... not give himself freely and fully to the acquisition of the new" (p. 36).

Experienced workers who enter professional education often present particular challenges to field instructors. "Because these students may have an investment in retaining the automatic responses and ways of working that have contributed to their perceived competence, the educational objective is to encourage conscious choice over intuition in practice" (Haffey and Starr, 1988). In analysis of their practice, experienced students can be encouraged to examine instances in which spontaneous responses failed to achieve desired outcomes. It can also help them to recognize that experienced professionals struggle with ambiguities and dilemmas too.

Many older students bring experience in personal psychotherapy to their social work education which may lead to a conception of the helping process at variance with social work practice. In such instances, field instructors need to be alert to the helping model of a student and prepared to explore and discuss differences from social work practice when they exist.

In summary, students over thirty now constitute a growing majority in M.S.W. education. Their resources in life experience and quality of motivation can lead to very productive engagement in the field practicum. At the same time, their increasing presence in social work programs challenges field educators to reexamine their teaching approaches. Especially important for older learners are field instructors who are sensitive to the range of transitional issues that are often paramount for them and expect their active participation in planning and implementing the full educational experience. Instead of reliance on a single tutorial relationship in the practicum, it is recommended that a range of opportunities to work with multiple teachers, to learn from peers, to observe and critique the practice of others, and to explore questions independently be provided.

## BIBLIOGRAPHY

Berkman, B. and Carlton, T. (1985) THE DEVELOPMENT OF HEALTH SOCIAL WORK CURRICULA: PATTERNS AND PROCESS IN THREE PROGRAMS OF SOCIAL WORK EDUCATION. Boston, MA: Massachusetts General Hospital Institute of Health Professions.

Clancy, C. (1985) The use of the andragogical approach in the educational function of supervision in social work. THE CLINICAL SUPERVISOR, 3:1, 75-86.

Foeckler, M. and Boynton, G. (1976) Creative adult learning-teaching: who's the engineer of this train? JOURNAL OF EDUCATION FOR SOCIAL WORK, 12:3, 37-43.

Haffey, M. and Starr, R. (1985) Teaching work-study students: curriculum delivery and program design issues. In DESIGNING A WORK-STUDY PROGRAM: WHERE SOCIAL SERVICE EMPLOYMENT

MEETS PROFESSIONAL EDUCATION, 85-95. Martha Haffey and Rose Starr (Eds.) New York: Silberman Fund.

Hidalgo, J. and Spaulding, E. (1986) STATISTICS OF SOCIAL WORK EDUCATION IN THE UNITED STATES. 1986. Washington, D.C.: Council on Social Work Education.

Hoffman, L. and Nye, F. (1974) WORKING MOTHERS. San Francisco: Jossey-Bass.

House higher education bill provides for older students. (Dec. 5, 1985) AGING SERVICE NEWS.

Knowles, M. (1972) Innovations in teaching styles and approaches based upon adult learning. JOURNAL OF EDUCATION FOR SOCIAL WORK, 8:2, 32-39.

Marshack, E. (1986) Task supervision: a quiet revolution in field teaching of MSW students. ARETE, 11:2, 45-50.

Pins, A. (1964) Whom are we educating? New York: Council on Social Work Education.

Rappaport, J. (1983) Mid-life women at social work school: a comparative study. DSW dissertation, New York University.

Sales, E.; Shore, B.; and Bolitho, F. (1980) When mothers return to school. JOURNAL OF EDUCATION FOR SOCIAL WORK, 16:1, 57-65.

Sarnat, R. (1952) Supervision of the experienced student. SOCIAL CASEWORK, 33, 147-152.

Shulman, L. (1983) TEACHING OF THE HELPING SKILLS: A FIELD INSTRUCTOR'S GUIDE. Itasca, Ill.: F.E. Peacock.

Sondheim, G. (1986) Problems of the mid-life returnee to social work school: a student perspective. Unpublished manuscript.

Sontag, S. (Feb. 1986) Fitting graduate programs to working adult problems. NEW YORK TIMES, Special Continuing Education Supplement.

Towle, C. (1984) THE LEARNER IN EDUCATION FOR THE PROFESSION. Chicago: University of Chicago Press.

# THE OPEN EXPRESSION OF DIFFERENCES IN THE FIELD PRACTICUM: REPORT OF A PILOT STUDY[1]

Frances B. Raphael and Amy Frank Rosenblum
*Virginia Commonwealth University.*

Preparing MSW students to debate and contribute to the major social policy issues of our time would seem to be central to the mission of social work education. Yet matters of vital concern to social workers only can be debated when the underlying issue of the freedom to air differences is emphasized in every social work arena. In the course of educating professionals, there is a need to examine whether the open expression of differences is valued as appropriate content for the educational experience. Has social work education over-emphasized commonalities at the expense of differences?

The field practicum is a fertile area within which one may examine whether differences actually are expressed. Students, as adult learners, are likely to experience differences with their field instructors. The differences may be minor, (an example would be an easily clarified misunderstanding), or they may be major (such as profound disagreement in point of view). Both student and instructor face dilemmas about this situation: The student wonders whether to suffer the disagreements silently or to share them with the field instructor; the instructor wonders whether or not to reach for these differences, and if so, when to do so.

Social work educators generally have assumed that the learning process moves beyond rote learning when a student stops merely absorbing information and begins raising questions for critical examination. In the practicum, when student and field instructor examine their differences and disagreements, one may observe the change that takes place in students: They move from simply taking in information to actively grappling with ideas and concepts. The airing of differences is generally seen as constructive, even essential to the making of a social worker. However, it has not been demonstrated empirically that differences are actually discussed. As a result of preparing an article on students at risk of failure in the practicum (Rosenblum & Raphael, 1987), and through experience as faculty field liaisons, the authors became aware that open expression of differences between students and field instructors was not always evident. It seemed worthwhile, therefore, to learn more about how differences between students and field instructors were handled in the practicum.

## LITERATURE REVIEW

The difficulty of researching open expression of differences may account for the dearth of studies on this subject. The relevant literature focused on several related issues: (a) Expectations for social work students regarding the expression of

[1]This article was first published in the JOURNAL OF SOCIAL WORK EDUCATION, Vol. 25, No. 2. and it is reprinted here with the permission of the Council on Social Work Education.

their differences from field instructors; (b) students' behavior in the context of field instruction in relation to the expression of differences; (c) factors of power and authority in the student-instructor relationship and the effect on student expression of differences; and (d), the attributes of the 'good' teacher in relation to the expression of differences.

The literature supports the idea that social work students should be expected to express their differences with field instructors. In some instances, authors thought this should occur from the beginning of the relationship (Judah, 1972). Others suggested that such expression is a developmental task to be accomplished over time (Germain & Gitterman, 1979). Wilson (1981) wrote that the quality of students' field performance might be evaluated partly in terms of their willingness to express differences. There was consensus that students **ought** to be expected to express their differences; opinion varied over **when** it might occur.

Rosenblatt and Mayer's well-known study (1975) dramatically revealed how students behave with respect to their differences and disagreements with field instructors. They found that despite "norms of communication that exhort students to be open and honest in supervisory sessions," none of the students in the survey openly confronted their supervisors (p. 187). This failure to express differences suggests a discrepancy between expectation and actual behavior and also offers a challenge to seek further understanding of the phenomenon.

In addition to the student's reluctance to confront the field instructor, there possibly may be a concomitant reluctance on the instructor's part: There may be some hesitance to encourage the emergence of differences, on the grounds that it might jeopardize the student-instructor relationship (Rosenblum and Raphael, 1987). Another aspect of the failure to express differences may have to do with the instructor's position of power: The student may be unwilling to take such a risk. Robinson described a tendency to "annihilate difference" (1949, p. 39) as a way of establishing identification in the early stages of the field instructor-student relationship; Studt (1954) wrote about the inclination to surrender leadership to the person possessing knowledge-derived authority. Nelson (1974) observed that students were more willing to risk venting their ideas when they felt themselves to be on a more equal footing with their instructors. On the other hand, some researchers have raised the specter of the punitive potential of authority (Raphael and Rosenblum, 1987; Wilson, 1981), by relating the student's reluctance to express differences to the power of the field instructor to grade student practicum performance. In fact, Wilson stated that the student may "fear retaliation" if "he or she disagrees with the supervisor on an issue" (p. 24).

The literature seems to affirm the value of teaching behaviors that encourage open expression of differences, despite the power differential that may impede the process. Over the years, writers on social work education have highlighted some of these behaviors. Some writers discuss the importance of actively struggling against the tendency to wipe out differences in order to permit each person to become wholly involved in learning (Robinson, 1949; Tropp, 1969). Others have advocated a teaching style that shares responsibility with the student (Selby, 1965; Somers, 1971). Perlman (1967) believed that the mark of a truly great teacher is the ability to allow differences to emerge. Shulman (1983) placed importance on the ability to present ideas in a manner that encourages challenge; he viewed it as a vital ingredient of teaching skill, and suggested discussing with students "how comfortable [they are] in taking the field instructor on" (p. 2). Others highlight the importance of field instructors bringing into the open **their** differences from students (Rosenblum and Raphael, 1987).

The literature clearly gives value to the open expression of differences as a part of preparation for social work practice. Less clear, however, is the extent to which it actually occurs and, when it does, the nature and content of these differences. This pilot study was conducted to explore the nature of differences that arise in the field practicum, how and when they emerge, how they are handled in the instructional process, and whether and when students and field instructors expect them.

## METHODS

Two versions of the same questionnaire were developed in order to obtain information from both students and field instructors. To tap the broadest possible range of responses, most questions were open-ended. The questionnaire covered the following areas: (a) When were differences of opinion first expressed? (b) What were the differences? (c) How did the field instructor and student each respond to these expressions? (d) How was the field instructor-student relationship affected? (e) How was the student's practice influenced? And (f), did the field instructor and student anticipate that the expression of differences would be a part of their work together?

The questionnaire was pretested on 15 field instructors and their students; a few questions then were modified for greater clarity. For example, on the original questionnaire, a question about the differences elicited general answers; as a result, the question was rephrased to ask the respondent to identify the issues specifically.

The questionnaire was sent to all master's level students and their field instructors of one large urban school of social work. The initial mailing took place in the twelfth week of the Fall semester, 1986. There were 246 students and 208 field instructors. The twenty field instructors who had more than one student were sent additional questionnaires. Two weeks after the first mailing, a follow-up letter was mailed to each recipient. The response rate was approximately 40%.

Alert to respondents' potential reluctance to give information about differences, the authors tried to find the least threatening mechanism for encouraging open and honest reporting. Some consideration was given to attempting to match students and field instructors, but because it might raise concerns about confidentiality, the plan was abandoned in the hope that there would be greater freedom to respond.

Both researchers read the responses to all open-ended questions. Upon mutual agreement, core themes were identified. For example, responses to the question "what was the difference about?" yielded such categories as: practice issues, procedural matters, process recording, etc. All responses were sorted according to core themes and categorized only after discussion and agreement between the two researchers.

## FINDINGS

### Number of Student and Field Instructor Responses Reflecting Student Expression of Differences

The questionnaire was sent to 246 students; 77 (31%) returned them. Only 37 (48%) reported expressing differences. Roughly half of the students who returned the survey or reported differences were in their first year; the remainder were in their second year of study. Of the 246 questionnaires sent to field instructors, 114 (46%) were returned. In 57 instances, the field instructors stated that their students expressed differences. In other words, nearly half of all respondents (students and field instructors) actually reported the expression of differences.

### Times Differences Arose

Among field instructors' questionnaires citing differences, 37 (64%) reported that differences primarily occurred between the third and eighth weeks of the first semester. Most students did not answer this question; of the 14 (37%) who did respond, 11 agreed with the instructors' time frames. Although the majority of students with differences (20; 54%) reported a delay of one day or less between awareness and expression of differences, a small number of students (4; 10%) reported waiting more than three weeks before bringing their disagreements to the field instructor.

### Causes of Difference

Among those respondents who identified the expression of differences, 17 (46%) of the students' and 34 (60%) of the field instructors' questionnaires delineated practice issues as the main source of differences. These included such matters as: Direction of a case, conceptual issues, clinical decisions, assessment, etc. Field instruction issues constituted the next largest category, involving such concerns as the nature and appropriateness of assignments, the need for feedback, for more support, for additional field instruction time, and so forth. Student role and process recording also were among the issues about which differences were expressed.

### Field Instructors' Responses to Students' Expression of Differences

When reporting about students' expressed differences, 40 (70%) field instructors' questionnaires emphasized a number of teaching techniques. Most frequently, they reported giving information, confronting the student, clarifying the issues and engaging in discussion. In some instances, negotiation seemed to take place; field instructors either compromised or yielded in response to student concerns. Whereas students' responses emphasized supportive aspects of the encounters, field instructors tended to give responses that reflected their roles as teachers.

## Student Perceptions of Field Instructors' Responses

The majority (26; 70%) of students with differences reported empathic responses from field instructors. Most of these involved listening to students and discussing their concerns. Some students included clarification and problem-solving. A minority of students (10; 27%) indicated that when differences were voiced, they received non-empathic responses. Some of these students said the instructor expressed confusion, frustration, or defensiveness, or even ignored the issues entirely.

## Effect on Field Instructor-Student Relationship

Although 16 field instructors' questionnaires (28%) suggested that discussion of differences had no effect on their relationships with students, 38 (67%) indicated that the relationships improved after such discussions. Field instructors' comments indicated that increased mutuality, trust, respect and collaboration resulted from the open and honest discussion of differences. Even when the field instructor perceived a negative reaction in the student, discussion ultimately induced constructive changes. Five students reported no effect on their relationship with the field instructor, but most students (26; 70%) agreed that there were improvements as a result of open discussion of differences. The students echoed the field instructors' feelings of increased mutuality, trust, and respect. They also mentioned a more relaxed atmosphere and an affirmation of field instructors' interest in student learning. In addition, the students suggested that their fear of instructor authority diminished, which fostered more collegial exchange. A small number of students (6; 16%), in their attempts to express differences, perceived instructors' reactions as impediments to the relationship. These students recalled a sense of impotence and lowered investment in the working alliance, or, in some cases, a measure of tension, struggle and confrontation. Their reactions ranged from reluctant capitulation to spurious acquiescence. It is worth noting that 5 of these 6 students were among those who reported non-empathic field instructor responses to the expression of differences.

## Effect on Student Practice

The majority of field instructors' responses (44; 77%) indicated that the open expression of differences had positive effects on their students' practice. These effects included: Increased sensitivity, greater open-mindedness, heightened self-awareness and appropriate self-disclosure. Some instructors attributed students' heightened practice proficiency to their increased willingness to accept help. Whereas a few instructors reported "no effect", no field instructor felt that the expression of differences had any detrimental effect on student practice. Although six students reported no effect on their practice, most students (20; 54%) thought the freedom to express differences had a positive effect. By differing with their instructors, they could clarify issues, reach higher levels of understanding, solve problems more easily etc. They emphasized increased motivation, heightened self-esteem and renewed confidence in their own judgement. On the other hand, 5 students (14%) indicated they felt that expression of differences had a negative effect on their practice. All 5 also had reported non-empathic responses by their field instructors. They described a variety of results: Reluctance to share ideas, diminished enthusiasm, uncertainty about their goals and fear of exposing their practice. One of the students cited paradoxical effects, stating: "I became more independent and responsible for my own work in response to the lack of field instructor support, but it left me more vulnerable to making mistakes."

### Influence of Expression of Differences on Overall Field Learning

The questionnaire inquired if the expression of differences affected student learning overall. Thirty eight students responded to the question. Most of students (23; 61%) felt an overall increase in learning. Comments from these students included: "...forced me to think clearly and for myself"; "gave me permission to confront differences"; "broadened my horizons"; enriched my training"; "growth producing". A small number (8; 21%) found no effect. Seven students felt their learning had been hampered by the expression of differences; they pointed to the effects of strain, caution or divisiveness. Some of these students reported negative effects on their practice. They attributed the following effects to the expression of differences: loss of confidence in their judgement with clients, lowered enthusiasm for their work, and resentment or inhibition in client interaction. One student took the differences "underground", talking to others instead of to the field instructor. The vast majority of field instructors believed the expression of differences increased learning. Instructors stated that expressions of differences: "are a part of life as well as student learning"; [students] "find them stimulating"; are "a natural part of supervision"; and enable "me to be a better teacher". A few instructors referred to the difficulties that differences create, but saw the gains as worth the struggle. One commented: "differences add much stress to students' learning but have brought out some fundamental issues that, if resolved, will make students more qualified social workers."

### Expression of Differences as Part of Field Instruction

The questionnaire asked if respondents expected the expression of differences to be part of field education. An overwhelming 85% (56 of 66) of students felt it was an integral factor in learning. Students commented that it was: "Necessary for learning"; "necessary to stand up for what you believe"; and "needed for growth." They also felt it was their "responsibility to be aware of differences", that "adult learners have the right to an opinion", and that "one must speak out when something is wrong." The remaining 10 students said they did not anticipate expression of differences would be part of their work with field instructors. Some stated that they never thought about it. One student thought questioning would be expected in the classroom but not in the field.

Of the 56 students who expected that differences would be encountered during the practicum, 30 said they discussed them with field instructors. The other 26 said they did not encounter differences. Differences also were expressed by seven of the students who did not expect them. Three students who did not expect differences stated that they had none. The field instructors were asked a related, though slightly different question: **When** should students be expected to voice differences? Four categories of opinion emerged in the 89 responses. The largest number of instructors (38; 43%) expected differences to occur before the eighth week of the first semester. Half as many (19) expected them between the eighth and sixteenth weeks. A sizeable number (26; 29%) saw no pattern: They could not anticipate when differences would arise, and said they would occur "whenever students felt comfortable." A few field instructors expected differences to arise during the second semester.

**Summary of Findings**

Although it is difficult to generalize from such a small sample, some general trends can be noted among those who identified differences. Differences were reported by half of the students and field instructors who responded to the questionnaire. Differences were discovered between the third and eighth weeks of the first semester and once recognized, were discussed promptly. The most frequently reported sources of difference were practice issues. Field instructors responded empathically and educationally to student concerns and students generally viewed these responses as supportive. The expression of difference was generally perceived to strengthen both student practice and the student-instructor relationship. In most of these cases, open expression of differences led to desirable outcomes, but when field instructors gave non-empathic responses to student expression of differences, those responses nearly always had negative effects on student practice and/or learning.

## DISCUSSION AND CONCLUSIONS

The literature asserts that open expression of differences is to be expected in field instruction; this pilot study confirmed that students and field instructors also held this belief. The respondents also believed that such differences are a natural part of learning. Furthermore, they expected expression of differences to take place by the **eighth** week of the first semester. It should be noted that whereas this view was widely held, only a limited number of students and field instructors cited actual disagreements, despite the fact that the questionnaire was distributed in the **twelfth week** of the semester.

Although one only can speculate, several possible explanations come to mind. Perhaps it is easier to value the concept of expression of differences than to observe and analyze one's own participation in such an exchange. Differences also may have gone unreported because they seemed so natural that they simply went unnoticed. One might consider the possibility that despite clear instructions to report both minor and major differences, some respondents only reported major or vituperative ones. One also might argue that, despite assurances of anonymity, the exposure of disagreement in an ongoing practicum might inspire fear of identification. Although students might be especially prone to such anxiety, field instructors certainly would not be immune: they may have been reluctant to place a very sensitive aspect of their teaching (potential conflict with students) under the scrutiny of a researcher. Another possibility is that since little attention has been paid to differences between field instructors and students; a request to document these differences may have seemed alien to the respondents. Perhaps the expression of differences occurred later than field instructors expected; obviously, the questionnaire could not record events that had not yet taken place. In some instances, the questionnaire may have seemed ambiguous or been misunderstood.

Despite the limitations of the study, some of the students' responses to open-ended questions may help explain why relatively few differences were expressed. Some students said they did not ask questions because they lacked sufficient knowledge to question authority. Others felt their task was to "listen and take in". Prior experience with rote education may have encouraged this point of view. Another factor might be assertiveness, which is essential to open expression of differences. If a student has a conciliatory nature and believes the field instructor (or, the authority figure) is the expert, he or she might hesitate before allowing differences to surface. Even those who tend to be assertive might be reluctant to confront an expert; they might not even recognize differences unless specifically encouraged to do so. Given the likelihood that most people do not easily assert their differences from authority figures, social work educators must do more than pay lip service to the open expression of differences. They need to find ways to enable differences to emerge. It is sobering to read the words of Cournoyer, "Regardless of method or setting, graduate social work education does not enhance assertiveness" (1983, p. 28). If the assertion of differences is not modeled within the instructional process, how can students learn that it is expected? Indeed, unless it is encouraged, graduate social work education may not be fulfilling its mission to prepare social workers for practice roles "geared to assertiveness and positive action" (Robertson, 1968, p. 57).

Students come to graduate school with well-developed attitudes about self and society. Genuine engagement with the field instructor enables the student to make use of life experience and reach a fuller understanding of client and community. An authentic field instructor-student relationship that permits each person to be himself or herself is not likely to be free of differences. Instructors need to demonstrate the belief that differences are normal, healthy and useful in the educational process; instructors should reach for them and encourage their expression. Behaviors such as allowing differences to emerge (Perlman, 1967), presenting ideas so they remain open to challenge (Shulman, 1983), and power sharing (Somers, 1971) all need reaffirmation. The desirability of the open expression of differences is supported by the results of this study. Most students who expressed differences felt it had positive effects on learning and practice; an even larger number of instructors noted improvements in their students. The data in this pilot study pave the way for further exploration. One finds a suggestion that both the expression itself and the manner in which it is managed are equally important. A number of questions deserve further consideration. They include: What elements tend to stifle the expression of differences? Is it sometimes appropriate to submerge differences between instructor and student? If so, under what circumstances?

One may wonder whether differences can always emerge naturally. It would appear that the expression of differences is something that needs to be taught. If so, the implications for social work education must be considered. Students may need more help in asserting their differences, and field instructors may need to learn to bring out differences that are not readily expressed. If we expect students to meet the needs of their own learning and begin to speak out in support of the values of the profession, it is crucial that attention be given to the best means for achieving those goals.

## BIBLIOGRAPHY

Cournoyer, B. R. (1983) Assertiveness among MSW students. JOURNAL OF EDUCATION FOR SOCIAL WORK, 19, 24-30.

Gitterman, A. and Gitterman, N. P. (1979) Social work student evaluation: Format and methods. JOURNAL OF EDUCATION FOR SOCIAL WORK, 15, 103-108.

Judah, E. H. (1972) Responsibilities of students in field instruction. In B. W. Sheafor and L. E. Jenkins (Eds.), QUALITY INSTRUCTION IN SOCIAL WORK, (pp. 144-160). New York: Longman.

Nelson, J. C. (1974) Relationship communication in early field work conferences. SOCIAL CASEWORK, 55, 237-243.

Perlman, H. H. (1967) And gladly teach. JOURNAL OF EDUCATION FOR SOCIAL WORK, 12, 41-50.

Raphael, F. B. and Rosenblum, A. F. (1987) An operational guide to the faculty field liaison role. SOCIAL CASEWORK, 68, 156-163.

Robertson, M. E. (1968) The role of students. JOURNAL OF EDUCATION FOR SOCIAL WORK, 13, 55-64.

Robinson, V. (1949) THE DYNAMICS OF SUPERVISION UNDER FUNCTIONAL CONTROLS. Philadelphia: University of Pennsylvania Press.

Rosenblatt, A. and Mayer, J. E. (1975) Objectionable supervisory styles: Students' views. SOCIAL WORK, 20, 184-188.

Rosenblum, A. F. and Raphael, F. B. (1987) Students at risk in the field practicum and implications for field teaching. THE CLINICAL SUPERVISOR, 5, 53-63.

Selby, L. G. (1955) Helping students in field practice identify and modify blocks to learning. SOCIAL SERVICES REVIEW, 29, 53-63.

Shulman, L. (1983) TEACHING HELPING SKILLS: A FIELD INSTRUCTOR'S GUIDE. Itasca, IL: F. E. Peacock.

Somers, M. L. (1971) Dimensions and dynamics of engaging the learner. JOURNAL OF EDUCATION FOR SOCIAL WORK, 16, 49-57.

Studt, E. (1954) An outline of social authority factors in casework. SOCIAL CASEWORK, 35, 231-238.

Tropp, E. (1969) AUTHENTICITY IN TEACHER-STUDENT COMMUNICATION. Paper presented at CSWE APM, Cleveland, OH.

Wilson, S. J. (1981) FIELD INSTRUCTION: TECHNIQUES FOR SUPERVISORS. New York: Free Press.

# THE GATEKEEPER ROLE IN SOCIAL WORK: A SURVEY

Carl Hartman, *Wayne State University*
Robert M. Wills, *Lafayette Clinic*

Rating a student's performance as unsatisfactory is one of the field instructor's most unpleasant and challenging tasks. He or she struggles with questions such as: "By what standards is this student's performance unsatisfactory?" "How would other field instructors rate the same work?" Maybe it's my failing to reach this student and not the student's failing that is at issue!" "What right do I have to block this student's professional aspirations?" "Maybe the problems I see are situational and will change with time and experience." "What external criteria do I have to justify my rating?" Field instructors and faculty advisors are confronted with such issues each time an unsatisfactory performance evaluation is considered.

Indeed, one of the acknowledged functions of field education is to identify potentially harmful behavior in apprentice practice and to screen out students if this behavior cannot change. Although screening out unsuitable candidates for the profession is clearly a key function of field education, this function is unsupported by clear criteria for evaluation.

Students who are unfit for social work by aptitude, maturity, or emotional stability are more likely to move through their academic training and enter the profession if these issues are not addressed--not only in social work but other helping professions as well. Woolliscroft, Stross, and Siva (1986) report that few candidates in internal medicine are judged as not being clinically competent by program directors. Langsley (1986) points out that although 13 percent of psychiatric residents will fail board exams on the first try, when training directors were asked to predict how many of their residents would fail, the prediction for the total group was only one percent.

Whether related to a presumed narcissistic injury, the need to see only the good in trainees, or anxieties related to honest evaluatory feedback, it is clear that in social work as well as other professions, field instructors entrusted with gatekeeping responsibilities need support in the form of standardized methods of evaluation. Field instructors must be helped to differentiate student responses to clients which are potentially harmful from work that reflects situational stress or work reflecting lack of training and experience. Permitting the impaired student to complete training and enter the profession where he or she will work with emotionally vulnerable, high risk clients, is professionally irresponsible and unethical.

Research consistently points to rigid personality and emotional disturbance in the practitioner as one of the major contributors to ineffective and deleterious practice.[1] However, field instructors have little empirical data to refer to when attempting to differentiate harmful student work from that which is substandard but not injurious. In order to fill this void, this study asked field instructors from a large midwest school of social work about gatekeeping attitudes and how they would rate problematic interpersonal anecdotes given three possible choices: the vignette most likely represents (1) a student responding to a situational stressor, (2) poor student work but probably responsive to intensive supervision, and (3) harmful student work which might be cause for removal from training if it becomes a pattern of interaction or does not change significantly. Thus, this study represents an initial effort to develop a consensus on what constitutes unacceptable behavior.

## OBJECTIVES OF THE STUDY

Several factors related to the field instructor's gatekeeping role were examined. The authors wanted to determine field instructors' experiences with and attitudes toward gatekeeping, whether or not their gatekeeping behaviors were congruent with their gatekeeping attitudes, and how field instructors would categorize examples of student performance. Specific objectives of the study were:

1. To determine the extent to which field instructors encounter resistance to removing a student from social work training.

2. To discover the range of field instructor gatekeeping attitudes and the extent to which this dimension predicts how they will view problematic student behavior.

3. To develop vignettes of problematic student performance and have field instructors rate them as examples of work influenced by situational stressors, poor work, or harmful work.

## PROCEDURES

A questionnaire, divided into three parts, asked for (1) demographic information and external factors affecting a field instructor's ability to fail the unsuitable student, (2) agreement or disagreement with fourteen attitudinal statements related to failing the unsuitable student, and (3) rating 20 problematic interpersonal activities as situational stress, poor work, or harmful work. Student responses to clients resulting from situational stress were considered as likely to improve without supervisory intervention or by modification of the learning environment. Poor work was regarded as requiring intensive supervision. Harmful work was viewed as resulting from deeply entrenched personality factors, possibly

---

[1] See L.E. Beutler, M. Crago, and T.G. Arizmendi, "Therapist Variables in Psychotherapy Process and Outcome," in S.L. Garfield and A.E. Bergin, eds., HANDBOOK OF PSYCHOTHERAPY AND BEHAVIOR CHANGE (New York: John Wiley & Sons, 1986), pp. 257-310; D.T. Mays and C.M. Frank, "Negative Outcome: What to Do About It," in D.T. Mays and C.M. Frank, NEGATIVE OUTCOME IN PSYCHOTHERAPY AND WHAT TO DO ABOUT IT (New York: Springer, 1985), pp. 281-311; S.W. Hadley and H.H. Strupp, "Contemporary Views of Negative Effects in Psychotherapy," ARCHIVES OF GENERAL PSYCHIATRY, 33 (1976), pp. 1291-1302; H.H. Strupp, S.W. Hadley, and B. Gomes-Schwartz, PSYCHOTHERAPY FOR BETTER OR WORSE (New York: Aronson, 1977).

indicating the student was unfit for professional practice. The 20 problematic interpersonal activities were selected from an initial list of 35 vignettes that were presented to 10 highly experienced social workers.

Questionnaires were mailed in April 1986 to all current field instructors in interpersonal practice settings associated with Wayne State University, School of Social Work, Detroit, Michigan. Descriptive statistics were calculated for the returned data.

## RESULTS

Ninety-four (78%) questionnaires were returned out of 120 mailed; one was unusable due to insufficient information. The high rate of return, together with the numerous unsolicited comments asking for results when available, impressed the authors with the depth of concern and the interest field instructors have in this topic.

Seventy-two percent of the field instructors were female and 87 percent were White. Thirteen percent of the respondents were Black females; there were no Asian, Hispanic, or Black male field instructors responding to the survey. Forty-five percent of the field instructors worked in mental health settings, 34 percent in family and child agencies, 13 percent in health care, and "others" comprised 11 percent. The respondents had been field instructors for an average of 6.5 years (range 25 to 1 years) and had been social workers an average of 12.8 years (range 35 to 2). The field instructors had supervised an estimated 1079 students collectively (range 1 to 140), for an average of 11.6 students per field instructor. Eighteen field instructors were involved with 22 students who failed the field practicum for performance problems.

### External Factors

Field instructors identified five external issues as preventing them from failing students felt to be unsuitable for the profession. Disagreements between the field instructor and the faculty advisor whether or not to fail the student were most frequently cited. Twenty-two percent of the respondents indicated that on at least one occasion the school decided to move the failing student to another practice setting in order to see if performance would improve. Thirteen percent said that on at least one occasion the faculty advisor refused to assign a failing grade when they had recommended one. Four percent of the field instructors noted that a student who would have been failed for field work performance was terminated for academic reasons. Apparently the influence of appeal processes and interference from agency administrators was rare. In only one instance did a respondent say that a student was given a failing grade but appealed and won. Likewise, only one field instructor reported interference from the agency preventing the assignment of a failing grade for poor performance.

**Table 1: Frequency with which Field Instructors Are Likely to Work with a Failing Student**

| Number of students instructed, lifetime | Percent of field instructors who thought they worked with a failing student |
|---|---|
| 5 or less | 9% |
| 6 - 10 | 20% |
| 11 - 20 | 63% |
| more than 20 | 94% |

From the above analysis, it is clear that a statistic based solely on how many students failed field practice misrepresents the actual experience of field instructors who deal with failing students. A truer index would combine three factors--students who were failed, students who were passed by faculty advisor against the recommendation of the field instructor, and failing students who were given a "second chance" in another practice setting. In the present sample, 35 field instructors (38%) reported this experience. Using the combined index, the likelihood of a field instructor encountering a failing student increased dramatically with the number of students supervised over a lifetime (see Table 1).

Isolating from this table the subgroup of field instructors who supervised five students or less, it is possible to obtain an estimate of the frequency with which field instructors identity students who are failing field practicums. Eight field instructors among this subgroup reported supervising a failing student. The total number of students supervised by this subgroup was 113. Assuming one failing student per field instructor in this subgroup, 7 percent of students who enter social work school will exhibit performance difficulties so severe that the field instructor will consider removal from training.[2]

## Field Instructors' Attitudes

Wilson (1981) suggests several factors that influence the field instructor's willingness to be a gatekeeper--self doubt, lack of commitment to standards, unwillingness to deal with the student's angry response. These and other factors were used to create a 14 item list that field instructors were asked to rate on a scale of 1 to 5 where 1 indicated "strong disagreement", 3 indicated "undecided", and 5 indicated "strong agreement." It was thought that high scores would indicate strong gatekeeping attitudes and low scores would indicate weak gatekeeping attitudes; thus, an index of "gatekeeper attitudes" would be created. The items and the mean score for each are listed in Table 2.

---

[2] We suspect the actual field work failure rate is far lower at most schools of social work. Records from Wayne State University, School of Social Work show that of approximately 1,500 field work grades given over a five year period, there were only 14 failures, a failure rate of less than one percent.

**Table 2:  Field Instructors' Attitudes to Factors which Inhibit Gatekeeping**
1 = Strongly disagree   3 = Undecided   5 = Strongly Agree

| Factors: | Mean |
|---|---|
| I would be willing to impose high standards on students whether or not other's do. | 4.3 |
| The lack of measurable practice standards in social work does not deter me from failing a student due to poor performance. | 4.2 |
| I am willing to confront a student's poor work at the risk of alienating the student. | 4.2 |
| I am willing to risk examination of my professional judgments in order to assert my right to fail an inadequate student. | 4.0 |
| I am willing to devote the time required to document failing performance. | 4.0 |
| I take seriously my power to block a student's professional aspirations. | 3.8 |
| One cannot be nonjudgmental with students even when teaching them to be nonjudgmental with clients. | 3.8 |
| I do not avoid the emotionality of failing a student. | 3.7 |
| As a field instructor I have a stronger obligation to the profession than to the student. | 3.7 |
| I can envision myself in this hypothetical situation: I feel the student does not deserve a passing grade. The faculty liaison believes the student has potential and will do better next year.  I insist that a third party evaluate the student's work. | 3.6 |
| I would pursue failing a student even if my agency director did not support it. | 3.6 |
| If a student's field work performance is very weak, I am inclined to consider "lack of aptitude for social work" more strongly than "lack of experience." | 3.5 |
| I would pursue all avenues to prevent a student who is performing inadequately in the field to enter the profession. | 3.3 |
| I would consider it unimportant if students avoid placement with me due to my reputation as a tough field instructor. | 3.2 |

It is clear from Table 2 that on the average, field instructors tend to espouse relatively strong gatekeeper attitudes.  Concerns over the vagueness or subjectiveness of practice standards and how other field instructors might hold lower expectation did not seem to be major issues deterring the respondents from dealing with unsatisfactory student performance.  Field instructors also seemed willing to have their professional judgments confronted by the students themselves, faculty advisors, and "due process" proceedings. Field instructors were somewhat more sensitive to bring labeled "tough," and were reluctant to be seen as "pursuing" the removal of an unsatisfactory student from professional training.

## TABLE 3: Field Instructors' Perceptions of Student Behavior

| SITUATIONAL STRESSORS | Sit. | Poor | Harm. | N |
|---|---|---|---|---|
| 1. Student is placed in a complex, multidisciplinary setting and feels overwhelmed. | .97 | .03 | .00 | 92 |
| 2. Student, assigned to an analytically oriented field instructor, feels unsupported and unable to learn in this setting. | .90 | .10 | .00 | 90 |
| 3. A young female student is upset by one foreign medical resident who discounts her contributions and cuts her off during staff discussion. | .82 | .17 | .01 | 92 |
| 4. Student was treated for cancer 5 years ago with no recurrence. Assigned to a client fatally ill with cancer, the student becomes upset and finds it difficult to manage the workload successfully. | .78 | .20 | .01 | 93 |
| **POOR WORK** | | | | |
| 5. Student interprets client behavior before the client is ready to understand its meaning. | .08 | .91 | .01 | 93 |
| 6. Student has a tendency to manage the client through advice. | .08 | .90 | .02 | 91 |
| 7. Student has difficulty making client contacts purposeful; student engages clients in social chat and other idle curiosity. | .04 | .89 | .07 | 92 |
| 8. Student focuses only on self-exploration to the exclusion of behavior change so as to distort or ignore reality factors. | .04 | .85 | .11 | 91 |
| 9. Student is unable to confront or give feedback to which the client will disagree. | .11 | .85 | .04 | 91 |
| 10. Student is scarcely aware of the client's past history as having bearing on the present. | .06 | .75 | .18 | 93 |

| | | | | |
|---|---|---|---|---|
| 11. Student tries to make clients like him/her at all times. | .12 | .69 | .19 | 91 |
| 12. Student gives reassurance whenever the client is hurting, no matter what the situation. | .28 | .67 | .04 | 92 |

### HARMFUL WORK

| | | | | |
|---|---|---|---|---|
| 13. Male student convinces a female client who feels she is unable to please men to have sex with him as part of the treatment. | .00 | .00 | 1.00 | 93 |
| 14. Student is very cold and distant, lacks empathy for client feelings, and remains uninvolved no matter what the level of emotional intensity. | .00 | .09 | .91 | 91 |
| 15. Student is unable to modulate his/her own anger. Hostile, provocative clients bring out marked aggressiveness in the student. | .03 | .21 | .76 | 91 |
| 16. After explicit warnings, a student's continual refusal to check his/her mail box for messages results in a severe crisis for the client. | .00 | .25 | .75 | 92 |
| 17. Student is very controlling and coerces people to change in preconceived directions. | .01 | .26 | .73 | 90 |
| 18. Student conveys virtually no sense of "hope" in the treatment process because his/her outlook is generally pessimistic. | .06 | .24 | .70 | 90 |
| 19. Student who has a bad record of absenteeism and tardiness is observed at a shopping mall when he/she is scheduled for a home visit. | .01 | .31 | .68 | 90 |
| 20. Student is insensitive to the degree of distress experienced by the client so that the ego disorganization of fragile, disturbed clients is ignored. | .01 | .49 | .49 | 91 |

## Assessing Problem Behaviors

Table 3 lists 20 problematic student activities and indicates the rate at which field instructors assigned each behavior to one of three categories: situational stressor, poor work, and harmful work. These items were presented randomly and without indication of prior categorization in the questionnaire. Here they are arranged in the group to which the expert raters assigned them during the questionnaire pretest. Responses were in high agreement with prior categorization by the expert raters, except for item #20. This item--"the student is insensitive to the degree of distress present in a fragile, highly disturbed client"--was divided equally into "poor work" and "harmful work" categories while the expert raters felt this was clearly harmful work. Only two items (#11 and #12) in the "poor work" category were identified by less than 70% of the field instructors.

Three of the items (#13, #16, #19) in the "harmful work" category involved concrete, open, and blatantly objectionable behavior that was thought to be obviously harmful. However, only sexual conduct with a client was identified as harmful by every field instructor. Repeated absenteeism, tardiness, and doing personal business on field work time was regarded as evidence of poor work by 31% of the field instructors, and 25% did not see harmfulness in repeated failure to check one's mail box for client messages. It may be that for some field instructors, the distinction between poor and harmful work is not critical in the sense that activity in either category is taken seriously and could result in a failing grade if not corrected.

Field instructors showed a remarkable ability to distinguish poor or harmful work (items #5 through #20) from situational stress. Sixty-one percent of the respondents did not see any of the "poor work" items as situational, and it was rare that anyone misidentified "harmful work" as situational. On the other hand, 12% of the field instructors (i.e., the 11 who misidentified 3 or more poor/harmful items, see Table 4) accounted for 85% of the poor/harmful items misidentified as situational. It appears that a small group of field instructors categorically treated problematic student behavior lightly. Under these field instructors, students who are unable to confront clients, or ingratiate, or lack awareness of important developmental problems, or manage clients through advice, or use interpretation without empathy are allowed to complete training under the assumption that this behavior will abate or modify without special attention.

---

**TABLE 4: Field Instructors' Tendency to Regard Poor and Harmful Work as Situational**

| NUMBER OF FIELD INSTRUCTORS | ITEMS MISIDENTIFIED AS SITUATIONAL | | |
|---|---|---|---|
| | POOR | HARMFUL | TOTAL |
| 57 | 0 | 0 | 0 |
| 15 | 1 | 0 | 1 |
| 2 | 0 | 1 | 1 |
| 3 | 1 | 1 | 2 |
| 5 | 2 | 0 | 2 |
| 1 | 2 | 1 | 3 |
| 2 | 3 | 0 | 3 |
| 1 | 4 | 0 | 4 |
| 1 | 3 | 2 | 5 |
| 3 | 5 | 0 | 5 |
| 2 | 6 | 0 | 6 |
| 1 | 7 | 1 | 8 |

Note: There were a total of 8 items each in the "poor work" and "harmful work" categories.

---

## CONCLUSIONS

Lidz (1981) draws attention to the fact that some personality types are "better suited for some occupations than others, and some are unsuited for certain occupations" (p. 379). Frank (1963) suggests "the choice of a career in psychotherapy may represent a way of solving the therapist's personal problems" (p. 184). Wilson (1981) states the issue succinctly: "Not all students who enter schools of social work should be social workers. Not all have the skills, aptitudes, interest, motivation, maturity, and emotional stability necessary to be a professional helping person" (p. 195). Sometimes personality development influences a person in such a way that the person can relate well in some situations but not others. Blumenstein (1986) makes a strong case for viewing the parentified child who enters the helping professions as possessing the capacity to care for others but lacking the capacity to withstand the multilevel conflicts of conjoint family therapy.

In social work, the task of identifying the student who is unsuitable for entering the profession due to inept or harmful interpersonal behavior, and the task of differentiating situational, poor, and harmful work, falls conjointly to the field instructor and the faculty advisor. But the gatekeeping task is not an easy or comfortable one; it raises a number of self doubts and personal-professional issues that are too frequently ignored in the field. Field instructors and faculty advisors who dare to exercise the gatekeeper role are subject to hostile reactions from students, challenges to their professional judgment, and inner doubts about where they stand in relation to other field instructors and faculty concerning gatekeeping attitudes and behavior.

In an effort to explore field instructor gatekeeping attitudes and to provide an empirically derived field instructor consensus regarding what constitutes terminable student performance, the authors surveyed a large sample of field instructors from a midwest school of social work. Although most field instructors were found to have fairly strong gatekeeping attitudes, gatekeeping activities may be inhibited by lack of support from faculty advisors and by the tendency of the school to transfer failing students to another setting. Field instructors provided a clear consensus on 19 of 20 vignettes of student/client interactions; items which may be used by field instructors for support regarding their own judgments and by field instruction trainers to orient new field instructors to three conceptual categories of student responses to clients.

Although the authors surmised that field instructor gatekeeping attitudes would differ widely, and that such attitudes would predict how student/client interactions were categorized by field instructors, findings did not support either hypothesis. Instead, the authors found a small group of field instructors who consistently misidentified poor and harmful student responses as situational. These field instructors may be less likely than others to recognize the student who by temperament, aptitude, or personality is unfit for social work. Such field instructors demonstrate their own pattern of denial and rationalization which prevents them from confronting problematic behavior and engaging the student in intensive supervision. Interpersonal difficulties with clients which present themselves subtly are ignored or glossed over, only the most blatantly harmful activities warrant intervention or termination from training. Field instructors in this group are weak gatekeepers because they fail to make critical judgments.

Likewise, it is surmised that a small percentage of faculty advisors may similarly misidentify poor and harmful student behavior as situational. Such weak gatekeeping faculty will consistently inhibit gatekeeping activities by field instructors, unconsciously sending messages during field visits which indicate an unwillingness to take problematic student responses to clients seriously and refusing to support the field instructor if a failing grade is proposed.

The major findings of this study are: (1) agreement exists on what constitutes inadequate field work performance, (2) problem behaviors can be reliably categorized as situational, poor, or harmful, (3) lack of clarity and direction from schools of social work inhibit field instructors from adequately fulfilling their gatekeeping role, (4) most field instructors espouse strong gatekeeping attitudes, (5) a small group of field instructors can be identified who see situational responses in student behavior that the majority of field instructors regard as poor or harmful work, and (6) the gatekeeping attitudes of this group of "weak" gatekeepers does not significantly differ from the majority. The vignettes in Table 3 may also prove useful in sensitizing new field instructors to the types of problems exhibited by students and the appropriate direction for intervention.

## BIBLIOGRAPHY

Beutler,L.E., M. Crago, and T.G. Arizmendi (1986) "Therapist Variables in Psychotherapy Process and Outcome," in S.L. Garfield and A.E. Bergin, eds., HANDBOOK OF PSYCHOTHERAPY AND BEHAVIOR CHANGE. New York: John Wiley and Sons, pp. 257-310.

Blumenstein, H. (1986) "Maintaining A Family Focus: Underlying Issues and Challenges," CLINICAL SOCIAL WORK JOURNAL, 14, pp. 238-249.

Frank, J.D. (1963) PERSUASION AND HEALING. New York: Schocken Books, p. 184.

Hadley, S.W. and H.H. Strupp (1976) "Contemporary Views of Negative Effects in Psychotherapy," ARCHIVES OF GENERAL PSYCHIATRY, 33, pp. 1291-1302.

Langsley, D.G. (1986) "Rating Clinical Skills of Psychiatric Residents," in J.S. Lloyd and D.G. Langsley, eds., HOW TO EVALUATE RESIDENTS. Chicago: American Board of Medical Specialties, 267-273.

Lidz, T. (1968) THE PERSON; HIS DEVELOPMENT THROUGHOUT THE LIFE CYCLE. New York: Basic Books, p. 379.

Mays, D.T. and C.M. Frank (1985) "Negative Outcome: What to Do About It," in D.T. Mays and C.M. Frank, NEGATIVE OUTCOME IN PSYCHOTHERAPY AND WHAT TO DO ABOUT IT. New York: Springer, pp. 281-311.

Strupp, H.H., S.W. Hadley, and B. Gomes-Schwartz (1977) PSYCHOTHERAPY FOR BETTER OR WORSE. New York: Aronson.

Wilson, S.J. (1981) FIELD INSTRUCTION: TECHNIQUES FOR SUPERVISION. New York: The Free Press, p. 195-198.

Woolliscroft, J.O., J.K. Stross, and J. Silva, Jr. (1986) "Clinical Competence Certification: A Critical Appraisal," in J.S. Lloyd and D.G. Langsley, eds., HOW TO EVALUATE RESIDENTS. Chicago: American Board of Medical Specialties, pp. 371-379.

# DIRECTORS OF FIELD EDUCATION: CRITICAL ROLE DILEMMAS

Lillian Hawthorne, *University of Southern California Emerita*
Reva Fine Holtzman, *Hunter College School of Social Work*

## INTRODUCTION

The need for more information, understanding and study of the role of director of field education has become increasingly evident. The practicum director occupies a pivotal position both in the social work education program an with the collaborating professional community. He/she carries educational and administrative responsibility for that important part of the student's learning experience which accounts for approximately 50% of the scheduled time. He/she also carries responsibility for the interface between the school and social work agencies; this involves visibility, communication, interpretation and linkage.

Despite this, there has been a relative paucity of study about this role and its issues. Perhaps this is not so surprising since field directors, as a rule, have not been expected, encouraged or assisted to engage much in research about their positions. Furthermore, academic faculty are probably unlikely to pursue field education issues as subjects for research in their own "publish or perish" quests.

The role of practicum director involves many diverse functions spanning administrative/coordinating responsibilities (e.g., placement recruitment, assignment, monitoring) as well as key educational ones (e.g., field curriculum development. Therefore a basic issue is whether this is perceived as an educational or administrative position. This has been further exacerbated by current pressures impacting on the position: 1) on the one hand, educationally to deal with changing client and student needs; and 2) on the other hand, administratively to satisfy accountability demands.

It is our hypothesis that field directors embark on this role with an identification as educators but that, over time, find that the position becomes increasingly administrative.[1] If this assumption is correct, then there are significant implications in four different areas. First is the effect on status (e.g., rank, tenure, advancement opportunities, rewards) for an administrative position within an educational institution. The question of status, in turn, effects the relationship between practicum directors and academic faculty and, therefore, opportunities for support, communication and collaboration. Second is the effect on job satisfaction and dissatisfaction due to the unanticipated changes in tasks, responsibilities and relationships. Obviously, if the experience of the role over time is that it has become different from what was initially sought or intended--especially if that difference is perceived to be one of devaluation--then professional self image and satisfaction will

---

[1] and can be a dilemma, as recently many field directors have changed title from Director of Field Placement to Director of Field Education.

be effected. Third is need for support systems geared to the realities and practicalities of the position, including appropriate advance preparation plus continuing resources for role management. Fourth is potential for turnover and burn-out as a result of the combination of preceding circumstances. Indeed, the data demonstrate that this has been, and continues to be, the case.

In summary, this central and crucial position contains critical dilemmas inherent in the role itself and in its perception by others. These dilemmas, in turn, have led to considerable inconsistencies about the expectations, functions, status, structure and even future of this role in schools of social work--inconsistencies which have significant implications for successful operation. Different schools have endeavored to resolve these issues in different ways, depending upon particular resources, philosophies, needs and goals. It is not expected that any single best or preferred arrangement can be discovered or would even be desired. However, the more information available about currently operating models, successful or unsuccessful, the more can creative ideas be developed to deal with these important concerns.

## REVIEW OF LITERATURE

Although literature specifically about the role of field director is still quite limited, despite its importance as a crucial component in the success of a school's practicum program, there has been increasing recent interest through a number of studies and articles. In addition, pertinent reflections about the practicum director can be extrapolated from some of the earlier or general literature about field education.

Some of the major writings about field education in the 1980's and 1970's were authored by Helen Cassidy, Ruth Werner and Margaret Schutz Gordon. These writers emphasized that the activities of the practicum director relate to the way a school defines its own field program, e.g., viewing it as a central and integral part of the curriculum with its own special learning mode or merely as an appendage requiring limited status and support. The recent 1982 work by Jenkins and Sheafor reaffirmed the significance of this range of definitions and perceptions for the role, position and tasks of the field director.

All of these authors identified such major activities of the practicum director as: decision making about use of agencies; placement planning; providing educational opportunities for field instructors; field curriculum development; liaison with agencies; developing policies and manuals; maintaining records; planning, implementing and coordinating field sequence objectives; trouble-shooting with difficult students and agencies; and keeping the dean informed. Some of these responsibilities were to be shared or delegated; some were to be solely the task of the field director. Some were clearly educational in nature; some were administrative; some were an interaction and combination of both.

In a 1984 article about the unique situation of the BSW practicum program, Earle Jones commented that, despite variations in descriptive terminology, the literature reflects a fairly persistent view of the director's role as containing administrative, coordinative and supportive functions; the precise nature and degree depending upon how the school defines and structures its program.

This overriding quandary about the priority allocation and intermeshing of the administrative and educational functions of the field director has been examined in several recent empirical studies. The 1984 Skolnik CSWE field education survey presented statistical and informational data about field directors in 1964 reporting programs--data which reflected an almost bewildering array regarding rank, title, tenure, background, duration. The 1984 Holtzman pilot study of New York field directors obtained data about the gender distribution in the position and possible implications of the preponderance of female directors for status and advancement. The 1985 Brownstein survey of field instructors documented a parallel educator-administrator dilemma which affected the title as well as perception and functions of the position. The 1986 Hawthorne report described a professional model of field administration which, in effect, attempted to resolve the dichotomy by creating a separate and distinct category, title and line.

What is so striking in the review of this literature is that the issues about the role of field director are as real and prevalent today as they were earlier, and as unresolved.

## PURPOSE AND DESIGN OF STUDY

Therefore this research study was undertaken to ascertain basic current data about the role of practicum directors, specifically in the following four major areas: 1) allocation of time and tasks; 2) kinds and degrees of satisfactions and dissatis-factions; 3) available and desired support systems; 4) patterns and predictions for the future of the position. Some of the specific items and questions were modeled in part on previous studies by Alfred Kadushin and Carlton Munson on supervisor functions and satisfactions.

The research questionnaire also sought demographic data about the field directors, including the following: 1) specific title; 2) number of years in position; 3) appointment and tenure status; 4) data and level of final degree; 5) size, level and auspices of social work program; 6) number of faculty engaged in field education tasks.

It was decided by the co-authors to begin with a limited survey of schools in two specific areas of the west and east coasts. Such a pilot research study would test out the feasibility of a more inclusive study and would also provide opportunity for refinement and revision of the research design. The choice of these two particular west and east coast areas also offered other advantages: 1) each area contained a large number of social work programs; 2) each of the co-authors had some familiarity with, and direct access to, the schools in these areas; and 3) it provided opportunity for comparison of possible geographic influences.

The pilot study questionnaire was sent to the field directors of 8 west coast and 9 east coast schools of social work. Responses were received from 15; of these, one chose, without indicating any particular reason, to answer only a limited number of questions. The two non-responses may possibly be attributed to the fact of new appointments to the position.

## SUMMARY AND COMPARISON OF DATA

All but one of the responding schools are CSWE accredited; that one still in candidacy status. Five of the schools represent private universities; 10 are public institutions. One school has an undergraduate program only; 5 have combined programs; the remainder are exclusively graduate programs.

The size of enrollment varied from a low of 140 to a high of 540 students; the average number in the west coast schools was 212; in the east coast schools was 369.

For purposes of space and brevity, the specific data from each group of respondents, and the accompanying tables, have been eliminated from this version of the paper.[2] Instead, the overall responses of the two groups will be reviewed, analyzed and compared.

## DEMOGRAPHIC INFORMATION

Two significant differences appear in the schools in the selected areas: size and auspices. The east coast schools of social work are considerably larger, in terms of student enrollment, and are more evenly divided between public and private universities. However, there seems to be no particular correlation between these differences and the survey findings.

There is considerable similarity in the title of the position held by both sets of respondents. The majority bear titles containing the terms "field education or field instruction". There is some significance to what the position is called, since the current titles represent a shift from the historical label of "field work" to the current emphasis on field education.

There is notable difference in the appointment line and duration in position of the two groups. In the west coast schools, only one practicum director carries a faculty appointment with tenure; whereas, on the east coast there are five, though only two are actually tenured. East coast respondents have also been in the position longer, by a factor of almost 2 to 1. These two differences may possibly be attributable to the fact that, overall, the east coast social work schools have longer established histories and traditions. Nevertheless in both groups, the number of years in position still indicates a considerable degree of mobility and turnover. Surprisingly, considering the above-mentioned differences, east coast field directors represent fewer earned social work doctorates than their west coast counterparts. However, there is inconsistency in both groups, probably reflecting differences in schools' perceptions of the role as administrative or educational.

Both groups, with one major exception on the west coast, describe traditional field administration models in which faculty members share certain placement, advisement or liaison responsibilities. However, specific information was not sought, or offered, about the effectiveness of these arrangements.

---

[2]This information may be available upon request.

## TASKS AND TIME

West coast directors report only one category which actually expends more than 40% of their time, i.e., practicum administration. Most of the respondents indicate spending 20-40% of their time on education and on coordination/consultation tasks. The least amount of time is allocated to research/publication and to general administration. None of these respondents single out any particular category preferred for a preponderance of time allocation. Instead, they indicate a preference for a more even distribution among education, coordination/consultation, community relationships and practicum administration. This indicates that east coast directors view their role as rather evenly balanced between educational and administrative tasks, and also that they find that their actual time allocation is not seriously incongruent with their preferred time allocation.

Among east coast directors the only category allocated more than 40% of actual time is either practicum or general administration. Most of these respondents report spending 15-40% of their time on coordination/consultation. Surprisingly, education is allocated one of the lowest percentages of actual time. The east coast respondents indicate preferences for spending more time on education and on research/publication and less on coordination/ consultation. Both the actual and preferred responses in this group reflect considerable and somewhat unexpected variation. This, plus the inconsistency in the number of responses, makes interpretation and comparison difficult. However, it seems clear in both groups that administrative tasks are more acceptable to the degree that they contribute directly to field education and carry some status.

## SATISFACTIONS AND DISSATISFACTIONS

West coast directors unanimously report that their greatest source of satisfaction is contributing to the professional education of students. Two other major satisfactions are: "ensuring quality and effective field education experiences" and "stimulation provided by professional colleagues". Items providing the least satisfaction are: freedom from direct teaching responsibilities and the physical aspects of the position. No specific item on the list is identified as causing great dissatisfaction, but several are selected in the "somewhat" category. These are: paperwork details; responsibilities interfering with educational time; loss or reduction of direct student and field instructor contact; high stress level; limited status, reward and career opportunities; insufficient collegial, administrative or financial support. These responses clearly indicate that the greatest degree of satisfaction stems from opportunities for providing and receiving educational growth and enrichment. Conversely, most of the dissatisfactions stem from obstacles or omissions interfering with educational functions.

East coast directors similarly report that contributing to student professional education is their greatest satisfaction. The only other item selected as strongly satisfying is ensuring quality and effective field education experience. Both of these, of course, are clearly and closely related. Being freed from direct teaching provides the least amount of satisfaction; most of the other items are scattered throughout the "somewhat" category. The greatest dissatisfactions derive from the lack of adequate resources and of administrative and financial support. Paperwork tasks, time interferences and insufficient collegial support also rank high on the category of "somewhat" dissatisfying.

There is striking similarity between the responses of the two groups to this question. In both groups, educational activities provide the most satisfaction, and lack of support and resources the most dissatisfaction. This correlation between degree of satisfaction and proximity to the primary educational process corroborates the implications of the data in the preceding question on actual and preferred time and task allocations. The similarities in responses also indicate a common basic perception of the role and a common definition of its positives and its problems.

## SUPPORT SYSTEMS

West coast directors report that the most available resource has been adequate preparation for the position and the least available, ongoing professional training. Basically they indicate a desire and need for all sources of support, either to a great or moderate degree, with equal emphasis on continuing training, support and cooperation. In other words, their expressed desire for a variety of support systems is general rather than acute or specific.

East coast directors indicate that all of the designated supports have been available to them, though mainly to a moderate rather than extensive degree. Their desired sources of support are quite similar to the actualities, except in one area, e.g., the need for more understanding and cooperation.

Although both groups express similar preferences for support systems, east coast respondents appear somewhat more satisfied with what is actually and currently available to them. This may largely be due to their area field consortium which offers a support network geared to role management strategies. This operating consortium may, in turn, be due to the aforementioned longer history and duration in position. In contrast, such an arrangement exists in a much more partial and rudimentary form on the west coast.

## PATTERNS AND PREDICTIONS

There are a number of striking and illuminating similarities in the comments of the two groups in the final section of the questionnaire. In describing changes in their respective schools, both especially note the following: 1) proliferation of different and part-time programs and schedules; 2) increased financial pressures on students and programs; 3) struggles to maintain standards while dealing with less experienced students and more needy clients. In their respective professional communities, they report: 1) increasing difficulties in maintaining quality field placements and field instructors in the light of declining commitment and resources; and 2) concern about diminished commitment to serving the needy and disadvantaged. There are also a few specific comments that appear to be unique to a particular area or a particular school, e.g., the issue of MFCC's on the west coast and the pressure for student interviews on the east coast. Overall, these changes are perceived as having negative impact on the role of field director, e.g., rendering the tasks more difficult, more complicated and more stressful.

In their final personal reflections, the two groups of respondents express similar ambivalence about the role, viewing their experiences as both challenging and frustrating. The following two quotations will illustrate. One west coast director describes "--- a key but lonely role--no one has greater impact and no one is more isolated ---." An east coast respondent describes field directors as "--- a special lot ---" and "--- a unique blend of educator-administrator ---" struggling to keep "---in synchrony the needs of faculty, students, and community field agencies ---."

## CONCLUSIONS AND RECOMMENDATIONS

Despite the limited scope of this pilot study, the data obtained are both informative and provocative. Overall, the responses highlight three special characteristics of the role of field director that merit serious attention: duality, centrality, and sensitivity.

The data confirm the broad variety of task, functions and responsibilities carried by field directors and the mix of education and administration involved in this spectrum of duties. This unique education-administrative blend underscores the dual nature of the role and its inherent dilemma which, in turn, affects job image, job satisfaction and job seniority.

The findings also confirm the key role of the field director in facilitating the student's professional education, particularly preparation for practice. This position is also central in its interface with academic faculty, professional agencies, other professional or educational institutions and with the community. In effect, the field director may be likened to the hub of a wheel which interacts significantly with all the "spokes" comprising the social work educational experience.

The third special characteristic of the position is its sensitivity. The role of field director is neither insulated, bounded, or static. On the contrary, it is particularly sensitive and vulnerable to changes in the school and professional environments, especially regarding expectations and resources. Indeed, there appears to be an inverse correlation between these two, e.g., the more limited the available resources, the greater the expectation of field education, which emerges as the current situation in both east and west coast areas.

These qualities of duality, centrality and sensitivity are closely interrelated with each other as well as with assumptions about future needs. Most of the respondents express strong commitment to the role as well as appreciation of its significance. At the same time, there is consensus and concern about the obstacles impeding the role fulfillment: 1) the need for more resources (e.g., financial, material, personnel, time); 2) the need for more support (e.g., from school administration, academic faculty, professional peers); and 3) the need for more recognition (e.g., status, rank, tenure, advancement opportunities).

The intent of this pilot study was to test both the need for, and feasibility of, future exploration of the role of field director in social work education. It is the conclusion of the co-authors that both of these have been demonstrated. The data from this limited sample appear to bear out the basic hypothesis about the ambiguity and dynamic tension between the educational and administrative natures of the field director's role. Consequently this raises a number of questions about current realities and future possibilities. How can and does the school define the role? What can and does the school provide to implement expectations? How can and does the school reward the role?

Since the sample in this study was admittedly limited, a larger source of information is needed, especially in geographical areas other than, and different from, the two metropolitan coastal areas already covered. Other changes also need to be considered in any further study. More demographic data about the field directors would be helpful, e.g., rank, gender, other responsibilities carried. Some of the questions need to be redesigned, both for greater specificity and clarity of terminology and for reduction of possible duplications. Such changes will help to minimize the uncertainties and ambiguities that appeared to limit some responses. Another inhibiting factor was apparently concern about confidentiality; therefore a future questionnaire will need to provide such protection. Finally a revised instrument could include some questions about particular programs or plans already being developed or utilized by various schools that offer promise of meeting special needs.

There are encouraging signs of the increasing respect and seriousness being accorded the practicum experience. Symposia such as this are an example, as are also the increasing number of articles geared to field education, and the development of regional field consortia and institutes. Within the overall practicum experience, no one is, or can be, more crucial than the field director. Therefore, we see a vital need for continuing study, understanding and articulation of this role.

## BIBLIOGRAPHY

Brownstein, Cynthia (1985) "The Social Work Educator: Social Worker and Professor?" SOCIAL SERVICE REVIEW, September, Volume 50.

Cassidy, Helen (1969) "Role and Function of the Coordinator or Director of Field Instruction", CURRENT PATTERNS IN FIELD INSTRUCTION IN GRADUATE SOCIAL WORK EDUCATION, edited by Betty Lacy Jones, Council on Social Work Education.

Downing, Robert and Sathazah, David (1984-85) "Survey in Field Instruction", University of Illinois at Urbana-Champagne.

Fellin, Philip (1982) "Administrative Support and Field Instruction",     pp. 101-115, QUALITY FIELD INSTRUCTION IN SOCIAL WORK. Bradford E. Sheafor and Lowell E. Jenkins, Longman Press, N.Y., pp. 136-143.

Gordon, Margaret Schutz (1982) "Responsibilities of the School:  Maintenance of the Field Program", QUALITY FIELD INSTRUCTION IN SOCIAL WORK. Bradford W. Sheafor, Lowell E. Jenkins, Longman Press, N.Y.

Hamilton, Nina and Else, John F. (1983) DESIGNING FIELD EDUCATION, Charles Thomas Publisher, Springfield, Illinois.

Hawthorne, Lillian (1986) "Developing a Professional Model of Field Administration: The USC Plan", Presented at APM, Council on Social Work Education.

Holtzman, Reva Fine (1984) "Women and the Administrative/Coordinator Position in Field Work in Schools of Social Work", Presented at APM, Council on Social Work Education.

Jenkins, Lowell and Sheafor, Bradford W. (1982) "An Overview of Social Work Field Instruction", pp. 1-2, QUALITY FIELD INSTRUCTION FOR SOCIAL WORK, Longman Press, N.Y.

Jones, Earle F. (1984) "Square Peg in a Round Hole: The Dilemma of the Undergraduate Social Work Coordinators", JOURNAL OF EDUCATION FOR SOCIAL WORK, Fall, Volume 20.

Munson, Carlton (1982) "Field Instruction in Social Work Education", JOURNAL OF TEACHING IN SOCIAL WORK, Spring/Summer, Vol. 1.

Schneck, Dean (1985) "On Field Education Models: Living with the Loose Ends While Weaving the Tapestry", Presented at APM, Council on Social Work Education.

Skolnik, Louise (1985) "Field Education Project", Council on Social Work Education.

Werner, Ruth (1969) "The Director of Fieldwork - Administrator and Educator", pp. 157-164, CURRENT PATTERNS IN FIELD INSTRUCTION IN GRADUATE SOCIAL WORK EDUCATION, Editor Betty Lacy Jones, Council on Social Work Education.

Wilson, Susanna J. (1981) FIELD INSTRUCTION: TECHNIQUES FOR SUPERVISORS. The Free Press.

# CONTRIBUTORS

**Richard P. Barth**, ACSW, Ph.D., is Associate Professor, School of Social Welfare, University of California at Berkeley and the Chairman of the School Social Work Program. He teaches graduate courses in child welfare research, policy, and practice. He is the author of several books and articles dealing with children's services, practice-research, and the training opportunities of social work students; and is an editor of **Journal of Social Work Education, Children and Youth Services Review,** the **Journal of Adolescent Research, and Social Work in Education.** Professor Barth is the winner of the University of Chicago's Frank Bruel Prize for excellence in child welfare scholarship, a Fulbright scholar, and a Lois and Samuel Silberman Fund Senior Faculty Award Fellow.

**Marion Bogo**, MSW, Adv.Dip.S.W., social work practice professor, is Field Practicum Coordinator, University of Toronto. Her teaching and research interests are the development and testing of curriculum models in laboratory and practice in a local, national, and international context; education of new field instructors; clinical social work practice with individuals and families.

**Mary Borecki**, MSW, is the Director of Alumni Development and Public Relations at the University of Connecticut School of Social Work. Her research interests are in the areas of child mental health, school social work, and public relations.

**Cynthia Brownstein**, ACSW, Ph.D., is the Alexandra Grange Hawkins Lecturer in the Graduate School of Social Work and Social Research of Bryn Mawr College, Pennsylvania. She teaches in the Clinical Practice, Family Treatment and Mental Health Policy at the Master's level and Issues in Practice at the Doctoral level. She has written widely about the social work profession including the field practicum and the liaison role.

**John J. Conklin**, ACSW, MSW, Associate Professor and Director of field education at the University of Connecticut School of Social Work has teaching and research interests in the field education, casework, and child mental health.

**Eddie Davis**, DSW, ACSW, is an Associate Professor in the School of Social Work of Wayne State University, Detroit, Michigan and teaches the first year core practice courses and social welfare policy in the undergraduate program. He has conducted workshops and training events, and given papers dealing with minority and migrant youth and family issues; social policy, administration and planning; and elder abuse. His current research interests center on youth violence and urban problems.

**Geraldine Faria**, Ph.D., is Assistant Professor and Field Coordinator in the Department of Social Work at the University of Akron (Ohio). She has teaching and research interests which include social work practice, learning styles, and other aspects of social work education.

**Ami Gantt**, Ph.D. is Assistant Professor at Mt. Sinai Medical School, Division of Community Medicine, and Assistant Director of the Hospital's Dept. of Social Work Services. Her areas of specialty include social work in psychiatry, particularly psychoeducation and research.

**Urania Glassman**, MA, MSW, is Assistant Professor at the School of Social Work at Adelphi University, where she has served as Director of Field Instruction. She teaches practice, group work, and a course for field instructors; and has authored numerous articles and presentations on field instruction and social group work. She recently co-authored a book, GROUP WORK: A HUMANISTIC APPROACH, with Ken Kates for Sage Publications.

**Bart Grossman**, MSW, Ph.D., has been Fieldwork Coordinator and Associate Adjunct Professor at the University of California at Berkeley School of Social Welfare since 1981. He was one of the founders, with Helene Fishbein and Dean Schneck, of the CSWE Field Work Symposium and co-chaired the Symposium from 1985 until 1990. Dr. Grossman has written and presented extensively on social work field education. He has also published on the evolution of alternative social agencies and public-private agency interaction in the delivery of social services. In addition to coordinating the practicum and teaching social work methods, Dr. Grossman is director of the Bay Area Social Services Consortium and the School of Social Welfare/Social Work at the University of California at Berkeley, San Francisco State University, and San Jose State University.

**Martha Haffey**, DSW, is an Associate Professor at the Hunter College School of Social Work of the City University of New York. She has had a long-standing involvement with work/study education, directing a work/study human service program for high school students and completing a dissertation on the topic for her Doctorate in Social Welfare. She has directed the One-Year Residence Program at Hunter since 1981. An active participant in the development of the National Committee on Part-Time Social Work Education, she had edited the committee's publication Topics and serves on its Steering Committee. She has presented papers on part-time and work/study education at numerous professional conferences.

**Carl Hartman**, MSW, is Associate Professor at Wayne State University School of Social Work. He teaches courses in marital therapy, human sexuality, case methods, models of practice and structured interaction. He currently chairs the Mental Health Concentration and Family and Marital Practice Graduate Certificate. Research includes Ethics in Social Work Practice, Personality Disorders and the Affect on Marriage, and Parallel Process Learning in Field Instruction.

**Lillian S. Hawthorne**, Emerita Professor, was Assistant Dean for Student Affairs and Director of Field Education at the University of Southern California School of Social Work until her retirement in 1988. She has teaching, research, and publication interests in supervision, field instruction techniques and skills, and training of field instructors.

**Reva Fine Holtzman**, DSW, Professor, Hunter College, has been on the faculty of Hunter School of Social Work since its inception in 1956. She has taught both on the Masters and Doctoral levels; and until 1981, was Coordinator of Field Work. She is currently the Director of the Center for Field Instruction. Primary interests in field education, instruction for practicum supervisors, including the initial seminar and advanced education via the Center. Her other research interests are in gerontology, human-animal bond concept, and terminal illness. She has served on the editorial staff of **The Clinical Supervisor** and the **Journal of Teaching in Social Work**.

**Nancy Johnston**, MSW, ACSW, is Director of Field Instruction at the University of Minnesota Minneapolis School of Social Work where she teaches the practicum seminar and one to two graduate courses per year. She also gives workshops and training for agency-based field instructors. Her research interests center upon social work involvement in the political process, field teaching and supervision, and care for the elderly mentally ill. Prof. Johnston has been chair of the Midwest Coalition of the National Association of Social Workers since 1987.

**Theadora Kaplan**, DSW, Assistant Professor of Social Work, is the Director of the Undergraduate Program at the Adelphi University School of Social Work. Her special areas of study are social work with children and domestic violence, and she has published articles and run workshops on such topics as group supervision, incest and social work with blended families. She is a board member with a liaison program of several Long Island school districts that provides social work services to children and families.

**Allie Callaway Kilpatrick**, Ph.D, is Associate Professor, School of Social Work, University of Georgia, where she teaches the family courses and serves as Coordinator of the University Interdisciplinary Graduate Certificate Program in Marriage and Family Therapy. She was Director of Field Instruction for seven years and a major research interest has been in field instruction. Other research interests include family issues such as sexuality and the family and family mediation, social work practice and education, and international social work.

**Judith Lacerte**, MSW, is currently Associate Professor and Graduate Practicum Director with the School of Social Work and Human Services at Eastern Washington University, and is also Director of the Alcohol and Drug Studies Program at the university. She has published other articles in the areas of practicum, agency training, and temperance issues.

**Judith Lemberger**, MSW, ACSW, is the Director of Field Work at New York University School of Social Work. She also serves as Project Director of NYU's Homeless Women's Shelter Project for the chronically mentally ill. Her research interests are field instruction, career patterns, and organizational culture.

**Nancy Levine-Jordano**, MSW, Licensed Clinical Social Worker (California), received her Masters in Social Work from Columbia University in 1979, and is presently completing her Ph.D. She has extensive experience in clinical supervision of students and staff with medical, hospital, mental health, and private practice settings. She is Director of Family Service of Contra Costa County in Walnut Creek and Richmond, California, and maintains an active practice in Oakland.

**Elaine F. Marshack**, DSW, Director of Field Education, Hunter College School of Social Work. In addition to directing the field program, she teaches practice and seminars in field instruction. Her research interests have been primarily in the field component of learning and the health area of practice.

**Marcia L. Martin**, Ph.D., is a faculty member and Field Instruction Coordinator at Bryn Mawr College Graduate School of Social Work and Social Research. Her research interests include supervision, theory, and practice, particularly focusing on learning styles, and social work service delivery to persons with AIDS.

**Robert W. McClelland**, MSW, MPH, is currently a doctoral student in Adult Education at The Ohio State University, and was formerly the Director of Admissions, Financial Aid, and Recruitment for the College of Social Work at The Ohio State University. He has held teaching positions at Eastern Washington University-Cheney, the University of Minnesota-Minneapolis, and the University of Wisconsin-Madison. His current interests center around health care and macro practice issues.

**Ellen Sue Mesbur**, MS, Ed.D., is currently Director of the School of Social Work, Ryerson Polytechnical Institute, in Toronto, Canada. Her background in social work practice and social work education includes a focus on social groupwork, gerontological social work, field education and adult learning.

**Sylvia Navari**, D.P.A. directs the field education program for the Division of Social Work at California State University-Sacramento. She has been on faculty there since 1987, After receiving her MSW in 1974, she worked in both public sector and independent non-profit human services. She earned her doctorate at the University of Southern California.

**Sidney Pinksy**, DSW, is the Director of Social Work Education, Training and Research at Long Island Jewish Medical Center, New Hyde Park, New York since 1975. He holds a B.A. from Rochester University, and both an MSW and DSW from Columbia University School of Social Work. He is an adjunct Associate Professor at Adelphi University and Columbia University Schools of Social Work. He is also a member of the Columbia University Field Work Advisory Board.

**Frances Raphael** is a retired Associate Professor, Virginia Commonwealth University with special interest in family social work practice, field and liaison activities, and health social work practice. She has co-authored articles and presented at various conferences on subjects related to the field practicum and the liaison role.

**JoAnn Ray**, Ph.D., Associate Professor with the School of Social Work and Human Services at Eastern Washington University, serves as Undergraduate Program Director and teaches research and practice courses. She has published numerous articles on child sexual abuse and program evaluation.

**Mary Ann Reitmeir**, MSW. As an Associate Professor of social work at Bemidji State University (Minnesota), Prof. Reitmeir coordinates the internship component of the social work program, and teaches courses in health care, the elderly and community organization. She also teaches in the Women's Studies and Applied Behavioral Sciences Graduate Program. At the current time, she is a doctoral student in social work with a supporting area in feminist students at the University of Minnesota beginning the dissertation process. Her topic is a qualitative student of women leaders of an Alinsky-modeled, grass roots organization.

**Linda Cherrey Reeser**, Ph.D., Associate Professor and Director of Field Education at Western Michigan University in Kalamazoo is author of several articles about social worker professionalization and activism and has recently published a book entitled PROFESSIONALIZATION AND ACTIVISM IN SOCIAL WORK: THE SIXTIES, THE EIGHTIES, AND THE FUTURE (Columbia University Press, 1990).

**Barry Rock**, DSW, is Director, Department of Social Work Services, Long Island Jewish Medical Center, New Hyde Park, NY (since 1984). He hold a B.A. from Queens College (CUNY), an MSW from the Adelphi University School of Social Work and a DSW from Hunter College School of Social Work (Graduate Center, CUNY). He is adjunct associate profession and member of the advisory boards at both the Adelphi and Columbia University Schools of Social Work.

**Ronald H. Rooney**, Ph.D., is an Associate Professor at the University of Minnesota, Minneapolis. He has been involved in field work supervision for 11 years. He is completing a book entitled STRATEGIES FOR WORK WITH INVOLUNTARY CLIENTS to be published by Columbia University Press.

**Ellen Rosenberg**, DSW, is Associate Professor, Adelphi University School of Social Work, and former co-Director of the Practice Research Center. She received her MSW from New York University School of Social Work and her DSW from Columbia University School of Social Work.

**Amy Frank Rosenblum** is an Assistant Professor and Assistant Director of Field Instruction, Virginia Commonwealth University School of Social Work. She has taught practice in both the graduate and undergraduate programs and has special interest in field and liaison activities. She has co-authored and presented at various conferences on subjects related to the field practicum and liaison role.

**Dean Schneck**, MSSW, is a Clinical Professor and the Associate Director for Field Education at the School of Social Work of the University of Wisconsin-Madison. He has over twenty years experience in various roles in social work education including agency field instruction, faculty field instructor, classroom teaching and field program administration. His practice background as a direct service worker and supervisor was in public child welfare. His primary contributions have been in field education, generalist practice and staff morale/job distress issues. He has served as co-chair of the National Field Work Symposium of CSWE for the past five years in an attempt to bring together field educators to examine and improve the quality of field instruction.

**Paul Shearer**, MSW, Board Certified Diplomate, practices clinical social work in San Francisco with an emphasis on psychotherapy and social research. He specialized in the challenges encountered by long-term survivors of the HIV epidemic and by those who serve them. A graduate of Fordham University and the University of Connecticut, Paul practices in medical, forensic, and private settings.

**Harrison Y. Smith**, Ph.D., is an Associate Professor of Social Welfare at the University of Kansas in Lawrence. He initiated the first research and published study of "The Role of Faculty Field Liaisons" and relative perceptions of field practicum directors at school and programs of Social Work.

**Rose Starr**, DSW, is an Associate Professor at the Hunter College School of Social Work of the City University of New York. She has been affiliated with the One-Year Residence Program at Hunter since the late 70's. Her dissertation for the Doctorate of Social Welfare involved research on faculty advising for work/study students and the development of innovative advising models. She has been an active member of the Steering Committee of the National Committee on Part-Time Social Work Education and co-chaired a recent Symposium. In addition to part-time and work/study education, her professional interests include community organization practice and teaching, entitlement advocacy, and intensive case management.

**Elaine Vayda**, MSW, Practicum Coordinator, School of Social Work, York University in Toronto, Ontario, has research interests which include legal aspects of social work education, practice education, and family policy issues.

**Robert Wertkin,** DSW, is an Associate Professor at the School of Social Work, Western Michigan University in Kalamazoo. He has current research interests in and has published articles on child welfare.

**Robert M. Wills,** MSW, is Director of the Marital Therapy Training and Research Clinic at Lafayette Clinic in Detroit, Michigan, and Adjunct Instructor of Social Work in Psychiatry at Wayne State University. He is actively engaged in clinical research and social work education, focusing primarily on marital therapy outcome, personality disorder studies, and field education in social work. He is a member of NASW, a clinical member of the American Association for Marriage and Family Therapy. a past president of the Michigan Association for Marriage and Family Therapy and an AAMFT Approved Supervisor.